Publications of the John Gower Society

XVI

*Vox Clamantis* by John Gower:
"The Voice of One Crying"

Publications of the John Gower Society

ISSN 0954-2817

*Series Editors*
R.F. Yeager (*University of West Florida, emeritus*)
Alastair J. Minnis (*Yale University, emeritus*)

*Editorial Board*
Martha Carlin (*University of Wisconsin-Milwaukee*)
David R. Carlson (*University of Ottawa*)
Helen Cooper (*University of Cambridge*)
Siân Echard (*University of British Columbia*)
Andy Galloway (*Cornell University*)
Brian W. Gastle (*Western Carolina University*)
Linne Mooney (*University of York*)
Peter Nicholson (*University of Hawaii*)
R.D. Perry (*University of Tenessee-Knoxville*)
Ana Sáez-Hidalgo (*University of Valladolid*)
Nicholas Watson (*Harvard University*)

This series aims to provide a forum for critical studies of the poetry of John Gower and its influence on English and continental literatures during the late Middle Ages and into the present day. Although its main focus is on the single poet, comparative studies which throw new light on Gower, his work and his historical and cultural context are also welcomed.

Proposals or queries should be sent in the first instance to the series editors or to the publisher, at the addresses given below; all submissions will receive prompt and informed consideration.

R.F. Yeager, Professor of English, *emeritus*
University of West Florida
byeager@uwf.edu

Alastair J. Minnis, Douglas Tracy Smith Professor, *emeritus*
Yale University
alastair.minnis@yale.edu

Boydell & Brewer Limited, PO Box 9, Woodbridge, Suffolk, IP12 3DF, UK

*Previously published volumes in this series are listed at the end of this volume.*

# *Vox Clamantis* by John Gower: "The Voice of One Crying"

Translated with notes by
Robert J. Meindl, Mark T. Riley and R.F. Yeager

D. S. Brewer

Translation and editorial matter © Robert J. Meindl, Mark T. Riley
and R.F. Yeager 2025

*All Rights Reserved*. Except as permitted under current legislation
no part of this work may be photocopied, stored in a retrieval system,
published, performed in public, adapted, broadcast,
transmitted, recorded or reproduced in any form or by any means,
without the prior permission of the copyright owner

The right of Robert J. Meindl, Mark T. Riley and R.F. Yeager to be
identified as the authors of this work has been asserted in
accordance with sections 77 and 78 of the Copyright,
Designs and Patents Act 1988

First published 2025
D. S. Brewer, Cambridge

ISBN 978-1-84384-754-0 (hardback)
ISBN 978-1-84384-755-7 (paperback)

D. S. Brewer is an imprint of Boydell & Brewer Ltd
PO Box 9, Woodbridge, Suffolk IP12 3DF, UK
and of Boydell & Brewer Inc.
668 Mt Hope Avenue, Rochester, NY 14620–2731, USA
website: www.boydellandbrewer.com

Our Authorised Representative for product safety in the EU is Easy
Access System Europe – Mustamäe tee 50, 10621 Tallinn,
Estonia, *gpsr.requests@easproject.com*

A CIP catalogue record for this book is available
from the British Library

The publisher has no responsibility for the continued existence or accuracy
of URLs for external or third-party internet websites referred to in this book,
and does not guarantee that any content on such websites is, or will remain,
accurate or appropriate

Erico W. Stockton,
*qui praeivit clarisque lampadibus viam illustravit*

# CONTENTS

| | |
|---|---|
| Acknowledgements | ix |
| List of Abbreviations | x |
| Note on the Translation | xi |
| Introduction | 1 |

### BOOK I
| | |
|---|---|
| [*Visio Anglie*] Text | 9 |
| Explanatory Notes | 71 |

### BOOK II
| | |
|---|---|
| Text | 87 |
| Explanatory Notes | 110 |

### BOOK III
| | |
|---|---|
| Text | 118 |
| Explanatory Notes | 184 |

### BOOK IV
| | |
|---|---|
| Text | 202 |
| Explanatory Notes | 239 |

### BOOK V
| | |
|---|---|
| Text | 250 |
| Explanatory Notes | 281 |

### BOOK VI
| | |
|---|---|
| Text | 287 |
| Explanatory Notes | 329 |

*Contents*

BOOK VII

   Text     343

   Explanatory Notes     385

   The *Cronica Tripertita*     393

Appendix 1: The Epistle to Arundel     395

   Explanatory Notes     398

Appendix 2: Known Manuscripts of the *Vox Clamantis*     400

Bibliography     403

Index     409

ACKNOWLEDGMENTS

The authors wish to acknowledge the role of the Gower Project in curating the first versions of the translation in on-line presentations of individual books on its website, for devoting an issue of *Accessus* (vol. 7, no. 2), its on-line journal, to the publication of the translation in that earlier form, as well as for publishing Robert J. Meindl's commentary articles on several of its various component books. The articles are "Semper Venalis: Gower's Avaricious Lawyers" (*Accessus* 1, no. 2 [2013], 1–64), "The Failure of Counsel: Curial Corruption in Book VI of the *Vox Clamantis* (*Accessus* 3, no. 2 [2016], 1–51), and "The Community of the Realm: Gower's Account of the Commons in Book V of the *Vox Clamantis* (*Accessus* 6, no. 1 [2020], 1–44). Gratitude is due also to the anonymous reader of the manuscript for Boydell & Brewer, and to Georgiana Donavin and Eve Salisbury, all of whom provided helpful suggestions that led to an improved translation.

# LIST OF ABBREVIATIONS

| | |
|---|---|
| ON | Old Norse |
| OE | Old English |
| Gr. | Greek |
| Lat. | Latin |
| *VC* | *Vox Clamantis* |
| KJV | King James Version of the Bible |
| GenPro | General Prologue to the *Canterbury Tales* |
| *CT* | *Canterbury Tales* |
| [C] | London, British Library, MS Cotton Titus A.xiii |
| [$C_2$] | London, British Library, MS Cotton Tiberius A.iv |
| [D] | Oxford, Bodleian Library, MS Digby 138 |
| [E] | San Marino (California), Huntington Library, MS HM 150 (*olim* Ecton) |
| [G] | Glasgow, University Library, Hunterian MS 59 (T.2.17) |
| [H] | London, British Library, MS Harley 6291 |
| [$H_2$] | Hertfordshire, Hatfield House (MS privately owned) |
| [$H_3$] | Oxford, Bodleian Library, Hatton 92 |
| [L] | Oxford, Bodleian Library, MS Laud (Misc.) 719 |
| [$L_2$] | Lincoln, Cathedral Library, MS A.72 (235) |
| [S] | Oxford, All Souls College, MS 98 |
| [T] | Dublin, Trinity College, MS D.4.6 (214) |

## NOTE ON THE TRANSLATION

This is a book for modern readers. It developed out of a recognition that Gower's Latin poem, the *Vox Clamantis*, is out of reach for most present-day audiences simply because it was written in Latin, a language increasingly little studied. Other attempts to render the *Vox* more widely available have been made – notably translations by Eric W. Stockton of the full poem in prose, and by George R. Rigg, of just the first Book, in verse.[1] Stockton's translation has long been out of print. Rigg's was limited to the *Visio Anglie* (i.e., Book I) and in a meter Gower did not choose. While both these renderings have many virtues, what seemed needed was a translation in straightforward language that more closely replicated Gower's metrics, kept his lineation, and accurately retained his paronomastic style.

Latin, however, is not the sole impediment to present-day appreciation of Gower's poem. The *Vox Clamantis* is very much a work of its time and place – albeit, like all significant literary achievements, replete with lessons for all time. Gower wrote as he did, and what he did, always intending to improve the society around him. He envisioned the audience he addressed to consist of people with a social status and education similar to his own, with little if any outreach beyond that: people, that is, similarly troubled by political and social events around them, similarly enclosed in a small and privileged cultural milieu. Such readers were obviously different from those of today – even the most scholarly – who may wish to experience Gower's powerful poem. Therefore, the present translation has notes of several kinds. Previous editions and translations have, of course, gone some way to meet this need. G.C. Macaulay, upon whose seminal edition this translation is based, offered notes for scholars as proficient in Latinitas as himself – a great resource, but beyond the skills and interests of a wider public today.[2] Stockton annotated his text extensively, but in many cases inaccurately – through no fault of his own, but due, rather, to the limited resources available to him in the early 1960s. Mirroring the man who produced them, the notes provided by David R. Carlson for Rigg's translation are

---

[1] *The Major Latin Works of John Gower: The Voice of One Crying and the Tripartite Chronicle*, ed. and trans. Eric W. Stockton (Seattle: University of Washington Press, 1962); *John Gower: Poems on Contemporary Events: The Visio Anglie (1381) and Cronica Tripertita (1400)*, ed. David R. Carlson, trans. A.G. Rigg (Toronto: Pontifical Institute of Medieval Studies, 2011).

[2] *The Complete Works of John Gower*, ed. G.C. Macaulay, 4 vols. (Oxford: Clarendon Press, 1899–1902), vol. 4, *The Latin Works*.

immensely learned, and aimed primarily at a specialist academic audience. And, of course, they cover just the first Book.

Annotations here take a different approach. Our goal is to offer information sufficient to make clear Gower's meaning in a given line or passage. Hence, in general, named figures from classical mythology, the bible, and ancient or contemporary history are identified succinctly but precisely. When Gower, as he often does, imports text from other writers or alludes to other works, annotations are intended as guides to sources, directing the reader where fuller contexts can be found. The existence of a note is shown with an asterisk. Notes for each Book are placed after the translation of each.

When using the notes, it is helpful to keep several points in mind. All biblical citations refer to the Latin translation of Jerome (the Vulgate Bible). Despite its differences from later English translations perhaps more familiar to many modern readers of English, the Vulgate is closest to the bible in the form that Gower knew it. The latter point foregrounds a difficulty common to all of Gower's sources: we cannot know precisely from which version of any text he worked, nor – thus – exactly what it looked like. This is true not only of the bible, but particularly so for Ovid's works, from which Gower excerpts most often. Variant manuscripts abound. Consequently, our annotations rely on, and have been checked against, the best and most accessible modern editions, as cited in the bibliography. Where no scholarly modern edition exists, as is the case for Godfrey of Viterbo's *Pantheon*, for example, a "best text" early printing has been chosen. Finally, G.C. Macaulay assigned single-letter identifiers to each of the eleven known manuscripts of the *VC*, which we have used in the notes. These are: Dublin, Trinity College, MS D.4.6 (214) [T]; Glasgow, University Library, Hunterian MS 59 (T.2.17) [G]; Hertfordshire, Hatfield House MS, privately owned [$H_2$]; Lincoln, Cathedral Library, MS A.72 (235) [$L_2$]; London, British Library, MS Cotton Tiberius A.iv [$C_2$]; London, British Library, MS Cotton Titus A.xiii [C]; London, British Library, MS Harley 6291 [H]; Oxford, All Souls College, MS 98 [S]; Oxford, Bodleian Library, MS Digby 138 [D]; Oxford, Bodleian Library, MS Laud (Misc.) 719 [L]; Oxford, Bodleian Library, Hatton 92 [$H_3$]; San Marino (California), Huntington Library, MS HM 150 (*olim* Ecton) [E]. "A-Text" designates first, and "B-Text" later, versions of the poem, as found in various manuscripts. These variations are indicated in the notes.

## QUOTATIONS FROM OTHER WORKS IN THE *VOX CLAMANTIS*

In the *Vox Clamantis* Gower draws on few authors expressly, but those that he did borrow from he knew very well. Listed are what we consider to be actual quotations, as opposed to passages possibly prompted by earlier works. For example, Gower's "mutatas...amoris...formas" (V. 47–8) may be inspired by the "mutatas...formas" of Ovid's *Metamorphoses* 1. 1, but we do not consider this a quotation. Similarly with Gower's "Sicut auis visco volutans se voluitur illo" (V. 145), perhaps inspired by "Non auis utiliter uiscatis effugit alis" (*Ars Amatoria* 1. 391), or his "Sic tibi fata volunt, non crimina..." (I. 1547), perhaps inspired by "sic erat in fatis; nec te tua culpa fugavit..." (*Fasti* 1. 481). The image of a bird trapped in birdlime or the idea that a disaster may have happened by fate, not by one's own fault, are common enough, and Gower's wording does not seem to derive from Ovid's. Lines directly and fully quoted are listed as *verbatim*. Lines with minor changes not affecting meaning – e.g., the interchange of "Dic," "Nam," or "Quid" at the beginning of a line, the change of "nec" to "non," and the like – are cited as "virtually *verbatim*." The notation "adapted" indicates that Gower made major changes to his source, which is nevertheless readily identifiable. We may have missed some quotations, particularly from long works like the *Pantheon*, of which no modern, scholarly edition exists. It is striking that no close quotations from the commonly read school authors (Cato, Statius) or from Virgil (*pace* Carlson, "A Fourteenth-Century Anglo-Latin Ovidian," 333) have been identified. (We certainly find reminiscences of Cato: *fistula auceps* [VC IV. 995] reminds us of Cato 1. 27, *Fistula dulce canit, volucrem dum decipit auceps*; [VC VII. 331] *Dum fueris felix* sounds like *Distichs of Cato* 1. 40, *Cum fueris felix, semper tibi proximus esto*; but we consider these to be commonplaces, not quotations. More reminiscences, not quotes, from Cato are mentioned in Carlson and Rigg, *Poems on Contemporary Events*, 357–8.)

# INTRODUCTION

### The Poem and its Genesis

It is difficult to know precisely when Gower began work on various versions of what eventually became the *Vox Clamantis*, but assuredly the accession of Richard II in July of 1377 focused and intensified his labors. The poem's initial purpose, to review the state of the realm, particularly in respect to the clergy, was reconceived to provide counsel for the young king Richard. The poet's first major work, the *Mirour de l'Omme*, directed to the Anglo-Norman-speaking world of Richard's predecessor, his grandfather Edward III, had covered much of the same material, albeit in a manner unsuited to Gower's new aim and audience. The poet may have thought that Richard, born in Bordeaux and affecting Parisian French throughout his life, would likely not have been impressed by the language of the *Mirour*. Latin would have recommended itself for many reasons, not least among them its prestige as the language of learning and serious literature. Possibly, too, Latin appealed as best suited to the instructional posture Gower adopts, in the manner of the influential pseudo-Aristotelean *Secretum Secretorum*, in which Aristotle, in Latin, schools the young Alexander in the essentials of statecraft. The appropriateness of Latin for such a poem would not have been lost on Sir Simon Burley, under whose tutelage the ten-year-old king was, when Gower was composing the *Vox*.

Internal evidence gives some indication of the stages of the poem's composition as it evolved over the course of a decade or so. The initial assemblage, the Alpha text [A], would seem to have been Books III–VI, the proposed critique of the three estates and a direct address to the king. Book III begins with a prologue that fulfills the rhetorical requirements of an introduction, and the conclusion of Book VI looks to have been an early attempt at a "wrap" of the poem's hermeneutical concern with the correct reading of texts of diverse sorts. The device of the three estates breaks down during development of these four Books. Gower actually designates five degrees of English society: clergy, gentry, the urban mercantile community, officialdom (from legal practitioners through judges and royal counsellors to the king himself), and plebs, the rural and urban working classes who receive little beyond collective criticism as mere necessary appendages of the gentry and the burgesses.

The poem's second manifestation, the beta text, frames the class critique with Book II (whose prologue suggests it once marked a beginning), which discusses the poem's central theme of human responsibility for history, and with Book VII, which develops teleologically and eschatologically the reading of history that ends Book VI. The prologue of Book II is filled with the exordial topoi[1] that we would expect to start a poem of the late Middle Ages and the remainder of the Book discusses at length the philosophy of individual responsibility that the poet urges upon the reader throughout the poem and in his other works generally. Book VII then becomes the poem's new conclusion.

When this second major compositional stage had been completed and Books II–VII were in hand, the Great Rising of 1381 occurred.[2] Gower then wrote the *Visio Anglie*, at first very likely as a separate poem, but eventually added it to the six-Book *Vox* as a prequel, shaping it to demonstrate in a contemporary context the hermeneutics of historical interpretation that he had espoused in the larger *Vox*. If we allow a reasonable amount of time for the composition of the *Visio* and its transformation into Book I, this third phase, the Delta text (Macaulay's Delta [Δ]) would have been completed sometime late in 1381 at the earliest, or more reasonably in 1382. The final form of the poem undergoes local revisions at various times during the 1380s to account for circumstances prompting a change in Gower's attitude toward Richard, whose performance as king made the poet increasingly critical of his reign and less optimistic about the country's future.

In 1400, after the forced deposition of Richard, Gower composed an account of Richard's fall, the *Cronica Tripertita*, clearly at first as an independent poem. Much of the *Cronica* relies on the "Record and Process," fostered as the official Lancastrian justification for the ascension of Bolingbroke as Henry IV in 1399 – hence how much of its vitriol reflects the true depth of Gower's disillusionment with Richard is difficult to assess. One possible indication is that, at some point, Gower appended the *Cronica* to some manuscripts of the *Vox*: of the eleven extant, four manuscripts attach the *Cronica*, which also survives once separately. With or without the *Cronica* as an appendix, Gower's major Latin project had occupied the poet for almost a quarter of a century.

## Versification and Sources

The *Vox Clamantis* is written predominantly in unrhymed elegiac couplets – "the first substantial Anglo-Latin work [in that meter] since Henry of

---

[1] On *topoi*, see Ernst Robert Curtius, *European Literature and the Latin Middle Ages*, trans. Willard R. Trask, Bollingen Series 36 (New York: Harper & Row, [1953] 1963), 79–105.

[2] Charles Oman, *The Great Revolt of 1381*, new ed. with a new introduction and notes by E.B. Fryde (Oxford: Clarendon Press, 1969), provides excellent background.

*Introduction*

Avranches" (d. 1260).[3] The first line of each distich is in dactylic hexameter and the second in dactylic pentameter. The pentameter line in Latin poetry is traditionally indented in order to mark it clearly and enhance the reader's recognition of the poet's skill at arranging materials in the rising and falling alternations of the distichs. Lines are frequently enjambed to disrupt a rhythm that otherwise becomes too easily predictable. Since Gower used indentation to mark paragraphing, editors until recently declined to employ the tradition to mark his pentameter lines. Our translation follows the edition of G.C. Macaulay, which took as its base text Oxford, All Souls College MS 98, collated with most other manuscripts. We have adopted the practice of David R. Carlson in his edition of Book I and indented the pentameter lines in both our text and our translation. Like A.G. Rigg in his translation of Carlson's text, we have marked Gower's paragraphs with a blank line left between them. Unlike Rigg, who translated Gower's elegiac distichs into blank verse, we have tried to replicate the original movement of Gower's Latin verses by rendering them in couplets of alternating iambic hexameter and iambic pentameter, thus to provide in English a reasonable approximation of the Latin original.

Gower's major literary sources have been identified more completely than heretofore, in any edition or translation. Ovid is his favorite classical author, and borrowings from *Metamorphoses*, *Tristia*, *Heroides*, *Fasti*, *Ars Amatoria*, and *Ex Ponto* are everywhere quoted, adapted and adjusted to his needs. In Book I, Gower leans on Ovid especially heavily. Peter Riga's *Aurora*, the *Speculum Stultorum* of Nigel of Longchamp (Nigellus Wireker), and Godfrey of Viterbo's *Pantheon* are likewise favorites; Virgil's *Aeneid* seems to shadow Gower's lines in a number of places, although in contrast to his borrowings from Ovid, Virgil's verses are very seldom quoted directly. Biblical references underlie Gower's text throughout. Most passages are prominent in canonical studies, but also familiar to an ordinary parishioner, recognizable with little special study. The Old Testament figures more prominently than the New, and direct biblical borrowings are generally from the *Aurora*. Biblical citations in the notes refer to the Vulgate text, as the version closest to what Gower knew. Asterisks at the ends of lines refer to words or passages discussed in the explanatory notes found at the end of each Book. Specific references to the text quote the Latin original, not the translation.

## John Gower, Man and Poet

By comparison with how much information we have about his friend and fellow-poet Geoffrey Chaucer, precious little is known about John Gower's

---

[3] A.G. Rigg, *A History of Anglo-Latin Literature 1066–1422* (Cambridge: Cambridge University Press, 1992), 287.

life. Chaucer's journey from the house of his merchant parents in the London Vintry to serve, first as a page, then later in the retinue of royal households, as an emissary and a soldier, and subsequently as a trusted administrator, variously responsible for the king's works and the wool staple, is well documented throughout.[4] Gower's biography remains a blank slate until he was at least twenty-one years old (if not a bit older). We know nothing of his parents or his place of birth nor its date, nothing precise of his lineage, or of his education. Although in his latter years he was demonstrably a man of some wealth, we cannot say for certain how he came by it. He married at least once, late in life and apparently happily, though in his lengthy poem in French, the *Mirour de l'Omme*, he hints at an earlier wife. He would seem to have had no children and, while his acquaintance in London and especially Kent was both wide and well-connected, apart from Chaucer and possibly the Oxford philosopher, lawyer, and poet Ralph Strode, we are at a loss to name his friends.

All this notwithstanding, bits of material evidence do exist on which we can construct a tentative life with some confidence.[5] The heraldic arms on his tomb in Southwark Cathedral – a tomb he likely designed himself – imply a relationship at least indirect with Sir Robert Gower of Brabourne, Kent, and other documents, related to a transfer of rents from property in London, claim a connection with the Northwoods, another family of Kentish gentry. This offers a partial solution to the mystery of Gower's education. A scion of such a background could be assumed to have learnt his Latin letters and probably French too in the household, since, as notice on his tomb also tells us, Gower lived during the reigns of Edward III (1327–77) and Richard II (1377–99), when many families of his class knew and used French, especially during the earlier years under Edward, when a young Gower would have been most receptive. And Gower was extremely well-read. His works show him familiar with a wide range of authors classical, ecclesiastical, and secular, in all three languages he wrote in himself – though none, perhaps, drew him more often or deeply than did Ovid. Gower's debt to Ovid is never so evident as in his borrowings, into the *Vox Clamantis* especially. But after such guesses about his childhood, the blank descends again: we have no record of Gower attending either Oxford or Cambridge, and in the absence of any documentary proof, speculation about any formal legal training must remain only that – speculation.

Indeed, it is not until 1364 that John Gower enters the public record, and then in a fashion that remains controversial. The cause was a transfer of land – one-half of Aldington manor and two marshes, all in Kent – by

---

[4] See *Chaucer Life-Records*, ed. Martin M. Crow and Clair C. Olson (Oxford: Clarendon Press, 1966).

[5] On Gower's life, see currently Martha Carlin, "Chronology of Gower's Life Records," and "Gower's Life," in *Historians on John Gower*, ed. Stephen H. Rigby with Siân Echard (Cambridge: D.S. Brewer, 2019), 3–120.

*Introduction*

one William de Septvauns to Gower, who paid William eighty marks, and another transfer to Gower's companion at the time, Richard de Hurst. The transfers brought official scrutiny, first because Aldington was held by William "in chief," meaning that until William was twenty-one and of age, the manor technically belonged to the king, and second because William would not, in fact, be of age until 1367. Only then could he sell or otherwise distribute lands inherited from his father, a knight whose ownership of Aldington depended, itself, on providing military service at the king's behest. The case was further complicated by charges presented that young William had "continually dwelt in the company of Richard de Hurst and the said John Gower, at Canterbury and elsewhere" from Christmas 1364 until Michaelmas 1365, "and during that time he was led and counselled by them to alienate his lands." Eventually the controversy made its way to parliament, which voided William's grants, and returned control of the properties to the king. In 1368, however, when William was in fact twenty-one, he deeded the half-portion of Aldington manor and the two marshes to Gower once again.

The case is particularly noteworthy because its ramifications extend in several directions. The manor at Aldington became Gower's chief residence until he relocated to London, sometime after 1382, and through it he derived his title as "esquire of Kent." It is because of Aldington that Gower gained a connection with Sir John Cobham (whose family owned Aldington's other half, and whose mistreatment by Richard II figures large in Gower's poem, *Cronica Tripertita*, attached in several manuscripts to the *Vox Clamantis*), and with another Kentish neighbor, Sir Arnold Savage, eventually among the witnesses of Gower's will. More significantly, quite likely Gower was living at Aldington in the summer of 1381, and witnessed first-hand the violence of the Kentish mob that swept through the county on its way to ravage London – thus providing the inspiration for the *Visio Anglie*, originally a stand-alone poem later conjoined by Gower as a new first Book to the longer Latin work he had then to hand, the *Vox Clamantis*.[6] This *Vox*, along with the *Speculum Meditantis* (the *Mirour de l'Omme*'s Latin title) and the *Confessio Amantis*, is one of the three large volumes supporting the head of Gower's effigy on his tomb.

But unequivocally, most important about the "Septvauns affair" is what it has to tell us, if anything, about Gower's character. John Gower is, after all, that same "moral Gower" into whose hands Chaucer placed *Troilus and Criseyde*, "to vouchen sauf, ther nede is, to correct," and earlier had entrusted with his financial affairs during his initial trip to Italy, in 1378. Chaucer's epithet has adhered to Gower, and over the years, depending on how one prioritizes the "moral," has impinged variously upon Gower's

---

[6] See Michael Bennett, "John Gower, Squire of Kent, the Peasants' Revolt, and the *Visio Anglie*," *Chaucer Review* 53 (2018), 258–82.

poetic reputation. Might we not ask how legitimately "moral" could a man be, who misled a youth for gain?

The question has particular pertinence for any assessment of Gower's poetry, since his stance in all his salient poetry from first to last is staunchly moralistic, even Cato-esque in its judgmental calling out of vices, as in the *Mirour de l'Omme*, and in the *Vox Clamantis* especially: consider that the latter's title, and Gower's authorial stance there, pointedly echo John the Baptist. In the *Confessio Amantis* as well, where Gower's turn toward exemplum form and fictional narrative mitigates to some degree the stern, moralistic voicing of the other major works, we find passages railing against corrupt clergy (monks and friars in particular), and of course John Wyclif and the Lollards; and there in the *Confessio* too, as in the so-called "epistle to the king" in the *Vox Clamantis*, Gower feels on solid enough ground to proffer behavioral advice to his sovereign.

Alas, the details of the "Septvauns affair" – though they have divided scholarly opinion for years – are, in the end, too murky to supply a basis sufficient for any final judgment about Gower's character. Nor are other cases recorded in the archival rolls definitive. Gower appears many times there, either as plaintiff or defendant, usually with counsel, but occasionally representing himself – a courtroom independence that, along with a prominent recourse to legal language, particularly in Book VI of the *Vox Clamantis*, has suggested to some that he had formal legal training. Unsurprisingly, most of these cases involve transactions of land, or suits to recover damages or debt. If Gower somehow inherited a measure of wealth, throughout his life he actively engaged in varieties of commerce – property deals and, perhaps, forms of money-lending, a practice then common enough among men of his status, and without stigma – to increase it. Such dealings too find their way into the poetry. The vocabulary of mercantile transaction, no less often than that of the law, also shapes his poetic voice, in the *Mirour de l'Omme* especially.

Thus in the end, to evaluate Gower the man we must first look again, briefly, at his tomb, and latterly to the poetry. Without question he would applaud our doing so, for the labor of his later years, if not of most of his life, was spent crafting a persona to stand as "John Gower" for all time. Certainly the tomb assembles his several aspirations for the viewer: his effigy, helmet and coat of arms at its feet, proudly displays a chain of gold "SSS," a gift from Henry IV; on panels behind are images of the virtues Faith, Hope, and Charity. His head rests on books representing his three major poetic works, as noted earlier, and bears a chaplet of four roses interspersed with "Merci IHS [Jesus]," evoking simultaneously his post-mortem hopes, his esquire's status, and a poet's laurel. The tomb is, then, a monument to both the unexceptionable Christianity and the worldly ambition of a complex individual, each element claimed with a certain measure of carefully coded pride.

Gower's poetic *oeuvre*, no less than his tomb, conveys these same messages when considered *ensemble*. The testimony of his manuscripts, some of which remain suggestive of direct authorial oversight, clearly demonstrates how he assembled originally shorter, independently conceived pieces with an eye to create the three epic-length books prominent on his tomb. The practice characterizes not only the making of the *Vox Clamantis*, but also the *Mirour de l'Omme* and the *Confessio Amantis*, as well. That these should be one each in Latin, French, and English, the three major languages of his day, was hardly lost on Gower. As noted by "a certain philosopher" (conceivably Gower himself) in Latin verses known from part of their first line as "Eneados, bucolis" and often included with Gower's Latin poetry by contemporary hands, Virgil wrote in just a single language, but Gower in three. (Perhaps the comparison was a gentle dig at Chaucer, too.)

Such inherent – and competitive – pride-of-place, so obvious in the gold "SSS" chain and armorial accoutrement pointedly present on the tomb, is unmistakable in much of Gower's poetry. His *Cinkante Balades* took aim at the *Livre des cent ballades*, a collection written by the foremost French nobility, to show what an Englishman could do in his version of their own language;[7] poems like the Latin *O recolende* and *In Praise of Peace*, in English, presume to advise the newly-crowned Henry IV in two languages he could read, lauding him profusely at the same time. (Gower ever wore his loyalties, to monarch or to his social class, visible on his sleeve.) But alongside the partisanship and intense social critiques, Gower also wrote poems of philosophical depth, plangent piety, and reflective, personal introspection. These should not be overlooked in any thoughtful account of Gower's *oeuvre*, or of the man himself. Of poetry of the first sort, *De lucis scrutinio*, justly termed a "tractatus" in its colophon, is a supreme example, as the Marian final section of the *Mirour de l'Omme* is of the second. To experience the third kind, poems in which Gower reveals himself vulnerable with a near-modern confessional intensity, consider *Est Amor*, a prothalamion of sorts composed evidently in 1398 on the brink of marriage to Agnes Groundolf, his only known wife, or *Quicquid homo scribat* (sometimes known as *In fine*), a now-blind man's reluctant farewell to composing further poetry, even while stubbornly asserting *mens tamen interius scribit et ornat opus* ("my mind writes within me and adorns the work").

John Gower died in 1408, probably on September 7 of that year.[8] He was buried in the chapel of St. John the Baptist, now the Harvard Room, in the Cathedral of St. Saviour and St. Mary Overie (Southwark Cathedral). Agnes, whom he named an executor of his will and who outlived him by an unknown number of years, was interred in the same chapel, in a sepulchre more modest, that no longer survives.

---

7   See Jean le Seneschal, *Les Cent Ballades: Poème du XIVe Siécle*, ed. Gaston Raynaud (Paris: Firmin-Didot, 1905).
8   On this date for Gower's death, see Carlin, "Gower's Life," 88.

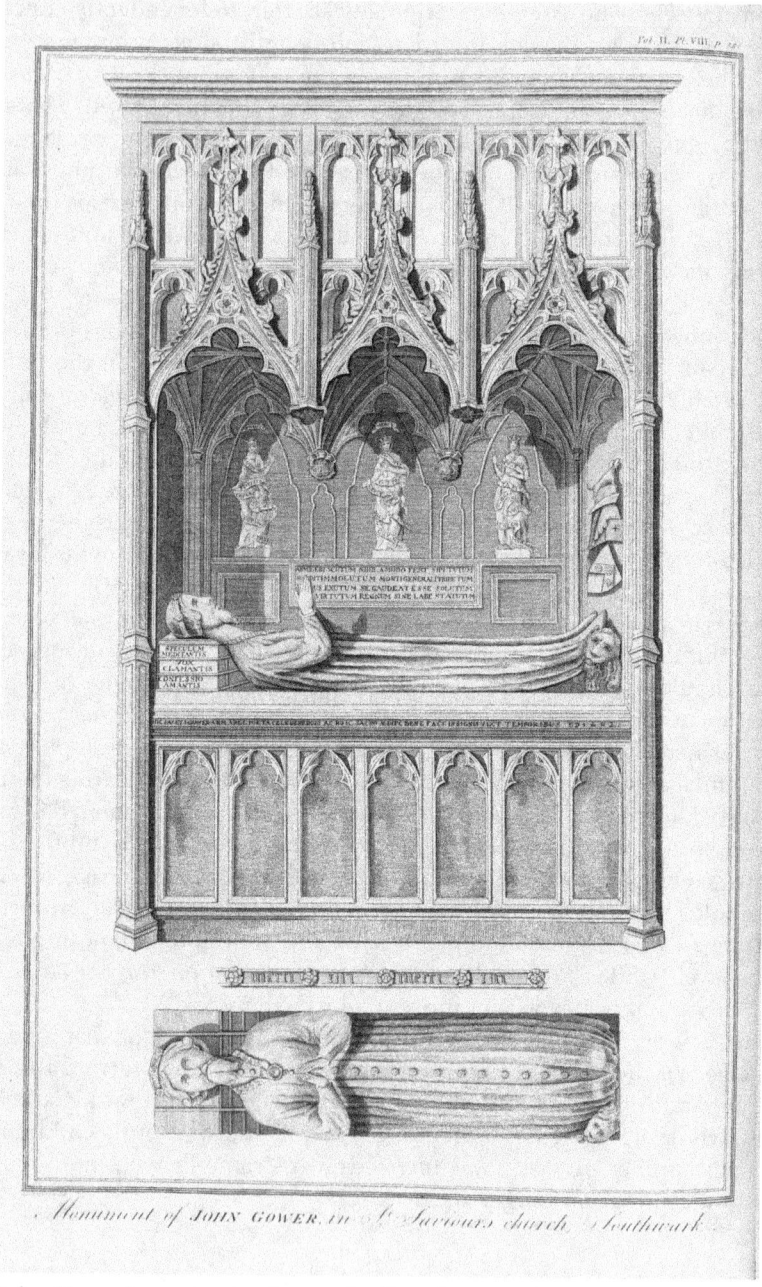

John Gower's tomb, chaplet, and effigy, from Richard Gough, *Sepulchral Monuments in Great Britain*, vol. II, part 2 (1796). By courtesy of The Lewis Walpole Library, Yale University.

# BOOK I

### Incipit

In two manuscripts, a prose incipit – "Incipit Cronica que Vox Clamantis dicitur" – appears ahead of the Prologue to the first Book. Evidently a later addition, but clearly authorial, it evidences Gower's attempt to smooth the integration of the freshly composed *Visio Anglie* into the extant six-Book *VC* as a new Book I.

### Prologue

The *Vox Clamantis* has the clear purpose of teaching the lessons of the past as a guide to the present, an intention it makes clear in this first of three prologues (Books II and III will have theirs too) and in frequent observations throughout the poem. That intention will be certified by an interpretation of Nebuchadnezzar's dream in Book VII, and retrospectively recertified in the poem's final form with a reading of the Great Rising of 1381, added late as Book I. In Gower's view, everything that is and happens must be read and interpreted for the guidance God provides, for the Divine knows and governs everything that is and happens. (Doubtless, Gower would have subscribed to George Santayana's dictum about history, "Those who cannot remember the past are condemned to repeat it," while perhaps rephrasing it to say that those who fail to read correctly the lessons of the past are not only condemned to repeat them, but condemned *simpliciter*.) Gower sets out to instruct the newly crowned boy-king in what can be learned from history and experience. These, along with Scripture and Nature, are replete with omens and portents sent by God to guide rulers if they but learn to read them. As old books have guided the author, he intends that his account will likewise mark the paths of proper conduct and be a guide to those yet unborn.

### Book I [*Visio Anglie*]

Gower's account of the Great Rising of 1381 is a biased description of events that evidences absolutely no sympathy for those who have brought it about. From his perspective, the Revolt constituted a demonically inspired threat to an order ordained by God. Those designated the bound servants of the free and the noble have turned upon their divinely placed masters, like Satan against God, and accordingly have forfeited whatever shaky claim to humanness they might have possessed. Their behavior has revealed their bestial natures and earned them the same severe repression that would be accorded animals who dared to attack humans. For a social and spiritual conservative like Gower, acceptance of the status quo constitutes obedience to the will of God. It is not for the oppressed to oppose what is, but rather to prosper in their stations, as far as possible, while remaining within the limits defined for them by the Creator's master plan. Thus the demand of the rebels' leaders for a royal charter abolishing villeinage was for Gower not only a political but also a doctrinal impossibility. That is why he presents the Rising starkly – and simplistically – as an unjustifiable revolt of serfs against freemen, even though he must have known, from reports or observation, that freeborn peasants, yeomen, and tradespeople from the towns also played major roles.

In Book I Gower's narrator frames his account of the revolt as a series of dreams, the content of which he records as the *Vox Clamantis*. Notably, the dreams maintain a certain verisimilitude in both chronology and events – an effect not achieved without juggling. The account identifies the narrator as an actual observer except in two instances: the wandering in the wilderness after the fall of the Tower of London, and the storm at sea. These episodes, he specifies, are presented *quasi in propria persona* (as if in his own person). Everything else purports to be the narrator's observations of what he saw in dreams. A basic outline of the narrator's progression therein can be reconstructed from the text. He says he sees the peasants abandoning their tasks, gathering in the fields (which are left untended) and flowing along the roads, destroying homes and looting in the towns along their way to the gathering at Blackheath, just south of Greenwich. There he sees and hears an address by Wat Tyler, observes the rebels making a demonic pact, watches them take up their rustic arms and march on London. He witnesses John of Gaunt's Savoy Palace destroyed in Southwark (ll. 929–30) and, across the river (New Troy is on his right, l. 879), St. John Clerkenwell and the Temple burning (ll. 931–4). He goes to his townhouse (l. 903), which isn't safe, and so flees to the Tower of London, where he sees the trial and execution of Archbishop Sudbury and others. Leaving the unsafe Tower, he returns to his townhouse, but it has been ravaged and he doesn't dare cross its threshold (ll. 1376–80). Then, again as if in his own person, he searches in vain for a safe place to hide because he doesn't dare attempt a return to his Kentish manor along roads that are manifestly unsafe (ll. 1409–10). Finally, he portrays, albeit within the dream of the Ship Vision, the downfall of Wat Tyler at Smithfield.

Verisimilitude or no, it must be registered that Gower's account of the revolt by no means tells the complete story. To begin with, he truncates events, ignoring the activities of late May and early June when the official attempts to gather the poll tax levied to fund the French wars set events in motion. He likewise ignores the bloody royal retribution that lasted throughout June and into July. Then at first he shadows only the Kentish rebels, until he notes the Essex rebels' fiery destruction of St. John Clerkenwell (located not far outside the city's east wall, near Aldgate), and the burning of "the sacred temples" (that is, both the church and the early versions of the law schools by that name, located in Westminster, west of the wall's Newgate) by the rebels from Suffolk. After the Kentish rebels destroy the Savoy, at the foot of the approaches to London Bridge, the bridge's keepers inexplicably open its portcullis, allowing the southern rebels to surge into the city and join forces with those from Suffolk and Essex. These latter had gathered at Mile End, entering the city through Aldgate, likewise opened to them (perhaps by Alderman John Horne of the Fishmongers), for reasons that remain unclear. It seems safe to conclude, however, that there was a considerable measure of sympathy in the city for the rebels.

The still-dreaming narrator then takes refuge in the Tower of London, from which he observes the abrupt trial and botched execution of Archbishop Simon Sudbury. Treasurer Robert Hales and a Franciscan physician, William Appleton, were likewise killed, although Gower does not mention them by name. Fleeing the Tower after seeing the bodies of the slain thrown outside the gates, he seeks hiding places in various locations, interacts cautiously with other fugitives while evading the rebels, and then takes refuge aboard an imagined ship that represents at once both the Tower of London and the nation. Again he undergoes, this time through the dual images of a storm and a maelstrom, the assault on the Tower. The ship survives the maritime threats when Wat Tyler, the leader of the Kentish rebels, is sacrificed to Neptune – a poetic retelling of Mayor William Walworth's disposal of Tyler with a blow of his sword on Saturday, June 15, at Smithfield, where the rebel leadership had come to meet with the king. The poet's version of the uprising thereupon works its way to the conclusion. The immediate crisis has passed, and the poet rejoices in the restitution of order, albeit soberly, for he believes evil yet lurks in the savage villeins' hearts. No detail is given about (although nodding reference is made to) subsequent events, during which some rebels are checked and dispersed by the London citizenry and others slaughtered by the forces of Henry Despenser, Bishop of Norwich. John Ball's and Jack Straw's deaths (the former, and perhaps the latter, was drawn, hanged, beheaded, and quartered in the king's presence) are not noted. But in answer to the narrator's prayers, the rebels received their just due from a unforgiving power elite.

Gower's version of events compresses the Rising into one week, which can be dated from Sunday, June 9, to Saturday, June 15, 1381 – a precision made possible by the poem's references to the onset of days and times of days correlated to the known date of the feast of Corpus Christi in 1381, June 13. This constitutes the poem's Thursday. The poet organizes the actions of the book around three visionary episodes: the narrator sees rebellious serfs transformed into beasts who gather and march on London; the narrator describes the sack of London, presented as the fall of Troy, and wanders a nightmarish landscape, searching in vain for a safe hiding place; the narrator boards a ship (the Tower) that is battered by perils on the sea and limps into port in a land devoid of peace.

Book I thus begins on Sunday night, June 9, 1381, with the sinking of the moon in the west. Lucifer, the morning star, rises and sets and then dawn breaks on the morning of June 10 (Trinity Monday) in Edenic England before the Fall – that is, the Revolt. The poet describes a bucolic landscape in which all is ordered and functioning according to God's plan, as administered by Nature. Evening sets in, and the poet, anxious for no apparent reason, falls asleep and has the first of his three visions. This begins, as the prose headnote to Chapter 2 specifies, on Tuesday morning. The narrator observes disorderly serfs, their tasks abandoned, on the move along the roads and through the fields. Before his eyes they change into domestic animals, their kinds reflecting their functions as serfs; these quickly lose their domestic traits, taking on, in a supreme instance of adynaton, the attributes of wild beasts. So transformed, they are both portents of coming evil and monsters, in the dual sense of Latin *monstrum*, the word Gower applies to them. The beasts wander about, frolic in the fields, and misbehave variously while passing along in the poet's representation of the rebel trek from the Kentish countryside to London, ravaging towns along their path. The end of Tuesday is marked (ll. 675–8) by an extended use of anaphora ("This was that day").

The mob congregates on Wednesday morning, June 12, to listen to the exhortations of Wat Tyler at Blackheath, whereupon at noon (l. 737) they set off to London and occupy it in the second vision. After taking the city, they sack it on Thursday, the feast of Corpus Christi (l. 919), which comes to an end in l. 950. Appropriating the homes of the well-to-do and drinking themselves into a stupor at day's end, the rebels ravage the city. The Troy episode continues as Friday, June 14 dawns (l. 953) and the rebels enter the Tower of London, which falls without resistance. At midday Archbishop Simon Sudbury is executed clumsily in a botched beheading that has him twitching on the ground as the rebels hack off his head (ll. 1079–80). The sack of the city is then further described by the narrator, who flees the Tower at high noon on Friday (ll. 1363–4). During the rest of the day and into the next morning he wanders and hides, presenting his ordeal as an extended wandering in the wilderness although it actually comprises just one day (Friday noon through mid-day Saturday).

In the third vision, which coincides in time with his experiences in the Tower and his frantic search for safety, the narrator seeks refuge aboard a "ship of tower" that immediately puts to sea. This ship is an hallucinatory melding of nautical details with the Tower of London, its travails also representing the plight of those that sought refuge there. It is thus both microcosm and macrocosm, a representation of the narrator's mind during the course of that last terrible night, tossed upon the raging waters of the Rising, and an emblem of England's endangered ship of state, threatened both within by revolt and without by French and Castilian coastal raids, ongoing since the 1370s. (The magnates' inability to protect coastal inhabitants from the depredations of the foreign fleets was, in fact, one of the causes of the Rising specified by the Speaker of the Commons in November of 1381.) Gower's ship is soon reduced to a floating hulk by the tempest and then almost swallowed by the maelstrom. Neptune, god of the sea, appears and, to end the storm, demands a sacrifice, forthcoming as the killing of Wat Tyler. God now calms the sea, the clouds part, the sun shines forth, and the ship finds a harbor, if not a safe refuge. Tyler's elimination (also struck by the mayor's squire, he actually died the next day) effectively put an end to the Rising when the peasants, in confusion and having been promised pardon, thereafter were dispelled and dispersed. Religious reflections and the voice of God ensure that we realize the entire event was the consequence of sin. The divine voice orders the poet to relate the events he has just experienced. He promises to write the work we have just read and ends with a cursory transitional passage to Book II.

*Vox Clamantis by John Gower: 'The Voice of One Crying'*

# INCIPIT: HERE BEGINS THE CHRONICLE THAT IS CALLED THE VOX CLAMANTIS

**In the beginning of this modest work, the author intends to describe how the peasant serfs rashly arose against the freeborn and the nobility of the realm. And because an affair of this sort was like an abominable and hideous \*portent, he says that he saw in a dream various mobs of the rabble transformed into different kinds of domestic animals. However, he says that those domestic animals, turning away from their nature, took upon themselves the savagery of wild beasts. Concerning the causes for which such outrages occur among humans, he discusses further according to the divisions of this book, which is arranged in seven parts, as what follows below will clearly show.**

## HERE BEGINS THE PROLOGUE OF THE FIRST BOOK

Ancient writings hold lessons for those yet unborn;
  Something that has happened commands belief.
Although common opinion may maintain that dreams
  Contain no content worthy of belief,
Nevertheless, works written in the days of old
  Certainly teach us to the contrary.
It is plain from Daniel that dreams do signify,*
  Nor was sleeping Joseph's vision groundless.*
Nay, the good angel who watches within a man*
  Always protects him with vigilant love,     10
And, although sleep may possess the outer body,
  He visits our inner mind and lends strength.
Often he reveals presages in sleepy dreams
  That men may know the causes of crises.
Hence I think that the dreams I saw in the nighttime
  Brought portents of a distinct circumstance.
What sort the vision was and when, in which king's year,
  These things you can find out in these writings.
If you should seek the writer's name, here I disguise
  My discourse, folded within three verses.     20
Take **Go**dfrey's first letters and bequeath them to John,*
  Let **W**ales conjoin to them its beginning.
Beheaded, let "**ter**" grant the remaining letters,
  Showing, when combined, the name's arrangement.
Propose, however, nothing in the scribe's praise, but

   Grasp for yourself what the writings provide.
For I write nothing in search of praise and my work
   Is not concerned with my reputation.
I shall address the plights my land lately suffered;
   It's righteous work to tell a nation's deeds.*        30
I'm allowed to weep, since I'll describe tearful times,
   That it be a guide for posterity.
As our state is doleful, so doleful is our song,*
   The writing suitable to its matter.
All of this work that is lachrymose, the reader
   Should understand, was written with my tears.*
My pen drips with these abundant tears as I write;*
   While I'm borne by zeal, heart and hand tremble.
When I try to write, the weight of the work presses
   My hand and fear then steals my strength away.       40
He who goes on with this work and its threatening times
   Will find nothing pleasant in the whole poem.
If the voice in my frail chest were to be firmer*
   And I had many mouths with many tongues,
It still would not be possible for me to tell
   Everything about the present day's ills.
My heart is so blocked by the pollution of sins*
   That my poem flows in a slower vein.
A journey to Rome is long for a pulled hamstring;
   A small book, hard work for a simple mind.       50
I ask pardon rather than praise, because my will
   Is good, if my sense too small for the task.
Add, my muse, order to the Latin I've gathered
   And grant, my mistress, words that suit your book.
True dreams indeed, filled with fear, I intend to sing,
   Whose meaning perturbs the depths of the heart.
May he whose name I bear, whom the isle of Patmos*
   Received in Revelation, guide this work.

## HERE BEGINS THE FIRST BOOK

### Chapter 1

**Here he clarifies at first in which king's reign, and also in which month and year, this event, whose course follows, befell him. Beyond that, he commends, according to how it used to be, the fecundity of this land where he then was, in which as well, as he says, delights of**

*Vox Clamantis* by *John Gower: 'The Voice of One Crying'*

**practically every kind came together. And he talks further about the loveliness of the season, and likewise about the peacefulness of the day, which, however, preceded a very terrible dream.**

It happened that, in the fourth year of King Richard,*
   When June proclaims the month to be its own,
The moon, leaving heaven, hid her light beneath earth
   And Lucifer, Aurora's spouse, arose.*
New light springs up from his setting and Aurora,
   Glowing from the nether regions, brings day.
She renews day with light and holds forth wondrous dawns*
   Since her light, fled, brings night and, returned, day.
Shining rays radiate from Phoebus reflected*
   And heaven's joyous face shines upon earth.      10
The shadows gone, bright Aurora beholds the morn,*
   And, seeing her blithe, all on earth adore.
Shining, she makes rosy-red doorways glorious,*
   And courtyards, with her freshness, full of pink.
Phoebus in his wain, agleam with shining emeralds,*
   Burns hotly in Cancer with a new fire.*
He makes all fruitful and full, feeds, favors, augments,*
   Gives life to all that sea and earth bring forth.
Each scent that rightly can, each beauty, shining light,
   Splendor, and display adorn his chariot.      20
Gold is the axle, nor is the pole otherwise,*
   And golden splendors shine on its curved wheels.
A row of silvery gems glitters along the yoke,
   Whilst chrysolite constituted its spokes.
Fiery stallions draw the Thunderer's chariot
   Behind them, hastening across the sky.
Refulgent in his royal robe, he sits enwrapped,*
   And all the world lies open to his sight.
Before his throne pass the four seasons of the year,
   Which are adorned with their various days.      30
Wreathed in white, Summer stands nearby, on his right side,
   And all the creation venerates her.
Everything blooms then, then is a new age of time,*
   And in the fields gamboling heifers play.*
Then is the field fecund, then the time of calving,*
   And, too, all creeping things renew their sport.
Flowers in the fields garb themselves in diverse hues,*
   And birds sing, warbling from their untaught throats.
The grass that has lain long hid finds the secret way*

*Book I*

By which to breezes it then lifts itself, 40
And the morning star then thaws out the frozen fields*
   And stirs the birds to fuss among their chicks.
Icy bristling winter has then shed its frosty*
   Locks and the earth has been restored to ease.
What it buried, winter yields up from icy cold*
   And fallen snow wastes in the warming sun.
The leaves return, shorn by the cold from off the trees,
   And summer's progress reigns in every grove.
It has soaked the soil with dew, gives earth grass, the woods,
   Leaves, and the trees, abundant, pleasing fruit. 50
It has renewed a thousand flowers with various crowns;
   Beneath its law the grassy field grows green.
Flora, her countenance joyous, visits her realm
   And the fields delight, with floral hues suffused,
With gathered violets, which earth grows sown by none,*
   The freeborn rustic maid adorns herself.
There were as many colors there as nature has,*
   And earth preens, painted with varied blossoms.
Oh! how I would have counted the colors bestrewn,*
   Yet could not, their abundance was so great. 60

In enclosed gardens just like paradise, fragrant
   White lilies grow mingled with red roses.
In the meadows are primroses, girt by hedgerows,
   And every herb that medicine approves.
The powers of the herbs are those that can bring health
   By their seed, by their juice, or by their root.
From the green sod the earth births a purple flower,*
   Which Nature embellishes by her laws.
Balsams, spices, cassia with nard, resinous
   Myrrh have all established their places here. 70
Purple violets, dewy roses, ever white
   Lilies contended to dwell in this place.
This place alone claimed for itself all that the air,
   The sea, and the earth cherished and held good.
Here is earth's splendor, its bloom, the glory of things,
   Which holds all the delights our custom seeks,
Planted with trees, sown with grasses, in every gift
   Surpassing what man desires for himself.
It's a second paradise there, for whatever*
   Human mind desires, blessed earth brings forth, 80
Abounding in flowing springs and pregnant with seed,

## Vox Clamantis by John Gower: 'The Voice of One Crying'

    Adorned with flowers and fruitful good things.
The ground, saturate with dew, takes on delightful
    Powers and fosters the different new plants.
Thence the grove is clothed with leaves, the garden with blooms,
    The meadow with grass, and the soil with sprouts.
The wood renews its foliage, and every meadow
    Greens that winter covered over with mud.
The west winds caress flowers that were born unsown*
    And bright warmth from above adorns the ground.         90
The season brought forth song among the birds and each
    Grove rings with various piercing voices.*
Repeating its song with its clear throat, the cuckoo*
    Calls and witnesses to the new season.
Aurora's messenger, the rhythmic lark, flutters
    Above and sings on high into God's ear.
The turtledove, joyous for the verdant season,
    Vows her compliant heart unto her mate.
Philomena in her complaint makes good her lost*
    Nature and with her notes proclaims her tale.         100
And Procne, too, sings about her sister's betrayed
    Maidenhood, so great are deceits in love.
A thousand thousand birds, like organs sound their songs,
    And just as many flowers scent the fields.
Between them they contend whether song to the ear
    Brings the more pleasure or scent to the nose.
But their suit was mild and their discord in accord,
    For both estates shine with equal merit.

When Nature fills all the woods with her law's sweetness
    And the songs of birds echo on all sides,         110
When the beauty of the flowers fills the broad fields
    And grassy plants nourish the flowery mead,
When sweet Eurus lightly breathes, sounding in the boughs,*
    And pure waters slap their banks with a sigh,
Then every creature joys in the peaceful season
    And fish take to the stream bed for the heat.
Enjoyment was renewed for everything alive
    By the pleasant breezes of the season.
And since seeing such things the eye is cheered, it takes
    Them to the deepest chambers of the heart.         120
And the ear, hearing this, prompts the sighs of the heart
    With which Venus calls love's aid to a lad.
Behold! such was the day which the lovely season
    Gave me to wander in my joyfulness.

## Book I

Everything has an end; thus evening at last came,
   When the sunset is wont to claim the day.
That still day completed its allotment of hours
   And songs ended, fell still with their sweet notes.
Night had sunk the sun's fiery rays in its darkness
   And sleep constrained a man to go to bed.          130
Then, with the dying day, I bowed my body down,
   Since sleep is wont to soothe the weary limbs.
Sadness after joy, clouds after Phoebus, sickness
   After times of good health will tend to come.
Thus the day once so bright had barely concluded
   Before the dark shadow of night arrived.
Behold! dark clouds hid the lurking constellations,
   A gold moon fled, and night then lost its fire.
Boötes had turned his cart 'round, with its pole slanted,*
   And had not set a straight course in the sky.       140
The ill-starred constellation, its center loosening,
   Sent Tartarus raging upon the earth.

Awakened from rest, my eyes not yet soothed again
   By sleep, which my mind's fear rising drove off,
Lo! sudden my hair stands, my flesh quakes, my heart's core
   Is numbed, and my senses turn to water.
Thus, tossing incessantly, I retrace in mind
   What the reason is for my sudden fear.
Thus wakeful abed, I ponder many things, pour
   Out my heart, my mind wandering about.        150
It was the time when all is still, when random dreams
   Rush into hearts as minds are slumbering.
But neither sleep nor dreams had as yet ensnared me
   When dread assured me evil was at hand.
It was midnight and heavy eyelids weight my plaints,*
   Yet relief for my eyes is slow to come.
Awake, I spent most of the night in worrying,
   Not knowing what fateful labor drew nigh.
I saw times that had passed and dreaded the future,
   And finally the shadows closed my eyes.        160
So when the frustrated night's greatest part was done,
   Sleep sudden overcame my weary eyes.
I had a little rest, until morning's star lit*
   Aurora's fire, and then I had my dreams.

## Chapter 2

**Here begins the dream, when he says that on a certain Tuesday he saw various mobs of the rabble, the first of which was seen suddenly to be changed into the likeness of asses.**

    By the time sluggish sleep had transfixed my still limbs,
        My spirit had already been snatched up.
    I thought I walked in fields to gather some flowers
        When Mars himself venerates his own day.*
    My way had not been long when near at hand I saw
        A host of very frightening portents,     170
    Many malicious sorts of the common people
        Wandering through the fields in untold mobs.
    And while my eyes thus looked upon the swirling crowds
        And I marveled at so much peasantry,
    Lo! the curse of God flashed suddenly upon them*
        And, changing their shapes, turned them into beasts.
    Those who before were human, of innate reason,
        Took the likeness of irrational beasts.
    Different shapes characterized different mobs
        And marked each by its own occupation.     180
    Since dreams signify, I'll show the wondrous events*
        That make me yet more fearful now I wake.

    I saw rebels, by sudden novelty, prideful
        Asses and nobody held their bridles.
    For, their hearts suffused with the fury of lions,
        They ventured forth in search of their own prey.
    For halters are useless and can't control their heads
        While the asses prance wildly through the fields.
    Lo! their racket terrifies all the citizens
        When they bray their hee-haws all together.     190
    The donkeys have become violent wild burros
        And what had been useful is now useless.
    They decline further to carry sacks to the towns;
        They don't want to bend their backs with the weight.
    Nor do they care for the coarse grasses in the hills,
        But from now on seek something more tasty.
    They drive others from their homes and want, without right,
        To have the rights of horses for themselves.

    The asses from now on presume to enjoy jeweled
        Saddles and to have their manes always combed.     200

*Book I*

As old Burnellus once so foolishly wanted*
  His own docked tail to be lengthened anew,
So these wretches seek in vain for new spacious rears,
  To be from behind alike lion and ass.
The ass adorned his back with a leonine pelt*
  And his vainglory overstepped all bounds.
Because his tail was not the equal of his head,*
  Against Nature he sought help for his lot.
Thus the foolish asses attempt to aggrandize
  Themselves with what Nature has denied them.                210
They did not care for the tail that she who bestowed*
  Their ears planted, but thought it was too vile.
The mind's foolish thinking is wont to ponder much*
  That hinders more than carries out its wish.
Innate stupidity gives birth to every grief
  Of a fool and guarantees a bad end.
Great things suit great people and small things, small people,*
  But those who are born low want to be grand.
A thought that has lasting effects is sudden born
  And lightly incurs an endless burden.                      220
So the foolish asses, whom arrogance stirs up,
  Refuse neglected duties set by every law.
The insanity in the air corrupted them,
  So they were changed, as if portents for me.*
Those whom I had known formerly by their long ears
  Bore long horns in the midst of their foreheads.
The two-edged sword does not cut more fiercely than those
  And they were drenched with the blood from fresh wounds.
They who, lazy by nature, were wont to loiter
  Ran at the fore with the quickness of stags.               230
Does the leopard not beat the ass at leaping light?
  Yet then the ass bested him at leaping.
The lowly ass had at that time a longer tail
  Than had, alas! the splendid lion himself.
Whatever the will of the asses bade had law's
  Force, and their new right put the old to flight.
But their asinine manner signified they were
  Dull and crude, because they had no reason.
When I saw the foolish creatures, I was afraid,
  And trusty foot would take me no farther.                  240

*Vox Clamantis by John Gower: 'The Voice of One Crying'*

## Chapter 3

**Here he says that in a second dream he saw a mob of rabble turned into oxen.**

    Behold! with them then came oxen whom no one dared
        To prick with a goad: everyone feared them.
    Against the rules of oxen, they spurned the plowman,
        And would not be led, for they had new law.
    Today a raging ox gores that just yesterday
        Was easily led by the horn to plow.
    They who had been lately tame refused their duty,
        Their brows raised aloft with menacing horns.
    They said they would no longer be yoked to the plow,
        But wanted to bear free their unbowed necks.          250
    Henceforth they will not eat chaff nor coarse straw either,
        But seek out where there's better sorts of grain.
    Since they've reformed themselves, Nature gives up their forms
        And transforms the oxen into monsters.
    They have the paws of bears, and tails just like dragons,
        So every person, fearful, shrinks from them.
    From their cavernous mouths they emit sulphurous flames,
        Which water can't quench when they issue forth.
    Devastating heat consumes whatever is touched
        By the flame, be it wood or be it stone.          260
    No herdsman is able to ward off these oxen,
        Which turn to ruin the countryside and towns.
    The jaws of the bulls of Colchis, which stronghanded*
        Jason slew, did not spew such sulphurous flames.
    With these flames, the oxen kindle more rustling roofs
        And devour them with the fire of their breath.
    The bull of Minos, which Neptune gave him, did not*
        So harm the plains, when he was raging mad,
    More than these oxen wasted fields and in towns caused
        Fearful damages in their mad frenzy.          270
    Neither Nessus, changed to a bull's likeness and by*
        Hercules conquered when he waged him war,
    Nor the centaurs, nor fierce Minotaur himself so*
        Warred upon men as in this fearful time
    These oxen did. Behold! abandoning their plows
        They brought about the violent deaths of men.

    Through the empty fields they leave the tools of their work*
        Scattered and plows hold no sway over them.

*Book I*

Behold! their rakes, hoes, and mattocks thus lie about,
   Plow beams and moldboards lack handles and ropes.    280
No yoke, coupling collar, nor halter is at hand,
   No alignment stake, plow tongue nor haft lends aid.
There is no use for plows and shares are forsaken;
   Harrows are not allowed to do their tasks.
Wagon and driver are gone and carts sit idle;
   They are of no further usefulness now.
The only road for the farmers' produce remains
   Lawless and they are untamed by reason.
Thus wherever you look lie lands without fieldhands*
   And abandoned fields that nobody claims.    290
If that's the way fields are going to be tended,*
   Granaries wait in vain their promised crops.
The ox is lion, leopard, bear, and it is plain
   That it does not remember its nature.
Now, because I saw the baleful oxen wander
   The furrow untamed, my mind was disturbed.
Oh alas! I said, the care of the fields will cease
   And there'll be fearful famine in my day.

## Chapter 4

**Here he says that in his dream he saw a third mob of rabble turned into swine.**

My sleep yet continued and seized my weary limbs,
   And heaped in addition more dreams on me.    300
Then raging crested swine, possessed by the devil,
   I saw milling about in great numbers.
A great assembly of them had come together,
   Corrupting the air with their foul ordure.
Lo! raging piglets imitated hogs; young boars,
   Their sires; and the sty held them no longer.
The boar makes a compact with his suckling comrade
   So they'll root up more soil working as one.
Sow and boar ally themselves with their fellow pigs
   To do more harm and cause more wickedness.    310
I saw the impure swine tear up the earth so much
   Scarce nothing was left whole to withstand them.
No swineherd was there, in the customary way,
   Who could drive them from the grainfields of men.

## Vox Clamantis by John Gower: 'The Voice of One Crying'

No one was there able to insert rings in their
   Snouts so that they can't dig their fearsome ruts.
And no one could affix about their bristled necks
   Restraints, but every road was free to them.
Nature so wanders along a crooked pathway
   That the swine have a wolf's ways, not a pig's.        320
Among them there was a boar that Kent had brought forth;*
   No country could produce one like to it.
Its eyes glow red and from its breast it exhales flames*
   From whose fire scarce a home was far enough.
Breath that sears the towns roars like lightening from its mouth*
   And it makes war with elephantine tusks.
When it squeals piercingly, hot foam, mixed with men's blood,*
   Streams forth across its brawny forequarters.
It gushes its hissing foam out upon the fields,*
   As well as fresh blood from some fellow's throat.        330
What its head strikes, however strong, falls to the ground;
   No one's able to survive its assaults.
Its fearsome neck bristles like a battle standard
   And in its rage it has a tiger's look.
Its hairs stand on end, like the stiff shafts of the spears*
   That carry the baleful banners of hell.
Like a laden cart groaning or a river's course
   Roaring, the boar goes by with a rumble.
This beast tramples upon crops growing in the fields*
   And treads the grain down into flattened straw.        340
The boar thereby grew so that no grass pasture could
   Produce savage beasts larger than the brute.
No place can be safe which such a beast menaces,
   Except heaven, where evil cannot go.
The beast's aroused anger exceeded hell's furies;
   At his coming the whole country trembled.
But from the north came another swine and it joined*
   The boar so they could both rip up deep ruts.
The Tegean wood did not bear such a fierce boar,*
   Although that one in Arcady was huge.        350
It did not so rouse Hercules' wrath in the hills,*
   Nor assault other people with such force
As these swine, seen in my dreams, who caused a thousand
   More damages in a thousand more ways.
That fiercely savage boar that Meleager slew*
   In woodsy lair was not so destructive
As these wrathful pigs, fitted with tusks as weapons,
   Who raged worse and caused more violent harm.

*Book I*

> Neither dregs nor lees pleased them, nor was swill as food
>    To the liking of the beasts we speak of.                              360
> They did not search out pods for themselves or acorns,
>    But pillaged the better things that they saw.
> Neither thick slops nor plain water was good enough
>    For them to drink, but they gulped down good wine.\*
> Since their nature was unaccustomed to the wine,
>    They lay like fallen trees from drunkenness.
> The greed of the pigs grew until rich folks in towns
>    Could scarcely enjoy their own food in peace.
> The sty is no longer a fit lodging for pigs;
>    They need a dirty bed and pillow too.                                 370
> They even tread in their filth beneath courtly roofs
>    And, in city's midst, attack those nobler.
> Once disfigured, they were now transfigured, and those
>    Who had been swine cultivate proud figures.
> They grunted just like lions who bellow loudly,
>    At whose sound Echo convulses the woods.
> They were the swine into whom the evil spirit\*
>    Entered, just as it says in Holy Writ.

## Chapter 5

**Here he says that he saw in his dream a fourth mob of rabble turned into dogs.**

> Afterwards I saw standing ten times a thousand
>    Barking dogs and the fields shook with their voice.          380
> Lo! the light's winged herald had issued forth his song\*
>    And the raging wrath of dogs beats the air.
> But a food scrap that falls from the master's table
>    Was not for these dogs, nor was any bone,
> No, they demand with their threats better nutriment,
>    And where they go they eat up all the fat.
> However, there are no well-bred dogs among their
>    Company, but curs whom no school has trained.
> They neither course in the chase nor bay joyously
>    To horns, nor abide that which isn't base.                        390
> They don't want to traverse the woods to seize the hare
>    Nor to drive with their energy the stag.
> Instead, they prefer to bark at the heels of men
>    From behind, and cause them much discomfort.

## Vox Clamantis by John Gower: 'The Voice of One Crying'

Cut and Cur course swiftly through the back alleyways,
   Leaving their vile huts out of viciousness.
The shepherd's dog is on hand and the one that guards
   The hall, barking at night; often they bite.
Every bakery and kitchen alike lets slip
   A broken chain to release its own dog.              400
And I saw the huge mastiffs of the butchers come
   And the dog from the mill didn't stay home.
The stables couldn't hold experienced barkers back,
   Who came as well and joined with their comrades.
There was a one-eyed dog, and a three-legged mutt
   Limped behind them and barked with his comrades.
The cur snarling in a hoarse voice then abandoned
   His dung pile and aspired to a new place.
These are the dogs it doesn't pay to stroke their backs,
   To pull their tails, or, playful, hug their heads,       410
For, angry all the time, they bare to you their fangs
   And in their rustic way don't hold with love.

They all join together, young and old, and as one
   Run about with their jaws ready to bite.
They walk in a proud manner with their tails erect;
   Nothing is safe from them that they can rend.
The jaws of the dogs are deformed by the tusks of boars;
   Their bite is pestiferous and grievous.
The more food they consume, the less they're satisfied;
   Insatiable hunger persists in them.               420
They for whom lodging in the night was manure
   Pampered their filthy limbs upon soft beds.
Their numbers were so great that none of them maintained
   Whatsoever regard for proper rank.
Oh! if anyone had heard them, how the world shook,
   Astonished by their voices far and wide,
He would have said then that the ears of no estate
   Had heard before the likeness of their howls.

And when the dogs' racket comes down to Satan's ears
   And the Inferno joys with the new sound,        430
Lo! Cerberus, the lower world's dog and hell's guard,*
   Cocks his ear and then in his joy goes mad.
And in his fury he bursts apart with fire
   The chains from his neck by which he was bound
And, leaping forth, he pierced at once the core of hell
   And swiftly hastened his journey to earth.

Book I

So comrade and peer allies with comrades and peers;
  A wicked leader leads the wicked dogs.
So a raging leader from hell makes everything
  Rage more and out of men he fashions dogs.     440
And when grieving Hecuba changed herself and took*
  A rabid dog's shape, she was not as fierce,
Indeed, as these mongrels whose anger raged, who bit
  And chewed on every limb that they could seize.
The dogs that hunted and rent Acteon, Cadmus'*
  Nephew, did not practice such wickedness.
That monstrous giant, Geryon, whom long ago*
  Spain birthed, bearing the heads of three canines,
Did not so sharpen his bloody teeth by the deaths
  Of men, nor was he then so destructive     450
That there wasn't yet more blood-soaked human slaughter
  By these dogs of which I myself now speak.
Such warfare was not waged by the murderous beast
  That Diana, exiled from the city,
Once sent to Athens to destroy its citizens,
  Nor did so many men succumb to it.
Cephalus' dog itself, which once drove the beast from*
  The city, did not have their endurance.
That's how these were, at whose vicious attacks every
  Citizen and freeborn man shook with fear.     460

## Chapter 6

**Here he says that in his dream he saw a fifth mob of the rabble turned into cats and foxes. He explains the cats as domestic servants. He explains that the foxes, the criminals freed everywhere from the prisons that were broken open, then became their comrades.**

Just when I thought I had seen it all in my dream,
  My onrushing vision showed new portents.*
Now I saw approaching foxes and cats without
  Number, who showed themselves peers of the dogs.
Nothing above or beneath the earth lies hidden
  From them, for indeed they see everything.
They dash about the fields and there probe the crannies;
  From woods and meadows they take what there is.
Not town, nor stone citadel, nor proper wall then
  Denies them entrance when they want to come.     470

They penetrate strongrooms and enter chests without
  A key, bringing all the booty to light.
With their long, fearsome iron teeth they gnaw every
  Handiwork so that nothing withstands them.
Medicine, moreover, cannot restore to life
  What their venom may infect with a bite.
Their bite is fatal; scorpions do no worse harm;
  Where they come, their companion, Death, comes too.

Lo! grey foxes determine to leave their woodland
  Dens and approach the city's wealthy homes.     480
Night-time thefts that are most often done furtively
  Broad daylight then makes manifestly plain.
Henceforth they don't value sheep nor a poor sheepfold,
  Nor does chicken or lamb please them as prey,
But those things in the city of greater value
  They seize, nor can any law restrain them.
The servile fox who dwelt beneath the ground ascends
  Into halls and seeks lodging everywhere.
Foxes, who were previously dogs' enemies,
  Make peace treaties by mutual accord.     490
Becoming wolves, they swiftly follow their prey's tracks,
  Who were normally more fearful than lambs.

The cat also joins with them and, leaving the barns,
  This rustic starts forbidden mischief.\*
Henceforth the cat declines to prey upon the mice;
  Its nature does not care to keep its ways.
Who is by right supposed to drive pests from houses
  Is then pesky and brings pests to houses.
The mice who once entered the city of Ekron,\*
  Where God's ark was, did not as sharply nip.     500
Madness did not so terrify the Ekronites
  Nor was there such a protection this time.
Nay, the awful fury I saw in these monsters
  Grieved and terrified the citizens more.

## Chapter 7

**Here he says that he saw in his dream a sixth mob of rabble turned into domestic fowl, mingled among which he says there were owls, that is, predators.**

*Book I*

It was a wonder to me when I saw such things
   And my mind's shock rushed unto my heart's depths.
There was not among the beasts any creature made,
   Of those born to servile circumstances,
But that I saw each sort amongst those in the fields
   And their mingling side by side was threatening.     510
Among ridges, hills, and out of the way places,*
   Every flock has escaped from burst stables.
The occupant of each kind of villeinage comes,
   Sprouted more thickly than plants from the soil.
When, fearful, I turned my eyes now here and now there,
   Espying all these marvels in their turn,
Lo! there came a mob of transformed domestic fowl,
   The leaders of which were cock and gander.
They who were wont to stay at home and tread the dung
   Presumed to usurp the rights of eagles.     520
The rooster took on the falcon's beak and talons;
   The gander would touch the stars with his wings.
Thus when law is exiled lofty matters succumb
   To base causes and worthy yield to vile.
Wherever the animals couldn't gain entrance,
   The birds flew above all to take the prey.

Suddenly I saw that the gander and the cock's
   Colors had changed and they'd taken new forms.
New plumage from the black raven transformed the cock
   And the gander, behold! turned to a kite.     530
They not only took on plumage foreign to them,
   But the same manner of behavior, too.
Whom nature had formerly fed at granaries,
   Satisfied with little, folly changes.
For they demand that they might eat the fat corpses
   Of human beings, which alone please them.
They who'd dutifully waited to be summoned,
   Awaited a hand to scatter their meal,
Behold! more fierce and rapacious than the falcons
   Thrust themselves forward to snatch prey by force.     540

The cock, who used to sing in the night so that all
   Were accustomed to joy in hearing him,
Crows hellishly and the horrid sound of his mouth's
   Terrible voice surpasses the thunder.
And fierce Coppa, following afoot, urges on*

> Her cock to every evil she thinks up.
> She does by her chatter what she can't do by deeds,
> > Herself stirs a thousand to base malice.
> And the gander abandons the goose that he treads
> > And everywhere he huffs at some new prey.     550
> The gander, who once in his natural state frightened
> > Nobody but children with his weak hiss,
> Now horrifies adults with his terrible sound
> > And tries to slash the bolder sort apart.
>
> And the wrath of the birds that had once spurned the owls
> > Ceases and now there is love between them.
> They determine the day is lawful for those whom
> > Night's dark shadow had granted furtive ways.
> The owl flies from confinement as the birds' comrade
> > And joins up with them freely in the fields.     560
> There'd been a time owls folded feathers together
> > To capture safely their prey through the air.
> However, this feathered rabble was using iron
> > To whet its pinions, from which men could die.

## Chapter 8

**Here he says that he saw in his dream a seventh mob of rabble changed into flies and frogs.**

> Uninterrupted slumber continued my dreams
> > And granted me many more things to see.
> That the monsters' madness be more fully replete
> > And that evil's wicked troop be increased,
> Lo! there comes every kind of flies, which swear to pierce
> > With stings and bites every healthy being.     570
> Lo! the wasps return that tortured Vespasian\*
> > Formerly and cause anew misfortunes.
> Then so great a raging horrid host of flies rose
> > That scarcely a man could hide from their bite.
> As hell rages, they drive poor wretches here and there,
> > Biting all things, inflicting injury.
>
> The frog, companion of the fly, besets many;
> > One flies to crime, the other hops behind.
> The mob of farmers Latona had turned to frogs\*
> > Returns and contrives ills with new furor.     580

## Book I

The revenge of the strange frogs was just terrible;
  In every house they did no little harm.
The frogs ate up all the food and all the fodder,
  And everywhere they spewed their vile poison.
These were the frogs barren Egypt had formerly*
  Abhorred and they caused just as much damage.
Not a wise man on earth was left unharmed by them;
  Philosophers lament the wounds they took.
The frog is bad, but the fly worse, whose violence
  Spreads and disturbs every place everywhere.     590
Oh grave punishment! than which none graver happened
  Before, from which decent men suffered more.
The noxious fly of Egypt was not more horrid*
  Nor did it terrify freeborn men more.
Yea! these flying furies searched out every chamber
  And dealt out injuries to upright men.
However, they harmed nothing base, but sought to hurt
  Those whom on earth freeborn status honored.
Thus like to like, a villein mob abets other
  Villeins, as malice joins up with malice.     600
The flies assemble, the wasps form into a ball;*
  They confound the air with their wickedness.
The fierce horsefly is there and gnats, houseflies, beetles;*
  The locust, since he bites, is their comrade.
Wandering lawless, they swarm hamlets and cities,*
  And there were no nets to impede their way.
There was no meat-preserving pot without its fly,
  Nor jar so shut a slight crack didn't show
That Prince Beelzebub, arriving, could get in
  And his army of flies along with him.     610
The torment from the various kinds of flies varied
  Then, who conferred injuries of diverse sorts.
This one struck, that one stuck, one bit, another stung,
  One hopped up and wounded with its poniard.
A grave plague, the fly, than which nothing more harmful*
  Ever lived or scourge more vicious on earth.
There was so much madness and frenzy on that day
  That no one could be safe in any place.
Flies suddenly became active from too much heat,
  Which hoarfrost previously suppressed with cold.*     620
Thus summer's heat in a sudden frenzy scattered
  Through the fields what brief winter had restrained.
Oh! what a wonder, when wandering locusts claimed*
  The labors of the ant belonged to them.

## Vox Clamantis by John Gower: 'The Voice of One Crying'

Oh! what a wonder, when the fly raged everywhere
  For its prey, more a raptor than the hawk.
Oh! what a wonder, when the filthy fly assumed
  The peacock's disdain with its proud feathers.*
Oh! what a wonder, when the fly with its small wings
  Would speed more swiftly than the lark with its.     630
Oh! what a wonder, when the feeble fly would try
  To outdo the crane in its might and flight.
Oh! what a wonder, when the fly ruled the lofty
  Eagle and aspired to take its place.
This was that day when beastly flies that had fangs came*
  Forth, which plagued the earth with their pestilence.
This was that day Fortune was not of any help;*
  There was no place flies could not get into.
This was that day the warhorse succumbed to the ass
  And in defeat was without its honor.     640
This was that day when the fierce hearts of the lions
  Were cowed in fear, pressed by the oxen's strength.
This was that day the foul pig contaminated
  All the neat and tidy fields with its filth.
This was that day when the dog became stronger than
  The bear and leopards could not face the cat.
This was that day when the swift wolf wandered freely
  Everywhere amidst the fields for its prey.

This was that day when everywhere the weak frightened
  The strong; the low, the high; the small, the great.     650
This was that day when suddenly the mighty oak
  Fell, knocked down lightly by a modest Straw.*
This was that day on which the fragile roofing Tyle
  Overcame the strong marble with its strength.
Behold the day a Straw was binding his own straws,
  Who thought that the grain was without value!
This was that day on which, when freedom was grieving,
  The villein rejoiced in his villainy.
This was that day which took the serfs onto the heights
  And cast down leaders not allowed as peers.     660
This day was the harsh stepmother of the virtues
  And the mother of all the world's evil.
This was the day that every wise man in the world
  Wished had passed by without having happened.

This was that day when all of us feared that God's wrath
  Was made manifest because of our sins.

This was throughout the earth that unique awful day,
    As if in fear of judgment it were full.
This was that day about which, if we speak truly,*
    No chronicle before had told the like.                              670
Alas, how awful! Alas, how sad and bitter!
    How confounded was that day with evil!
May heaven's vengeance, grave and swift and manifest,
    Devastate those through whom that day thus raged.
May that day delay, return never in our time,
    May there be no reason it ever would.
If there is anything we should ask of this day,*
    I beg that it not return to this place.

## Chapter 9

**Here he says that in his dream he saw, when all the abovesaid furies had gathered together, that a certain grackle, in English a jay (which is commonly called Wat) presumed the status of governor of the others, and in truth \*this Wat was their leader.**

When such a host of marvels, in manner fierce beasts,
    Had joined as one like the sands of the sea,                 680
There was a jay-bird, taught in the craft of speaking,
    Whom no cage had been able to keep home.
Here, spreading his wings while all looked on, he maintained
    Though unworthy that his was the chief role.
Just as the devil led the legions from the pit,
    So this wicked man led the wicked mob.
A fierce voice, wild face, the very image of death,
    These were the features of his appearance.
He silenced their mutterings; they all fell silent
    That the sound of his voice be better heard.                  690
He climbed atop a tree and said to his compeers
    These words in a voice from his gaping maw.
"O servile race of wretches, whom the world long past
    Subjugated to itself by its law.
Behold! the day has come when the villeins rise up
    And force freeborn to give up their places.
Down with preferment! Down with law! Let no powers
    Which once existed endure in the world.
Let that law cease that was wont to subjugate us
    By right, and let our court from now on rule."               700

## Vox Clamantis by John Gower: 'The Voice of One Crying'

The mob falls silent and ponders the speaker's words,
   Pleased by the manifesto from his mouth.
The rabble lent his treacherous words their deceived
   Ear and did not see what the end would be.
For when he had been elevated by the plebs,
   He drew the entire land unto himself.
Now, since the plebs unwisely bowed their necks to him,
   He calls the people here and takes command.
As the tide is often suppressed by a high wind*
   And as a wave swells from a whirlwind's blast,       710
So the jay-bird sways the others by his voice's
   Fervor, incites the people's mind to arms.
The foolish people do not know what their court is,
   But what he orders has the law of force.
He said, "Strike, slay, unleash wrong!" and someone strikes, slays,
   Wrongs and no one speaks out against killing.*
All those whom that Fury summons prick up their ears,*
   Listen, and drawn to the voice throng the road.
Thus many poor men, urged by the prompting Fury,
   Often put their hand into the fire then.       720
"Let it be so," they all proclaim in a loud voice;
   That sound was like the roar of the ocean.
Taken aback by the huge racket of their voice,
   I could henceforth scarce keep my trembling feet.
Nevertheless, I saw from afar how they made
   Their mutual compact by clasping hands.
They said that the peasant mob would destroy on earth
   Whatever of the freeborn sort exists.

When this was said, they all walked together as peers
   And hell's wicked commander led their way.       730
A black cloud that was stirred up by hell's furies comes,
   Which rains down, pours in their hearts, every sin.
And thus the earth became wet with the dew of hell
   That from this time forth no virtue could grow.
But every vice that a faultless man shrinks back from
   Grows, and from that time forth it fills their hearts.
By then the noonday devil had made his approach*
   And on a sad day spinning arrows fly.
Satan released is there himself and likewise all
   The errant multitude of paupered hell.       740
Behold! ignorant hearts have lost their sense of shame
   And feel no fear of crime or punishment.

*Book I*

When I saw Erebus' leaders led the world,*
   Heaven-given rights were of no avail.
The more I saw them, the more fearsome I thought them,
   Unaware what the end would have to be.

## Chapter 10

**Here he says he saw in his dream that the cursed progeny of Cain had joined with the aforesaid, together with a multitude of the servants of King Ulysses of old, whom Circe changed into beasts.***

The heat was great, the madness fierce, the mob immense
   When the Inferno raged as one with earth.
Like sea sand was the foul council of the monsters,
   Pouring from everywhere, without number.         750
That offspring of the demon's lineage was enraged,
   Rendered horrid to men, rebel to God,
Scornful of authority, savage for slaughter,*
   As is the wolf which famished rends the sheep.
At once every abounding sin of the worst sort*
   Erupted and the air poisoned good men.
The seven generations Cain himself begot*
   Are numbered there with their comrade furies.
Dreadful, foul, quick to do wrong and slow to do right,
   Each does in his own way his very worst.         760
A depraved creation ignores approaching doom;
   Everything they do they share equally.
Always loving sin, they were the agents of ruin
   And rage like butchers hell-bent on slaughter.
Isaiah, Isidore, Apocalypse all tell*
   And mighty Sybil mentions in her books*
That Gog and Magog was said to be their surname,
   Among whose sorcery is every sin.
These furies do not know what king or law might be;*
   They are restrained by no rule or order.         770
They fear no men nor, bowing, worship any gods,
   But do that which the world holds most shameful.
This filthy tribe is wont to feed on human flesh*
   And feral life provides them their shambles.*
The dark species has many shameful practices*
   Which set the wicked mob bad examples.
This raging madness consequently joins as one

*Vox Clamantis by John Gower: 'The Voice of One Crying'*

    Those raging furies I mentioned before.
Ulysses' comrades, whom Circe turned into swine,*
    Have also come and are joined up with them.     780
Now they wear the faces of men, now the transformed
    Heads of beasts that are devoid of reason.

## CHAPTER 11

**Here he says, according to the vision of his dream, how he heard their diverse names and horrid voices. He also tells of *John Ball, who goaded them on to every wickedness and was regarded among them as a prophet.**

    Wat summons, Thom comes to him, nor does Simm hang back;
        At the same time Bet and Gibb bade Hykk come.
Colle rages, whom Geff helps to make mischief ready;
    Will vows to go with them on a rampage.
Grigg steals while Dawe distracts; their companion is Hobb;
    Lorkin thinks to be no less in their midst.
Hud smites those Jud strikes, all the while Tebb threatens them;
    Jack pulls down homes and kills men with his sword.     790
Hogg shows off his strut because he thinks he's become
    Greater than the king in nobility.
Their prophet Ball teaches, whom a malign spirit
    Has taught, and he was then their highest school.
As many madmen as I've recognized by name
    There were still, as I recall, some others.
They shout out often in portentous deep voices,
    Making their noises in their different ways.

Some bray in the beastly manner of the donkeys;
    Some bellow out the lowing of oxen.     800
Some the horrible grunting of the pigs issue
    Forth and shake all the earth with their rumble.
The foaming wild boar gnashes and makes huge uproars;
    The croft boar grunts, too, and adds his racket.
The fierce barking whipped up the winds in the city
    As the harsh voice of the raging dogs flies.
The hungry fox wails and the sly wolf howls on high
    As well and summons together his like.
Nor does the cackling gander beat with lesser sound
    Ears that shudder, pierced by a sudden pain.     810

The wasps are abuzz and their sound is horrendous;
  No one is able to number the swarm.
They roar together in the manner of maned lions
  And all that was bad before becomes worse.
Lo! the boorish racket, the loud din, the foul brawl;
  Such fearsome sound was never heard before.
Rocks resound with the uproar, air bounces the sound,
  And Echo takes the noise and sends it back.
The fierce noise frightens nearby places with its din,
  Where all fear that an evil fortune comes.                    820
The perversity of this time had touched many*
  And many more were stunned by the monsters.
At the storm's front, the jay, before whose name the earth
  Trembled, struck terror in all the bigwigs.
Rumor flew forth and leaders were busy with talk,
  But there was no wise counsel from the wise.
The unheard of situation weighs on stunned ears
  And in the mind by ear stark fear arrives.
They try to doctor it, but the wound is deadly
  And there's no cure without a doctor's hand.                  830

## Chapter 12

**Here he tells, according to the vision of his dream, how the abovementioned madmen appointed heralds and tribunes among themselves, and how their old and young were armed.**

Amongst them they establish heralds and tribunes
  And order that their will should be the law.
By herald's voice they proclaim this their law, that all
  Houses be burnt down that speak against them.
Their own wicked that don't support their wickedness
  Shall be beheaded and their homes burned down.
They name those who aid and abet their crime and rage,
  Upon whose hands that work should then depend.
And that's why I saw so much damage inflicted
  When their herald shouts in their fool's forum.               840
This peasant intoned, a building was set on fire,
  Sound exploded, and the house was aflame.

This raging peasantry decreed that all who could,
  Both young and old, were required to bear arms.

Those who are elderly carry ancient fence posts
  Or poles rather than be without something.
Worn by their advanced age, they crutched their limbs with sticks,
  Those whom, like sheep, a cough marked in passing.
Here comes a peasant with a quiver upside-down,*
  Here broken bows, here a torch without light. 850
Whoever bore a distaff thought that he was armed,
  So even old men, feeble, rage in arms.

But those among the peasants whom youthful years drive
  Bear whatever crude tools there are to hand.
They carry axes and scythes rotted out with dark*
  Rust, which slash necks wide open with their edge.
Half a sheath barely covers the sword one peasant
  Carries and with which he smites the freeborn.
A spade turns into a sword, a stick is shaken
  Like a spear, and there's a hatchet handy. 860
Many a bow is twisted, bent by smoke and age,
  And many a shaft flies without feathers.
Hayfork and shovel are carried as if lances
  And an iron maul is borne as a sword.
Some peasant had said, "These are suitable for our
  Shoulders," and having muttered went his way.
So the youngsters cavort like puppies through the fields
  And think that they're more agile than the beasts.
The sling was there to hand as well, and smoother stones,*
  With which villeins have behaved threateningly. 870
When there is nothing else, in their ferocity*
  Some carry clods and branches torn from trees.
Some part bear rocks, nor did some lack spears in their rage,
  And with deadly intent they wage fierce war.
They say this ignorant progeny drenched the land
  Profusely with the blood of wiser men.
Step by step they made their way with a steady pace,
  Where Will alone, not Reason, bade them go.

## Chapter 13

**Here he tells, according to the vision of his dream, how and when the aforementioned madmen, goaded on by the devil, entered *New Troy, that is, the city of London. For just as Troy was once laid waste, so this city at that time was left forsaken, deprived of all consolation, to its utter shameful sorrow.**

## Book I

Then on my right hand I thought that I recognized
   New Troy, which looked like a widow in shock.                       880
Once encircled by its walls, it now lay open,
   Bolts in the city gate left unseated.
A thousand wolves advancing, and amongst them bears,
   Decide to leave the woods for city homes.
There was no monstrosity or lineage sprung up
   On the estates, whose rage could grieve the earth,
But that it came and grew, like the rain from the south,
   Every kind of madness from every side.
Then those appear in plain, wide open places who
   Lurked before and were greeted by their peers.                      890
A huge ferocious beast has left the wood and marsh,
   Raging more from hunger than with madness.
Yet it rages then from madness in the waste town,
   Which reels that such unheard of evil comes.
With rustic rage this woodland beast vows that, as one,
   Law cast aside, they'll overthrow justice.
The number of perdition's slaves is so great there
   That scarcely any dam can contain them.

When fury drives a task, there will be no restraint,
   For it plunges into all things proscribed.                          900
They hasten of their own accord, stop for nothing,
   So no one can impede the way they take.
We hand over all, open wide our doors to foes,*
   And put our trust in faithless betrayal.
As a keen horse neighs, prances to the ringing brass,
   Warlike, unaware that evil draws nigh,
So the savage peasantry, heedless of perils,
   Begins and fails to see what end will come.
The serfs' council, which is gripped by every fury,*
   Seeks to clasp triumphant hands with others.                        910
So the rustic mobs draw furiously nigh the town
   And, like the sea's flood tide, they enter it.
Oh! what a great event and notable wonder
   Occurred upon the entry of this threat.
Grand palatial halls in the city are transformed
   And altered altogether into huts.
And the basest huts suddenly become the halls
   By Chance, turned now in judgment most unsound.
Lo! it was Thursday, the Feast of Corpus Christi,*
   When madness girt the city's every side.                            920
One peasant ringleader at the forefront eggs on

The others, urging them to follow him.
Aided by many men, he tramples the city,*
    Strikes down the citizens, and burns their homes.
He did not screech alone, but drew thousands with him
    And involved many thousands in his crime.
His words rally their rage and, savage for slaughter,
    He shouts "Burn, Kill!" in the ears of the crowd.
What had been a safe way rages, roaring with fires,*
    And there's no passage to the long castle.                    930
The Baptist's house, bereft its spouse, falls to the sword*
    And is soon turned into fiery ashes.
Sacred temples flared with the fires of wickedness*
    And impious was mixed with pious flame.
With their hearts quaking, stunned ministers were weeping
    And fear had snatched the strength from their bodies.
He whose terrible right hand hurls fierce thunderbolts*
    Commands that the sky torment earth with fire.
If some house survives and is able to fight off*
    Peril unscathed, it makes God pious vows.                     940
I need not ask if the raging rabble lusts for*
    The city's wealth and loots during that time.
As many ants are wont to take in a thin line*
    The grain they light upon to earthen barns,
So the swarm of madmen haul their loot through the town
    And no one could reckon up their number.
One held, one yanked, one rested, another ransacked,
    And many hands quickly gathered their loot.
However, Bacchus, getting to them, soaks their guts
    In wine, and that brought Thursday to an end.                 950
Night fell, their eyes and minds were aswim in the wines;*
    Limbs twitched, but feet didn't go anywhere.

After Aurora put the starry fires to flight,*
    Lo! waxing grief now prepared fresh insult.
If Jove's violent wrath had harmed before, Venus*
    Then moved by her fury does twice as much.
The madmen dash about like lightning from the south;
    Where they come, woe and alas! they have peers.
Then in accord wolf, dog, and bear hunt together
    In the city, where they have made their lairs.                960
Behold that old Calchas, whose wisdom was greater*
    Than everyone's, did not know what to do.
Antenor could not then broker alliances
    By peace treaties, for rage dissolves his work.

Book I

No space separates a righteous man from a fool;
  Thersites' heart is just like Diomede's.
The words composed for eloquent Ulysses' tongue
  Fell flat nor was his delivery inspired.
And since Fate seems to resist so many efforts,
  Everyone hands the reins over to Chance.            970
Arms don't do much good, neither spear nor use of horse,
  And good old-fashioned bravery is gone.
As a raging lioness, leaving her nursing cub,*
  Falls upon the cattle nearest to her,
So peasant beasts, leaving the salutary law,
  Fall fiercely upon the foremost families.
The calamity befell everyone alike,
  But it did not ruin everyone the same.

Oh! the decadent nature of our first city,
  You who let the mob's madmen take up arms.         980
Oh! how backward matters are, when the wretched knight
  Quakes and feral rabble have time for arms.
The battles of Thebes, of Carthage, and Rome itself*
  Were not filled with more fury than were these.
Capaneus did not prevail, nor Tydeus;
  Neither one of them launched a fierce attack.
Palamedes did not prevail nor brave Ajax,
  And Agamemnon's sword was not in charge.
Victorious Troy fell, lay vanquished in defeat;
  Like a lamb to a wolf, Troy became prey.           990
The villeins attacked, the city's knights did not fight;
  Troy lacked Hector, and Argos, Achilles.
Hector's or Troilus' boldness did not conquer then,
  But, conquered, they submitted cravenly.
Priam did not bask in his accustomed honor;
  Though lord, he suffered what the serfs dealt him.
Hecuba's chambers then could scarce have any peace,
  For sorrow stirred the fearful hearts in them.
Nor could Ilion then, within its high towers,
  Protect anyone against the madmen.                 1000

*Vox Clamantis by John Gower: 'The Voice of One Crying'*

## CHAPTER 14

**Here he tells figuratively, according to the vision of his dream, about the death of the Archbishop of Canterbury.**

> Oh! High Priest Helenus dies, cut down by the sword,*
> Who saved the Palladium from Troy's altar.
> At first he pleads that his life should be granted him,
> But fails to stir cruel hearts for the better.
> What he says is enough if Grace could touch their ears,
> But they don't think his words have any weight.
> What he said on his own behalf ran out their ears
> And inclined the mob more to villainy.
> A mutter sounds, is raised at once to a mighty
> Uproar, and it is full of sedition.     1010
> The vicious plebs bring men of virtue to trial
> And a filthy mob crowds the sacred court.
> Faith wages war with Fraud, Virtue with Villainy,*
> Wickedness with Duty, Rage with Reason.
> Impiety, the guest, gets no gentle inputs*
> From its heart; Love leaves its mind, an exile.
> God knows that these wild men are worthy hell's endless*
> Fires and wickedly vagrant from reason.
> Oh! the sorrow in deeds, Oh! sorrow's wicked deeds.[1]*
> These are the evil deeds of hell, not man.     1020
> This was not human wickedness, since the devil
> Brought such a vicious deed from hell to earth.
> The plebs, forsaking the love of Christ, rage so wild
> Since the crude mob denies God the Father.
> Here Virtue retreats, the host of Vice advances.
> One leaves its place, the other seizes it.
> Goodness falls, Pity perishes, all Decency
> Goes into exile, and Good takes to flight.
> Here Love and Rest, Peace and Harmony of the Mind,
> And Hope and Faith abandon their mansions.     1030
> Both Temperance's kindly manner and modest

---

[1] ll. 1019–23 are written over an erasure in SCHG. D has the following, which TH2 have also but with a different l. 1021 ("The highest demon rules them, not Holy Spirit"):

> Not prickly bramble, but shining olive, lovely
> Fig, and coaxing vine incur their hatred.     1020*
> The Highest Lord doesn't rule them, nor Holy Spirit,
> Neither the law nor Christ then governs them,
> Because they do not hold their Maker in esteem.

*Book I*

Sense of Shame have built their homes far away.
Patience has conveyed itself to a better seat
   And its comrade Humility follows.
The Virtues' troop dispersed, a fierce mob of cruel plebs
   Raises a pitiless hand 'gainst Simon.
And when a powerful assembly had gathered,
   A large crowd rushed to this mortal contest.
At once from afar, some of those who stood aside,
   Awaiting the end of the matter, shout,          1040
"The death sentence applies, let him be put to death,*
   Let his blood be upon us for all time."
Words were also spoken against this opinion,
   But the foolish common voice condemned him.
His foes rush forth and violate the Lord's altars,
   Surrounding on all sides the prelate's death.*
Without any pity, merciless butchers shout,
   "He shall be done away with by our hands."
Grabbing him, they severed his neck with a halberd;
   No belief there reveres the laws of Christ.        1050
But he endured all their outrage submissively
   And, while he suffered greatly, was composed.
The curse of Christ, so earned, will not forget the ones
   Who so treat the head whose members they are.
Four confederates conspired in Thomas's death,*
   A hundred thousand delivered Simon's.
A king whose heart was moved grieved for Thomas's life
   And a king grieved the last day of Simon's.
A king's wrath was the death of Thomas, but the rage
   Of a whole mob was the cause of Simon's.       1060
An unlike cause there was, yet one death for the two
   And each righteous man suffered unjustly.
His neck unharmed by the swords, the one's head perished,
   Which God's altar received and accepted.
With his head left intact, the other's neck took blows,
   Whose passion occurred in an open square.
A knight was chiefly guilty of Thomas's blood;
   A peasant furnished arms for Simon's death.
Leaders who were not in awe of the Church of Christ
   Were the cause of the martyr Thomas's death.      1070
A villainous sort opposing the realm's justice
   Brought Simon's final day in the city.
Thomas fell by the sword in the mother's bosom
   And Simon in a mob of his children.
A king could have saved Thomas, but regal power

Lacked the might to save the life of Simon.
The death of Thomas was avenged and now vengeance
   For Simon's death looms daily at the gates.
The sun at its highest now made meager shadows;*
   At mid-day the ephod was soaked in blood.*           1080
Thus an innocent victim, the axe at his neck,*
   Suffering, pulses the earth with purple blood.
The father of the soul is bereft his body;
   The shepherd leaves the fields, slain by his flock.
The guardian of the soul was left without a guard;
   The children whom the father rears kill him.
The crozier bearer, first among priests by office,
   Was here forsaken and hung on the cross.
The doctor of the laws perishes without law,
   And the jaws of the flock grind their shepherd.       1090
He dies before his time, without sins or reason,
   He whom both Nature and God alike grieve.
Though subjugated by the false law of the serfs,
   He walks, a freeborn man, eternal ways.*
Though he fell physically, his manly courage
   Restores him spiritually to God.
His temperateness, whatever rage did outside,
   Endured within him in his innocence.
Though his wisdom is reft from the world, his virtue
   Gains a place in heaven with The Wise One.        1100
Although Justice seems cast down, by it he ascends
   To the stars and abides with God on high.
They have brought to life the one whom they thought to kill;
   They took him from the world but not from God.

Oh! who knew, in times gone by, such wicked events
   As are mirrored in the prelate's murder?
He'd served the commons before, through many good deeds,
   And the mob gladly hates him in return.
In all his years, Nestor did not know such evil,
   Which, because rare, is even more striking.         1110
But acts that occurred formerly don't weigh on me
   As heavily as those seen at present.
For the disaster I saw happen in my time
   Resulted in more grievous frightful acts.
Oh! the consequence of sin perpetuated,
   The mob's course of conduct these days teaches.
I believe them worse than Cain, who only killed his
   Brother, for that one had been their father.

## Book I

I do not know who deserves praise for such a deed;
   I do know fallen Troy allowed such crime.*     1120
What one does, another aids, and another nods
   So that bad and worse could become the worst.
The man who commits a crime and his accomplice,
   The law requires, should be tried as equals.
O you city who dares stone prophets entrusted
   You, there's reason enough that you should grieve.
But the rustic madmen of the plebs above all
   Begot this crime when they first did mischief.
Oh! the cursed hand of him who struck off the head,
   His sin frightful, his torment eternal.     1130
O you who've committed such a crime God forbade,
   Traitor, what pain, what death do you merit?
Oh! your insane fury, rustic folk, violent plebs;
   Your wicked plot goes past all wickedness.
Say with what impudence you accomplish such crimes;
   No one's equaled your guile and treachery.
Hie hither old men, flock here you flowering youth,*
   Behold what arms the wicked peasant bore.
Beat your breast, pour out your tears, bewail the dead man*
   Whose incredible death is here set forth.     1140
Like a serpent whose tail writhes when it's beheaded,*
   He who had been our head spasmed and died.
A furious death took place at the sacred altars,*
   The prelate shown less honor than a beast.
Take heed, you who are yet to come, and let this time's
   Incredible case instruct all the earth.
Let those who tend the Church beware by this instance,
   Lest earth usurp divine office right now.
What Cassandra like a prophet used to predict*
   Came true in the city to grave effect.     1150
God's nurturing hand allowed evils to happen,
   But God alone knows what his reason was.
All were stunned by such an unwarranted demise,
   At least those whom reason drew to God's love.
Priam was unable to save Helenus, for
   At that time the king's regnal laws fell still.
But when in time's course the king learned what had happened,
   He lamented and grieved with his heart's love.
The king grieved for the deed, but could not impair fate
   Nor bring to Holy Church its justice due.     1160
I saw the bodies thrown before the sacred gates;*
   There was no place free of iniquity.

## Chapter 15

**Here he describes further, according to the vision of his dream, the different persecutions and murders that the aforementioned madmen committed in the said city, which was at the time, alas! almost defenseless, and how the news of this sort of thing terrified neighboring cities.**

> The citizens who were prominent at that time
>   Fell at the hand of death, laid out like sheep.
> Corpses dispatched by death were never carried off,
>   But everywhere lay strewn about the streets.
> And so no relics should remain for men, the mob
>   Trampled the dead bodies, rent limb from limb.
> The corpses of the dead rested hung upon walls
>   And brutes, like brutes, denied them sepulture.                   1170
> That was a grim plague, when the earth was soaked in blood
>   And where a spring bubbled blood made it red.
> Death rages at the door, pounds on the gates of law,*
>   And the peasants themselves rule life or death.
> Whatsoever was strong succumbs beneath their hands;
>   The highest city falls, buried in gore.
> They waste the food they find in towers overthrown
>   And wreck the better things they recognize.
> There was new woe, lament, and overwhelming grief;*
>   The wicked refuse to honor the king.                              1180
> Old men, whom age had guided through a hundred years,
>   Wept for the calamity one day brought.
> More than fish want water, the madmen desire blood,
>   Nor does it help to beg peace and mercy.
> If a father spoke beseeching words for his son,
>   He fell, both alike at a word hewn down.
> If you sought mercy and wept the sea's waves for it,
>   Those tears would not have carried any weight.*
> Then the mob burns with ungovernable anger;*
>   No prayers succeed in restoring pity.                             1190
> When prayers are spent, the raging peasant becomes more
>   Violent and does the worst that he can.
> No boar amidst the woods, as savage in his wrath,*
>   Tossed with his foaming jaws the coursing dogs.
> Before you could have said one word to the madmen,
>   You'd have found your head severed by their tools.

*Book I*

Confounded by the terror of sudden collapse,
   The freeborn scarcely acknowledge their own.
The freeman flees and wanders, but finds no safe place,
   Neither city ramparts nor forest lairs.                      1200
Seeking safety, he draws nigh a thousand houses,
   But in no place can he find peace and quiet.
Now here, now there, like a rain cloud in his movements,*
   The freeman goes, but nowhere is he safe.
Men sleep in holes and choose the pits of Avernus
   Rather than perish, if they can but hide.
But the woods fear the woods and the fields fear the fields,*
   Town fears town, and nothing knows what is what.
How sudden those furies, the actions of which God*
   Abhorred, spattered the set table with blood!            1210
They drenched with drops of blood the food strewn everywhere;*
   No room or bed chamber was a safe place.
Then nothing, unless in the pit or in the sky,
   Could be secure by virtue of its place.
Every foreigner was their prey, smashed in the mouth
   By peasants attacking with biting swords.
Oh! the sorrow in the wife when she sees death's sword,
   By which her man would fall, although guiltless.
He holds her in his arms, dries her tears with kisses;*
   "Let us seek heaven's heights," she says, "as one."         1220
The flowing locks spread on her neck absorbed her tears,*
   And her lips quivered with her trembling sobs.
Thus I often saw, with grieving heart, women's cheeks
   Grow wet when they were bereft of their men.*
They often wrung their hands, and often tore their hair,
   And with their nails they slashed at their own skin.
But he who was the author of such savagery
   Rejoiced at their grief and would add to it.
Thus did these monstrous men cold-bloodedly rejoice;

Reports, drifting through the uncertain towns, broadcast
   Rumor's murmur and caused stout hearts to quake.
The public carnage with its grave outcome is told
   And no one knows whom Fortune will fell next.
The merciless sword, whose hand no golden gifts
   Could then buy off, lo! terrifies men more.
A bitter thirst besets and twists men's burning guts,
   While fear dries up the chambers of their hearts.
The undefeated man whom no one before could

Conquer was conquered then by grievous fear. 1240
The blood, like rain, and the earth tinted red by blood
   Disconcert still more the bold man's courage.
But there's no potion at hand to cure his disease,
   Nor does someone hasten to his rescue.
No one conjures up help in his bitter distress;
   Each one thinks his death hangs in the balance.
The leaders' hands are still and don't oppose the day's
   Wrath, but meekly accept every evil.
The strength of no powerful man was then secure;
   Nay, the wicked tail oppressed its own head. 1250
Then the house of every man seemed to be mourning
   Nor was any man safe from death's cancer.
He dipped his blades, raised high, in a great deal of blood,*
   The country peasant when he took to arms.
Merciless, he will spare neither boys nor women,
   Wastes property, farms, rights, markets of all.
No one gets mercy beneath his ferocity;
   His onslaught terrifies the whole country.
For all the mob of rabble favored the madmen,
   Nor was there one freeborn that opposed them. 1260
There was not in the whole kingdom one lance or sword
   In a knight's hands, with which he'd do his work.
When the fury grew, when the peasant mob swelled up,
   The knight that wavered then became quite meek;
The mild gentry yielded and gave way before wrath,
   And the villainous ground down the upright.
The foot takes the mind's place and error has the law's,
   No doctor has a cure for the disease.
Thus neither the shield nor lance of nobility
   Avails to uphold their ancient honor. 1270
Hollow justice ceases and no longer maintains
   Due rights in an untamed savage's heart.

Time does not grant any remedies for fury,
   For drunkenness rushes to every crime.
Who might wish to reproach these evils, but couldn't,
   Poured forth their tears in token of their thoughts.
From the bottoms of their hearts, they all summoned up
   Their tears and waited for the end to come.
Eyes that were dry before and filled with gay laughter
   Burst out in tears that flowed just like water. 1280
Who were before used to weep on no occasion

Book I

Have instructed their eyes that they should flow.
Grandfathers wept, sisters wept, and their brothers wept;*
   Their eyes saw nothing but the grief they bore.
"Alas! Oh woe!" they said, everything full of grief,
   Everything full of the worry of fear.
Someone, weeping, cries out, "How will this end for me?"
   No one knows at daybreak what night will bring.
"Help us I pray," one says, "and free us from our fear;*
   Remove our wretched fate, O God!" he says.     1290
The villein tells the freeborn, "Great power is ours,"
   He said, "and your privilege has now ended."
O class appalled by death's chilling apparition,*
   How fickle Chance has brought you such evil!
The reason is laid up in the storehouse of God
   Why such a great storm struck down freeborn men.

Peace and quiet perished because lowly creatures
   Waged shattering wars with a fierce spirit.
I saw those seek prey themselves who before had been
   The prey, but no prey could stand against them.     1300
For I saw that the smallest cubs drove off the lion
   And that the leopard could find no safe place.*
The flock of sheep point their sharp horns at the shepherd
   And they're soaked in red blood spilled from his heart.
When they put aside Christ's faith and when they rampaged,
   They thought the church and the brothel the same.
The treasonous folly of the time then denied
   All that God or Nature themselves required.
It did not fear God nor reverence the world's rights,
   But declared every wicked crime legal.     1310
Thus any semblance of order turned upside down,
   And no estate knew what status it had.

The thistle grew higher than the spikes of the grain;
   The weed devastated and spoiled the fields.
Lot is captured, the shepherd seized, the farm pillaged
   And He who sees all lets the world go blind.
Then the saintly are punished for the people's sins
   And this madness holds what's sacred wicked.
These sinful men deserve to be demons' subjects
   Since they did not fear either man or God.     1320
Deserving of their grief, the wicked plebs mutter
   And cause much dissent among the people.

Presuming the rights of priests and usurping their
   Offices, they incurred the wrath of God.
The fury of this plague blitzed indoors like a storm;
   Outside, the fearsome mob thundered with roars.
The madmen shout as one, the mournful earth answers;
   Alas! that such ills happen in this time.
No happy face is then seen upon the city;
   Each visage reflects its heart's bitterness.                1330
There is no quiet for its troubled mind and no*
   Aid comes so it can be restored to health.
Thus the Trojan's ancient love is changed to anger,*
   And song, suppressed by dirge, stills everywhere.
Laughter has turned into tears, all honor into
   Disgrace, and what sufficed before now fails.
Tears bathe faces and the heart shudders with alarm;
   Grief swallows all that had been happiness.
You would have seen some weep and lie upon the ground,
   Battered by their own and others' sorrows,                1340
And many times they stretch their arms up to heaven
   As if there's a cure for evil on high.
Who had been good is tormented for his goodness;
   Lament abounds, fresh sorrow everywhere.
"We have lost everything," they say, for in the town
   No one gets the respect his rank expects.
The wise men of the law who flourished in those days
   Lost their heads when the sword was put to them.
And those whom the madmen considered the lawyers
   They felled with like blows, slashing their bodies.       1350
Blame flew shrieking and horrified their fearful ears;
   A wise man didn't know what rights he had.
Every crime blossomed, goodness withered, the law fell
   Ill, and the king lacked wherewithal to rule.
Insane cruelty, which no one had seen before,
   Caused these and more bizarre evils in town.
This fury trampled our fatherland under foot
   Not only in cities but everywhere.

## Chapter 16

**Here he laments as if in his own person, according to the vision of his dream, the sorrows of those who saved themselves by hiding in the woods and caves for fear of those times.***

## Book I

So when I saw these things, ghastly horror gripped me*
    And it seemed to me that my life was done.           1360
The image of death stabs constantly into my
    Vitals and like a sword stirs all my guts.
And now high noon had contracted the slim shadows;*
    Evening and dawn were equally distant.
Three times, yea four, I saw the bodies of comrades*
    Flung down, their death a portent of my own.
Seeing the faces of others dripping with gore,
    I was struck with the fear of my own death.
Watching the cruel hands, the eyes devoid of the light*
    Of law, I said, "This is the end of us,"            1370
Since beasts had seized the government and arms of men,
    And there was no equity in their laws.
This becomes for me the surest cause of anxious
    Fear and the start of a worse fate for me.
For since I had seen the leaders yield to the serfs,
    There was no more hope for help from the Fates.
Those who broke out of Gehenna broke into my*
    House, taking away the laws of order.
Thus fleeing, I sudden left the site of the ruin;*
    I did not dare to cross my wrecked threshold.       1380

And then, leaving my home, through the alien fields
    I ran, where I put up in wild woodlands.
I fell often, stabbed in the back by people's tongues,
    Guilty although I'd committed no crime.
I was charged in absentia, my cause, although just,*
    Perished because no one defended it.
Then, making my weary way along hostile paths,*
    I sought, alone, to find a secure way.
Fear at this madness nevertheless lent my feet
    Wings, and in fleeing I was like a bird.*          1390
Thus wandering here and there where chance was taking me,
    In great distress I tried several places.
Silently, on stealthy foot, eyes wide, ears aching,
    My hair standing up stiff, my heart trembling,
Like a frightened boar, hemmed in by the baying pack,*
    Dismayed, I thought to find some distant place.
Ah! how often did I lie to myself and say*
    I'd set a time suitable for my plan.
Though it would be better for me to go someplace,
    My foot stays fixed in the midst of the road.       1400
In my grief I saw nothing suitable; I saw*

No fields; no lush garden looked right to me.
My mind is distracted and I cannot decide*
   What place offers a better chance to live.
Scarce trusting in myself, changing in one moment
   My prayers a thousand times, my heart wavered.
If safe places there were, I'd gladly go to them;
   Where my body can't go, my mind takes me.
But when I thought I would go home during daytime,
   My foe seized the roadway and I couldn't.                1410
I feared I would be seized if I set out at night,
   So at no time was there a time for me.
The enemy was on the right, pressed from the left,*
   And both sides terrified me with like fear.
Ah! how often seeing madmen I sought shadows,
   My ear ever open to its fullest.
Ah! how often I hid in woods, scarce dared the caves,
   Fearing at night what the morning might bring.
Ah! how often fear struck my mind, saying to me,
   "Why do you flee? You'll live but short time here."*     1420
Ah! how often I failed to heed what I now was;
   What I had been still held me in its grip.
Often during the day, when the sun was brightest,
   Night came untimely to my fearful eyes.*

Dreams that mimic my state of affairs frighten me*
   And my emotions wake to my losses.
My feelings dissolve with sleep-inducing worries,*
   As fresh wax will do when set near a fire.
Unless some better image restores me in sleep,*
   I see my native land's abandoned homes.                  1430
Like a hare, I traveled oft through slanting shadows
   Where there's a wooded hollow in a vale.
A field devoid of trees and open on all sides*
   Caused me to feel unsafe at any time.
A dense old forest untouched by any hatchet*
   Became safer for me than any church.
Then unaccustomed exertion tired me, so that
   I could scarce here or there take halting steps.
Thus fleeing my own home, my mind recoiled from caves,
   But bore that evil to escape a worse.                    1440
Putting aside my pride, without any shelter,
   I made a bed of grass combined with leaves.*
If I could have, I would have hid below those leaves,

*Book I*

Since nothing then was safe above the ground.
Hiding somewhere by day, trembling at every sound,*
  I fled, aware of the dangers I saw.
Fending off hunger with nuts, I covered myself
  With grass and leaves, nor did I move a hand.
Grief was the cure for my mind and tears were flowing
  Like sustenance into my stomach's pit.               1450
Then my food was grass, then my impulse was to run
  To deep forests, since castles were no help.
I fed my hunger with my sweat and with my tears,*
  And numbness made that food enough for me.

Grieving, I was afraid most of the time; the cause
  Of my great fear, above all, was God's wrath.
Since I was alone, I was sad, without solace,
  Compelled to walk wandering on unknown paths.
Thus hidden places multiply hidden sorrows*
  Without a companion to lighten care.              1460
But since sorrow alone brings joy to an exile,
  I am able to put on a sad face,
So tears bring joy to tears and so does grief to griefs
  While I grieve what no one can remedy.
And tears arising in my breast slide down my cheeks*
  Since hope has become hostile to my fate.
My tears are endless except when numbness blocks them,*
  And a stupor just like death binds my breast.
Then dread checks both my gushing tears and inner voice
  In a condition something like a trance.            1470
Reaching toward the sun's light, I extended my arms
  And they signed what my tongue could not manage.
And when my spirit's fierce ardor had dried my tears,*
  My sighs proclaimed that now it was their turn.
I was pale as a sheet; roiled by evils within,*
  My mind shook like the surface of the sea.
The ghastly color in my face revealed outside
  What hid in the depths of my teeming brain.
Fear and terror, the madness in my anxious face,
  Made me look like someone I didn't know.         1480

While my mind sorrowed, my body complained, its bones
  Protruded forth, and no food pleased my lips.*
I seemed now to have lost my human countenance
  And my wan features showed the marks of soil.

## Vox Clamantis by John Gower: 'The Voice of One Crying'

The blood forsook my brain and color, my body,*
   And dirt looked more attractive than I did.
Because my body had been dried up a long time,
   It had but thin skin to cover my bones.*
I'd been fearful in my mind so long that I lost
   My appearance and became someone else.           1490
I had only scarcely held onto my right mind
   Since no good fate swore to keep faith with me.
I was not free to share my thoughts with anyone;
   Nay, rather my mouth, quiet, held its words.
If happenstance conveyed some comrade here to me,
   Together we blended sorrowful tears.*
It was rare that I was consoled by friendly words*
   Because scarcely one friend was faithful then.
It was a doubtful time, when none had a sure friend
   Such as he had been accustomed to have.          1500
The man who had borne me true love previously*
   Ceased then, however, in an adverse time.
Then I sought out faithful brothers, but not the ones*
   Their father would have wished that he'd not sired.
About to speak, I'd think myself amidst plotters
   And, looking at the ground, say but few words.*
I frittered away empty moments with bland words
   When chance compelled me to speak with someone.
Many times a mild response discourages wrath;*
   Safety came then from non-committal words.        1510
And often, when struggling I wished to proffer words,
   My tongue faltered, frozen by forebodings.*
Not to burden others by asking for the news,
   My tongue avoided the wretched events.*
Often I wanted to speak my mind, but I feared
   I'd give myself away and held my tongue.
Alas! dreary fate stubbornly pressed me, wretched,*
   And no gentler hour came in my misery.
If a wretched life is a kind of death, I think*
   My life at that time was the same as death.         1520
Thus wherever I look, there's nothing but death's mark,*
   Which I think no man able to remove.
I often wished I'd die rather than see such sights,
   Or that I could be safe from these monsters.
I determined to die, since it's written, "Death frees*
   All, which it releases from evil's threat."
"O grief of Fortune," I said, "spare me further pain,*

## Book I

 Allow me to live fully or to die."
But the only goal I had was the hope of death;
 I did not dare approach my home's threshold.    1530
Then sudden came murmurs to my mind's recesses
 And often for grief brought such words as these:
"O you who will not live to see the break of day,
 How much better your fortune is than mine.*
Alas! since my death won't occur in my own bed,*
 There'll be no one to mourn me when I'm dead.
If my spirit will now go forth into the sky,*
 No friendly hand shall oil my limbs reposed.*
But if my lot has fulfilled those years that it owed*
 And the end of my life has sudden come,    1540
Lo! God, you know that I do not refuse your dooms:
 When you smite, I endure what I've deserved."

And when my raging grief overwhelms me the more
 And I'm still tossed about by my bleak lot,
Behold! Wisdom says, sympathetic to my grief,*
 "Leave off, I pray, your tears, and be patient.
The Fates don't want your reproaches, but trust that God
 Has knocked you down that he might lift you up.
Guiltless, you endure God's wrath, not his punishment.*
 Fear not, for every sorrow has its end."    1550
With such-like and similar instances, Wisdom
 Advised me to be patient, without dread.
But my mind was aware, although I'm free of fault,*
 Only a doubtful safety could be hoped.
No craft was great enough to bring back happy times
 And take from me the wrath of the divine.
There had been such great discord in my weary mind
 That I could scarcely preserve my senses.
What then was in my mind, or what ought to have been,
 When neither death nor life seemed a sure thing?    1560
Now this, now that, I thought of in my unsure mind,*
 On a day that brought me no peace or joy.
Since my despair was greater when I was asleep,
 I said the following in a low voice:
"Cruel sleep, why have you held me helpless in your grip?*
 I should have been taken by death at once."*
And so my mind quarreled often with my sorrows.
 "Why do you weep?" it said, "you'll soon be gone."*
So my wretched body was worn by wakeful cares,*

|   | |
|---|---|
| Which dreams allowed my waking mind to bear. | 1570 |

   Which dreams allowed my waking mind to bear.     1570
Fear overwhelmed me, and I stood, sad, without light,*
   And all the color drained out of my face.
Bowled over by the mighty storm of such miseries,*
   I often became senseless, like a stone.
As my mind returned, however, my griefs did, too,*
   Since life could not dislodge death from my mind.
Wanting to die, I feared the forebodings of death;
   My mind told me nothing would get better.
I would have complained aloud, but my grief-filled bowels
   Stopped me, and allowed no words at the time.     1580
My voice's strength was checked by my sobs, and my tongue,*
   Fearing the onset of tears, curbed its way.
My death is life, my life is death, which is sweeter
   Than life, and love of death smacks of living.
Alone, forlorn, hopeless, almost bereft of life,*
   I considered if my lot were certain.
Such marvels I endured then, which I scarce recall
   Now, could not be told in an entire year.
If someone wanted to know what happened to me,*
   What I'd tell them would take no little time.     1590
Thus continuously, in wide-ranging sorrows,
   I endured those weary and savage times.

## Chapter 17

**Here, also according to the vision of his dream, he describes as if in his own person the various torments that occurred to those who took themselves to the Tower of London in the hope of safety, and of the breaching of that same tower. He figures the aforesaid tower to be like a ship in danger near *the whirlpool of Scylla.**

When I perceived that law had forgotten the earth,
   And rumors of evils rose everywhere,
Lo! the shock in my dreams then more and more provoked
   Fear and often led me on doubtful ways.
As I feared what I should do, unsure what might be
   Safe, that wrath led my eyes to cast about.
Not far off, I saw a ship, and I ran towards it,*
   Hoping that my lot would be safer there.     1600
Behold! I saw a ladder and I climbed aboard,
   Where a kind sailor found a place for me.

## Book I

I saw how many others of the freeborn class
    Boarded the ship, whom total fear possessed.
There was from top to bottom scarce any degree
    Of those who were then of noble lineage,
But that, fearful, they climbed that ship upon the sea,
    Where they sought peace, if any there might be.
But whatever others did, I had always one
    Concern: that I escape the madmen safe.     1610
Having boarded the ship, with timid mind I prayed
    That fair winds would give me following seas.\*
My prayer calls on Christ, whom the winds and sea revere,\*
    That he give me smooth passage through the sea.
"Be thou my guide, Star of the Sea, be thou my cure,\*
    If you lead where the waves go, I'll be safe."

When the waves of the sea had carried us offshore
    And the ship's course had found the best currents,
I told myself that I was fully quit of earth's
    Furies, but as for that my hope was vain.     1620
For just when my hopes had been raised that I would find
    Peace, suddenly sorrow's cause was at hand.
Its terrible face hidden in the tarry murk,\*
    The sky aloft makes war upon the straits.
The blasts of the four winds roar so loud the anchor
    Was unable to hold our helpless ship.
Beside himself, on sodden wings, Notus flew forth,\*
    Whose guttering caused furious damage.
Earth's power could not hold those heavenly waters
    Which Libra, pendent above, was surging.\*     1630
Thus they're hurled relentlessly upon the surface,\*
    Whence the sea's swollen waves conquer the land.
Heaven raged against our ship with discordant winds
    And the sea's driven wave crashed on our oars.
Thunder resounded, a squall line poured from the sky;\*
    A host of troubles tossed our ship about.
Juno's swollen messenger put on her diverse\*
    Colors and flung down water diverse ways.
It is not a sweet drop that she pours, nay, rather
    Foul, bitter, sharp, vile, sour, and unhealthy.     1640
This fluid lacks a decent taste, stabs the drinker's
    Vitals, and all his guts looses at once.
Oh! happy the man who then avoided such rain,
    More noxious than the Styx or Phlegethon.\*

## Vox Clamantis by John Gower: 'The Voice of One Crying'

No matter how I was tossed, I clung to the ship,
   Which almost sank in the sea's raging wrath.
Owls went for a swim with larks in this water's flood,*
   Wolves with sheep, and the unjust with the just.
Our plowing hull suffered this sudden water's force,
   Which rushed upon the castles and the deck.            1650
The great whales grew fearful of such a huge torrent
   When more and more the ocean's wrath increased.
Enormous downpours pelted from the bursting clouds,*
   And the lightning's wrath sounded midst the sky.
You'd think the sky had all collapsed upon the strait,*
   And Iris frighted all lands with her threats.
The swollen sea climbed up the expanse of the sky*
   As if it wished to leave its proper place,
The while it spread out, growing white with hissing foam,*
   And took below what had been up above.              1660
Now when it churns the tawny sands up from the depths,*
   The water's surface takes a yellow hue.

The torments that the seas or winds could conjure up
   They furnished with huge waves and grievous gusts.
The waters of the sea merge with the heaven's air*
   And, mixed with rain, saltwater surges up.
The sails are sodden from the rains; their cover helps*
   No single head to keep itself dry then.
The war of the winds agitates the foaming waves,
   Which Auster rolls along in constant surge.*          1670
The winds sent from on high are the lords of the seas
   And render aimless the course of the ship.
Foul night spreads over us, and bright lightning itself*
   Gives light to the dark with its flashing fires.
When during the night the sea began to whiten*
   With crests, and Eurus raged headlong in arms,*
The captain shouts, "Run to the yards!" and orders us,*
   "Let go the topsails of the ship at once!"
He orders this, but adverse gales countermand him;*
   The sea's uproar does not let him be heard.          1680
Others, however, hasten to manage the oars;
   Some shore up the ship's sides with their efforts.
One pumps out the flood, pours the sea upon the sea;
   One removes spars, which flail without restraint.
The winds go to war and roil the raging narrows,
   Rendering useless men's further efforts.

*Book I*

Such a bold evil force had overwhelmed his ship
    That the crazed man lost his wavering courage.
Terrified, he did not know the situation*
    Since fear from his frozen mind iced his heart.             1690
The men cry out as the rigging and cordage groan;*
    The captain attempts no more with the oars.
The sea was all, and the shores receded from it,*
    And the deep bears its portents to the throne.

## Chapter 18

**Here he tells, according to the vision of his dream, how the storm increased so greatly that everybody on the aforementioned ship doubted there would be sure relief without God's intervention, and above all anyone from the freeborn class in particular entreated God devoutly.**

Twinned colors paint the vault dark grey and rusty red*
    And heaven's wrath is spread out everywhere.
Wrath thunders aloft, the abyss beneath ruptures,
    And the earth spews out rivers from its guts.
The clouds pour down unheard-of sheets of rain; our ship
    Takes from all quarters countless heavy seas.             1700
Adrift, our vessel doesn't know what its fate holds
    And swims amidst oceans of sea and rain.
The sea confounds minds with terrible mutterings –
    The fearful sound alone terrifies us.
The sky is so o'erspread with darkness grievously
    That we can't see our hands before our eyes.
Then there come from the sky omens that threaten death
    And all await what the fates wish for them.
The air aloft is filled with flames from the Furies,
    And frenzy on all sides spurs the waters.                 1710
Then the flaming fire discharges ferocious sounds
    And shoots an ember like a lightning bolt.
The fire-spewing flow so confused us that all
    Fell still and silently bowed down their heads.
Our skill failed us, our spirits fell, our strength faltered,
    And we were left without a shred of hope.
Then, beyond this, a huge sea beast coming arose*
    From the sea, snorting waves from its nostrils.
Just like a ship fitted out with a ramming prow,*

## Vox Clamantis by John Gower: 'The Voice of One Crying'

It plowed the waters, striking all with fear.                                        1720
The fierce creature has a broad wave beneath its breast*
  And demands for itself the right of way.
Brother of Scylla, it's madder than Charybdis,
  And sought, just like hell's maw, what it might gulp.
Seeing this, a bold man loses his inner heart's
  Strength, which dread suddenly snatches away.
And now the helmsman, raising his hands to the stars,*
  Neglecting his skills, begs for help in prayer.
The wind defeats his craft and he no longer holds*
  The reins, so an errant ship plows the strait.                                     1730
As if sick with fever, we found food abhorrent
  And without health our minds spewed out their sense.
Hands and eyes open, we stretched our arms to heaven;
  With sorrowful minds, we begged assistance.
Some wept, some were struck dumb, some called upon the saints,*
  And all invoked their God for salvation.
The captain, commending everything to God, said,
  "May Heaven's Master rapidly send aid!"
A seam opened, offering lethal waves entrance,*
  And all thought it an opening for Death.                                           1740
I saw Scylla, and then I saw Charybdis, too,*
  And both sides aspired to devour our ship.

Oh! how then was the Tower of London this ship's
  Likeness – because a savage storm shook it;
A tower lacking a wall, where rock took paper's
  Form, which dirty flies pushed through and entered;
A tower where the gate declined to set its bars,
  Whose chamber bore shameful penetration;
A tower open to madmen, where each peasant
  Entering in looted goods and quarters;                                             1750
A tower where strength capitulates to weakness;
  A tower where courage assists no man;
A tower hoping for aid, its defenses gone,
  And left without counsel unto itself;
A disgraced tower and foul bloody patricide,
  Whose nagging fame will last as long as time;
A tower whose leopard's cave was broken into,*
  Which, driven forth, left like a faithful lamb;
A tower where a rotted Tyle oppressed the Crown,*
  Whose puny foot stood on a mighty head;                                            1760
A tower redolent of ill health, not frankincense,
  Lament, not joy, filled up with loathsomeness;

*Book I*

A tower divided of tongue as Babel was,
   A tower like that Tarshish ship asea.*
So the tower submits, crushed by vice's maelstrom,
   Not knowing where to find the righteous way.
Everyone grieves, but not like me, since shipwrecking
   Scylla has its sights on my bitter ruin.
Waking as if with eyes shrouded in sleep, I saw
   These signs that made me fear harms yet to come.     1770

There's no doubt that I was terrified and alarmed
   When in those dreams I thought I bore such things.
Brought into doubtful dangers, how oft did I say
   That the ocean was safer than my ship?*
Shaken, I was afraid of Eurus and Zephyr,*
   Frigid Boreas and hurtling Notus.
These four winds throughout the four quarters of the earth
   Blow and nobody can withstand their blasts.
Our fortune is driven by hurricane force winds*
   And no one's lot could be grimmer than mine.     1780
Wretched, I thought about the fates that were dealt me*
   And deemed that evil came by my own fault.
Thus thinking to myself, I said beneath my breath,
   "My own fault brought me what I now suffer."
There were no sins hidden in the vault of my heart
   That I did not call one by one to mind.
My heart called to mind the commission of my sins
   And what it saw stimulated my prayers.
There was not a saint whom my tongue did not implore
   When the portents seen asea forecast doom.     1790
Ready to appease with my prayers the burning wrath
   Of God, I offered up these words with tears.

"O Founder of the human race, Christ Redeemer,*
   Without whom on earth naught is better, or good,
You spoke, and all things were established by your word;
   You bade, and all created things appeared.
In your word the heavens are provided their form
   And your spirit then made all this splendor.
Through you are the waters and also their fixed bounds
   And every kind of fish that's in the seas.     1800
The air with its birds you created by your word
   And gave the wind breath in four directions.
You made earth with your almighty divinity,
   Which the order you arranged made stable.

## Vox Clamantis by John Gower: 'The Voice of One Crying'

Through you live all the terrestrial living things
   And everything that crawls is 'neath your law.
Just so, you made man at the end in your image,
   Rational, that he surmount all your work,
Who, urged to transgress your commandment by that old
   Serpent, perished from a bite of apple.      1810
But so by your mercy you redeem him from death,
   You were become flesh from the Virgin's flesh.
And thus, parent of our kind, by earthly love you
   Were made, whence you'd be more beloved by us.
Since I believe that you are my God and parent,
   I beg you, gentle Father, guide my fate!
Since it did not shame you to bleed upon death's cross,
   Thus in my time of troubles, Christ, forbear!
You who snatched Paul from the sea, Peter from prison,*
   Jonah from the whale's belly, think of me!      1820
God never leaves those who hope in him, visiting
   The sick, cheering the exiled, lending aid.
I've sinned, I return; I beg you, forgive this wretch!
   The time has come to comfort the wretched.
Spare, I pray, your lightning and put away your bolts,*
   Which cause so much distress to wretched me!
"Oh! I implore you, to whom I send my prayers,
   Let my tearful voice in your divine ear.
Already near cast down by earth, I'm cold and sick;
   If saved I may be, I'll be saved by you.      1830
"O God!" I said, "put your hand to our splintered oars
   And grant me, shipwrecked, refuge on your shores.*
May she who cured the human race with Christ's coming
   Provide me to my cure a mother's aid.
I pray you, kind God, that she mediate for me,
   Who bore a flower without being deflowered.
Why don't you free me from the troubles I endure?
   Lo! we're dying; behold! a plague threatens."
While I was prostrate in my prayer, more coming blows
   Awaiting, without hope and health I feared.      1840
Then suddenly a blow struck our ship, which almost
   Foundered, nearly swallowed by Scylla's wrath.*
But the kindly strength of prayer withstood the maelstrom's
   Thirsty mouth, wherefore it was not sated.
We remained in uncertainty as to our fate;
   We had neither reasonable hope nor fear.
He perishes more gently whom waves gulp right down*

Than he whose strong arms beat the fearsome seas.
Yet all plead incessantly, offering up vows
   Kneeling, and cast aloft their pious prayers.     1850

## Chapter 19

**Here, according to the vision of his dream, he conceives of a certain divine voice shouting on high, and how God, placated by prayers, finally stills the storm, and how as if in a fiery sacrifice \*the jay, that is Walter, the captain of the madmen, was killed for his crimes.**

Our outcry, tears, and constant groans arose on high
   And God's mercy did not overlook them.
Accordingly, Neptune, god of the sea, appears
   To calm the waves and demand sacrifice.
Our offerings and our prayers availed, for which the god,
   Appeased, nodded to our vows and our pleas.
Thus, while the tempest on the swollen sea raged on
   And deadly dangers were plain to be seen,
The spirit of righteousness moved Mayor William\*
   In his thinking to the depths of his heart.     1860
Grasping fast his sword, he toppled with it that proud
   Jay and with that he brought things to an end.
One bird died that a thousand thousand live again
   And Neptune stopped up the sea's raging mouth.
Thus, although late and compelled by crimes committed,
   Our grieving ill-starred ship took up its arms.
Lo! the jay is dead. They did not die unavenged
   Whom he struck with his beak for a weapon.
The cutthroat who killed with the sword perished by it;\*
   The evildoer set the example.\*     1870
Having heaped crime upon crime and corpse upon corpse,
   The reaper gathers in the crop he sowed.
The dead man's spirit departed on gentle winds;
   God alone knows if it went to the pit.
Since he had taken up warfare so bestially,
   The prayers of the foolish peasant were void.
Since what had been wanted on high had been fulfilled,
   His cursed lot ceased from its rampages.
Perhaps that day would have been error's pinnacle
   If God had denied his aid with that death.     1880
What a great comfort the mighty victor brought me,

Who raised on high what the Fates had cast down.
Blessed the hand that offered required sacrifice
  By which the sea's tempest, conquered, was stilled.
Even as the sea's waves raged the most, since God wished,
  Salvation's welcome hour came from above.
That God had removed his wrath for the time being,
  A voice made an announcement from on high.
From the midst of the air, borne by the divine voice,
  Such was then unto our ears related.                     1890
It said, "Behold! I will allow you yet some time
  And postpone my sentence out of mercy."
At this, Scylla, submissive, checked its gaping jaws;*
  What it had first gulped, it spewed forth at once.
Thus, God bidding, our ship, which the savage maelstrom
  Swallowed, was raised, clinging, from ocean's depths.
Thus its earlier harsh heaving has been subdued,
  Such a force comes from the celestial voice.*
And, faltering, I am as revived by its words*
  As, flush with wine, a pulse grown strong again.           1900

The sailors give a cheer, some surge aloft, and each
  Rushes swiftly to tend to his duties.
On the cusp of life and death, they quickly correct
  The course to where they deem it safe to go.
They raise the small portion of the sails that remained
  Intact so that they then could steer the ship.
The waters' maw and flood were so overwhelming*
  That the earth scarce returned the waters calmed.*
But he who walked the sea afoot, compassionate,*
  Curbing the horrors, granted happy times.                1910
He constrained the seas and closed the sky's openings,
  And bade the angry waters to recede.
The north wind blew the clouds away, the spray settled,*
  And thunder's booming voice rampaged no more.
He calmed the sea's waters, returned them to their bounds,
  Lest the sea's wrath o'erwhelm our crippled craft.
And then he showed earth the sky, and the sky, the earth*
  And checked the raging furies of the sea.
Then peace returns as waves retreat, shores re-emerge,*
  And safety is restored to the righteous.                 1920
The powers of darkness fled from the new-cleansed sky*
  And long-awaited day shines brightly forth.
The risen light revealed solid earth with its rays*

*Book I*

And our ominous plight came to an end.
The sea keeps its shore, channels contain their rivers,*
   New paths are opened to the rule of law.
Thus, as God wished, when the wave is more moderate
   Our anxieties are tempered by joys.
All then praise Christ that he did not let the maelstrom
   Overwhelm them, but that he restored them.    1930
Then on bent knee, with my hands up to the heavens*
   Outstretched, I said, "Glory be, Christ, to you!"
Repeating this, I cast off the freezing fear's reins
   And new hope smooths a joyous way for me.
Since the sea had been stilled and the wind was friendly,*
   Hope returns, lifting sailors' downcast hearts.
The crew regain their strength, and one quaking sailor
   Steers, attempting to reach a safe harbor.
The mariner has new sails put before the winds,*
   Hoping better luck, and the canvas flaps.    1940

## Chapter 20

**Here he talks about that ship still seen in his dreams, that is, about his still agitated mind. It was as if he himself, fantasizing in his thoughts, had investigated every corner of the world, looking for peace of mind like a ship adrift at the mercy of the winds. At last, he says, he reached parts of Greater Britain, where peace is scarce. He also tells how the voice in his dreams commanded that he write everything he had seen and heard about the world in that search. With that the dream is ended.**

Still my eyes closed in sleep, in which my dreams ever
   Pictured a ship that searched for a safe port.
Fear could not readily leave my wandering mind
   Before it might come safely into port.
The oars on both sides had been shattered by the winds,
   And the ship held its course where Fortune led.
On the lookout for peaceful shores, it searched every
   Quadrant, but it could find no safe harbor.
But the swirling waves of the sea at last brought it
   To a port where, alas! wickedness raged.    1950
Thus in fleeing Scylla it faced no lesser risks
   When an island more dangerous took it in.
This was a broad island, protected all around,
   Which was fruitful, girt by ocean's waters.

## Vox Clamantis by John Gower: 'The Voice of One Crying'

When we arrived in port, I disembarked and went
   Ashore at once, where a tremendous crowd
Of people came running to meet me, one of whom
   Happened to be worthy above the rest.
I asked him, "Tell me, what island is this, who are*
   These people, and why do they act this way?"        1960
Lo! that old man, who was standing at the harbor,
   Answered my questions with these fearful words:

"This used to be called the isle of exiled Brutus,
   Which Diana gave him out of pity.
The practice of the people who live in this land
   Is to hold more with discord than with love.
For since this people has sprung from various tribes,
   It has the faults of its diverse make-up.
They are handsome in form, but by nature,
   Lo! they are fiercer than the savage wolf.*        1970
They don't fear the laws, overthrow what's right by force,
   And, bellicose, put Justice to the sword.
Uncivilized by laws, this folk plots frauds, uproars,
   Wickedness, armed conflicts, plagues and nuisance.
The men from the localities of this country
   Have hearts more turbulent than the ocean.*
This land has arisen from various sources,
   But it always has blood, slaughter, and war.*
Its torn-up fields grow but the sorrowful wormwood,*
   Whose fruit shows how bitter this country is.        1980
I think if they would only love one another,
   There'd be no folk more righteous 'neath the sun."

I heard many more things and they all disturbed me;
   Alas! renewed grief now incites my heart.
Just when I thought that God would be sweeter to me,
   There was Fortune's bitter apparition.
When I saw how relentless my fate was, I cracked,
   My modest hopes, crushed by great fear, collapsed.
Thus pierced by the iniquitous shafts of Fortune,
   I felt in my heart nothing but sadness.        1990
I had reached port, yet was terrified by that port,*
   The unsafe land more dreadful than the sea.
Thus tossed right back on disconcerting land and sea,
   I don't know how I'll make a safe escape.
Thus I suffer the snares of both man and the sea,*
   Swords and waves constituting my twin fears.*

*Book I*

Why did I escape so many swords? Why did no
   Threatening storm overwhelm my wretched head?
Now my hopes died, since Chance had led me to abide
   In such a port where peace cannot be found.            2000
Color had left my face, atrophy shrunk my limbs*
   (My downcast mouth had taken little food).
Just as slender stalks are shaken by a light wind*
   And poplar leaves shivered by a cold breeze,
When I wished to go on, I was all atremble,
   With a pain just like childbirth in my heart.
When I lament, the tears follow upon my words
   And earth receives the water from my eyes.
May God be my witness, who makes my feelings reel,
   I don't know what more to do in this world.           2010
So once again, convulsed anew from my heart's depths,
   I fell like a dead man down on the ground.
And when at last I raised from the dirt my eyes and
   Body, I looked behind and to each side,
And lo! there was utterly nothing; like shadows
   Ship and crowd were gone, and I was alone.
Seeing I was alone, I grieved yet all the more
   And my spirit became melancholy,
When suddenly the celestial voice I had heard
   Before proclaimed these words that follow here:       2020

"Sorrow will do you no good; if it behooved you
   To fear harm while you circled the earth's seas,
You must still watch yourself closely, for you've landed
   In a hostile isle where peace rarely thrives.
All the less, therefore, should you strive for earthly gains,
   For this world offers no rewards for peace.
If strife should assail you without, in inner peace,
   God helping, control yourself with patience.
When madness rushes in, give way to fury's rush;*
   All onslaughts are most difficult at first.             2030
Leave off struggling, let the winds direct your canvas,*
   And let your rudder take you as tides bid.
Whether the earth is warmed up by day or the stars*
   Shine cold, watch for which straits the winds stir up.
When you look around to see how times go, believe
   Nothing you've seen unless it's close at hand.
There's divine power at play in human affairs*
   And the present hour rarely shows what's true.
Be cautious always and know that what seems joyous

Can become dolorous while you're speaking. 2040
Who is silent is strong; who says a lot in haste
  Will bring shame enough down upon himself.
Leisure restores the body, which it nourishes,*
  And too much labor will do you damage.
Nature celebrates moderation, but a man
  Who indulges himself always wants more.
So I admonish you, when leisure gives you time,*
  Hasten to write what you have seen and heard
In this vision, for dreams can render the future's
  Judgment." And behold! after saying this, 2050
The sound of the voice is heard no more, and with that
  It chanced that the rooster then, in his way,
Delivered his song to the dawn, at which I was,
  Waking, dumbfounded now my dream was gone.
I could scarcely understand if what I had seen
  Had been within my body or without.
But now, because I wake alive, with all fear gone,
  My hopes in the Lord are even greater.

## Chapter 21

**Here waking he gives thanks to God, who saved him from the sea in his dreams.**

As I saw the world more clearly with waking eyes,
  That day was clear, the clouds were driven off, 2060
As I saw the madmen suppressed by ancient law,
  A broken way restored by law anew,
As I now patted my body's parts all over,
  Happy my head was still on my shoulders,
Old friendships returned with the passing rush of wrath
  And the rights of men were at last restored.
Revived by my heart's restoration, I offered
  Songs of praise to the Lord's celestial throne.
But yet I confess my courage had not returned,
  I'd borne such sudden troubles recently. 2070
Who's been harmed like a fish by a treacherous hook*
  Will think there are barbs in all of his food.
He's scarce safe today who came to grief yesterday;
  A shipwrecked man fears even calm waters.*
Thus when I recall I had been in great danger,
  My previous plight warned me more could follow.

## Book I

Thus when I'm asea, I know I'll recall that storm
   Because I can't get it out of my mind.

Alas! that I am forced to recall the sorrow
   Of that time when misery was everywhere.     2080
Now, because I escaped alive from that madness,
   I render with joy songs of praise to God.
Mary, Star of the Sea, who calmed the bitter flood
   Lest I perish, her I praise now I'm safe.
Above all I'm glad Scylla did not swallow me,*
   Into whose gullet I had been put whole.
I'd survived among dangers amidst enemies,
   But I'm free now because of God's mercy.
I have passed through the dens and by the fearsome jaws
   Of beasts, but I was not gripped in death's bite.     2090
Like a rose among thorns that avoids the sharp stabs,
   I was plucked from the swords of murderers.

Thus when the peasantry had been bound fast in chains
   And lay suffering underneath our foot,
The ox returned to the yoke, seed grew in the plowed*
   Fields, and the villein desisted from war.
Satan's power likewise lay crushed by divine might,
   Though it lurks yet in untamable serfs.
For always till forever serfdom lies in wait
   For a chance to subdue the freeborn class.     2100
For the fierce peasantry is not gentled by love,
   But, bitter, ever bears a hostile heart.
Now crushed, the slavish plowman fears, but does not love,
   And harms in a trice the man who feeds him.
Let the goad of fear be firmly driven in him
   And let weights oppress those whom peace drives mad.
A sensible man who's prepared is not deceived;
   From past troubles, he discerns future harm.
But God's right hand did mighty work, in order that
   A day filled with fury would pass me by.     2110
The trap was sprung, from which I escaped, a free man,
   And I awoke just like a man renewed.
Just as I sudden fell, all of a sudden God
   Relieved my fall, steadied my faltering foot.
I now see that dream is alive; I think it is*
   My life, and this great new fact fills my heart.
Heaven saved me, no matter it sent much lightning;*
   That tempest frightened but did me no harm.

## Vox Clamantis by John Gower: 'The Voice of One Crying'

You who mercifully gave me counsel to live
   When love of death was in my wretched breast,     2120
It behooves me that, alive, I now render you
   Praise, God, since you are more than life to me.
I ask, God, that you renew my joy since the gate
   Of happiness has long been closed to me.
Oh! if my land, which the sea did not swallow up,*
   Would know it should render prayer owed to God.
The Lord has punished, but then not delivered it
   To death's cancer, for his wrath stayed its hand.
Whatever praise others offer, I'll not be still,
   Whom God plucked from the rage of the sea's maw.     2130
For since my mind drank in all of those raging waves
   In which it tossed, released it spews them out.
Although the wave of the sea took me, I praise God
   That my wit did not succumb to the flood.
Whilst my mind recalls, it will record the details,
   Which, as if waking from a kind of dream,
I fearfully conceived; however, I've not found
   Rest, and bear everything in inmost heart.
We did not give the dream those hours that it requires;*
   Granted, I but imaged troubles in dreams.     2140
O wakeful dreams! in which no vision such as mine
   Was of a sleeping but a waking sort!
O wakeful dreams! you who have brought true dreams to me
   From which every man yet to come can learn.
O wakeful dreams! whose significance has henceforth
   To be retold in troubled poetry.
Since the voice ordered me to write all that I saw,
   I will apply myself with all my heart.
Now let the old work proceed that erstwhile was mine,
   Recent concerns be pushed aside for new.*     2150

# NOTES TO BOOK I

"Incipit Cronica que Vox Clamantis dicitur": This prose *incipit* appears in two manuscripts, evidently as a later addition, representing an attempt to integrate the newly written *Visio Anglie* into the extant six-Book *VC*, as a new Book I.

## Incipit

In line 3, *monstrum*, translated here as "portents," from the early fourteenth century in French and English also meant "monster" in the modern sense. Both were used by Gower: e.g., "monstra" l. 224, "monstris" l. 254, "monstrorum" l. 567, below; *Mirour de l'Omme*, ll. 2465, 8195, etc.; *Confessio Amantis*, I. 435, V. 5275. This word will be translated in these two ways throughout, depending upon context.

## Prologue

l. 7: cf. Daniel 2; but Gower probably also has in mind Daniel 8–9.

l. 8: cf. Genesis 37: 5–10, 40–1.

l. 9: probably based on Psalm 91: 11–12.

ll. 21–3: anagram for the name "JOHN GOWER": add to John the first two letters of "Godfrey" [GO] + beginning of "Wales" [W] + "ter" without its head [ER].

l. 30: *verbatim* Ovid, *Tristia*, 2. 322.

ll. 33–4: *verbatim* Ovid, *Tristia*, 5. 1. 5–6.

l. 36: adapted from Ovid, *Tristia*, 1. 1. 14.

ll. 37–8: adapted from Ovid, *Tristia*, 4. 1. 95–6 (l. 96 in GDLTH$_2$ only).

ll. 43–4: virtually *verbatim* Ovid, *Tristia*, 1. 5. 53–4.

ll. 47–8: virtually *verbatim* Ovid, *Ex Ponto*, 4. 2. 19–20.

ll. 57–8: comparing himself to John of Patmos, divinely commanded to write what he sees in a vision, cf. Apocalypse 1: 9–11. Notably John, despite his visionary gift, describes himself (Apocalypse 1: 9) as "frater vester et particeps in tribulatione" ("your brother and your partner in tribulations"), a theme of commonality Gower carries forward throughout the *VC*. Macaulay's suggestion that Gower "may have had some thought of the formula 'seint John to borwe'" (*Works*, IV. 371) is in error; that expression refers rather to John the Baptist, and moreover may, by the latter fourteenth century, have developed a sense of lovers' perfidy – cf. *Confessio Amantis*, V. 3416 and Chaucer, "The Squire's Tale," *CT* V. 596.

## Book I

l. 1: i.e., June 23, 1380 to June 23, 1381. The so-called Peasants' Revolt, or the Great Rising, began May 30, 1381 in Essex and was finally put down that November. In the poem, however, Gower treats only six days.

l. 4: adapted from Ovid, *Heroides*, 18. 112. Lucifer (actually the planet Venus) is the morning star – though it seems unlikely that Gower, who borrowed much of this passage from Geoffrey of Viterbo's *Pantheon* (where Lucifer is not specifically so mentioned), found the demonic association inappropriate in this context. Aurora is the dawn.

ll. 7–8: cf. Godfrey of Viterbo, *Pantheon*, col. 28.

l. 9: *verbatim* Ovid, *Metamorphoses*, 2. 110; cf. also *Confessio Amantis*, IV. 979–1034.

ll. 9–13: cf. Daniel 10–11.

l. 11: virtually *verbatim* Ovid, *Metamorphoses*, 7. 703.

l. 13: virtually *verbatim* Ovid, *Metamorphoses*, 2. 113.

l. 15: virtually *verbatim* Ovid, *Metamorphoses*, 2. 24.

l. 16: Cancer, the fourth sign of the Zodiac, extends from June 22 to July 22.

ll. 17–18: Godfrey of Viterbo, *Pantheon*, col. 28.

ll. 21–4: adapted from Ovid, *Metamorphoses*, 2. 107–9.

l. 27: virtually *verbatim* Ovid, *Metamorphoses*, 2. 23.

l. 33: *verbatim* Ovid, *Fasti*, 1. 151.

l. 34: *verbatim* Ovid, *Fasti*, 1. 156.

l. 35: virtually *verbatim* Ovid, *Fasti*, 3. 241.

ll. 37–8: *verbatim* Ovid, *Tristia*, 3. 12. 7–8.

## Notes to Book I

ll. 39–40: virtually *verbatim* Ovid, *Fasti*, 3. 239–40.

ll. 41–2: adapted from Ovid, *Amores*, 1. 6. 65–6.

l. 43: virtually *verbatim* Ovid, *Metamorphoses*, 2. 30.

ll. 45–7: virtually *verbatim* Ovid, *Fasti*, 3. 235–7.

ll. 55–6: virtually *verbatim* Ovid, *Tristia*, 3. 12. 5–6.

ll. 57–8: virtually *verbatim* Ovid, *Fasti*, 4. 429–30.

ll. 59–60: virtually *verbatim* Ovid, *Fasti*, 5. 213–14.

l. 67: *verbatim* Ovid, *Metamorphoses*, 13. 395.

ll. 79–80: virtually *verbatim* Nigel of Longchamp, *Speculum Stultorum*, ed. Mann, ll. 1037–8.

l. 89: *verbatim* Ovid, *Metamorphoses*, 1. 108.

l. 92: adapted from Nigel of Longchamp, *Speculum Stultorum*, ed. Mann, l. 510.

l. 93: adapted from Nigel of Longchamp, *Speculum Stultorum*, ed. Mann, l. 515.

ll. 99–102: Philomela = nightingale; Procne = swallow. Cf. Ovid, *Metamorphoses*, 6. 667–70 and *Confessio Amantis*, V. 5551–6047.

l. 113: Eurus, associated with autumn, is the east wind.

l. 139: *verbatim* Ovid, *Metamorphoses*, 10. 447; Boötes, constellation known variously as the ox driver, plowman, or wagon-driver.

l. 155: adapted from Ovid, *Fasti*, 4. 549.

ll. 163–4: adapted from Ovid, *Metamorphoses*, 4. 629–30.

l. 168: Tuesday, June 11, 1381. Tuesday = from OE "Tiwesdaeg," Tiw being a Germanic god of war; hence "Mars' day" (cf. French *mardi*, Spanish *martes*, etc.). Gower's chronology of the revolt in the *Visio* is notably exact.

l. 175: "malediccio": cf. Deuteronomy 28: 15.

l. 181: adapted from Ovid, *Metamorphoses*, 9. 496.

l. 201: "Burnellus/Brunellus": chief character in Nigel of Longchamps's *Speculum Stultorum*, from which Gower quotes often throughout the *VC*.

ll. 205–6: adapted from Nigel of Longchamp, *Speculum Stultorum*, ed. Mann, ll. 61–2.

l. 207: *verbatim* Nigel of Longchamp, *Speculum Stultorum*, ed. Mann, l. 83.

l. 211: virtually *verbatim* Nigel of Longchamp, *Speculum Stultorum*, ed. Mann, l. 133.

ll. 213–14: virtually *verbatim* Nigel of Longchamp, *Speculum Stultorum*, ed. Mann, ll. 139–40.

l. 217: adapted from Nigel of Longchamp, *Speculum Stultorum*, ed. Mann, l. 159.

l. 224: "monstra": cf. Incipit, above, and note.

ll. 263–4: cf. Ovid, *Metamorphoses*, 7. 100–21; ultimately derived from Apollonius of Rhodes, *Argonautica*, ll. 210–59; Gower may have known the Latin version of Gaius Valerius Flaccus, if at all.

l. 267: cf. Ovid, *Ars Amatoria*, 2. 24.

ll. 271–2: cf. Ovid, *Metamorphoses*, 9. 98–133; also *Confessio Amantis*, II. 2145–307.

ll. 273–4: cf. Ovid, *Metamorphoses*, 8. 169–71.

ll. 277–9: adapted from Ovid, *Metamorphoses*, 11. 34–6.

ll. 289–90: virtually *verbatim* Ovid, *Ex Ponto*, 1. 3. 55–6.

l. 291: virtually *verbatim* Ovid, *Metamorphoses*, 8. 293.

l. 321: "unus erat quem Kancia": veiled reference to Wat Tyler, rebel leader from Canterbury.

l. 323: *verbatim* Ovid, *Metamorphoses*, 8. 356.

l. 325: virtually *verbatim* Ovid, *Metamorphoses*, 8. 289.

l. 327: *verbatim* Ovid, *Metamorphoses*, 8. 287.

l. 329: *verbatim* Ovid, *Metamorphoses*, 8. 417.

l. 335: *verbatim* Ovid, *Metamorphoses*, 8. 285.

l. 339: virtually *verbatim* Ovid, *Metamorphoses*, 8. 290.

l. 347: "Ex aquiline...venit alter": veiled reference to John Ball, renegade preacher from York.

ll. 349–50: cf. Ovid, *Heroides*, 9. 87; Virgil, *Georgics*, 1. 15; Arcady, location of Mt. Eurymanthus, home of the boar; see l. 350 below, and note.

l. 351: i.e., Hercules' fourth labor; cf. Ovid, *Metamorphoses*, 9. 191–2; Virgil, *Aeneid*, 6. 801.

l. 355: cf. Ovid, *Metamorphoses*, 8. 271–317, 414–19.

l. 364: adapted from Nigel of Longchamp, *Speculum Stultorum*, ed. Mann, l. 696.

## Notes to Book I

ll. 377–8: cf. Matthew 8: 28–32; Mark 5: 1–13; Luke 8: 27–33.

l. 381: virtually *verbatim* Ovid, *Fasti*, 2. 767; cf. also Prudentius, "Ales Diei Nuntius," sung at Lauds on Tuesdays and Thursdays in the Sarum Breviary.

l. 431: the three-headed, snaky dog Cerberus guards the gates of Hell; cf. Ovid, *Metamorphoses*, 10. 21–2; *Heroides*, 9. 94–5.

ll. 441–2: cf. Ovid, *Metamorphoses*, 13. 404–7, 567–71.

ll. 445–6: cf. Ovid, *Metamorphoses*, 3. 228–52.

ll. 447–8: "Gereon": three-headed (sometimes dog-headed) giant inhabiting what is now Andalucia; cf. Ovid, *Metamorphoses*, 9. 184–5; *Heroides*, 9. 92.

l. 457: "Cephali canis": Cephalus' magical dog Laelaps always caught its prey: "feram": the "beast" is the Teumessian fox, which magically could never be caught, sent to punish Thebes and driven out by Laelaps; cf. Ovid, *Metamorphoses*, 7. 763–93.

l. 462: "monstra": see l. 224, above, and note.

l. 494: adapted from Ovid, *Amores*, 3. 4. 17.

ll. 499–502: cf. I Samuel 5: 6, where the mice are a plague sent in punishment for abducting the ark of God.

ll. 511–12: Nigel of Longchamp, *Speculum Stultorum*, ed. Mann, ll. 529–30.

l. 545: "Coppa" = a common name for a hen; in the Reynard the Fox tales, a daughter of Chaunticleer; see also "Coppock," Nigel of Longchamp, *Speculum Stultorum*, ed. Mann, cxxxiii, n. 279.

ll. 571–2: Vespasian was cured of a life-long infestation of worms/wasps (L. "vespa" = "wasp") in his nose after professing belief in Christ; cf. Jacobus de Voragine, *Legenda Aurea*, St. James the Less (May 1).

l. 579: cf. Ovid, *Metamorphoses*, 6. 343–81.

ll. 585–6: frogs were the second of seven plagues invoked upon Egypt: cf. Exodus 8: 1–14.

l. 593: flies were the fourth plague invoked upon Egypt: cf. Exodus 8: 21.

l. 601: *verbatim* Nigel of Longchamp, *Speculum Stultorum*, ed. Mann, l. 555.

l. 603: adapted from Nigel of Longchamp, *Speculum Stultorum*, ed. Mann, l. 526.

l. 605: adapted from Nigel of Longchamp, *Speculum Stultorum*, ed. Mann, l. 533.

ll. 615–16: adapted from Nigel of Longchamp, *Speculum Stultorum*, ed. Mann, ll. 397–8.

l. 620: adapted from Nigel of Longchamp, *Speculum Stultorum*, ed. Mann, l. 394.

ll. 623–4: cf. Avianus, *Fabulae*, 34.

l. 628: adapted from Nigel of Longchamp, *Speculum Stultorum*, ed. Mann, l. 528.

l. 635: adapted from Nigel of Longchamp, *Speculum Stultorum*, ed. Mann, l. 423.

ll. 637–9: adapted from Nigel of Longchamp, *Speculum Stultorum*, ed. Mann, ll. 439–41.

ll. 652–3: stramine = "straw" hence an allusion to the rebel Jack Straw, who may have led the revolt in Essex and thence to London; beheaded in 1381 at Smithfield, according to Froissart and Thomas Walsingham, *Chronica Maiora* (Taylor, Childs, Watkiss, I, 498– 9), which includes Straw's (probably spurious) confession; "tegula" = "tile," here "Tyle" to emphasize the play on [Wat] Tyler. See note to Ch. 9 heading, below.

ll. 667–8: adapted from Nigel of Longchamp, *Speculum Stultorum*, ed. Mann, ll. 413–14.

Ch. 9 heading: "Wat," a contemporary colloquialism for "jay bird," here identifying rebel leader Wat Tyler; cf. l. 653 above, and note; cf. also Chaucer, *CT* GenPro I. (A) 642–3.

l. 669: virtually *verbatim* Nigel of Longchamp, *Speculum Stultorum*, ed. Mann, l. 441.

ll. 709–10: adapted from Ovid, *Fasti*, 2. 775–6; cf. also *Confessio Amantis*, VII. 4754–5123.

l. 716: adapted from Ovid, *Fasti*, 2. 44.

ll. 717, 719: the three Furies = Alecto ("implacable"), Tisiphone ("avenging murder"), Megaera ("jealousy").

ll. 737–8: "demon meridianus" = "noonday devil," associated with the sin of Acedia; "sagita volat": on both, cf. Psalm 91: 6 (Vulgate).

l. 743: Erebus ("darkness"), often synonymous with the underworld/hell; cf. Ovid, *Metamorphoses*, 5. 543.

Ch. 10 heading: "progenius Chaym": cf. Genesis 4: 11–16; "servorum... Uluxes": the sorceress Circe transformed half of Ulysses' men into swine: cf. *Odyssey*, 10; Ovid, *Metamorphoses*, 14. 273–90.

l. 753: *verbatim* Ovid, *Metamorphoses*, 1. 161.

ll. 755–76: based on Godfrey of Viterbo, *Pantheon*, col. 266, individual lines as follows: *VC* 757: adapted from epigram Part II, "Septem progenies Cain in diluvio periere," cf. Genesis 4: 17–24; from *Pantheon* Part XI, "De Goth atque Magoth...": *VC* 765–6: *verbatim Pantheon* XI. 5–6; *VC* 767: virtually *verbatim Pantheon* XI. 2, cf. Apocalypse 20: 7–8; *VC* 769–70: adapted from *Pantheon* XI. 8–9; *VC* 773: *verbatim Pantheon* XI. 7; *VC* 774: virtually *verbatim Pantheon* XI. 15; *VC* 775: *verbatim Pantheon* XI. 16.

ll. 779–80: cf. Ovid, *Metamorphoses*, 14. 280–1.

Ch. 11 heading: John Ball, English priest, critical of the Church hierarchy and imprisoned for preaching social equality; released by the rebels, preached at Blackheath a sermon beginning "When Adam delved and Eve span/ Who was then the gentleman?" Cf. Thomas Walsingham, *Historia Anglicana*, edited by Henry Thomas Riley, London: Longman, Roberts and Green, 1864, vol. II, page 32.

l. 821: adapted from Ovid, *Metamorphoses*, 1. 211.

ll. 849–50: adapted from Ovid, *Amores*, 3. 9. 7–8.

ll. 855–64: cf. Thomas Walsingham, *Chronica Maiora* (Taylor, Childs, Watkiss, I, 412–13): "Some of these had come together to conquer the kingdom of England, having only staves, some with swords covered with rust, yet others had only battle-axes; some had bows which were very old, and had been made redder than ancient ivory by smoke but had only one arrow each, and many of these arrows had but one feather."

l. 869: cf. I Samuel 17: 40.

ll. 871–3: adapted from Ovid, *Metamorphoses*, 11. 29–30.

Ch. 13 heading: "nouam Troiam": common terminology for London, original probably to Geoffrey of Monmouth, *Historia regem Britanniae*; cf. *Confessio Amantis*, Pro. 37; *Cronica Tripertita*, I. 58–9.

ll. 903–4: virtually *verbatim* Ovid, *Ars Amatoria*, 3. 577–8.

l. 909: virtually *verbatim* Ovid, *Metamorphoses*, 8. 421.

l. 919: Corpus Christi is a movable feast celebrated each year on the second Thursday after Pentecost, commemorating the Last Supper. In 1381 it fell on June 13.

ll. 923–4: adapted from Peter Riga, *Aurora*, Machabeorum 33–4.

ll. 929–30: these lines contain coded references to the London presence of John of Gaunt – a particular target of the rebels. "via salva" = "Savoy," the name of Gaunt's palace on the Thames which was burned to the ground during the revolt; "longum castrum" = "Lancaster." Cf. Chaucer's similar configuration, "long castel," *Book of the Duchess*, l. 1317.

l. 931: the "Baptist's House" ("Baptisteque domus") = the Priory of St. John of Jerusalem, Clerkenwell, sacked and burnt to the ground by a mob perhaps in search of the prior, Robert Hales, who had been appointed

Treasurer of England in February 1381, and was widely blamed (albeit erroneously) for implementing the third poll tax in four years which sparked the uprising. As the same mob ransacked and destroyed the Temple Bar in search of legal documents, that seems at least an attendant motive in both places. Hales, along with Archbishop Simon Sudbury, was seized and beheaded on June 14 in front of the Tower of London.

ll. 933–6: adapted from Ovid, *Fasti*, 6. 439–42.

l. 937: *verbatim* Ovid, *Metamorphoses*, 2. 61.

ll. 939–40: virtually *verbatim* Ovid, *Metamorphoses*, 1. 288–9.

ll. 941–8: Gower's report of looting seems unobserved (as he seems to acknowledge: "Est nichil ut queram" ["I need not ask"]), but inevitable in the circumstances. Walsingham, *Chronica Maiora* (Taylor, Childs, Watkiss, I, 418–19), relates that the rebels at the Savoy obeyed explicit orders of their leaders to destroy, not loot, anything of value; in the event, however, it seems unlikely this discipline prevailed elsewhere, if indeed it did there. Both Walsingham and Knighton (Martin, 214–17) concur with Gower that inebriation was widespread.

ll. 943–4: virtually *verbatim* Ovid, *Tristia*, 5. 6. 39–40.

l. 951: adapted from Ovid, *Fasti*, 6. 673.

l. 953: *verbatim* Ovid, *Metamorphoses*, 15. 665.

ll. 955–6: Thursday: (Jove's day – L. "dies Iovis" [cf. Span. "jueves," Fr. "jeudi"] – or "Thor's day" [ON "þórsdagr"], both Jove and Thor ruling the thunder; Friday: Venus' day – L. "dies Veneris" [cf. Span. "viernes," Fr. "vendredi"]). I.e., the atrocities of Thursday June 13 were doubly exceeded by those of Friday June 14.

ll. 961–1000: it is difficult to know whether contemporary individuals were intended by named Greeks, Romans, Thebans and Trojans in these lines, although they may have been recognizable, at least as types, to Gower's readers. References in ll. 997–1000 to "Hecuba's chamber" ("Hecube thalami") potentially allude to the rebels' entry into the rooms of Joan, widow of the Black Prince and mother of Richard II; ll. 999–1000 may describe the retreat of Richard and his court into the Tower of London. Gower's sources seem to be Benoît de Sainte-Maure, *Roman de Troie*, and Guido della Colonne, *Historia destructionis Troiae*.

l. 973: adapted from Ovid, *Metamorphoses*, 13. 547.

ll. 983–92: adapted from Peter Riga, *Aurora*, I Kings 555–62 (Vulgate).

l. 1001: Helenus, as the introduction to Ch. 14 states, represents Simon Sudbury, Archbishop of Canterbury and Chancellor of England, be-

## Notes to Book I

headed by the rebels on June 14 in the courtyard in front of the Tower, along with Robert Hales (see note to l. 931, above).

ll. 1013–14: *verbatim* Peter Riga, *Aurora*, Genesis 1129–30.

ll. 1015–16: virtually *verbatim* Peter Riga, *Aurora*, Genesis 1133–4.

ll. 1017–18: adapted from Peter Riga, *Aurora*, Judicum 213–14.

ll. 1019–23: adapted from Peter Riga, *Aurora*, Judicum 215–18 (lines only in Oxford, Bodleian Library, MS Digby 138).*

ll. 1041–2: cf. Matthew 27: 22–5.

l. 1046: *verbatim* Ovid, *Fasti*, 2. 228.

ll. 1055–78: the comparison is between two Archbishops of Canterbury: Simon Sudbury and Thomas Becket (canonized 1173), the latter martyred by a sword-blow to the head in Canterbury Cathedral by four knights, purportedly to please Henry II. Henry subsequently publicly mourned Becket, doing penance at his tomb in 1174.

l. 1079: *verbatim* Ovid, *Metamorphoses*, 3. 50.

l. 1080: cf. Exodus 28: 6–43.

ll. 1081–2: virtually *verbatim* Ovid, *Tristia*, 4. 2. 5–6.

l. 1094: *verbatim* Ovid, *Fasti*, 1. 122.

l. 1120: i.e., London, "New Troy"; cf. Ch. 13 heading, l. 1333 below.

l. 1137: *verbatim* Peter Riga, *Aurora*, Genesis 1205.

l. 1139: *verbatim* Peter Riga, *Aurora*, Genesis 1207.

l. 1141: *verbatim* Ovid, *Metamorphoses*, 6. 559.

l. 1143: adapted from Ovid, *Metamorphoses*, 7. 603.

l. 1149: Cassandra, gifted with prophetic power but cursed by never being believed, predicted that if Paris went to Sparta and returned with Helen, Troy would be destroyed: cf. Guido delle Colonne, *Historia*, 6. 384–403.

l. 1161: Ovid, *Metamorphoses*, 7. 602.

l. 1173: "gates of law" ("ostia iuris"): Walsingham, *Chronica Maiora* (Taylor, Childs, Watkiss, I, 420–1), writes of the destruction of Temple Bar, "where the more well-to-do legal apprentices had their lodging" ("locum...in quo apprenticii juris morabantur nobiliores, diruerunt"). Nevertheless, Gower's reference seems too general to fix firmly.

ll. 1179–80: adapted from Peter Riga, *Aurora*, Machabeorum 45–6.

l. 1188: *verbatim* Ovid, *Heroides*, 3. 4.

l. 1189: adapted from Ovid, *Metamorphoses*, 5. 41.

ll. 1193–4: adapted from Ovid, *Ars Amatoria*, 2. 373–4.

l. 1203: adapted from Ovid, *Metamorphoses*, 4. 622.

l. 1207: adapted from Ovid, *Metamorphoses*, 8. 585.

l. 1209: adapted from Ovid, *Metamorphoses*, 5. 40.

l. 1211: virtually *verbatim* Ovid, *Metamorphoses*, 14. 408.

l. 1215: *Anonimalle* (Galbraith, 175), Froissart (Macaulay, 255, col. 2) and Walsingham, *Chronica Maiora* (Taylor, Childs, Watkiss, I, 430–1) all note that London's Fleming population was especially targeted. Nonetheless, it seems likely Gower meant what he says here: anyone identified as "not English" was vulnerable.

ll. 1219–20: *verbatim* Ovid, *Fasti*, 3. 509–10.

ll. 1221–2: *verbatim* Ovid, *Amores*, 3. 9. 11–12.

l. 1224: virtually *verbatim* Ovid, *Heroides*, 5. 68.

l. 1253: adapted from Ovid, *Metamorphoses*, 7. 599.

l. 1283: virtually *verbatim* Ovid, *Heroides*, 8. 77.

l. 1289: *verbatim* Ovid, *Metamorphoses*, 9. 775.

l. 1293: *verbatim* Ovid, *Metamorphoses*, 15. 153.

l. 1302: see l. 1757 below, and note.

l. 1331: *verbatim* Nigel of Longchamp, *Speculum Stultorum*, ed. Mann, l. 1301.

l. 1333: "amor...vetus Troie" = Londoners.

Ch. 16 heading: "as if in his own person" ("quasi in propria persona"): compare *Confessio Amantis* gloss margin l. 60: "Hic quasi in persona aliorum quos amor alligat, fingens se auctor esse Amantem" ("Here as if in the person of others whom love binds, the author, feigning himself as the Amans [the Lover]...").

l. 1359: adapted from Ovid, *Metamorphoses*, 14. 198.

ll. 1363–4: *verbatim* Ovid, *Ars Amatoria*, 3. 723–4.

l. 1365: Ovid, *Metamorphoses*, 14. 206.

l. 1369: adapted from Ovid, *Metamorphoses*, 14. 200.

l. 1377: "gehenna" = hell; cf. Matthew 5: 29–30, 10: 28, 23: 33, Mark 9: 43 (Vulgate).

## Notes to Book I

ll. 1379–80: adapted from Ovid, *Tristia*, 5. 4. 33–4.

ll. 1385–6: *verbatim* Ovid, *Heroides*, 20. 91–2.

l. 1387: *verbatim* Ovid, *Metamorphoses*, 14. 120.

l. 1390: *verbatim* Peter Riga, *Aurora*, Judicum, 199–200.

l. 1395: virtually *verbatim* Ovid, *Metamorphoses*, 4. 723.

ll. 1397–8: *verbatim* Ovid, *Tristia*, 1. 3. 53–4.

ll. 1401–2: virtually *verbatim* Ovid, *Fasti*, 5. 315–16.

l. 1403: adapted from Ovid, *Metamorphoses*, 15. 27.

ll. 1413–14: virtually *verbatim* Ovid, *Ex Ponto*, 1. 3. 57–8.

l. 1420: virtually *verbatim* Ovid, *Heroides*, 3. 24; cf. l. 1568, below.

l. 1424: *verbatim* Ovid, *Ars Amatoria*, 2. 88.

ll. 1425–6: *verbatim* Ovid, *Ex Ponto*, 1. 2. 43–4.

ll. 1427–8: virtually *verbatim* Ovid, *Ex Ponto*, 1. 2. 55–6.

ll. 1429–30: virtually *verbatim* Ovid, *Ex Ponto*, 1. 2. 47–8.

l. 1433: *verbatim* Ovid, *Metamorphoses*, 3. 709.

l. 1435: virtually *verbatim* Ovid, *Metamorphoses*, 3. 28.

l. 1442: virtually *verbatim* Ovid, *Heroides*, 5. 14.

ll. 1445–7: virtually *verbatim* Ovid, *Metamorphoses*, 14. 214–16.

l. 1453: virtually *verbatim* Ovid, *Metamorphoses*, 4. 263.

l. 1459: adapted from Ovid, *Remedia Amoris*, 581.

l. 1465: *verbatim* Ovid, *Metamorphoses*, 2. 656.

ll. 1467–8: *verbatim* Ovid, *Ex Ponto*, 1. 2. 27–8.

l. 1469: virtually *verbatim* Ovid, *Metamorphoses*, 13. 539.

l. 1473: *verbatim* Ovid, *Metamorphoses*, 8. 469.

l. 1475: *verbatim* Ovid, *Metamorphoses*, 4. 135.

l. 1482: *verbatim* Ovid, *Tristia*, 3. 8. 28.

l. 1485: *verbatim* Ovid, *Heroides*, 14. 37.

l. 1488: *verbatim* Ovid, *Tristia*, 4. 6. 42.

l. 1496: virtually *verbatim* Ovid, *Heroides*, 5. 46.

l. 1497: adapted from Ovid, *Fasti*, 5. 237.

ll. 1501–2: adapted from Ovid, *Ex Ponto*, 4. 6. 23–4.

ll. 1503–4: adapted from Ovid, *Tristia*, 3. 1. 65–6.

l. 1506: *verbatim* Ovid, *Fasti*, 1. 148.

l. 1509: "Iram multociens frangit responsio mollis": A commonplace, but one of the very few lines to quote the Vulgate directly: cf. Proverbs 15: 1: "responsio mollis frangit iram."

l. 1512: *verbatim* Ovid, *Heroides*, 11. 82; cf. *Confessio Amantis*, III. 143–336.

l. 1514: adapted from Ovid, *Heroides*, 13. 86; cf. *Confessio Amantis*, IV. 1901–34.

ll. 1517–18: adapted from Ovid, *Heroides*, 3. 43–4.

l. 1519: adapted from Ovid, *Ex Ponto*, 3. 4. 75.

l. 1521: adapted from Ovid, *Tristia*, 1. 11. 23.

ll. 1525–6: cf. probably Romans 6: 20–3.

l. 1527: adapted from Ovid, *Metamorphoses*, 1. 264.

l. 1534: adapted from Ovid, *Tristia*, 5. 4. 4.

ll. 1535–6: adapted from Ovid, *Tristia*, 3. 3. 39–40.

l. 1537: adapted from Ovid, *Tristia*, 1. 5. 11.

l. 1538: adapted from Ovid, *Tristia*, 3. 3. 44.

ll. 1539–40: adapted from Ovid, *Tristia*, 3. 3. 29–30.

ll. 1545–8: adapted from Ovid, *Fasti*, 1. 479–82.

l. 1549: *verbatim* Ovid, *Fasti*, 1. 483.

l. 1553: adapted from Ovid, *Fasti*, 1. 485.

l. 1564: *verbatim* Ovid, *Heroides*, 14. 52.

l. 1565: virtually *verbatim* Ovid, *Heroides*, 10. 113.

l. 1566: adapted from Ovid, *Heroides*, 10. 114.

l. 1568: *verbatim* Ovid, *Heroides*, 3. 24; cf. l. 1420, above.

l. 1569: *verbatim* Ovid, *Metamorphoses*, 3. 396.

l. 1571: virtually *verbatim* Ovid, *Metamorphoses*, 14. 210.

l. 1573: *verbatim* Ovid, *Metamorphoses*, 7. 614.

## Notes to Book I

l. 1575: *verbatim* Ovid, *Metamorphoses*, 9. 583.

ll. 1581–2: *verbatim* Peter Riga, *Aurora*, Genesis 1171–2.

l. 1585: virtually *verbatim* Ovid, *Metamorphoses*, 14. 217.

l. 1589: *verbatim* Ovid, *Tristia*, 1. 5. 45.

Ch. 17 heading: "voraginem Cille": Gower frequently combines, or confuses, Scylla and Charybdis in independent composition, perhaps following Alain of Lille: cf. *De planctu Naturae*, metrum 8. 1–2; when working from classical sources, he differentiates, e.g., l. 1741, below, but not always – cf. ll. 1842, 1893–4, below.

l. 1599: adapted from Ovid, *Metamorphoses*, 14. 218–19.

l. 1612: virtually *verbatim* Ovid, *Heroides*, 19. 52.

l. 1613: cf. Matthew 8: 23–7.

l. 1615: "stella maris" ("Star of the Sea"): one of the many names of the Virgin; cf. note to l. 2083, below; *Mirour de l'Omme*, l. 29925: "O de la mer estoille pure."

l. 1623: *verbatim* Ovid, *Metamorphoses*, 1. 265.

l. 1627: adapted from Ovid, *Metamorphoses*, 1. 264; "Nothus" = south wind (cf. Latin Auster); notably, a rain-bringer.

l. 1630: *verbatim* Ovid, *Fasti*, 4. 386.

l. 1631: *verbatim* Ovid, *Metamorphoses*, 1. 282.

l. 1635: virtually *verbatim* Ovid, *Metamorphoses*, 1. 269.

l. 1637: virtually *verbatim* Ovid, *Metamorphoses*, 1. 270; "Nuncia Iunonis" = Iris, the rainbow.

l. 1644: "Stige...Flegetonte": two rivers of Hades, the former marking the boundary, the latter of fire.

ll. 1647-48: image based on Ovid, Metamorphoses 1. 304.

l. 1653: *verbatim* Ovid, *Metamorphoses*, 11. 516.

l. 1655: *verbatim* Ovid, *Metamorphoses*, 11. 517.

l. 1657: adapted from Ovid, *Metamorphoses*, 11. 518.

l. 1659: *verbatim* Ovid, *Metamorphoses*, 11. 501.

l. 1661: *verbatim* Ovid, *Metamorphoses*, 11. 499.

l. 1665: adapted from Ovid, *Metamorphoses*, 11. 519–20.

l. 1667: adapted from Ovid, *Metamorphoses*, 11. 519.

l. 1670: "Auster" = south wind; cf. l. 1627, above and note.

l. 1673: adapted from Ovid, *Metamorphoses*, 11. 521.

l. 1675: *verbatim* Ovid, *Metamorphoses*, 11. 480.

l. 1676: "Eurus" = east (or south-east) wind.

l. 1677: adapted from Ovid, *Metamorphoses*, 11. 482.

ll. 1679–85: adapted from Ovid, *Metamorphoses*, 11. 484–91.

l. 1689: *verbatim* Ovid, *Metamorphoses*, 11. 492.

l. 1691: *verbatim* Ovid, *Metamorphoses*, 11. 495.

l. 1693: *verbatim* Ovid, *Metamorphoses*, 1. 292.

ll. 1695–700: adapted from Peter Riga, *Aurora*, Genesis 597–600.

ll. 1717–24: cf. l. 1764, below, and note.

ll. 1717–18: adapted from Ovid, *Metamorphoses*, 4. 689–90.

ll. 1719–20: adapted from Ovid, *Metamorphoses*, 4. 706–7.

l. 1721: adapted from Ovid, *Metamorphoses*, 4. 690.

l. 1722: "right of way": Gower's knowledge of the *lex maris* is extensive: conventionally, distressed ships had right of way; hence the maelstrom violates contemporary maritime law.

ll. 1727–8: *verbatim* Ovid, *Tristia*, 1. 11. 21–2.

l. 1729: *verbatim* Ovid, *Fasti*, 3. 593.

ll. 1735–6: adapted from Ovid, *Metamorphoses*, 11. 539–40.

l. 1739: virtually *verbatim* Ovid, *Metamorphoses*, 11. 515.

l. 1741: "Cilla...Caribdis": cf. Ch. 17 heading, above, and note.

l. 1757: "spelunca...leopardi": In heraldry leopard = "lion passant guardant" and substitutes for the lion on the royal English arms; hence here, and above, l. 1302, identifies Richard II.

l. 1759: "tegula" = "tile," used here to implicate the rebel leader Wat Tyler; see also note to Ch. 19 heading, below.

l. 1764: cf. Jonas 1: 3–5 (Vulgate); cf. ll. 1717–24, above.

l. 1774: adapted from Ovid, *Fasti*, 2. 98.

ll. 1775–6: adapted from Ovid, *Amores*, 2. 11. 9–10; Zephyr = west wind; Boreas = north wind.

ll. 1779–80: *verbatim* Ovid, *Tristia*, 5. 12. 5–6.

l. 1781: *verbatim* Ovid, *Metamorphoses*, 14. 213.

ll. 1793–818: these lines draw heavily on Genesis 1–2, the Nicene Creed, and Psalm 103.

ll. 1819–20: cf. Acts 28: 15–44; Acts 12: 3–17; Jonas 2 (Vulgate).

ll. 1825–6: adapted from Ovid, *Tristia*, 2. 179–80.

l. 1832: *verbatim* Ovid, *Tristia*, 1. 5. 36.

l. 1842: see Ch. 17 heading and note, above.

ll. 1847–8: virtually *verbatim* Ovid, *Ex Ponto*, 3. 7. 27–8.

Ch. 19 heading: "Walterus" = Wat Tyler, killed at Smithfield June 15, 1381, by William Walworth, Mayor of London; see ll. 1859–63, below, note to l. 1759, above.

ll. 1859–63: see Ch. 19 heading and note, above.

l. 1869: cf. Matthew 26: 52.

l. 1870: adapted from Ovid, *Ars Amatoria*, 1. 654.

ll. 1893–4: cf. Ch. 17 heading, above, and note.

l. 1898: *verbatim* Ovid, *Fasti*, 4. 542.

ll. 1899–900: *verbatim* Ovid, *Ex Ponto*, 1. 3. 9–10.

l. 1907: *verbatim* Godfrey of Viterbo, *Pantheon*, col. 98.

l. 1908: *verbatim* Godfrey of Viterbo, *Pantheon*, col. 98.

l. 1909: cf. Matthew 14: 24–5.

l. 1913: *verbatim* Ovid, *Metamorphoses*, 1. 328.

l. 1917: *verbatim* Ovid, *Metamorphoses*, 1. 329.

l. 1919: adapted from Ovid, *Metamorphoses*, 1. 345.

l. 1921: virtually *verbatim* Ovid, *Metamorphoses*, 5. 286.

l. 1923: adapted from Ovid, *Metamorphoses*, 9. 795.

l. 1925: *verbatim* Ovid, *Metamorphoses*, 1. 343.

ll. 1931–2: adapted from Ovid, *Metamorphoses*, 13. 410–11.

l. 1935: *verbatim* Ovid, *Metamorphoses*, 13. 440.

l. 1939: *verbatim* Ovid, *Metamorphoses*, 13. 419.

ll. 1959–82: these lines allude to Geoffrey of Monmouth, *Historia regum Britanniae*, I. 11, in which Brutus, on the deserted island of Leogetia, learns from Diana in a dream that his destiny is to colonize Albion, an island inhabited only by giants, whom the Trojans confine to caves; thereafter the island is renamed Britain, in Brutus' honor.

l. 1963: "Brutus": see note to ll. 1959–82, above.

ll. 1970–2: virtually *verbatim* Ovid, *Tristia*, 5. 7. 46–8.

l. 1976: *verbatim* Ovid, *Tristia*, 1. 11. 34.

l. 1978: *verbatim* Ovid, *Tristia*, 1. 11. 32.

ll. 1979–80: *verbatim* Ovid, *Ex Ponto*, 3. 8. 15–16.

ll. 1991–2: *verbatim* Ovid, *Tristia*, 1. 11. 25–6.

ll. 1995–6: virtually *verbatim* Ovid, *Tristia*, 1. 11. 27–8.

ll. 1997–8: *verbatim* Ovid, *Tristia*, 3. 2. 25–6.

ll. 2001–2: virtually *verbatim* Ovid, *Heroides*, 11. 27–8.

ll. 2003–4: virtually *verbatim* Ovid, *Heroides*, 14. 39–40.

ll. 2029–30: adapted from Ovid, *Remedia Amoris*, 119–20.

ll. 2031–2: adapted from Ovid, *Remedia Amoris*, 531–2.

ll. 2033–4: *verbatim* Ovid, *Heroides*, 2. 123–4.

ll. 2037–8: *verbatim* Ovid, *Ex Ponto*, 4. 3. 49–50.

l. 2043: virtually *verbatim* Ovid, *Ex Ponto*, 1. 4. 21.

ll. 2047–50: cf. Apocalypse 1: 19 (Vulgate).

ll. 2071–2: *verbatim* Ovid, *Ex Ponto*, 2. 7. 9–10.

l. 2074: adapted from Ovid, *Ex Ponto*, 2. 7. 8.

ll. 2085–6: adapted from Peter Riga, *Aurora*, Evangelium 585–6.

l. 2095: adapted from Ovid, *Fasti*, 1. 703.

ll. 2115–16: virtually *verbatim* Peter Riga, *Aurora*, Evangelium 587–8.

ll. 2117–18: adapted from Peter Riga, *Aurora*, Evangelium 745–6.

l. 2125: adapted from Peter Riga, *Aurora*, Evangelium 747.

l. 2139: adapted from Ovid, *Ex Ponto*, 1. 5. 47.

l. 2150: adapted from Ovid, *Remedia Amoris*, 484.

# BOOK II

Book II gives a legalistic veneer to the entire poem when Gower labels it, in the prose headnote, a *libellus*, a word which means both "little book" and a petition entered to initiate a lawsuit in an ecclesiastical court. Gower calls upon the outcry of the *vox populi* (the people's voice) to sustain his complaint, which is based on the violation of religious and moral values that in his view has led to the present deplorable state of circumstances. Prior to Gower, *vox populi* has an obscure but apparently lengthy non-biblical history linking it as a commonplace equivalent to *vox dei*. Although the earliest documented appearance known of the two together is in a letter from Alcuin to Charlemagne dated ca. 800, its origins are doubtless earlier.[1] Closer to Gower's time, Canon 8 (*Qualiter et quando*) of the Fourth Lateran Council (1215), for instance, explains its authority as a component of inquisitorial procedure in response to widely circulated accounts of clerical abuse:

> Ex quibus auctoritatibus manifeste probatur, quod non solum cum subditus, verum etiam cum praelatus excedit, si per clamorem et famam ad aures superioris pervenerit, non quidem a malevolis et maledicis, sed a providis et honestis, nec semel tantum, sed saepe, quod clamor innuit et diffamatio manifestat, debet coram ecclesiae senioribus veritatem diligentius perscrutari.

> By these authorities (Luke 16: 2 and Genesis 18: 21) it is plainly proven that not only when a subject cleric but also when a prelate transgresses, if it should come to the ears of a superior through the outcry and comment, not indeed of the wicked and malevolent but of decent and upright persons, not once but often, the truth that the outcry points to and the defamation discloses ought to be diligently investigated in the presence of the senior authorities of the church.[2]

---

[1] See George Boas, *Vox Populi: Essays in the History of an Idea* (Baltimore: Johns Hopkins University Press, 1969).

[2] Latin text from *Constitutiones Concilii quarti Lateranensis una cum Commentariis glossatorum*, ed. Antonio Garcia y Garcia, MIC Series A: *Corpus Glossatorum* 2 (Vatican City, 1981), 54–7. Cited in Kenneth Pennington, "Introduction to the Courts," in *The History of Courts and Procedure in Medieval Canon Law*, ed. Wilfried Hartmann and Kenneth Pennington (Washington, DC: Catholic University of America Press, 2016), 3–29 (at 20, n. 63). The translation is our own.

Of course, in the larger *Vox*, Gower will cast his net over the whole of his world, not just the clergy, no matter how much he will assail their particular faults in Books III and IV. However, the people cry out for somebody to do something about decadence and decay everywhere, and Gower will duly report their clamor to the boy-king. The charges against all aspects of society will be couched in the language of religion and morality, formulated as well with an eye towards the methodologies of the medieval sermon, with avarice and lust given positions of prominence. Eventually all of the sins come in for their due share of the blame, nonetheless. Addressing such a critical survey of society and government to the king is fraught with danger, however, and it should be noted that Gower's watchword throughout is caution. He will reiterate at the poem's end that he means to designate no particular individuals, meaning only to invite his readers to investigate their own consciences concerning the question of responsibility for the national misfortunes.

The prose headnote to the second Book's prologue is clearly intended to elide the opening of a poem that had been fashioned at an earlier point with the subsequently added *Visio Anglie* – the dream-vision that became Book I. The dream-vision and admonitory voice are referenced there, and related to the clamor of the people. The prologue itself, now to Book II, renounces the muses of tradition, presenting instead a double invocation to God and Christ before embedding a host of introductory rhetorical tropes, a catalogue of humility *topoi* familiar to most late medieval readers.[3] The prologue concludes with what was at one point in the compositional process the first mention of the poem's title, but this comes now after the 2500-plus lines of Book I, thus in consequence standing out oddly.

The main item of business in Book II then becomes the rejection of Fortune, under all her various names and aspects, as the agent that has caused England's misfortunes and that has the power to dispose of humans by her own authority. Although people commonly blame their lots on Fortune, Gower like Boethius will insist everywhere on the individual's responsibility to make correct choices along the path to judgment. The proof of his proposition, abundant in the Scripture he cites at length – usually at second-hand – is sustained by biblical hermeneutics, according to which God in his three persons (and no one else) disposes of men by the terms of his doctrine. God created the universe and now governs it in the smallest details. When circumstances suggest otherwise, faith buttressed by the contemplation of God must prevail over puny human reason. Gower adheres to the proposition, developed by Abelard in his *Ethica* and adopted by the Church as doctrine, that God will judge people by the deeds resultant upon their intentions, and accordingly assign them appropriate sentences. Through him, the righteous eventually prosper

---

[3] On these see E. R. Curtius, *European Literature and the Latin Middle Ages*, trans. Willard R. Trask, Bollingen Series 36 (New York: Harper & Row, [1953] 1963), esp. 79–105.

and the wicked are cast down. This God, who resists representation in man's futile attempts to visualize him except by the cross upon which he certified his divinity, is the true author and arbiter of creation, the sole judge of man's actions. Man's conduct, not a whimsical Fortune, determines his end.

*Vox Clamantis by John Gower: 'The Voice of One Crying'*

# HERE BEGINS THE PROLOGUE OF THE SECOND BOOK

**Here he says that, now awake, he intends to write what he saw and heard about the world just as he received it from the voice in his dream, and he calls this petition \*The Voice of One Crying, because it was created as if from the voice and clamor of all, to which end he invokes the assistance of the Holy Spirit in his task.**

    I have seen and noted many different things
        My mindful pen now wants to write for you.
    I don't invoke muses at the start, make offerings
        To gods, but sacrifice to God alone.
    God of the soul's spirit, kindling the breast's senses,
        Inflame your servant's heart unto its depths,
    And in your name, O Christ, I shall cast forth my net
        That my mind may catch what's pleasing to it.
    I pray this work, begun to the praise of your name,
        Enjoys through you a successful ending.     10
    I beg you, the one who reads these words, handle them
        Respectfully, not mindful of my faults.
    Accept in them the matter, not the man, the thought,
        Not the form, for I'm a wretched fellow.
    Yet often in a worthless mine something precious\*
        Turns up that, removed, has a pleasing use.
    Whatever in these words plain virtue offers you,
        Take, and ask peremptorily no more.
    If my pen dripping in your ear irritates you,
        Let it be medicine that soothes your hurt.     20
    If I don't use fancy words, so that the meters
        Are elegant, examine what they mean.
    And if, untaught, I have done poorly, forgive me,
        You who read this, and take what lies within.
    If incorrect meters lead my verses astray,
        Take my prayers as suiting what my mind means.
    Whatever formal rhetorical leaves they lack,
        The fruit of their matter shall not be less.
    Though these verses formally have but modest worth,
        The strength of their content will be greater.     30

    Although dull sense may hinder me, without a blush
        I'll offer what my artlessness affords.
    Knowing little was once great shame in an old man\*
        For the gravity of the time he'd lost.
    But if old age now knows or teaches what it sees,

*Book II*

    The voice of youth scarce gives it a welcome.
What old men write, although zealous in its fervor,
    Is rarely able to please youth enough.
However, although canine jaws may bark insults,
    I will not flee but sing indeed my song.          40
Suck your oil from the rocks and honey from a stone,*
    And take the sweet notes from my untaught song.
Whatever morals Scripture furnishes within
    Ought to have a place for instruction's sake.
He who put words in an ass's mouth is my hope*
    That my mouth for a fact speaks to his praise.
Let thus my simplicity's detractor depart,
    That gnawing envy not consume my words.
Let readers' ears be free of strife and obstructive*
    Mutters end! Envious throng, cease your work!      50
Yet if Sinon should rant and the serpent rear up,*
    I mean to do what my pen has begun.
The eye is blind and the ear is as good as deaf
    That conveys to the heart's depths nothing wise.
And the heart that does not teach what it knows is like
    A glowing coal hidden beneath ashes.
A light shining beneath a bushel does nothing,*
    Or sense in a heart refusing to speak.
If little, it's fitting I write the few things that
    I know, helping another to know them.        60
A man of modest means, I'll give a modicum*
    That helps a bit rather than not at all.
No one's so poor he's unable to give something;
    If I cannot give gifts, I'll give my words.*
To the man trusting in the Lord no achievement*
    Is impossible when his work means well.

The one whom Christ's grace enriches is never poor;*
    Nay, whom God augments will have sufficient.
Great feats are often accomplished by modest sense;
    Little hands often manage great estates.        70
A little light often dissipates deep shadows,
    And rivulets deliver sweet waters.
Nothing is hard for one who wishes to do right;
    May God thus provide the words that I want.
I do not speak the words that follow on my own,
    But bring them like an informed messenger.
As honeycomb is gathered from many flowers*

And seashells are gathered on diverse shores,
So diverse mouths have bestowed this work upon me*
   And various visions are my work's cause. 80
I confess that my songs were strengthened in writing
   By the examples of learned ancients.
The name of this volume shall be *Vox Clamantis*,
   For the book brings word of today's distress.

## HERE BEGINS THE SECOND BOOK

### Chapter 1

**Here he tells how, according to what he has heard from the clamor of the commons, the estates and governance of the world have changed mostly for the worse in these parts, and how everyone blames Fortune for this.**

I will use my tears as a kind of ink, in which*
   Heavy-hearted I'll write with a new reed.
Solomon said man's empty and all's vanity*
   And nothing gives surety but loving God.
Whosoever are born, the voice of pain comes first,
   For everyone starts life with a loud wail.
Temptation plagues everybody after the font,*
   The devil's craft, carnal war, avarice.
We stand and fall, breathe and die, flower and wither;
   No place is stable for us in the world. 10
We all begin to die when our mothers cast us
   From their wombs and a brief hour concludes us.
Crying plagues infants; school, youngsters; lust, young adults;
   Ambition, men; and avarice, oldsters.
Not a single day brings to us so much success
   That grief will not harm us in some respect.

But if there can be happiness upon the earth,
   God long since granted that we be happy.
Of all that his hand on high could grant his creatures
   He conferred on us this prosperous place. 20
The glory (if that's what it is) of all this life
   Has been enhanced for us above the rest.
Once the talk was everywhere that God had favored
   Us especially, more than any folk.
And the rumor throughout the world was that our days

Were more blessed than any people's. But look
How disgracefully have disappeared our good old
   Days, for a bitter day now torments us.
As swiftly as blessings of better fortune rose,
   Just as rapidly have they tumbled down.                 30
We flowered quickly, but that flower was fleeting*
   And that brief fire of ours was made with straw.
Suffering and care, fortune not matching our conduct,*
   Cause what was high to fall lawlessly down.
Our praises used to proceed throughout great nations,
   Which, by our changed lot, now present dangers.

For that cause, many ask why our state of affairs
   Today is worse than once it used to be.
They ask why so many more grave and unusual
   Problems assail us now than yesterday.                40
For nothing in the land happens without a cause,*
   Just as Job taught, who endured much travail.
Nevertheless, everybody says they are not
   The cause, as if nobody were guilty.
In fact, they now call fickle Fortune to account,
   Maintaining that she is more guilty here.
Everyone now blames Fortune because she changes
   And reverses quickly what was before.
And anyone can discern by our example
   That what was sweet has now become bitter.            50

## Chapter 2

**Here he rebukes Fortune and deplores her inconstant outcomes.**

O you who call yourself Fortune, why do you cast*
   Down so viciously those whom you raise up?
To those you've been a loving mother you become
   By your guile a harsh lying stepmother.
Your lot has dispersed in wrath those whom you've built up;
   What you've united, you've scattered to harm.
If there were any shame in your deceiving face,
   You would not be so hostile to your friends.
You were a blooming rose, but, a stinging nettle
   Burning, you now grieve those you once refreshed.       60
Your wheel is much too fickle and with sudden moves

It changes opulence for poverty.
But I would climb the wheel's top from the bottom up
   Rather than slip and fall from high to low.
God forbid high to low! From low to high let me
   Ascend, for slips from prosperity smart.
For I think to have been happy is the worst pain*
   That can afflict a wretch in a lifetime.

How true it is that much is given those who have
   And those who have little must give it up!    70
This is shown in us, to whose glories all people
   Alike, as it were, once bowed down their necks.
There was no land where we were not held in honor,
   But now our praise of yore has disappeared.
For every land once wanted to have peace with us;
   Now everywhere our enemy seeks wars.
Who formerly appeared with a smooth forehead, lo!
   Comes thrusting his horns with hostile intent.
And he who had been horned, his head now turned aside,
   Harmless without his horns, scarce holds his place.    80
What had been a fortunate land in all respects,
   They say, has already lost its fortune.
But say, Fortune, if you do prove to be to blame –
   Though I do not believe you are the cause,
Even if the people's voice falsely credits you –
   I'd still say that I think you are nothing.
Whatever others do, I can't believe in fate,
   At least while God has power over all.
I shan't believe that you, Fortune, impact on me,
   Like people who mutter you are their fate.    90
Nonetheless, I've determined on this page to show
   Your false image, though it's nothing to me.

## Chapter 3

**Here he describes Fortune according to those who say Fortune is Fate and Chance.**

O Fortune, hear what is openly said of you;
   Fickle at heart, you're neither here nor there.
You are two-faced, the one of which contorts and looks*
   Askance, and from that one your wrath thunders.
The other beams with a happy mien and they who

## Book II

Behold it receive everything prosperous.
Thus your odious face and your loving visage
    Relieve anxious hearts and oft crush happy.             100
You weep with the first face and smile with the second,
    Or vice versa, but we never know you.
You wear two faces on earth because you're fickle;
    It's fitting you don't walk straightforward paths.
If your prosperity makes me happy on earth,
    Just when I think I'm safe, just then I fall.
In grief's shadow, the mind oft fears uncertainties
    When lo! tomorrow new joy comes to me.
Everything is dependent on your slender thread\*
    And those who trust in it will be deceived.              110
For if the blink of an eye is quick, yet quicker
    Is the headlong fall from your pendant fate.

No gifts can help that are able to retain you
    And no home is safe that stands in your orb.
You are heavier than stone, lighter than a breeze,
    Sharper than a thorn, softer than a rose.
You are lighter than the sere leaves when without weight\*
    They flutter, dried out by the shifting winds,
And there is less weight in you than the dried-out tips
    Of wheat burnt crisp by unrelenting suns.             120
You're now bright day, now a night replete with horror;
    You're peaceful now, tomorrow you're in arms.
Now your lot beams with joy and now pales with bitter
    Pangs, as you, fickle, may grant good and bad.
You grant each reward with a free or stingy hand;
    You take from whom you wish and bring their doom.

Iris has not as many colors in her clouds\*
    Or the month of March as many seasons
As you, your times divided in a thousand parts,
    All of them painted a different color.               130
Your love is more deceptive than any harlot's
    And like the sea's wave you ebb and you flow.
No one knows at night what your morning wish will be,
    For your mind doesn't know how to focus.
You wander every nation, but stay long in none,
    And you behave just like a whirling wind.
Your kisses do not show that you've made peace with me\*
    Because you don't end in the way you start.
Your cutting is without a root nor is its bloom

Praised for lasting long, for sudden it wilts. 140
Your wisdom confers nothing that proves permanent
　And each of your gifts is untrustworthy.
Your prosperity is neighbor to ruination
　And your glory, such as it is, is brief.

## Chapter 4

**Here he talks further concerning what people say about fickle Fortune. In the end, however, he concludes that those things which befall people are neither by *Fate or Chance, but according to their merits or faults.**

All who seek the joys of the world are deluded,
　For Fortune can't give honey without gall.
Fortune is Envy's good comrade, although, never
　True to anyone, she remains fickle.
What ignorant wretch could not know Fortune's doings?
　She steals what she gives, topples what she lifts. 150
Fortune regulates her sphere like the rambling moon,
　Which suddenly wanes and swiftly waxes.
She waxes, she wanes, nor in turn is she constant;
　She's now beneath and now above the earth.
"I'll rule, I rule, I've ruled, I am devoid of rule";
　Thus for a short time that path fools us all.
Her dooms are allowed to destroy all they ordain
　And change the days' moments in countless ways.
Beware of Fortune's favor, because her round wheel*
　Spins and sends low what had been borne on high. 160
She spurns whom she calls, casts down whom she lifts, spins all,
　Claims guile for her own characteristic.
Fortune wanders with a twisting, uncertain step*
　And day-by-day abides in no one place.
Whatever good Fortune has given, she takes back,
　And who was just now fat is sudden thin.
When Fortune aids and smiles benignly with her face,*
　Then wealth follows every lucky kingdom.
When she flees, it flees, and one who had been circled
　By flocks of companions becomes unknown. 170

The year's changing season by its example shows
　How changeable Fortune is in her ways.
Fortune is not such a friend that she won't deceive,

## Book II

Since her wheel's law rules her deceitful deeds.
Her wheel continually turns smoothly through its
   Gyre and never remains fixed in one place.
Her wheel does not exempt anyone in the world;
   Her wheel restrains, releases, and binds all.
You won't turn her with prayers, appease her with a bribe;
   Nobody will move her with any tears.            180
Not your sex, your free status, your rank or your age,
   Nothing compels her to feel merciful.
Citizen and farmer, king, peasant, light and dark,
   Learned and lewd, the rich and poor alike,
Meek and rash, pious, wicked, the just and unjust
   Are all judged the same when Chance is the judge.
She fells some, frees some, lifts some to thrust to the depths;
   She summons each one, whom she mocks in turn.
She jests and toys with things until her slippery wheel
   Slips and everything slips along with it.          190
This capricious wheel spins about so much in its
   Motion that nothing can remain at rest.

Her capriciousness upsets all the hopes Fortune*
   Gives and she never grants us a fixed place.
Alas! why was such power given such a one
   To whom no rights on earth were rightly given?
If she has any law, it's said to be deceit,
   For by law she should have no dominion.
That's what they say who think that she controls by chance
   Everything that our God has created.          200
For Fortune is naught, nor is Destiny or Fate,
   And Chance plays no role in human affairs.
But we all make our own destiny, incur chance
   As we please, and bring about our own fate.
And a free mind calls acts it does of its own will,
   With diverse results, by Destiny's name.
For Destiny is always handmaid to the mind,
   Which choses what its own renown shall be.
If you want good, good fate ensues; if you want ill,
   You cause by your mind's impulse an ill fate.       210
If you lift your mind to the stars by virtue's aid,
   Fortune takes you to the top of her wheel.
But if you're borne down by the weight of your vices,
   You'll take your fortune with you to the pit.
It's best that you decline the lesser destiny
   While your soul is free to follow either.

## Chapter 5

**Here he speaks according to the Scriptures and alleges how all creatures serve and obey the righteous person.***

God said that he would give to them prosperity
  Who would observe what he commanded them:
Fruitful fields and vineyards overflowing with grapes,
  A due mingling of sunshine and shower.           220
They would curb the stars and make Saturn show favor;*
  Who'd been a plague would be a remedy.
The sword would not run loose within their borders; nay,
  They'd put all wars to flight by their virtue.
Thus peace, thus a sound body, and thus abundance
  Are righteous persons' the while they dread God.
When righteous they arose, their good luck rose with them,
  And if they fall their good luck rightly fails.
If they're perverse, their prosperity will reverse;
  If they're evil, they shall garner evils.           230
Thus God disposes our seasons by our merits,
  As his narratives show if you pay heed.
Descending to men on earth, angel Raphael*
  Flew down from heaven to heal blind Tobit.
Conquered hell's demons cannot withstand a righteous
  Person's command, but are become servants.
And the celestial elements, subdued by right,*
  Tend righteous persons and fulfill their prayers.

By virtue of God, wise persons will rule the stars*
  And all of heaven's might will attend them.         240
Orbits and cycles and all the spheres on high, too,
  Are at the foot of those that God assists.
The sun stood in Gibeon for righteous Joshua
  And was unable to maintain its path.
At Joshua's command the sun's wheel did not dare*
  Run, but stood fixed, uncertain of its course.
Indeed, an emissary star announced Christ's birth,*
  By which God gave his peace to the righteous.
We read that Saint Gregory cured an airborne plague*
  In Rome by means of prayers that brought relief.    250
Moses struck the sea with his rod, it split apart,*
  And the people entered it dry on foot.
When Peter's firm faith began to believe in Christ's*

*Book II*

Words, the sea's wave made a way for his feet.
For Elisha, iron sunk in swirling waters*
  Hastened to return upon the surface.
The fiery furnace took the three Hebrew youngsters,*
  But the flames, conquered, spared them without harm.
For blessed Hillary, the earth that had been flat*
  Rose up and a lofty seat received him.                      260
Moses ordered streams in the desert to flow forth*
  From dry rocks, that the folk and cattle drink.
The king of the Macedonians joined cleft mountains;*
  God granted this because of righteous prayers.

The strength of the righteous conquers every wild beast,*
  The snake and lion, too, whom it subdues.
Babylon knew by this that Daniel was righteous*
  And Rome saw that Sylvester was sacred.*
And the birds of the air fell by Moses' command*
  And became food for the people of God.                      270
A fish saved Jonah for three days in its belly*
  'Til it spewed him out at Nineveh's port.
Thus it's plain that all of God's creatures come under
  Righteous persons and are subject to them.
How rich, how happy with their great gift are humans,
  To whom alone all the world owes service!
Happy, above all, they for whom all that the world*
  Holds rises up and obeys their commands!
But if righteous persons should act unrighteously,
  They will experience a turn for the bad.                    280

## Chapter 6

**Here he tells and relates how, according to the Scriptures, all creatures oppose and disobey sinful persons.**

When David committed wickedness, pestilence*
  Thickened the air and scattered his people.
And fire utterly consumed Sodom for its sins,*
  And Korah's house was burned down for his crime.*
The watery flood arrived because of our sins,*
  In which every kind suffered and perished.
And earth's solid parts were liquified by their sins
  When cleft ground swallowed Dathan and Abiram.*

And the Lord's angel put Syria's hosts to the sword*
    And made their leader Lysias take flight.                          290
By night the demon Asmodeus slew Sarah's*
    Seven wicked husbands, for God wished it.

Fortune cannot bring the unrighteous well-being,*
    For creation and Creator deny it.
Fortune takes from the righteous nothing of value,
    For God provides them aid and Fate nothing.
Who gave strength to Sampson, wisdom to Solomon,*
    His good looks to Absalom? Lo! indeed
Nature gave them their bodies, and she'll have them back;
    God's grace alone bestowed the soul's virtues.                   300
It's thus clear that Fortune bestows nothing on us,
    Or takes aught away since she grants nothing.
When Solomon governed such a peaceful kingdom*
    And when he possessed so many riches,
When David stood against the giant Philistine*
    With his sling, did not God bring this to pass?
And when the days of the dying Hezekiah*
    Were prolonged and death departed from him,
And when Susannah was found innocent of guilt*
    And Esther was honored among her folk,*                  310
Say, what good luck did Fortune confer on them then?
    None, I think, nor do I ask who caused it.
You cannot venerate Fortune and worship God,
    Nor can Fate be good if it does evil.

In what way was Pharaoh able to blame Fortune*
    When many of his men died for his rage?
Why did Nebuchadnezzar live among cattle,*
    His shape changed, unless he had been sinful?
What of Saul, who destroyed his kingdom and himself?*
    Did he not sin against God's commandment?               320
Did not perchance white leprosy fell Azariah*
    When he usurped the temple priest's functions?
What might Ahab say? When he took Naboth's field,*
    His avarice was the cause of his death.
Or Rehoboam? Since he scorned the elders' counsel,*
    He beat his breast to have his realm sundered.
Or Phineas and Hophni, whom war's sword scattered*
    And God's Ark was seized? They had sinned before.
And why did Eli, toppling back with broken neck,*

Fall from his chair when the reports stunned him? 330
Fortune's lot could not bring such endings upon them,
  Which happened to them because of their sins.
Who did evil earned in the end evil rewards,
  For evil by right does in the evil.

When the Hebrews sinned, venerating images,*
  God's wrath delivered them up to their foes.
Forsaking images, they begged heaven with prayer
  And God made their enemies show their backs.
Then the Jewish kings prevailed over everyone
  When they did not transgress the laws of God. 340
The Jewish people under arms always conquered
  Their enemy's forces when they were good.
But when they had transgressed, then their foe everywhere
  Began to scatter them, conquered, captive.
Thus whatever is meant to be among mankind
  Happens according to merit or fault.
So the dice tossed in the world will fall differently
  Since God's wont to put his hand in the game.

## Chapter 7

**Here he talks about God, the Highest Creator, who is triune and unitary, in whose knowledge and disposition all created beings are ruled.**

God alone, who governs all, is omnipotent;
  Abiding everywhere, he foresees all. 350
All the things to come are always present to him
  And he sees them made before they are made.
God was Father before the begotten and, first*
  Creatures begotten, Mover and First Cause.
All that is had its time appointed to exist,
  But God existed before there was time.
God is everything that is, was, will be, that he*
  Brings forth, but he exists outside of time.
No times can hold themselves coterminous with God,
  But it's plain he's Lord God by prior right. 360

God is the Father, the Son, and the Holy Ghost;*
  The three names thus proclaim his three persons.

Whatsoever the person, he's called Lord and God,
  Sole God and at the same time only Lord.
There are the three persons, but only one being;
  These three are one, not three, but three in one.
One essence abides in these three, one God is three;
  Here nothing can be either more or less.
One mind in three, only one being in the three,
  One goodness in the three, one wisdom trine.           370

Fire, heat, and motion may appear to be three things,*
  But a burning fire always has all three.
Father, Son, and Holy Ghost in the deity
  Are three and at the same time denote one.
So when the Lord says, "Let us make man," he teaches*
  Very clearly what the faith should maintain.
Here the one Creator affirms the three persons*
  While he remains one in his deity.

## Chapter 8

**Here he talks about our Lord Jesus Christ, the incarnate son of God, through whom we are reformed from wicked to good.**

Now it's right we believe in the incarnate son,*
  Jesus Christ, whom we worship devoutly.           380
The son took on the task; from the paternal mind,
  God, from his bosom he came down below.
He proceeded, not receded, from the father,
  Came to the world below but kept the stars.
Always he was of the Father, in the Father,
  With the Father, the same as the Father.
Made flesh, he assumed flesh, although he did not cease,
  Assuming it, to be what he had been.
Thus the flesh and the Word are made one, so that they're
  True God throughout, two persons of the same.           390
He always remained what he was; what he was not,
  He took from the Virgin's flesh and was that.
A work equal to this work is nowhere seen, no
  Honor, Mary, is thus equal to yours.
Weak in his flesh but hardy in his deity,
  Less than Father by flesh, peer by godhead,
Here he eats, hence is eaten; here feeds, thence is fed;

## Book II

Here is ruled, hence rules; here cannot, thence can.
Here he lies in a manger, seeks his mother's breast,
   Hence the heavenly order swears him God.                400
Here a narrow stall holds him 'neath a wretched roof,
   Hence a guiding star leads kings unto him.
Here thirstiness, hunger, tears, travail and sorrow,
   But at the end he could endure his death.
A priceless possession offered for a price, God
   Himself was betrayed and sold for some coins.
Delivered alive, he broke up the hungry tomb;
   Then, seeking his Father's realm, he arose.
And when the end of the world has come, he'll mete out
   By his judgment to all what they have earned.         410

Thus perfect man and at the same time perfect God
   He fulfills fully what befits them both.
That he nursed on a breast shows he's truly mortal;
   That a new star announced him shows he's God.*
He's seen to be man since a stall held him, God since
   The three honored the one with threefold gifts.
That poor be rich; an infant, God; a king, homeless;
   The Almighty demands to feed on milk,
Takes lodging in a stall, he whose home is the world's
   Framework, whose bedchamber is the sky's roof.        420
He came so that bread can hunger and rest can toil,
   Fountains run dry, so health can suffer pain,
Light be hidden by darkness, the sun lack its light,
   So glory can be sad and life can die.
Thus moved by love he bore these things of his own will
   So that God might become man, in our flesh.
Just as weak Adam became our first sorrow's cause,
   Our mighty God has made our task joyous.
The sin of the first Adam wounds everyone born*
   'Til the second Adam's water heals us.               430
The first Adam governed the beasts, birds, and serpents;*
   Our second Adam bestrides everything.
The Fall in the old days led to tearful places;*
   The New Law makes a way to joyous sites.
So those persons who wish to be saved must believe
   And not know more than is permitted them.

## Chapter 9

**Here he says that everyone ought to believe firmly and not probe the grounds of faith more than is seemly.**

When God brought forth the creation out of nothing,
   He was God alone and without witness.*
Since he wished to create alone, he wished alone
   To know, and he shared this work with no one.      440
No material, exquisite shape, unchanging
   Structure has anything of our reason.
Submit your mind to faith, since a mortal likeness
   Can't grasp the eternal judge's mysteries.
Sorrow, death, and tears do not know happiness, life,*
   And joys, nor do humans know God's business.
Shadows don't receive the sun; blind people, the light;
   Our lowly mind can't take the heights of God's.
Of course, you ought never probe the splendid mystery*
   Of the Holy Spirit, which you can't reach.      450

Or since it's not for us to know the world's ages,
   Why do we strain to know the creation?
To fathom proven faith by means of our reason,
   Will not be a task for human powers.
It's not a human task that we transcend the stars,
   Which mortals cannot achieve by reason.
Virtue's conveyance alone pierces to the heights;
   It flashes past the stars, abides in God.
Let one who's wise be more modest in these matters
   And ask to be able to have true faith.      460
Evil oft activates genius; it's not for us*
   To know what God himself construes on high.
It's better we not know some things; supreme matters
   Vex the senses, so be soberly wise.
Let one entrust to faith what one can't to reason;*
   Let a firm faith give what reason cannot.

Exalt faith, for true faith hears, believes, and hopes what*
   It can't see: that's our way, life, salvation.
And faith gives the proofs of things that cannot be known,
   Which cannot be grasped by mind nor reason.      470
True faith seeks whatever's true and earns everything;*
   What is held possible, true faith can hold.

*Book II*

The tongue stills, the mouth becomes dumb, the mind falters,
   Ears don't hear; nothing's here but faith alone.*

## CHAPTER 10

**Here he says that no trust should be placed in a graven or molten image, nor should such be worshipped, but that a repentant mind may be more quickly moved to the contemplation of the one God by the sight of them in church.***

What's one spark to the sun, or one drop to the sea,
   Or what can ashes be to the heavens?
But God wants us to worship him with loving heart,
   The vast by the slight, highest by lowest.
Loving him, let there be no due measure or bound,
   For nobody has loved him to his worth.           480
He teaches whatever is right but smooths what's harsh,*
   The broken heals, the fallen lifts, routs sin,
For the cross with its nails, suffused with rosy blood,*
   Is salvation when Satan is expelled.

Whoever contemplates Jesus should put aside
   Old behavior and tend to better things.
Through this name life is given to all and no one
   Can be blessed without Jesus' name alone.
There's no saint like this Lord, who makes sinners holy,*
   And who alone was free from every stain.         490
And there's none other but you, for they're all nothing
   Which a golden shape falsely proclaims gods.
Thus through you the Church blesses us, lavish of goods,*
   And the Synagogue is bereft of goods.

O cursed folk, traitor to God, indeed pagans,*
   Whom disbelief keeps from being holy,
Whom Christ's true faith abhors, for outside the true law
   Of the Creator, they worship mere wood.
They are made to bow down, prostrate themselves, adore
   Wood, forgetting about their Creator.         500
Wood, stones, whatever they see in a carved image,
   That is what they declare to be their god.
Humans, whom God raised up, lie prone before embers
   And pray to a statue carved from a post.
They pray for wealth, beg for help, implore with their hands

## Vox Clamantis by John Gower: 'The Voice of One Crying'

Things their hands made, which, mute, do not reply.
How empty and wretched their reason and their sense,
   That the masters of things make things their god!

O you confused in mind, remember the lesson,*
   By whom man was made in the beginning.                 510
Recall to mind the high honor that God bestowed
   On you once when he first gave you being.
Wasn't the world made in the beginning for you*
   And its riches subject to your command?
The world was made not to be loved, but for your use,
   To be your servant, not to be your god.
So, what reason persuades you that what the workman*
   Melts in fire or planes in wood is a god?
O wretch! why do you call your empty idols gods,
   And, made in God's likeness, fall before fakes?            520
Alas! this madness to worship mute gods when they
   Know nothing is the worst of all the sins.
Why attribute salvation to such images
   That do not have motion, touch, taste, nor sight?
What's less to a rational being than a brute?
   What's less to living kind than what ne'er lived?
One tree-part makes furrows, another an idol;
   Part cooks your soup; and it was all one tree.
Look how I debase two parts, but cannot explain
   By what reason the third should be worshipped.          530
"Let he who makes them and he who has faith in them*
   Be made like them," thus God himself commands.
The sculptor is worth more than the sculpture. Workers
   Who worship their work are very foolish.

We use our sculpted figures otherwise, I think,*
   Not by weakening God's laws in our worship.
We have them in order that we be more mindful
   To give the saints our deepest reverence.
For we believe in God, not in the gods, nor does*
   The Gentile rite hold us: away with it!               540
But when some make and decorate statues for gain
   So that they think to get gifts from the plebs,
When they who, devoted to gold, contrive such work,
   I don't think such craft has any merit.
And when God spoke to Moses upon the mountain,*

*Book II*

The people saw no figure of their God.
For if the people had seen such an appearance,
   Perchance they would have sculpted that same form.
But God, who spurned the honor of such a sculpture,
   Did not want his shape noted any way.             550
But I think God's image is flesh joined to reason,*
   Through which he lays claim upon his worship.

In crucified Jesus' honor, the cross's sign
   Pressed in our minds should be worship enough.
The cross's strength conquered hell and, Satan cast down,*
   The cross repaired the burden of our fall.
The cross is true salvation, venerable wood,
   Death's death, life's door, eternal ornament.
It purifies the breast, cleanses the mind from blight,
   Brightens the heart, and makes the body pure.       560
It gives sense, augments strength, both takes away the fear
   Of death and prepares the heart for battle.
Freedom returns in the cross and, the foe conquered,
   That power dies that erstwhile brought us death.
Religion, rite, and worship join all the people's
   Sacred things fittingly, one in the cross.
Eden's gates open in the cross; the flaming sword*
   Ceases to be guard of that distant place.
Behold how many figures prefigure the cross,
   How every page predicts it beautifully.           570
Wondrous is the tree's power, where the high father's
   Only son was drawn that he might suffer.
By the cross's power Christ harrowed hell and thence
   He recovered the sheep that had been lost.
By the cross's power he rose to heaven and
   In the father's light reached his starry realms.
The glorified flesh, which bore his pains on the cross,
   Presides in heaven by the seat of God.
By virtue of the pious cross and divine love,
   Grace rises in the Church with the New Law.       580

## Chapter 11

**Here he says that, since God alone created everything, God alone should be worshipped by his creatures, and also that it is most reasonable that he alone governs everything and judges humanity as he wills, according to its merits and defects.**

Always he is, was, and will be one triune God;*
   For him there is no beginning or end.
Yet he gave everything a beginning and end;
   Through him is all and without him, nothing.
Sufficient to himself, he can do what he wills;
   He ordains and what he ordains becomes.
I want him at whose command all creation serves,
   And I believe my God is heavenly.
When God's hand is open, it pours out abundance;
   When he turns it away, he takes all back.       590
Wise, he allocates all things with rightful judgment,
   For God himself can't want or be wanting.
It's likewise right, since God created everything,
   That he have jurisdiction over all.
Since all things were created by God's will alone
   Is Fortune able to undo God's work?
She who played no role at the start, nor will at last,
   I think will have no role in the meantime.

Who made the earth's mass, the heaven's revolving dome,*
   Or the stars move? Surely, was it not God?       600
Who gave taste to the springs in the sweet flowing streams?
   Who made the seas bitter? Was it not God?
Earth's Founder wanted beings for what he founded
   So that the whole creation would serve God.
He dressed the earth with plants and the plants with blossoms;
   He caused the blossoms to swell into fruits.
With great devotion, he took care to enrich earth
   And to make it abundantly fruitful.
Nor was he satisfied that the earth was wealthy
   In rivers, springs, gardens, flowers and buds.       610
He resolved to vary new things, form diverse shapes,
   And separate them by their appearance.
The earth received living beings of diverse sorts
   And groaned with the weight of its new burden.
He assigned each a place appropriate to it,

*Book II*

 According to its properties gave each,
Mountains to these, valleys to those, woodlands to these,
 To many the plains giving habitat.
Birds took to the air; fish claimed for themselves the sea;
 Cattle, the flatlands; savage beasts, the wilds.    620
Craft suggests forms for the work and the Craftsman shapes;
 The whole structure proceeds from his hands' skills.

Fortune contributes nothing, but since God alone\*
 Creates all, he alone rules creation.
Nothing is luckless and nothing is blessed by Chance;
 God grants humans his gifts for their merits.
Whatever happens, the wise who ponder Scripture
 Will not say Fortune is responsible.
I truly affirm, whatever happens on earth,
 Whether good or evil, we are the cause.    630

# NOTES TO BOOK II

### PROLOGUE

Heading: "Vox clamantis": the title derives from the Vulgate "vox clamantis in deserto," used to describe John the Baptist: cf. Matthew 3: 3, Mark 1: 3, Luke 3: 4 and John 1: 23.

l. 15: adapted from Nigel of Longchamp, *Speculum Stultorum*, ed. Mann, l. 14.

l. 33: adapted from Nigel of Longchamp, *Speculum Stultorum*, ed. Mann, l. 1133.

l. 41: the primary reference is to Jacob in the desert: cf. Deuteronomy 32: 13; but cf. *Mirour de l'Omme*, ll. 7549–51, there attributed to "le psaltier."

l. 45: "He who put words in an ass's mouth" = God. Cf. Numbers 22: 21–33, Balaam and his ass; cf. *VC* III. 531–2.

ll. 49–50: adapted from Ovid, *Fasti*, 1. 73–4.

l. 51: the context implies that for Sinon Gower had in mind an individual known to him, but at this distance precision about whom seems impossible, lacking further clues. The absence of a holographic text adds to the uncertainty. While portions of Macaulay's base MS, Oxford, All Souls College MS 98 (S, which we follow here), were the work of a scribe evidently close to Gower, the MS as a whole cannot qualify as authorial. The reference clearly posed difficulties for subsequent scribes: L has "Symon etcetraque," D "si non excecraque." Stockton (p. 375) chose to follow L and interpret accordingly "Simon" = Simon Magus, which is ingenious but unlikely. In the most complete version of the tale, Sinon was a Greek who, feigning desertion, convinced the Trojans to accept the Horse, later releasing the hidden soldiers and using a signal fire to guide the Greeks waiting in their ships (cf. *Confessio Amantis*, I. 1172 ff.) to attack before taking part himself in the sack of the city. Yet the story, as originally part of the epic cycle, had many sources by Gower's time: e.g., Guido delle Colonne (*Historia destructionis Troiae* XXX. 155 ff.) has Sinon just a soldier concealed inside the Horse; Dictys Cretensis (*Ephemeridos belli Trojani* V. 12), merely the one to light the signal fire. Virgil relates Sinon's lies at length (*Aeneid* II. 79 ff.) but presents him only releasing the hidden Greeks from the Horse. "Excetra" = Gr. "serpent" is uncommon in medieval Latin; in combination with Sinon it may hint at Gower's source, and hence his reference here. Stockton accepts the capitalization in S as Gower's (inexplicably, given the variance in the MSS elsewhere), reading "the old Serpent," i.e., Satan. In the immediate context (cf. ll. 48, 50), that Gower means the serpent to embody envy is a likelier possibility here: a comparison is Giotto's depiction of the vice in the Scrovegni frescoes.

ll. 57–8: for the light beneath the bushel, cf. Matthew 5: 15; Mark 4: 21; Luke 8: 16, 11: 33.

l. 61: cf. *Mirour de l'Omme*, ll. 16531–2, describing Moderacion, the fifth daughter of Mesure, who counters Prodigality: "Si molt avera lors molt enprint,/ Du poy petit measurement."

l. 64: virtually *verbatim*, Ovid, *Ars Amatoria*, 2. 166.

ll. 65–6: a commonplace, probably originating in Mark 9: 23.

ll. 67–8: another commonplace: cf. II Corinthians 8: 9.

ll. 77–82: common metaphors for products of *compilatio*: florilegia, etc. The bee/honey/hive for literary sources can be traced to Longinus and was familiar from Quintilian (e.g., *Institutio oratoria* I. x. 7) but probably best known in the fourteenth century from Seneca, *Epistulae morales*, 84 – and from Ovid. See following note.

l. 78: virtually *verbatim*, Ovid, *Ars Amatoria*, 3. 124.

## Book II

l. 1 "incausti specie": cf. *Confessio Amantis*, VIII. 2212–13.

l. 3: cf. Ecclesiastes 1: 2 and 12: 8.

ll. 7–8: virtually *verbatim* Peter Riga, *Aurora*, Exodus 245–6.

ll. 31–2: virtually *verbatim*, Ovid, *Tristia*, 5. 8. 19–20.

l. 33: *verbatim* Ovid, *Tristia*, 5. 5. 47.

ll. 41–2: cf. Job 5: 6: "Nihil in terra sine causa fit" (Vulgate); and also *Mirour de l'Omme*, ll. 26857–9: "Seint Job nous dist expressement/ Qe riens sur terre est accident/ Sanz cause."

Ch. 2: ll. 51–90: the description of Fortune relies heavily on Boethius, *Consolation of Philosophy*, II. Prosa 1.

l. 67: a commonplace, possibly drawn from Boethius, *Consolation of Philosophy*, II. Prosa 4: "in omni adversitate fortunae infelicissimum genus est infortunii fuisse felicem."

ll. 95 ff.: "facie bina": Fortune's two faces, one smiling, one frowning, or at times half white/half black, were medieval commonplaces; cf. Petrarch, *De remediis utriusque Fortunae*.

l. 109: virtually *verbatim* Ovid, *Ex Ponto*, 4. 3. 35; a common metaphor: cf. *Mirour de l'Omme*, ll. 10948–50 (attributed to "Orace"); *Confessio Amantis*, VI. 1514; also *Troilus and Criseyde*, III. 1636.

ll. 117–20: virtually *verbatim*, Ovid, *Heroides*, 5. 109–12.

l. 127: Iris is the goddess of the rainbow.

ll. 137–8: cf. Latin verses following *Confessio Amantis*, II. 1878, describing False-Seeming: "Quod patet esse fides in eo fraus est, que politi/ Principium pacti finis habere negat."

Ch. 4 heading: "sorte aut casu": cf. Boethius, *Consolation of Philosophy*, IV. Prosa 6.

ll. 159–61: cf. Godfrey of Viterbo, *Pantheon*, col. 265.

ll. 163–4: virtually *verbatim* Ovid, *Tristia*, 5. 8. 15–16.

ll. 167–70: adapted from Ovid, *Tristia*, 1. 5. 27–30.

ll. 193–4: virtually *verbatim* Nigel of Longchamp, *Speculum Stultorum*, ed. Mann, ll. 581–2.

Ch. 5 heading: "scripturas": It is likely Gower had no specific scriptural passage in mind, as the sentiment of what follows is near-ubiquitous, cf. e.g., Deuteronomy 28: 1–14, Joshua 1: 8, Psalm 112 (Vulgate), Job 36: 11, Isaiah 60: 5.

l. 221: Saturn's attributes are complex and contradictory. Ovid and Virgil praise the "Golden Age of Saturn" as a time of universal peace and prosperity – an interpretation Gower knew. Alternatively, when linked with Cronos, who consumed his children at birth (cf. *VC* III. 923; *Confessio Amantis*, V. 835–69) until Jupiter was able to evade discovery and imprison his father, his influence was considered malevolent; it is this latter Saturn that astrology reflects (cf. *Confessio Amantis*, VII. 935–46), and is the intention here.

ll. 233–4: cf. Tobias 5–6 (Vulgate).

ll. 237–8: these and the following nine lines may all be based on Joshua 10: 12–13, ll. 243–6 in particular; Gower, however, appears to have been reading Peter Riga, *Aurora*: see ll. 245–6, below, and note.

## Notes to Book II

ll. 239–74: cf. *Mirour de l'Omme*, ll. 27013–96; *Confessio Amantis*, VII. 511–20.

ll. 245–6: *verbatim* Peter Riga, *Aurora*, Josue 169–70; cf. *Mirour de l'Omme*, ll. 27014–18.

l. 247: cf. Matthew 2: 2–10; cf. *Mirour de l'Omme*, ll. 27019–21.

ll. 249–50: Pope Gregory I "The Great" was said to have purified the air in Rome in CE 590, thereby putting an end to a deadly pestilence, by leading a procession bearing an image of the Virgin through the streets while entreating her to pray for the populace. The air as the procession passed each point was purified (cf. *Mirour de l'Omme*, ll. 27022–4), and in front of Hadrian's tomb – now the Castel de Sant'Angelo – Gregory had a vision of an angel (in some versions St. Michael) wiping and sheathing a bloody sword, indicating that the plague was finished; see Jacobus de Voragine, *Legenda Aurea*, for March 12. Gregory's story had lasting interest for the English since in 597 he commissioned Augustine of Canterbury to convert King Aethelberht of Kent to Christianity.

ll. 251–2: for the parting of the Red Sea, see Exodus 14: 21–9. In fact, Moses extends only his empty hand over the water, both to part and to close up; with his rod he brings water from the rock of Horeb (Exodus 17: 5–6, Numbers 20: 7–11; see *VC* ll. 260–1, below). That he used his rod to part the sea is a common belief, however, seemingly based on God's command in Exodus 17: 5, "And take in thy hand the rod wherewith thou didst strike the river." Cf. also *Mirour de l'Omme*, ll. 27079–80.

ll. 253–4: cf. Matthew 14: 28–31; *VC* III. 319–20; *Mirour de l'Omme*, ll. 27037–9.

ll. 255–6: cf. IV Kings 6: 5–7 (Vulgate); *Mirour de l'Omme*, ll. 27040–2.

ll. 257–8: cf. Daniel 3: 12–30. The "tres pueros Hebreos" are Shadrach, Meshach and Abednego.

ll. 259–60: St. Hilary, bishop of Poitiers (d. ca. CE 367), when denied a seat equal in height to those accorded other bishops by the ostensibly heretic Pope Leo I, sat on the ground, saying "Domini est terra"; the ground rose up, providing Hilary an equivalently high seat; see also *Mirour de l'Omme*, ll. 27031–6; Jacobus de Voragine, *Legenda Aurea*, for January 13. Hilary is the patron saint of lawyers; the spring terms of the English and Irish law courts, and the universities of Oxford and Dublin, are called Hilary term in acknowledgement.

ll. 261–2: see note for ll. 251–2, above.

ll. 263–4: Alexander the Great, encountering a savage people (often identified as the Ten breakaway Tribes of Israel, and later the peoples Gog and Magog) at a juncture in the Caucasus, sought unsuccessfully to contain them in Asia by building what became known as "Alexander's Gate." Ultimately he entreated help from God, who moved the mountains, closing off passage into Europe. The story has many variants and was widely known: e.g., Peter Comestor, *Historia scholastica*; Archpresbyter Leo, *Historia Alexandri Magni* (*Historia de preliis*); Matthew Paris, *Chronica majora*; *The Wars of Alexander*; and Gower's probable immediate source, Godfrey of Viterbo, *Pantheon*, supplemented by *Historia de preliis*.

ll. 265–6: cf. Psalm 90: 13; *Mirour de l'Omme*, ll. 27046–8.

l. 267: cf. Daniel 6: 16–23; also *Mirour de l'Omme*, ll. 27049–51.

l. 268: cf. *Confessio Amantis*, II. 3551–96, Pope Sylvester I's miraculous cure of Constantine's leprosy and the Emperor's Christianization; but as this tale ends with the "poisonous" Donation of Constantine – a *bête noire* of Gower's – and given the specific context here, the more likely reference is (as also *Mirour de l'Omme*, ll. 27053–5) to Sylvester's binding of a dragon, thus saving Rome and causing the pagan priests who previously had served Constantine to become Christians: cf. Jacobus de Voragine, *Legenda Aurea*, for December 31.

ll. 269–70: cf. Exodus 16: 13.

ll. 271–2: cf. Jonah 1–2; *VC* I. 1819–20; *Mirour de l'Omme*, ll. 27056–60.

ll. 277–80: cf. *Mirour de l'Omme*, ll. 27065–72.

ll. 281–2: cf. II Samuel 24: 10–17; *Mirour de l'Omme*, ll. 27073–84.

l. 283: cf. Genesis 19: 24–5.

l. 284: cf. Numbers 16: 30–5; *VC* VI. 1228; *Mirour de l'Omme*, ll. 2344–7.

ll. 285–7: cf. Genesis 7.

l. 288: cf. Numbers 16: 25–33; *VC* VI. 1227–8; *Mirour de l'Omme*, ll. 2341–3, 27077–8.

ll. 289–90: cf. II Maccabees 11: 1–12.

ll. 291–2: cf. Tobit 3: 8.

ll. 293–302: these lines are built around Boethius, *Consolation of Philosophy*, II. 4–7.

ll. 297–8: Samson: cf. Judges 13–16; Solomon: cf. III Kings 3: 9–12; Absalom: II Samuel 14: 25.

ll. 303–4: Solomon reigned for forty years in peace and prosperity: cf. III Kings (Vulgate), describing both.

ll. 305–6: cf. I Samuel 17: 32–51; *Mirour de l'Omme*, ll. 2173–84.

## Notes to Book II

ll. 307–8: cf. IV Kings 20: 1–6 (Vulgate); Isaiah 38: 1–8.

l. 309: cf. Daniel 13.

l. 310: cf. Esther 1–16 (Vulgate).

ll. 315–16: cf. Exodus 14: 27–8; *Mirour de l'Omme*, ll. 27079–81.

ll. 317–18: cf. Daniel 4: 30; *Confessio Amantis*, I. 2785–3042.

ll. 319–20: cf. I Samuel 13: 9–14; 15: 10–35; 26: 21; 31: 1–13.

ll. 321–2: cf. II Paralipomenon 26: 16–21 (Vulgate). NB: Paralipomenon = Chronicles in KJV; Azariah = Uzziah; in the Vulgate Azariah = Ozias.

ll. 323–4: cf. III Kings 21: 1–22, 28–9; *Mirour de l'Omme*, ll. 4957–61; *Confessio Amantis*, VII. 2527–685.

ll. 325–6: cf. III Kings 12: 6–24; II Paralipomenon 10: 1–15; *Confessio Amantis*, VII. 4027–146.

ll. 327–8: cf. I Samuel 2: 12–17, 4: 11. L. 328 "Archaque capta fuit" may owe something to 4: 11 "Et arca Dei capta est."

ll. 329–30: cf. I Samuel 4: 17–18. Eli (Heli, Vulgate), the aged father of the wicked priests Hophni and Phineas, breaks his neck falling backward out of his chair upon hearing of their deaths, and of the capture of the Ark of the Covenant by the Philistines.

ll. 335–8: *verbatim* Peter Riga, *Aurora*, Judicum 5–8.

ll. 335–44: cf. *VC* VI. 871–902.

ll. 353–74: Gower was clearly working with an open copy of Godfrey of Viterbo's *Pantheon* while writing these lines, sometimes borrowing *verbatim* (e.g., l. 353 "Ante creaturam genitor deus et genitura," ll. 357–9, 361–3). It is not always possible to determine whether Gower was modifying, or directly quoting, from his text (e.g., ll. 371–4), absent a modern critical edition of the *Pantheon*, and given that significant differences exist between early versions. In the edition used here throughout: ll. 353–4: *Pantheon* col. 11; ll. 357–9: *Pantheon* col. 9; ll. 361–3: *Pantheon* col. 11; ll. 371–4: *Pantheon* col. 12. Cf. also *Confessio Amantis*, VII. 73–120.

ll. 375: cf. Genesis 1: 26; *VC* VII. 511.

ll. 377–8: virtually *verbatim* Peter Riga, *Aurora*, Genesis 141–2.

ll. 379–92: lines based broadly on the Nicene Creed.

l. 414: cf. *VC* I. 1615, 2083; *Mirour de l'Omme*, l. 29925. Stockton suggests Godfrey of Viterbo, *Pantheon* "Nata maria stella, regina Maria novella" as a source for l. 414, but references to the Virgin in these terms were universal and commonplace from the ninth century at least (e.g., "Ave Maris Stella," attributed to Venantius Fortunatus, Vespers hymn sung on Marian feast days); the ultimate source is III Kings 18: 44.

ll. 429–30: *verbatim* Peter Riga, *Aurora*, Exodus 1271–2; cf. I Corinthians 15: 45–8.

ll. 431–2: *verbatim* Peter Riga, *Aurora*, Genesis 243–4.

ll. 433–4: *verbatim* Peter Riga, *Aurora*, Numeri 419–20.

ll. 438–9: assuming that *VC* was written earlier than *Carmen super multiplici viciorum pestilencia* (ca. 1395–7), Gower transferred these lines to the latter poem, where they appear *verbatim*, ll. 56–7. For several other instances of the same, see below.

ll. 445–60: cf. *Carmen super multiplici viciorum pestilencia*, ll. 60–75 *verbatim*.

ll. 449–50: *verbatim* Peter Riga, *Aurora*, Exodus 85–6; "sacri flatus": here, the Holy Spirit; see further note to Book III, Prologue, l. 106, below. This, along with several other variants, confirms Gower's MS of the *Aurora* as a first edition (late twelfth/early thirteenth century), without the later changes made by Peter, or the additions of Aegidius Romanus (late thirteenth/early fourteenth century).

l. 461: adapted from Ovid, *Ars Amatoria*, 2. 43.

ll. 461–3: cf. *Confessio Amantis*, Pro. 352–4.

ll. 465–6: cf. *Carmen super multiplici viciorum pestilencia*, ll. 76–7 *verbatim*.

ll. 467–70: most of the ideas here throughout are commonplaces of Christianity, familiar to any regular churchgoer, and wouldn't demand recourse to a bible text to employ. As such they are prime examples of Gower's generalist approach to scripture. The basic underlying texts here are Matthew 7: 24 (l. 467) and John 14: 6 (l. 148); cf. also Mark 4: 23–4 – but none of his readers would have required precise *loci* to understand his points. See also l. 474, note, below.

l. 471: a possible derivation from Mark 9: 22.

l. 474: cf. Mark 4: 23–4, and note to ll. 467–70, above.

Ch. 10 heading: Gower articulates the orthodox position of the Church, that denied images agency in the manner of idols, but accepted them as aids to contemplation. It is possible lollard criticism prompted his carefulness here; see below, ll. 535–8.

l. 481: cf. Luke 3: 5; *VC* III. 252 and (contrastingly) *VC* IV. 324.

## Notes to Book II

ll. 483–4: *verbatim* Peter Riga, *Aurora*, Judicum 79–80.

ll. 489–92: *verbatim* Peter Riga, *Aurora*, I Kings 61–4.

ll. 493–4: *verbatim* Peter Riga, *Aurora*, I Kings 85–6.

ll. 495–508: cf. *Confessio Amantis*, V. 1497–590.

ll. 509–12: cf. Ecclesiastes 12: 1, which seems to provide the originary idea.

ll. 513–14: cf. Psalm 113: 16 (Vulgate B version; KJV 115: 16).

ll. 517–34: adapted from Psalm 113 (Vulgate).

ll. 531–2: cf. Psalm 113: 8 (Vulgate B version; KJV 115: 8).

ll. 535–8: see above, Ch. 10 heading, and note.

ll. 539–40: "ritus/ ...gentilis": i.e., the rituals of those who are neither Christians nor Jews; cf. Matthew 10: 5–6.

ll. 545–50: possibly derived from Exodus 33: 18–23, although not seeing the face of God is explained differently there.

ll. 551–2: cf. Matthew 23: 16–19.

l. 555: the role of the cross in "conquering Hell" is described in the second part of the (apocryphal) Gospel of Nicodemus, probably complete by the fifth century CE. Gower would have considered it orthodox, although the line itself hardly justifies his direct knowledge of the text, as the Harrowing of Hell was a generally acknowledged event.

ll. 567–8: cf. Genesis 3: 24.

ll. 581–4: as in most of chapters 10–11, these lines draw on several bible passages: e.g., cf. Genesis 1–3; Psalm 95: 11; John 1–3.

ll. 599–622: cf. Genesis 1; also cf. Boethius, *Consolation of Philosophy*, V. Prosa 6.

ll. 623–30: cf. *Confessio Amantis*, Pro. 520–8; 544–9; 905–9; Boethius, *Consolation of Philosophy*, II. Prosa 6.

# BOOK III

Book III opens with a prose headnote once intended, apparently, as a transition from the dream and the voice of Book I, offering further evidence of Gower's composition process. The headnote is followed by another prologue that briefly summarizes the second book's argument against Fortune, and reasserts the legalistic tone of the poem by terming it a *libella* (l. 13). What follows thus suggests this as the point at which Gower began writing. The prologue's second paragraph introduces the notion of the three estates that will be the subject of this and the ensuing three books, followed once again by a humility *topos* not unlike that found in Book II. The reader is again asked to overlook the author's inadequacies, God's assistance is again summoned to the work, which is again sent forth into the world with the author's hope for its acceptance, Christ is called upon once again to be the poem's guarantor, and – in a gesture rooted in classical metaphor – the poet casts off his mooring lines and apprehensively sets sail. Perhaps not quite as detailed as the second Book's prologue, this one nevertheless touches all the requisite bases and could just as well stand as the poem's actual beginning, which at an early stage of development it was no doubt meant to be.

The subject matter of Book III is the secular clergy. Its first concern is the prelates – the cardinals, archbishops, bishops, certain deacons and even sub-deacons – who are considered the princes of the Church. The papacy is criticized at length. Despite the efforts of the reform popes who followed Leo IX (CE 1049–54), especially Gregory VII (CE 1073–85), Church leadership at Rome became increasingly imperial. It should be noted that Gower's criticisms of the prelacy aside from the pope are directed in large measure towards bishops, whose similar unrighteous deviations from their responsibilities he roundly attacks. (His use of the general term *praesul* rather than the more specific *episcopus* seems driven to a large extent by metrical considerations.) There follows a stern critique of curates, the parish priests who are governed by the prelacy, and then of a miscellaneous category of priests that includes unbeneficed mass priests and university scholars. Throughout, Gower's first concern is with individuals in the *ordo sacra* (holy orders) who are entrusted with the *cura animarum* (the cure of souls) that is embedded during the papacy of Innocent III in the ritual observance of the sacraments as their specific responsibility (see ll. 1983–96). Lesser functionaries who were likewise *clerici*, the throngs who comprised the ecclesiastical proletariat, play little part in the poet's critique. His target is worldly priests in the Church who have allowed the concerns of the secular world they inhabit to overpower their commitment to the ritual observance of the sacraments and other duties of the priesthood to which they are sworn for the betterment of the people.

The pope, in a passage that has been adapted at its end to specify the anti-pope Clement VII, comes in for especially keen criticism. The revised versions of the opening lines, moreover, show clearly how Gower, having finished Book III in the main before the Great Schism of August 1378 came to his attention, attempted to account for the event by adapting his materials to the limited extent his text allowed without a major disruption. When Gregory XI died in March 1378, the college of cardinals met in April and elected Urban VI, a competent functionary of modest origins who by his prior service appeared to be amenable to the direction of his betters. Little could have been farther from the truth. Urban, prickly and quick to take offense, almost immediately revealed his unsuitability for effective rule. The cardinals met again in August, electing the aristocratic Clement VII as Urban's replacement. Urban declined to step aside, however, and, since canon law had no procedure in place for such a situation, the Church found itself with two popes. Clement took up residence at Avignon, which had only recently been vacated by Gregory XI when he returned papal offices to Rome after the so-called "Babylonian Captivity," a period of sixty-seven years when seven popes, all French, held court under the close eye of the French king. To the English, Clement and his successors appeared merely pawns of the French court. England accordingly supported Urban VI as the true pope, despite his demonstrated incapacity. Although Gower had finished Book III for the most part before the Great Schism occurred, he was able to adjust his text to some extent to take developing circumstances into account. Whichever pope Gower intended initially – perhaps simply a figure of composite abuses – the lengthy speech put in his mouth in the critique of the papacy has the purpose of revealing the depth of corruption at the papal curia, whether in Rome or Avignon. Gower depicts the pope living like a worldly emperor, neglecting his spiritual functions while pursuing the world and the flesh.

At the core of Gower's criticism is the way ambition corrupts the integrity of the clergy that ministers to the world and – failingly – lives in it, and for it. The highest officials of the Church occupied positions in its hierarchy, and wielded wealth and power, not unlike those of the secular hierarchy, in which they often also served by virtue of their administrative skills. Leading figures of the Church are commonly encountered in service to the monarchy and occupy the highest positions at the king's court at the same time as they served the Church at the highest levels. Simon Sudbury, for instance, was not only Archbishop of Canterbury but also Lord Chancellor of England, and Robert Hales, the Prior of the Hospitallers, was also the king's Treasurer and Admiral of the West. Lesser clergy sought service at baronial courts. But celibates serving the Church in lifetime appointments, in what is called "subjective perpetuity," found themselves in different circumstances than did the nobility they resembled in terms of wealth and power. Ecclesiastical holdings are not hereditary, and unlike manorial lords prelates do not exist in supportive family contexts, committed to the succession of name and title across generations. Instead, they relied upon the men they appointed to choice positions under their control, that is, the *nepotes* (relatives) and *clientes* (supporters) who comprised their *familiae* (households) and affinities, to support their administrations. The sale of these positions (a practice considered a sin that came under the general heading of simony) and the maneuvering for them, the bribes paid just to be considered for candidacy, were ongoing scandals in the Church. The sale of offices, benefices and indulgences is everywhere on Gower's mind as he critiques his way through the ecclesiastical hierarchy and condemns its worldly ways. Everywhere he sees the secular clergy committed to the *imitatio imperii* and not to the *imitatio Christi* as reflected in the image of the good shepherd.

Gower also takes issue with the "third book" of the Church, that is, the ecclesiastical positive law that had come to supplement the laws of the Old and New Testaments. Comprised of the commentary of the church Fathers and other authorities, as well as the determinations of early popes, the *lex positiva* was gathered by Gratian into his *Decretum* (ca. CE 1140) and subsequently supplemented by the *Compilationes* of additional texts. Over time, these were added to the canon law until decretals began to give way to conciliar decrees and papal bulls as the primary vehicles for the issuance of church law. Gower both criticizes canon law and uses it in his commentary. The position of St. Ambrose and Pope Gelasius on the respective powers of church and state, the Gelasian dyarchy (known as the "two swords") of spiritual and imperial rule is the basis of his discussion of what belongs to Christ and to Caesar, respectively, as well as his criticism of those clerics who, like knights, led a warfaring life (ll. 577–650). Medieval students of the *ius canonicum*, and hence of Gratian as a basic text, encountered the controversy directly because Gelasius' famous letter to the emperor Anastasius (*Duo sunt quippe*) was incorporated into the *Decretum* (D. 96 c. 10). Boniface VIII's bull on papal supremacy, *Unam Sanctam* (ca. 1302), arguably the most famous (or in Gower's view, infamous) medieval document ever written concerning church and state, is scathingly noted (ll. 909–18) in the course of Book III's papal critique. Gower's sympathies, like Dante's in the *De Monarchia*, lie with secular rulers. *Licit Heli*, Innocent III's well-known decretal (ca. CE 1199) on simony and the need for bishops to bring the criminous to account, is the likely referent of Gower's criticism of the prophet Eli for his inappropriately gentle treatment of his wayward sons (ll. 1143–59). Other references to ecclesiastical documents, controversies, and positions abound. Gower registers his support for disendowment, the shedding of ecclesiastical wealth (ll. 283–301), also promoted by John Wyclif, summoned from Oxford by John of Gaunt in 1378 to preach in London against the corruptive riches of the Church; no less vehemently, Gower airs his opposition to warfaring clerics epitomized by Henry Despenser, the Bishop of Norwich. While the "Fighting Bishop's" forces slaughtered many rebels in 1381, the "crusade" he led two years later proved disastrous. Justified as a rescue of the Urbanists of Bruges from attack by heretical French Clementists, in reality the campaign was widely recognized as self-serving, and was quickly co-opted by English commercial wool interests.

Chaucer's good "parson of the town" receives scant attention in Gower's portrayal of England's curates, whose sins mirror those of the prelacy, played out on a smaller stage but driven by the same worldly desires. Securing a profitable benefice occupies a priest more than fulfilling its obligations once it is in hand, he argues. Living a secular life, such curates spend their time acquiring the world's possessions and seeking its pleasures. If possible, such a cleric will fatten his income by procuring a second parish, to be administered by a hireling substitute priest paid on the cheap. Thus freed of responsibility, the worldly cleric could frequent the courts of local magnates, ride to hounds, or engage in trade, all the while living richly and unchastely. Those priests unsuccessful in acquiring parishes hire themselves out as mass priests, and, driven by avarice, sell their services for a fee to earn the money they use to satisfy their secular desires. Gower has no use for such as these who, although garbed in the traditional garments worn to remind them of the world's temptations and guard against them, continue along their sinful path, cheating their parishioners out of the sacramental benefits a proper priest bestows (ll. 1983–96). Gower weighs in on the question of the efficacy of sacraments administered by sinful priests when he remarks that those who should receive spiritual benefit are instead left worse off (ll. 1895–6), judging such sacramental shams worthless. Although there are as many priests as stars in the night sky, he says, only two in a thousand give off any light (ll. 2029–30). Most priests take holy orders to avoid the strictures of the common law and strenuous labor, all the while receiving the basic necessities of life. The handful of good priests who do serve their parishioners faithfully will, however, be richly rewarded (ll. 2043–8). The book concludes with a brief account of good priests, who are motivated by the love of scriptural studies and the virtues.

The portrayal of the priest who studies and subsequently teaches *ars* in the schools is one of Gower's best comic pieces. It satirizes not only the individual priest's lustful inclinations, but also the broadening of the curriculum in the universities, traditionally theology and civil/canon law, to include secular literature, the sub-text of which, it was argued, also contained God's word if read correctly for its allegorical meaning. Gower's scholar-priest remains committed to the form of whatever text he studies, which becomes the figures of the females who are allowed to attend the classes of the schools where he studies and subsequently teaches. The bilingual pun on *ars* throughout is but one of the most noticeable of the portrait's many bawdy touches.

Vox Clamantis *by John Gower: 'The Voice of One Crying'*

# HERE BEGINS THE PROLOGUE OF THE THIRD BOOK

**Because what we call prosperity or adversity in the world befalls us not because of Fortune but by God's fitting judgment of our own merits and faults, here he says that he intends in what follows to write about the condition of humankind, how they behave themselves at the present time, just as he saw and heard in the dream mentioned earlier.**

    Since a good or bad lot is meted out to us
       By merit, more to these and less to those,
    Since the world is divided into three estates,
       Which makes the lots of all seem like Fate's work,
    And since a bad lot nowadays stems from our sins,
       Let us each weigh the records in our case.
    Whatever our standing, let it be recognized:
       A bad lot befalls us for what we've done.
    I won't fault individuals, but reproach the sins
       That we see are responsible in them.          10
    What I say isn't just mine but what the folk's voice*
       Gives me, which everywhere bemoans our lot.
    I say as the crowd says and in making my case
       Lament no class is righteous as before.
    Let all beat their own breasts and see accordingly
       If they're acquitted of what's in my charge.
    I don't know who can claim they're innocent since folk*
       Shout now that every class is affected.
    Indeed, widespread and serious sin has tainted
       With cases the times, us, and our places.         20
    But I'll not generalize from a particular
       Nor do I propose to fault some one class.

    We know there are three estates, among which on earth
       In their own way all live and do service.
    No estate's the party at fault, but blame assails
       Those who violate an estate's virtue.
    I write what all say, since I don't want anyone
       Should think these ideas are mine alone.
    He who censures vices praises virtues so that
       Good people stand out in their goodness more.         30
    As white set against black will stand out more clearly
       So also do good things against vices.
    Lest it grieve the good if the author talk of bad,
       Let a patient heart's scales weigh the balance.

*Book III*

Truth declines coloration, since an indictment
   Should be true, not pled with alluring guile.
If some bit of sense be in me, I pray that God
   Himself increase it to a fruitful store.
Let what good my scribbles contain seep from the fount*
   Of good: let God grant the good someone writes.          40
Let God grow in his servant the good his works do;
   Let us strew worthy seed, God send the grain.
O'erwhelmed I confess I sink, but Hope promises
   That I will come to a good conclusion.
What Hope promises, Love embraces, and as well*
   Faith provides her assistance and counsel.
She suggests, urges, persuades, pledges my labor's
   Fruit, and exhorts, "Begin, let the work start."

Where my sense is lesser, add yours, O God, and turn,
   I pray, your merciful face to my prayers.               50
That this pen venture nothing rashly by itself,
   I pray, God, grant your favor to my start.
I do not pretend to touch sidereal seats
   Nor seek to write high heaven's mysteries,
But instead I'll probe present evils, which upon
   This earth the common human voice laments.
Since a profitable sermon suits adverse times,
   I offer good words for a wicked day.
Let no whisperers impute scandals by which they
   May refute my book's words in hearers' ears.         60
Let no malicious critic rouse wrath against me,*
   Whilst I'll speak but to guilty transgressors.
Let lift, I pray, thy helping hand my frail carriage
   That my wheel may run on a trued axle.*
May thy favor aid me and relieve my efforts
   When in my trembling breast the work gets stuck.
Everything that is harmless in its proper place*
   Is able to corrupt a wicked mind.
That I prove capable and others may profit,
   God knows, will be the prayers of my labor.          70
Behold and grasp their contents from the words themselves;
   No hatred persuades me to write this work.
If this book will be attacked by its enemies,*
   I ask they be unable to rend it.
Go, my book, behind him who frees all his servants;
   Let no evil tongue interrupt your way.

If, book, you pass freely by envious voices,
  Others shall inflict no scandals on you.
My voice will not be hesitant, for all the folk
  Will be the greatest warrant of this voice.                              80
If I'm guilty of making frequent excuses,*
  Forgive me; shipwrecked, I fear every strait.

O Wise One, without whom the world's wisdom is naught,
  Into whose service my offerings bring me,
I pray you in an urgent time, merciful Christ,
  Grant I write readily the lines I've sought.
Let my pen refuse what's turgid, decline to write
  What's false, but show what now I see is true.
Beware lest it falter at first, but fittingly
  Let what's placed at the poem's start suit the work.                     90
Let naught here offend the reader unless what my
  Writings offer is true or near the truth.
In you who are true let my pronouncement be true;
  Let there be no deceit discerned in it.
Let the word both fit the matter and serve the sense,*
  Be pleasant, having somewhat of profit.
Let flattery be gone, let my account not lisp,
  Let no praise accrue to me without thine.
Grant I speak that vice decline and virtue henceforth
  Wax, that in the world man become more pure.*                           100
Guide thou my steps, increase thou my understanding,
  Reveal thou the sense, and rain words on me.
And since the world's state is arranged in order trine,
  Favor thou my writings in series trine.
These offered you, I sound the deep, a new sailor,*
  Praying you, Holy Spirit, guide my sails.*

## HERE BEGINS THE THIRD BOOK.

**Here he discusses how the state and order of the world consist in three degrees, which are, as he says, Clergy, Knights, and Husbandmen, by whose error the misfortunes of the world occur to us. He begins with the error of the clergy, chiefly in the rank of prelates, who are more powerful than the others; and he talks first about those prelates who preach Christ's teaching and practice its opposite.**

Book III

## A-Text

Cleric, knight, and farmer comprise a trinity;
   One teaches, one fights, and one tills the fields.
If we look first at what the clergy are, behold!
   The world, fleeing all others, clings to them.
In the first place, prelates come before followers,
   For the ways of the learned should be more secure.
Many nowadays do instruct with sober words,
   But their words do not agree with their deeds.
Jesus began by doing good and then teaching,
   But that way doesn't work for prelates now.**　　　　　10
He was a pauper, but they are heaped up with gold;*
   He granted peace and they have fostered war.
He was generous, but they are tight as money chests;
   Work occupied him, but leisure suits them.
He was meek, but they are more furious than fire;
   Humble, he endured, but they would prevail.
He was compassionate, but they pursue vengeance;
   He bore his pains, but they flee out of fear.
He was a virgin, but scarce one of them is chaste;
   He's the good shepherd; they devour the flock.**　　　　20
He spoke the hard truth, but they require soothing words;
   He was righteous; they see things as they wish.
He was constant, but they're shiftier than the wind;
   He opposed evils, which they tolerate.
With stomachs full, they praise the abstinence of Christ;
   He asked for plain water; they drink fine wines.
And as many sumptuous foods as the mind can
   Conceive, they condone to fill their stomachs.**　　　　28

## B¹-Text

Cleric, knight, and farmer comprise a trinity;
   One teaches, one fights, and one tills the field.
If we look first at what the clergy are, behold!
   By its example now all earth is stunned.
Schism shows plainly that today there are two popes;*
   One is schismatic and the other good.
France would venerate the false pope and upholds him,
   But England keeps the true faith everywhere.

Since I'm writing of this to readers everywhere,
   That's good news for the good but bad for bad.*   10

Christ's every rule denies the pleasures of the world,*
   But prelates transgress now in this respect.
Christ was a pauper, but they are heaped up with gold;
   Humble he endured, but they would prevail.
Christ was meek, but foolish pomp makes them arrogant;
   He brought peace, but nowadays they wage war.
Christ was compassionate, but they pursue vengeance;
   Mercy made him mild, but anger moves them.
Christ spoke the hard truth, but they need flattering words;
   Christ was righteous; they see things as they wish.*   20
Christ was constant, but they're shiftier than the wind;
   He opposed evils, which they tolerate.
Our Christ was chaste, but they are seldom virtuous;
   He's the good shepherd; they devour the flock.
With stomachs full, they praise the abstinence of Christ;
   They wear soft clothing and he goes barefoot.
They couldn't prepare finer dishes for themselves
   If they burned offerings at Bacchus' feast.*   28

## $B^2$-Text

Cleric, knight, and farmer comprise a trinity,
   But I intend to write of prelates first.
Schism shows plainly that today there are two popes;*
   One is schismatic and the other good.
France would venerate the false pope and upholds him,
   But England keeps the true faith everywhere.
Since I'm writing of this to readers everywhere,
   That's good news for the good but bad for bad.
When I inquire among Christ's prelate successors,
   No order remains what it used to be.   10
Christ was a pauper, but they are heaped up with gold;*
   He brought peace, but nowadays they wage war.
Christ was generous, but they are tight as money chests;
   Work occupied him, but leisure suits them.
Christ was meek, whereas they are very aggressive;
   Humble he endured, but they would prevail.
Christ was compassionate, but they pursue vengeance;
   He bore his pains, but fear puts them to flight.

Our Christ was chaste, but they are seldom virtuous;
    He's the good shepherd; they devour the flock.                  20
Christ spoke the hard truth, but they need flattering words;
    Christ was righteous; they see things as they wish.
Christ was constant, but they're shiftier than the wind;
    He opposed evils, which they tolerate.
With stomachs full, they praise the abstinence of Christ;
    He asked for plain water; they drink fine wines.
And as many sumptuous foods as the mind can
    Conceive, they condone to fill their stomachs.
Since food goes well with sex, and sex likewise with food,
    Venus, well fed, stands next to Gluttony.                    30

Christ himself upon the mount spurned every kingdom;
    Nothing but earthly glory pleases them.
He was a simple man in his habits and now
    The prelates make their money their morals.
But their wealth and insane desire for wealth have grown
    And when they can have most, they look for more.
Once they meditated more on the law of God,
    Whence the deity showed his face to them.
Now their concern for honors occupies them more;*
    Wealth comes to them, but there's never enough.          40
Their worth is now their wealth, income confers honors,*
    And abject poverty is the sole crime.
When rich people speak up, then every ear listens;*
    In poor people's mouths, no opinion counts.
If they lack income, wise people's sense is worthless;
    Today your rents count for more than your sense.
Paupers are fools, although they speak with Cato's tongue;
    Rich people, wise, although they're ignorant.
In their opinion, poverty's contemptible
    In all people even if they are good.                      50
And though rich people are of a perverse nature,
    They will not be adjudged to be wicked.
No arts, trustworthy pledges, gracious tongues, talents,
    Nor righteousness can exist without wealth.
There are no needy wise; property bestows sense;*
    Poor people who are wise are simply poor.
Whom the world condemns, lo! we condemn them also,
    And when they die, to the devil with them.
But we consider those worthy of our praises
    Whom the world's wealth leads to the earth's riches.    60

And so the prelates inwardly prefer the world
  Though outwardly they act like God himself.

We praise the good old days, but we enjoy our own;*
  The old ways do not suit us as a guide.
Then deadly crime did not drive Justice into flight*
  And she's now rapt from earth to those above.
Blessed souls renounced the world and all their concern
  Was to mount into the mansions above.
Neither Venus nor wine broke those sublime spirits,
  Who preferred to covet their God within.          70
But you can see many souls in these modern times,
  Who, far from Christ's praise, bear themselves proudly.
Now they pander to their own sleek pampered bodies,
  Although not with the joys born of the faith.
Not God's pious order, these grandees should admit,
  But false piety's shade alone suits them.
That's what prelates endure to gain the faith's rewards,
  Whence we repute them to be holy men.

## Chapter 2

**Here he speaks about those prelates who lust for carnal things and live luxuriously, without limits.**

Lo! Thomas's office remains, but his zeal is lost;*
  Martin's blessed rule is almost vanished.          80
He who was the shepherd becomes the hireling
  With whose flight the wolf scatters wide the flock.
The head no longer prevails with his sword nor does*
  His pampered flesh prevail with a hair shirt.
The prelate prefers the dishes of the fleshpots;*
  For manna, he would have leeks and onions.
Alas! the Church's breast nourishes such these days
  Who seek vain earthly things, not what's divine.
The flesh in their pots represents their carnal deeds,
  Which lust cooks, as it were, in clerics' flesh.          90
The kin to flesh are lust, vainglory, arrogance,
  Ambition, envy, drunkenness, strife, fraud.
With belly full, amorous flesh longs for the use
  Of Venus and seeks her carnal chambers.
And thus they cannot reach the peaks of the virtues
  Whilst wicked love of the belly rules them.

*Book III*

Tumescence, leisure, fine bread and persistent sin
   Subvert Sodomites; prelate, beware them.
But whatever prelates say these days to my face,
   The law of their own whim still governs them.          100
If they please the world and render the flesh pleasures,
   Then the soul's virtue will seldom please them.
The feast spread out, there Bacchus is poured into gold,*
   The goblet honored more than the chalice.
The vain man shows off gold cups, boasting his table,
   Where he can delight in his vain honor.
His hall open to all, his tables groan with food,*
   And he provides plenty to eat and drink.
The long rank of his clients shines in face and clothes,
   The mob attendant on his slightest nods.            110
The waste of the world scarce satisfies short bellies
   And the hall clamors with calls for servers.
Only for rich men, not others, are feasts prepared;
   There's no place for a poor man at a feast.
Empty piety is conquered by belly's greed;*
   The office ours, its burdens are ignored.

And so the greedy prelate dares praise Christ's fasting
   Though he himself does nothing similar,
And all that the sea, land, and air furnish for vice
   His wanton appetite seeks out and takes.          120
His hungering soul mortifies and his delight
   Of the flesh stuffs to surfeit his mouth's maw.
So, belly full, he's happy at his lavish feasts
   In daytime, but strumpets please him by night.
And when Bacchus has blushed both his bibulous cheeks,
   Venus' goads bring out his hidden horns.*
Thus the man's splendid virtue, thus his blessed life
   When, fed with delights, he sleeps with his whores.
He fears no chills of Acheron whom the warm bed
   Of debauchery heats up with its love.            130
And so he enjoys indulgence in various sweets
   And caters everywhere to his desires.
And so in jest, lust, wine, and sleep the blessed one
   Consumes the empty seasons of his life.
He doesn't know the body that he feeds and spoils
   May feed a torch of fire eternally.

## Chapter 3

**Here he talks about those prelates who hunger for earthly profits, delight in the honor of prelacy, and seek an episcopate, not that they serve but that they may rule.**

No one who's true is able to serve two masters,*
   But a prelate in office does just that.
He calls himself the eternal king's servant, but
   He serves and waits upon an earthly king.          140
Peter was keybearer of heaven, but this one*
   Asks for himself the king's exchequer keys.
He who's "devout" is covetous, who's "meek" is proud,
   And he who's "heavenly" cares much for earth.
He would therefore cling to both Christ and to the world:
   Christ will be his friend; the world, friendlier.
Who's dearer of the two, trial is often held,
   But there's no question who'll be the closer.
If he shows to the world the semblance of goodness,
   The depths of his heart rarely have any.          150

God declared merciful whatever is helpful,
   But anger provokes us to ball our fists.
I want to behave justly, but become angry*
   And anger ensuing ruins my good start.
I chastise the flesh, support the needy, but then
   Vainglory steals from me this nascent good.
God's wrath spews out, without any merit attained,
   This brew of secular glory and wrath.
Virtue is thus turned to vice, the world rejoices,
   And Christ passes away to no profit.            160

Holy orders once demanded a prelate serve;
   Now the cherished miter suits one who'd rule.
God's wrath was once lessened and wickedness o'erlooked
   By the prelate's prayers for a sinful folk.
Now our Moses does not lift up his hands in prayer,
   Wherefore Amalek plagues us with his sword.
When Moses raised his hands, victory came to Joshua,*
   And when he lowered them, he was beaten.
Entreating heaven for the plebs with hand, tears, prayer,
   The prelate at that point wards off the foe.      170
But if the prelate drowse, by torpor overcome,

## Book III

The folk, subdued, fall easy into sin.
Anyone can see in Moses' prayers what fruits\*
   The righteous one's suppliant word may have.

The good shepherd's moved by compassion for his flock\*
   And takes on his own shoulders his sheep's weight.
Although he is free of all their defect, he takes\*
   The ailments of his charges on himself.
Christ shows that he has not committed sin himself,
   But is said to bear guilt for his charges.         180
It's not his fault the folk offend, but he takes on
   Their sins in order to take them away.
But now they say there are such prelates in the world
   Who speak this truth without practicing it.
For they who harm themselves with their own sin seldom
   Are another's salvation by their cure.
They can't fulfill the wholesomeness promised to God
   Who give their all to worship of the world.

The prelate is supposed to cure his needy flock;
   When he sees sores, he ought to anoint them.         190
But if the prelate knows magnates are afflicted,
   He dares not anoint them, for he's afraid.
If the rest sin, so what if they're able to pay?
   He squeezes men and women by the purse.
He picks the flock's pockets and leads it in thistles\*
   So that there'll be some plucked-out wool for him.
The sinner's purse eases the sins of his body,\*
   So the new laws of the prelate proclaim.
Lust that is repeated puts profits on the books;
   Sins are resident when the purse permits.         200
When your purse is pregnant, you're free to impregnate;
   Your purse's offspring grant you laws suppressed.
So it is fear and profit that remit our sins;
   Every act is relaxed beneath their hands.
For profit thus the prelate relaxes his laws
   And grants us the right to practice our sins.
So Mammon's wicked coin grants us dispensation,
   But can't assure us eternal mansions.

Now a judge fumes if ordinary lechery
   Occurs and he can't charge the defendant.         210
If dissolute lay people should lie together,

The priest shouts in the church and it shudders.
But if a cleric has an affair, it's hushed up,
   Since he's both judge and party to his case.
So now the Gentile gods subvert the Almighty's
   Law and grant me leave to sin even more.
And so they grieve others pressed underneath harsh weights;
   How lightly *onus* weighs on their shoulders!
The wife found in adultery's pardoned, by which\*
   Parable Christ teaches us forgiveness.            220
But a golden purse doesn't redeem such a sin,
   For which a contrite spirit holds the cure.
There's no tear nowadays that's able to wash out
   Sins should a purse not know market value.
The purse validates sin and purges penalty;
   It's as powerful as the Curia.

## Chapter 4

**Here he talks about their positive laws, which, although they are not necessary to the cultivation of the soul, nevertheless burdensomely impose endless constitutions upon us almost daily to their profit.\***

Does Christ indulge me in advance for sinfulness?
   No, he shows me mercy after I've sinned.
Or has Christ prohibited anything that's not
   A sin? He does nothing of such a sort.            230
But now their new decretals forbid many things
   That neither Moses' law nor Christ's bans.
But what they tell me today is sin they remit
   Tomorrow if I pay; wherefore I charge
Either it is that something's sinful in itself
   Or it's only bad because it's proscribed.
If it's a sin, then why, before it's committed,
   Can it be legitimized by money?
If it's lawful, then why does their positive law
   Hold stringently that it should be condemned?        240
I don't think this is justly done, but whim decrees
   That profits be made by accusations.
He does a just thing justly who judges cases\*
   Well, not for love of coin but love of God.
Whatever's bound on earth by Church's laws for just

Reason, I believe it's fitting to bind.
But since God welcomes nothing unjust, no one else
   Can establish what God himself denies.
Lo! Simon attempts to renew his flight aloft;*
   He should much fear that he'll plummet anew.                   250

Merciful, Christ came not to set snares in mankind's*
   Path but rather to point out the straight way.
We, however, make crooked out of straight, rough from
   Smooth, and return sin for his compassion.
The law of Christ indeed was soothed by his mercy;
   Positive law is rife with penalties.
Christ's simply stipulated law is wrapped in but
   Few words, whence his yoke brings a gentle weight.*
However, infinite provisions in our law
   Are burdensome and seem to have no end.                    260
Christ's law is very generous, but in our law
   No pardon is *gratis*, without profit.
All is for its sake, and that's why positive law,
   Which the clergy founded, is big business.
The more birds that a fowler seeks to snare, the more*
   He desires to multiply his nets.
The more the clergy augment their positive laws,
   The more constrained the people's path on earth.
The more we walk tight paths, the sooner a false step
   Trips us, and then the clergy trample us.                   270
The more the clergy subject the world to themselves,
   The more the Church makes profits in the world.
The richer the clergy become, the more prideful,
   Issuing whatever laws they might wish.
The sun denotes the Church, the moon, the Synagogue,*
   But now our guardians look to neither.
They keep neither the injunctions of the Old Law
   Nor the new ones that Christ added to them.
Once a prelate was steadfast, holy, without sin,
   Helpful to the folk, worthy before God.                     280
But nowadays, when he can grasp the idle world,
   He doesn't heed the people's praise or God's.

## Chapter 5

**Here he talks about prelates who neglect spiritual possessions for the temporal goods of the world.**

    That same angelic voice that once terrified Rome\*
        On high, lo! sounds now in our world anew.
    In Sylvester's time, at the moment Constantine
        Bestowed the earthly world upon his Church,
    The angel said, "Poison is now sown in the Church
        When the terrestrial world becomes God's house."
    So it happened as he said; when property came
        Into the clergy's hands, poison adhered.      290
    So now all of them love their returns and reckon
        Carefully what's available to them.
    Church's law means nothing to them while they scramble\*
        To extend their castles and their holdings.
    They hunger for the world, but in holy orders
        All they want is a title from the Church.
    In the angelic orders, it's said, are Powers
        And Dominions, and such you see on earth.
    Since the clergy are unable to be angels,
        They make their own hierarchy down here.      300
    Because the prelates hesitate to grasp heaven's,
        They will enjoy the honor of this world.
    Christ said to Pilate that his kingdom was not of\*
        This world; the prelates do not follow him.
    But, unlike him, they all want to obtain kingdoms
        And to conduct wars among men for them.
    They don't want to wage wars with heathens for the faith,\*
        Not even to spread the Law's sacred words.
    But if so much as a Christian opposes them
        In earthly affairs, then they wage fierce wars.      310
    Since without Christ the clergy now take up worldly
        Arms in the Church, they will be without law.
    "You shall recognize them," Christ has said, "by their fruits,"\*
        And that precept is absolutely true.
    However the clergy mask the positive law,
        Their ways will be shown by their public acts.
    Peter's shadow healed the sick, but neither our light,\*
        Our voice, nor prayer can offer any help.
    Peter went upon the calmed waters with dry feet,\*
        But now the billows overwhelm our faith.      320
    We are ordered by the law of Christ to correct

> Through our prayers the one who persecutes us.
> But we, apart from God by new positive law,
>    Threaten to bring the vengeance of the sword.
> Thus we have destroyed those whom we are bound to teach
>    And lose the profit that Christ gained for us.
> "Vengeance is mine," God has said, but because the pope*
>    Is God on earth, he takes his vengeance first.

## Chapter 6

**Here he tells how Christ granted and bequeathed peace to his disciples. He says, however, that nowadays with their positive laws prelates institute and prosecute, even against Christians, wars for earthly goods.***

> Before the time of his death, Christ gave and bequeathed
>    To all his disciples his peace to have.    330
> And since they then desired nothing but Christ only,
>    They bore everything in Christ's gentle peace.
> But since now they desire only the idle world,
>    The world provides them the wars that they have.
> And since the clergy now lead a warfaring life,
>    God, the author of peace, doesn't help them.
> Christ said to Peter, "Whosoever of men kills*
>    By the sword in the end will die by it."
> I believe Christ's meaning cannot be mistaken
>    Although the clergy's sword does the killing.    340
> They strike with the sword; if anyone strikes back, then
>    Their new book's positive law condemns him.
> Behold! Peter preaches, but the modern pope wars;
>    The one seeks souls; the other, greedy, wealth.
> The one was killed for God's law, but the other one
>    Kills and God himself has no law for that.
> The one urges faith by simpleness, not violence,
>    But the other calls up arms on parade.
>
> God does not want our complaint to be impatient,
>    For he will avenge the ills we suffer.    350
> We've restrained enemy armies and hostile words
>    When vengeful anger didn't know our ways.
> Christ's conduct is not tested in easy matters,
>    But deep faith proves itself in a hard time.

The meek patience struggling in Christ in his sorrow
   Is truly the stuff of praise in our time.
Christ was patient when he bore every abuse, but
   Anger stirs us now for the least reason.
Every work flourished when a more noble clergy
   Left everything up to the will of God.                      360
The old piety implanted the faith, but now
   Vengeful wrath uproots those fathers' proud deeds.
"The sword does not save and he who trusts in the bow\*
   Will not be saved by it," affirmed David.
But we dispute the testimony of David
   The while a priest's hand is filled with a sword.
Moses' ark availed men of old, but that taut arc\*
   Prevails for us that, drawn, slays folks on earth.
God put a bow in the heavens that it might sign\*
   A covenant of peace to every race.                       370
When we, however, draw our bow in other lands,
   It leaves a bloody sign of exiled peace.
God aids those whom he will, but our clergy in arms
   Would find salvation by their knightly ways.

O Christ, you bound Satan by your mighty power,[1]\*
   Whom we, behold! by clergy loose anew.
When he was loosed, he absolved all those who'd been bound,
   Wherefore none comes to pay his vows to God.
The monk ignores the abbot and cloisters can't hold
   The prior to the form of the order                      380
While the priest holds a prostitute on his right side
   And, ready to arms, a sword on his left.
Who in such a world has better indicated
   That, strongly armed, he's ready to wage war?
When Nature urges it to coitus, every brute
   Will battle readily in its frenzy.
If this be the cause for which a priest takes up arms,
   War will be eternal, peace farther off.

The knight's office is not to incense the altars
   Nor the priest's to prosecute wars of state.               390

---

[1] A gloss occurs at this point in the text in manuscripts SCHGD: "Here a note about the clergy's war in Flanders in the time of King Richard, because there not only secular but also regular priests [i.e. canons], just like lay people, sought plunder in mortal battles."

If clergy can bear the sign of triumph in war,
   What's the purpose then of a true knight's deeds?
We see the clergy, who ought to pray, do battle;
   They have the cure of wars and not of souls.
If a man should injure you time and time again,
   Should it be said that he's your physician?
Or should a physician make you constantly ill
   So that good health grows ever more remote?
Ordinary experience teaches that all
   Which makes me more ill is bad medicine.                   400
If they should go to war who ought to work for peace,
   I cannot safely walk the path of peace.
It's said that something's fortune is known from its end:*
   The issue proves the case when it's in doubt.
How the end will be, or what fortune will ensue
   In the clergy's warfare, God himself knows.

## Chapter 7

**Here he tells how the clergy ought to be compassionate and patient in the love of God and neighbor, and not bellicose.**

Virtue is stronger in adversity and lo!*
   In darkness light is wont to be brighter.
Patience is the noble way to win; he conquers
   Who lasts; if you'd vanquish, learn to endure.            410
Your squire and standard bearer will be Christ himself
   If you are upright and learn to endure.
Others are commanded to fight with swords and spears;
   We should fight with faith, hope, and charity.
The law's foe can do nothing to the Lord's servant;
   Serving holy orders, he'll win his case.
Likewise, when you've been filled with proper instruction,
   You'll be able to put your foe to flight.
When you're girded with lofty works against the foe,
   You'll drive off hostile bolts with Scripture's spears.   420
Let Isaiah and Jeremy battle for us,*
   Daniel and Joel, David and Samuel.
The law of the Gospels, Paul's voice, the prophet's word,*
   These are the three whence our salvation comes.

Lo! David thought to found a temple to the Lord,*
  But heard from him, "You'll not be my builder.
You're a man of blood; therefore, you'll not be able,
  Blood-stained, to make me a worthy temple."
A blood-shedder, embracing the crimes of the world,
  Can't be God's temple because of his wars.     430
Such a one does not raise a shrine, a holy church,
  Nor erect a home for the Holy Faith.
For hatred is death, just as the Scripture declares,*
  And he who hates his brothers kills his own.
How therefore can we, stained with the blood of the folk,
  Be the servants of the altar of God?
Christ wishes life for the sinner, not that he die,*
  But be converted that he live with God.
And we kill with the sword, for the things of the world,
  Those to whom the blood of our Christ gave life.     440
The laws which Christ established were compassionate
  And sought nothing of the world but its heart,
Not the flesh of the heart but that spirit love serves,
  And he asserts that these laws are his own.
But we, to the contrary, demand the bloody
  Heart's flesh because our wrath is very fierce.
I don't know if we can conquer the world by such
  War; this I do think: it displeases God.
For God despises the church of an evildoer,*
  Beneath whose hand he lets nothing prosper.     450

Christ's faith and an inner love of brother grant strength*
  To those who've learned to overcome the world.
Brotherly love bestows peace, preserves agreements,
  Binds friendships, and perpetuates the faith.
Brotherly love won't want another's goods, pursue
  Claims, nor know how to cling to what it owns.
Brotherly love does not seek to be harmed, or harm;
  It makes no plaint nor gives cause for a plaint.
He wrongly avenges pain who increases grief;
  God himself opposes clergy who fight.     460
For love of world always oppresses everyone,*
  While God's hand preserves his own from the foe.
Fear of God is the first wisdom, salvation's first*
  Way, the first light that provides first rewards.
In eternal contract, this fear embraces love;
  By that same contract, love is joined with fear.

*Book III*

> The one can't be separated from the other,
>> For fear is considered the same as love.
> He is Father, hence loved; he is Judge, thence is feared;
>> Both this fear and love bring many blessings. 470
> It's not a slave's fear but a son's, and it begets
>> Not punishment but proffers great rewards.

> All people who love Christ fear him, and they who fear
>> Commit no outrage whence they provoke God.
> This love inspires people to look to the heavens
>> And judges that the world's joys are empty.
> It's a wonder, therefore, that the clergy's discord
>> Doesn't resolve itself with this love's help.
> Holy Writ teaches virtuous love pleases all,
>> And not ambitious worldly distinction. 480
> For, indeed, the world hampers its own devotees
>> And in the end they gain little from it.
> According to the Old Law, the Levites possessed
>> No lands and the world did not seduce them.
> Their only concern was to be open to God
>> For the peace of the people, and naught else.
> Therefore it is not good to take up the world's wars
>> Since God's gentle and loves peace's blessings.

## Chapter 8

**Here he also tells how it in no way suits prelates to wage war impatiently against a Christian people; they should, instead, subdue all the world's wickedness only by their prayers, with God's mediation, and without the force of anger.**

> Wonder seizes me when I ponder thoughtfully
>> How merciful was the teaching of Christ! 490
> The rule of Christ taught everything that is peaceful,
>> But our avarice makes everything fierce.
> Reason asks me reasonably, repeatedly,
>> Why warlike men should be in the clergy.
> There are many reasons that it shouldn't be so
>> And Christ teaches many words of warning.
> Even done for the world, if you check the outcome,*
>> The wisdom of the world speaks against it.
> For when peaceful and not covetous of honor,

Clergy were distinguished by peace of mind.                         500
If worldly warlike struggle should suit the worldly,
   That furor should be far from the clergy.
Things positive for some are proved to harm others:
   What stands this one upright knocks that one down.
The clergy's mysteries do not suit laymen well
   Nor do laymen's weapons suit the clergy.

Let others wage war and patience rule the clergy;*
   Whoever sound trumpets, quiet suits us.
The more gently victory comes to anyone
   The greater will be the victor's glory.                     510
It doesn't pay for those who can bind everything
   With words to lay on hands in any way.
There's no need of arms where the blessed voice triumphs;*
   War is naught to one who conquers with prayers.
For clergy, whom God has preferred with such a gift,
   It is enough to proffer spoken prayers.
Let those who desire peace wait patiently in peace;
   The world can't aggrieve those God himself aids.
In case you object, I'm obliged to answer you:
   "Wars are for those who should be warriors."                 520
Oh! how cruel the outcomes that lack of patience has,*
   From which headlong exits are often hard.
Haste, as I recall, brings heavy shame upon those
   Whom their own laws govern apart from God's.
And foolish vexation has often harmed a fool,
   Who then pays for a charge with his own head.
The individual who prefers his strengths to those
   Of Christ and thinks to win a war with them
Will be all the weaker, and when he thinks he's won,
   Lo! conquered, he's been beaten from the start.              530

Balaam wished to complete his trip, but lashed by whips*
   And seeing things divine, his ass delayed.
Thus, because our will has something headstrong in it,
   Its effect cancels out a helpful act.
How human affairs differ in their circumstance*
   Is taught everywhere by the way things end.
How the gravest peril can rise for the least cause*
   Is clearly taught by a matter's results.
There's need for much control in difficult matters;*

## Book III

One ought not rush one's step in grave affairs.     540
Wise Cato mandates walking softly in duress,*
    For going too quickly slows matters more.
As long as Fortune labors in doubtful affairs,*
    Patience will accomplish more than furor.
The clergy properly teach such things to others
    When they preach – but then act as if they're blind.

Shame befouls the learned ones whose sin assails them
    And they will hear no praise in times to come.
There's no excuse for it but our prosperity,
    Which far too long has held us in its grip.     550
And in our joys we garnered less understanding:*
    Our greed doesn't let us see that we're blind.
Abundance many times deceives foolish people
    And afflicts them with ever greater want.
What sweet repose was once for clergy free of blame,
    Today it's bitter care that teaches them.
We should fear pleasure more in our happy moments –*
    It hastens oft a restless heart to sin.
How near we are to ruin on happy occasions*
    And how easy the fall, no one perceives.     560

A will that's pleased with little should not deem it small;*
    The way things end will teach us what they were.
Nor should one deem that something's great when at some time
    That same thing could be lost by circumstance.
Let the headstrong learn and those who don't want to wait,
    Lest their hands rush them to their own downfall.
Experience of what the clergy does shows well
    That a worldly cure is of no value.
Hollow people who shine with honors and neglect
    The honors' burdens are like unto mules.     570
They're not an honor to God when pride weights their minds,
    But rather when they keep God's required laws.
"Who is not with me is considered against me;*
    Who gathers without me scatters in vain."
These are the words of the law of God and their weight
    Gains or loses naught by positive law.

## CHAPTER 9

**Here he says that, just as it does not suit temporal lords to usurp to themselves governance in spiritual affairs, so it does not suit the clergy's prelates to undertake wars and suchlike temporal matters, which lead to worldly pride and avarice.**

 Signet ring and crozier attend the papal rule,
  Which holds them as spiritual symbols.
 Caesar's scepter symbolizes worldly office;\*
  With it, worldly affairs come under him.    580
 Tending our souls, the pope condemns or gives them life,
  But Caesar by his right rules our bodies.
 Caesar is not permitted to torment our souls;
  That matter is not within his power.
 Nor is it seemly the pope weary men's bodies
  With wars, for that task is not in his realm.
 Let everyone do the work for which he has come,
  At the least he who bears the chief burden.
 He who has souls in his care is more exalted
  And his precedence will glorify him.    590
 Whatever the pope does, his office does not err,
  The man may falter, but the office not.
 For that sacred office transcends the world and his\*
  Right hand carries the keys of the kingdom.
 And hence he opens the sky and locks the foul pit:
  His law tends what's above or what's below.
 What he ties is bound and what he frees will be free:
  He holds thus his power over our souls.

 Those things which are Caesar's the law wishes rendered\*
  To him and those that are God's given God.    600
 You should bow down your head to Caesar and your soul
  To the pope and thus render each his own.
 Caesar cannot possess the papal state nor can\*
  The pope take Caesar's empire for his own.
 It is not for Caesar to do spiritual things
  Nor should the pope try to bear Caesar's arms.
 Let the pope keep his and Caesar his, that both their
  Laws should stand deemed by reason coequal.
 If Caesar usurps the papal law to himself,
  The pope does not permit him, but resists.    610
 So what is to the pope a war that is Caesar's?
  The Church's God was a lover of peace.

But since the pope ransacks the world with his armies,
   He'll find its manner like that which he seeks.\*
If you oppose the world, it responds and that which
   You proffer it, it gives right back to you.

The faithful, whom the Church itself had first endowed,
   Now, intolerant, it kills with cruel arms.
Peasants love a farmer, knights a fierce warrior,\*
   Sailors, a pilot for a ship in peril.                        620
Christ loves peace and peace claims the clergy for its own,
   So clergy should hold themselves merciful.
Shameful are those who retreat and don't stand their ground,\*
   Shameful, who abandon a distressed ship;
More shameful those who, for the world, reject Christ's law,
   Who in the place of peace establish war,
So that all the kingdoms the name of Christ o'erflows
   Wage wars more vile than the treacherous Goths.\*
It should be enough that lay people wage their wars
   Without a clergy fierce with their own swords.            630
Whatever the laic should do, I can't excuse
   The clergy, whom Christ's model holds to peace.
But the world's goods, which are as fleeting as shadows,
   Cause heinous wars when Christ is set aside.

What's done spiritually in human affairs
   The clergy claim to have as their duty,
And the greater glory that's in worldly affairs
   They claim as a property of their swords.
So now the clergy have two wings to aid their flight,
   But the wing of the world pleases them more.            640
Thus seeds of stinging nettle dilute the pepper\*
   When a secular clergy wed the world,
And the people suffer and their spirit sickens
   When haughty clergy join the greedy world.
It's not enough for them to vex a peaceful folk;
   They disturb God Almighty with their wars.
"Thou shalt not kill," it's written, but no one's able
   To find a safe place left upon this earth.
Say, therefore, where our due is; 'mongst such uncertain
   Properties, which are you able to keep?               650

The lineage of his birth mother proclaims Christ,\*
   By law, heir of the land where he was born.
If something in this world should be our property,

## Vox Clamantis by John Gower: 'The Voice of One Crying'

It would be the part Christ's entitled to.
But these days pagan intruders have it, for which
   They pay no tribute to our exchequer.
We don't wage war against these folk, attack neither
   Them nor their property; our law is still.
No bull admonishes us there, no broad decree
   Urges us, nor does our sword give battle.                 660
Let Christ claim those things there that are his, if he wants,
   And let him wage war for his property.
So we don't disrupt our leisure for distant wars,
   Nor send a legate there for Christ's dower.
But on our brethren, whom the water signs reborn,*
   We wage open war for worldly holdings.

The mandate of Christ is that the clergy shall preach*
   And thus earn their spiritual reward.
I don't read that the clergy should take up arms for
   Worldly gain, but forbear for love of God.               670
The clergy's preaching is unable to convert
   The pagans and they gain no profit there.
Rather, they gain for themselves castles, homes, and towns,
   To acquire which they wield arms forcefully.
Thus they reject the spiritual that suits them
   And flag unsuitably where they should watch.
But those of the world's earthly things that Christ had called
   Inappropriate, they appropriate.
Taking the unfitting and rejecting the fit,
   The clergy disown judgments that God gave.             680
For the prince of this world has come and we obey*
   Him because he brings abundant profits.
Our greedy minds abhor the poverty of Christ
   Lest it disturb our bodily repose.
Our heart takes no solace from his humble patience,
   For this denies our proud ostentation.
Nothing will harness us except our own free will,
   Whose flimsy bridle has to lead our flesh.

It's the law's author that seems to despise the laws;
   He doesn't keep the ways that he teaches.             690
He who's the first taken in sin condemns all sins;*
   Reproaching others, he behaves yet worse.
Who'd know the faults of others should first know his own
   And amend what his own sin has contrived.

*Book III*

Who bears the keys of Peter to unlock heaven's\*
   Gates closes them first to men upon earth.
The more I ponder this, the more I'm stupefied,
   For what his light reveals, his dark obscures.
The taste of one thing pollutes a thousand others;
   The rest are tainted by its evil smell.                      700
He is Pride, a duke riding in a high carriage,
   Menacing with his face, eye, voice, and hand.
Envy follows, a mob in sour affinity,
   A pallid thing, dark scourge and bitter plague.
Mercy, the champion once wont to remit our sins,
   Is now Avarice seeking fleeting gain.

How grim is the plague, how dolorous the name Pride,
   The root of sin, of evil fount and source!
The fount of wickedness, the cause of all sorrow,
   The virtues' vice, a falling leap to hell,               710
Avarice's host, prodigal poverty, fraud's
   Beginning, wrong thinking, a wicked love,
Mental unrest, neighborly conflict, death's mistress,
   Shifty minds, wayward reason, vain honor.
These are the very properties of Pride itself,
   Considered the chief resident of hell.
Where this chief evil reigns, he takes each wretched head\*
   And makes it the companion of his tail.
By it the head of things was made to serve the sins;
   We, who were free, learned to bear this grave yoke,     720
Not that of the Lord, which is said to be easy,\*
   But one the hateful foe imposed on us,
Not that by which the freedom of salvation's sought,
   But one which weighs us down in servile state.
The prime work, the prime splendor, with primacy's place
   Endowed, we became perdition's prime work.
Alas! say what is the cause of such a great fall:
   The impulse of a proud mind was the source.
Oh! the proud mind, dire presumption, to have the place
   Of the High King, to be the Judge's peer,          730
To be the Maker's equal, not to imitate
   But rival God, not follow his goodness.
For such reasons it is needful that arrogance
   Be purged and duty done with humble heart.
Dismiss what is doubtful, hold to the fact that Christ
   Was a peacemaker and declared no wars.

## Vox Clamantis by John Gower: 'The Voice of One Crying'

If the head of the Church strays from the sacred path,
  Lo! the head's sin makes the members sinful.*

The priestly order did not make wars in the name
  Of Christ, but persisted with piety.                          740
Beaten with clubs, they declined to beat anyone
  And conquered all by acting patiently.
And they conquered evil with good, for Christ was their
  Duke and gave the just the justice they sought.
Peter asked for spiritual gifts in his prayers
  And by his worthy prayer thus won his wars.
This was victory for the Most High's right hand, who
  Brought about through God's powers what he sought.
For all things were tempered mercifully and weighed
  Justly when Peter offered up his prayers.                   750
Thus those who, pondering, would expect Christ's mercy,
  Should neither pompous be nor lightly glib.

Peter said that he had no silver and no gold,*
  But that God gave more precious gifts to him.
He told the lame man he should rise, and he arose,
  He should walk and go, and he went at once.
Now what is this to us? Because if someone ask
  We should heal him thus, we don't have the cure.
Our haughty minds lack kind hearts with which worthily
  To pray; God yields to humble entreaties.                760
Those who'd been gentle are embittered in their wits
  And persons decked in flowers lack true blooms.*
We are splendid in gold and wanting in virtue,
  For we've resolved to pursue things of gold.
If some have gold, it's agreed that they have what counts
  And thus in this world they're blessed people.
It's as if the world flows into the clergy's maw
  And in their jaws they gulp down all the gold.
Not one tiny drop, however, flows back to help
  The poor, for, tight-fisted, they keep it all.               770
Christ gave himself to the folk as a precious gift,
  But we, ingrates, deny them what we have.

O Head of the Church, remember the times of Christ,
  If he gave such examples as you set.
He saved the sheep and brought them out of death to life,
  Which you torment and pitilessly kill.

He bade Peter to forgive sins seventy times*
  Seven and he himself spared the accused.
But at the first offense you strike with avenging
  Sword and spare no one for the sake of love.     780
Lo! Rachel wept and had no solace for her grief*
  When one born of her womb departed her.
O chosen kind, sacred tribe, why by your judgments
  Do you cause greedy scandals in the world?
Alas! the Church's goods, which are owed to the poor,
  He dissipates in wars who governs them.
Alas! from a clergy distant from mercy's law,
  Who once was Church's head becomes its tail.*
And health becomes sickness; life becomes death; rising,
  Falling; law, crime; and the father, the foe.     790

## Chapter 10

**Here he asks why, since prelates write about and teach those things that pertain to peace, they to the contrary attend and are devoted to those things that pertain to war. To which question, however, he himself subsequently responds.**

I've seen Rome's clergy have written thus in their books:
  "Read my writings that you might live better.
Do you wish to serve God, to know that which he asks?
  Read this and then you'll know what that should be.
Love, seek, trust, and strive to revere God in your mind."*
  By their book's witness, that's what clerics bade.
"Since life is short, flee all the pleasures of the flesh,
  Preferring heavenly gifts for your soul.
Serve justice, let your law be impartial to all;
  Do to others what you want for yourself.*     800
Love the Lord with your whole heart and with your whole soul;*
  Likewise let there be love for your brother.
Love of God truly begets the love of brother
  And divine love grows with brotherly love.
Take to the wretched the gifts that you owe to Christ;
  Bear no arms nor wage wars that harm someone.
Be pious and patient and your restraint will be
  To all a model of peace that it last."
When I read such things, I am felled by amazement
  That I see warfare among the clergy.     810

So I wanted to ask the clergy if someone
  Would give me a reasonable answer.
The question raised, a cleric took it up, arose
  And offered these things to my inquiries.
Establishing his was the acme of honor
  Of the Supreme Pontiff, here's what he said:

"Earthly power divided governance with me
  And I tend realms subject to heaven's law.
But since the earth is near to us and heaven far,*
  Let the earth that is so close please us more.                 820
My hall is grand and splendid with beautiful art,
  The bedroom elegant and its couch soft.
So that what I demand please my tongue, fine platters
  Of the better food are mine; I drink wine.
From every wholesome kind of the fowl and the fish,
  I'm given foods that are pleasant to have.
Every variety of wine yielded by grapes
  I get, that among them I never thirst.
I have harmonious songs, drums, and a merry muse;
  A minstrel renders ditties full of jests.                      830
The better things sea and land beget or air shapes
  Are in the market for me as I wish.
I have a bower, secluded parks with fountains,
  And I can have all I want from the world.
I have a fruitful spot in the fields endowed me,*
  Fine castles, the city's highest honors.
My woods contain beasts for the having, the air, birds,
  And the sea's waters teem with diverse fish.
But the places and the creatures are not enough
  For us unless we get gifts of gold coin.                       840

"Behold my great gates, which a guard watches closely
  That no pauper shall gain passage through them.
My court spurns with this warning those whom it rejects:*
  'Stay out, you wretches; weep outside my gates.'
Let the guard shut out that hand that does not hold out
  Presents; let it not experience our ways.
But those who want secretly to be our friend let
  Give gold, without which no offering pleases.
The hand that's full will more likely be asked inside;
  The empty, not so honored, kept outside.                       850
I free, I bind all things, I reign with highest crown,

## Book III

I'm lord of earth: what more could I wish for?
Everyone calls me Lord, worships the living me,
   So I walk every land a second God.
Our throne is the highest, from which our hand bestows
   Blessings and curses upon all alike.
And so with our power reverenced everywhere,
   We're great in the Church, greater in the world.

"We speak and things are done, we command and behold!
   Gifts, begot of sudden profit, pile up.                     860
We've taken all the realms of the world Christ renounced,*
   Which despotic vainglory granted us.
By the earth thus exalted we've drawn to ourselves
   All the things that are replete with pleasures.
So the state we've assumed approves what we are, as,
   Weaving our idle times, we grieve the earth.
Christ gave us a pleasant yoke, a light load, but we*
   Give out the graver burdens that are earth's.
We give the people laws, but aren't checked by the Law;
   Law that suits me shall have the force of law.            870
It's not for humans to judge I sin throughout earth,
   Just so they allow the acts that please me.
And if for these things the world be rebel to me,
   Behold! my hand is made stronger by war.
For these reasons likewise I, the pope, make answer,
   That by my wars I cast mere mortals down.

"Dissension once arose among the disciples;*
   Christ's precept of the child soothed their concern.
But by no means is someone able to steer us
   To true peace; our pride does not permit that.         880
Upon the cross transfixed did Christ endure his death
   And his passion was man's true salvation.
This patience of Christ was an example to all
   That we be each other's loyal comrades.
But we appoint the cross a token of vengeance
   And charge that it be borne to the folk's death.
And so we take mercy from a merciful sign
   And what was life will now be a new plague.
Thus what were once salvation's banners are now death's
   And the cross that brought peace now wages war.      890
And so we bear the Lord's cross, but don't follow him
   With any thought to why he bore the cross.

## Vox Clamantis by John Gower: 'The Voice of One Crying'

What virtue cannot do, brute strength will now supply,
   Not morals show the way but mortal war.
Our left will erode what our right hand once built up
   And thus a humble faith will hatch no eggs.
The harvest that others have gathered we now strive
   To scatter; our fierceness will devour earth.
So the Lord's uncultivated vineyards don't get
   Our labors and our hand becomes warlike.     900
The ox that mercy tells us to pull from the pit*
   Our savagery leads us to cast within.

"Judea reveals the reward that Peter brought*
   And people proclaim the wealth Paul bore them.*
But we do not come with our hands empty of gold,
   For spiritual profit is nothing.
Whatever the future may bring, we fear no sins
   Now as long as the world will be our friend.
For war will aid our task so that our name is held
   Above all names where honor's uncommon.     910
By Mohammed's law a man shall die by the sword*
   Who refuses to keep his name sacred.
So we now set forth a decree, wrapped in a sword,
   That our name hence be first in every land.
The one who opposes the decree of Caesar*
   Is not considered his friend in this world.
The one who does not acknowledge our lofty name
   Is death's child, guilty upon the sword's edge.

"So we have come to bring the world the sword, not peace;*
   We do everything new despite the harm.     920
So the head now savages and aggrieves the limbs,
   Which by its office it should do no harm.
So a father now becomes Saturn to his sons*
   And kills those whom his own law should sustain.
So, too, the shepherd, who by rights should feed the sheep,*
   Plunders his own sheepfold and devours them.
Thus like a savage judge we try the world by fire*
   And get more riches from base metal purged.
Let the clergy sell their garments and purchase swords
   And each order leave off its sacred tasks.     930
Thus let us extol our name among the nations
   So others fear that wars may come their way.
Let pastoral staff be transformed now into spear,*

*Book III*

    Miter be helm, and peace rush to slaughter.
Let serve who will, for we want preference above
    All men; let another bear the burden.

"Thus we who bear the name of the Supreme Pontiff
    Have deemed in our blind heart to pursue arms.
Whatever their souls may do, we aim to subdue
    The world's bodies, helped by positive law.*        940
Its commentary lets our hand take up the sword
    With which it may wage its far-flung battles.
Therefore let everyone fear to say nay to us:
    In our wars both our hand slays and our tongue.
But yet we receive into our peace all heathen
    Peoples, lest we be afflicted by them.
We prefer to move our armies against Christians,
    Who are now scarce able to claim their due.
Peter cut off an ear and Christ made good that wound*
    To the condition it had been before.        950
But our anger takes off a head, a wound from which
    We know no one returns to the same state.
Therefore our sentence is graver than Peter's was
    And our sword is more mighty than his sword."
Thus the one called Clement now lacks all clemency*
    And goes about bearing a headless name.

## Chapter 11

**Here he talks about those prelates who presume a holy name for themselves, but appropriate for themselves earthly possessions and then do not come to the aid of others by imparting charity.**

    "An angel, it is read, at one time to Saint John*
        Said, when he fell down and paid him homage,
'Beware that you don't do that to me, God's servant;
    Worship, instead, the Lord with all your heart.'        960
Though a celestial dweller upon earth spat out
    Such honor, our court claims it for itself.
So the knee is bent and kisses then soothe our feet*
    As if another foot of Christ were there.

"Christ once instructed that none of his disciples*
    Should take the name of father for himself.

In heaven, those who are holy proclaim 'Holy'
   The Worthy who sits the throne in honor.
However, we bear both names among the folk and
   'O father, O holy one,' all shout, 'hail!'                             970
A great power has been given to us by Christ,
   Which the world is everywhere eager to enhance.
Be that as it may: whoe'er binds heaven,*
   We know quite well that we can bind the world."
For now positive law proposes that the Church,
   Eager for war, can claim what's its by force.
But what the clergy seizes and keeps from others
   No man can take away from the clergy.
What the clergy have they put to their own uses,
   But want to have lay people's shares as well.                     980
They maintain that all their own goods are sanctified
   And let no lay person put hands on them.
They want to take a share of the laity's profits,
   But do not wish to share in its losses.
If love should be common, let all things be common,*
   For plainly each one can help the other.
But since the clergy are not a commons of love,
   What land they have they would keep for themselves.

By the Old Law, a man can't consecrate to God*
   Whatever he has plundered from a foe.                               990
But the clergy have pillaged regions that our Church
   Takes and claim these as sacred possessions.
Thus the clergy tax the laity, but nobody
   Can amerce them and so the new laws state.
The shepherds do not feed the sheep, but, fed by them,
   Gulp milk and meat like they're just other wolves.
Thirsting for pounds, they do not hunger for their books*
   And think the Book of Mark a one-mark book.
They care for their sums, not their Summae, and they think*
   The choice wines more divine than the sacral.                   1000
They pursue the love of women but not the way
   Of virtue and would plow only such soil.
Their honor is not from onus; their bodies gleam*
   With honors, but they won't lift their burdens.

*Book III*

## Chapter 12*

**Here he speaks about the simony of the prelates, and how these delicate fellows, calling themselves the Church, impose heavy burdens on others, and, furthermore, how they vex the laity with monstrous taxes for any little whim.**

    As God is my witness, who won't enter sheepfolds*
        By the gate is branded thief and robber.
    So clergy in the Church, advanced by simony,
        Likewise behave in a thievish manner.
    Nor can anyone please Christ conferring stolen*
        Goods; rather, God confounds his hands henceforth.     1010
    Therefore the fisc can seize the things Christ does not want;
        Since they are worldly, the world shall have them.
    For when the clergy are abusive of their law,
        The laws say they deserve to be deposed.
    The clergy call themselves the Church, as if they'd say
        Laymen shan't touch her, that office is theirs.
    The clergy in their arrogance want to be tried*
        In secret and not by the common law.
    They preen themselves, oppress and rob others, urged on
        By the new-fangled make-up of their law.     1020
    I can see that these days worldly pomp hides under
        The guise of the divine; God's laws don't stand.

    What is Holy Church but a faithful band of men?
        It's clear the laity, whom the faith nurtures,
    Are part of the Church, and the clergy, no better
        Unless they live better. Who says me nay?
    Only one faith, one baptism, one God abides,*
        So one Church unites us and holds us fast.
    Just as one leather sack may contain many grains,
        Just so one faith gathers many people.     1030
    Why then do the clergy want to have for themselves
        Holy Church's name, like another God?
    They hang the weight of law on the necks of others,
        But decline to burden their own shoulders.
    They allow to themselves all that's forbidden me;
        They take their leisure while I sweat with toil.
    Their deeds point the way to the commission of sins,*
        But their words say otherwise in your ear.

Hence a confused folk question if they should believe
   More in the clergy's words or in their deeds.     1040
When they forbid me that of which they should be charged,
   I hardly believe them, since they're guilty.
Thus I see that the clergy's proud new men destroy
   What the Faith gave through humble men of old.

These men teach submission to a blow on the cheek*
   So that people abide more patiently.
But if you should infer something grave about them,
   They'll soon curse your soul with mortal censure.
He who kills a soul by a death penalty would,
   If he could, first destroy the body too.     1050
The shepherd does more damage than the wicked wolf
   By butchering the sheep that he should heal.
They bear heaven's keys, but they don't enter themselves,
   Nor let us enter, whom they lawless rule.
Nor do they till the people's minds with doctrine's plow*
   Nor do they do the work that suits their tasks.
They want to sit at the right hand of blessed Christ,
   But they don't want, O Christ, to bear your cup.
These fishermen cast their nets widely for profits,
   That they catch the world, not solace for souls.     1060
Living badly, they give examples to lay folk,
   Who follow just as by their manner taught.
The sheep are infected by the shepherd's blind spots;*
   Together they fall sightless in the pit.

## Chapter 13

**Here he tells how the prelate ought to cast light for the people entrusted to him, not only by his teaching, but also by his good deeds.**

Who walks in ignorance does not know where to step,*
   Like those who can't see the way they must keep.
And when the people are untaught, they cannot see
   That their prelate does not keep God's precepts
When he doesn't teach Scripture or do pious deeds
   But shows by his vices he's sunk in sin.     1070
When his lantern dies out, without light in the night,
   When the prelate's acts are without virtue,
Then he leads the folk astray and the blind follow

Lightless the blind so their downfall ensues.
Therefore let them kindle their lights more brightly, they
   Who are leaders, that we may see the road.
A lit lamp does three things: it lights, it heats, it burns;*
   The prelate likewise does the same three things.
He shows the light by his life, the heat by his love,
   And when he rebukes sinners he burns them.          1080
When he binds the folk to him in heart, tends and feeds
   The sheep with blessed prayers, he pleases God.
And if some prelate worries, who is gripped by fear
   Lest that wolf Satan enter his sheepfold,
Let him feed his sheep with such holy examples*
   That in their mouths they taste sweet honeycomb.

Often a trumpeter used to go forward and
   A duke spurred his fighting men with its blast.
You, O prelate, who are a spiritual duke,
   Should give forth words consonant with God's law.          1090
Let loose your deep voice just like a trumpet sounding
   And let your tongue guide the flock's deeds with words.
Shout out, do not hold back, show the people their sins,
   But be yourself a good example first.
When taste abiding in a constant stream is sweet,*
   We gratefully drink waters from its fount.
When the life of the clergy is more blessed in Christ,
   The words which they teach will be more blessed.
God's word never comes back empty, but when sent forth*
   Bestows double talents of profit gained.          1100
God's pure word, administered by a faithful heart,
   Piercing heaven's gates, brings gifts back to earth.
The suffering souls that possess such a curate
   Will find, if they wish, salvation's sound path.
They who savor nothing on earth, but seek heaven
   And hunger and thirst after God alone,*
Who are drawn to books, not the gleam of pounds sterling,
   Whom God's altar feeds, not the sight of gold,
Will reap without end the enduring things they've sowed
   Since they've earned a fit reward for their work.          1110
Those who teach what is right and act accordingly
   Make it easy to do that which they say.
When the starting gate is raised, a good horse runs well*
   If it has others to pursue and pass.

## Vox Clamantis by John Gower: 'The Voice of One Crying'

The Scriptures of the Old Law should be kept in mind
  So a good shepherd can find examples.
This wisdom became memorable enough when
  Jacob set out some withies for his flock.*
Partly he bared them by stripping away the peel,
  Partly he left them covered with the bark.           1120
Whiteness shines in the withies when the peel is stripped,*
  When pastors pull brilliant words from Scripture.
When they grasp the letter only, they keep the peel
  And then they feed the sheep the simple sense.
But why would pastors set forth models they reject?
  That they might advance these, not those they hold.
We count for nothing one whose own life or teaching
  Will not help him in guiding the people.
But there are those who, offering unwise teachings,*
  Urge schism's great dangers upon the folk.           1130
Because of an untaught teacher, students often
  Get no virtuous profit from a school.
Thus unfit prelates, although they have abundant
  Doctrine, won't be effective without deeds.

Some overzealous men ravage more than a fire
  And, like a bear, press savagely the sheep.
When he rebukes someone harshly, such a teacher*
  Harms those whose salvation he ought to be.
He wounds the guilty, but then doesn't staunch their wounds;
  He makes yet worse that which was bad before.           1140
Thus the words of a proud prelate cannot heal us*
  Since authored by a man flawed in his ways.
And then there's the prelate who, as if he approves,
  Scolds so mildly the sinner doesn't heed.
Eli scolded sons with a father's tenderness,*
  Not a pastor's, not with a grave tenor.
By loyalty in his words to his sons, Eli
  Was impious, and condemned for their sins.
A pastor who does not scold his subjects thus earns
  God's wrath on high and will deserve his gaol.           1150

It's been written, "The blessed kept the middle way;*
  You should not seek great heights nor sound the depths."
The prelate should not tire us too much with harsh law
  Nor too much grant by weak indirection.

*Book III*

If the horseman's light hand has also no firm touch,
  The horse, when checked by reins, often resists.
A medicine now takes away, now bestows health;
  There's nothing helpful that can't also harm.
But a worthy prelate who grasps the reins will guide,
  Choosing his time, the journey where it's safe.   1160
A sinner oft awakens through a mild sermon
  Who'd be more unresponsive to harsh words.
From time to time it helps that the prelate's just wrath
  Relentlessly press reluctant rebels.
A fierce sickness can oft be tamed by bitter herbs
  And a sharp thorn bush bears tender roses.*
When it's renewed by plowing, hard earth, overturned,
  Has oft a pleasing softness at its top.

The prelate is anointed with symbolic oil
  And he should observe the meanings it has.   1170
Four things it does – penetrate, light, feed, and anoint –*
  A worthy bishop ought to consider.
He cannot penetrate without virtue of force,
  But that virtue, penetrating, pleases.
For when tenderness has been united with force,
  The prelate's way shall be gentle and stern.
Let him lack anger that he avoid harmful sin;*
  Let oil bedew and holy love anoint him.
Thus the more sublimely the teacher's voice strikes hearts
  Within, the more forcefully it moves them.   1180
The oil's nature weighs out these virtues equally;
  While its force penetrates, it gently rules.
It's light, food, balm for the blind, the hungry, and sick;*
  It pours out radiance, feeds and comforts –
Light by example, food when it feeds the needy,
  And balm when it spreads sweet words to peoples.
By David's witness, this is the oil of gladness*
  The Father used when he anointed Christ.
They're not anointed who share the sin of Simon,*
  Who buy or sell and don't say Masses free.   1190
Who sins in such ways is exiled from God's people,
  For Christ casts such men out of his temple.

## Chapter 14

**Here he tells how, according to some, signs of the Antichrist have appeared in the Roman Curia, chiefly from avarice.**

> On the verge of speaking, my mind pauses in fear;
>   Frightened it labors and trembling falls still.
> For if it's granted me to touch upon this vice,
>   Christ and all Rome alike shall be witness.
> Rome gnaws at ungiving hands, spurns and detests them,
>   So everyone takes a gift for a gift.
> God is not a respecter of persons; rather,*
>   More graciously, he looks to a man's deeds.                1200
> But only those whom the world enriches with gold
>   Receive our grace and no other people.
> Who puts down a rich payment carries back increased
>   Rewards, for the whole Curia favors him.
> The one to be anointed won't enter in there
>   Unless a bit of gold greases a palm.
> A wealth of morals confers nothing without gold,
>   For no virtue of the poor deserves aid.
> If you knock with gold, you'll get in and you'll have what
>   You seek, and your gift will get you a gift.              1210
> If you want generosity, be generous,
>   For if you sow few, you'll reap few rewards.*
>
> What shall a wise man do? A fool joys in a bribe.*
>   Let clergy who know speak to this matter.
> Bribes, believe you me, both men and the gods accept;
>   A great man in the world is soothed by gifts.
> But when Simon pays his bribes to obtain the world,*
>   His concern will not be Christ's advancement.
> That the thirsty come freely to his waters, Christ*
>   Urged and lo! he has slaked them at his fount.            1220
> But any thirsty man will not drink from our founts
>   Without a gift of money given first.
> To sell quid pro quo is the manner our Curia
>   Keeps and with Simon's help it flourishes.
> Our Curia knows nobody without a bribe
>   And an empty hand will come back empty.
> A layman who gives outweighs a theologian;
>   If you should give me gifts, I'll give you some.
> If Matthew, Mark, Luke, and John don't bring any gifts,

*Book III*

  They'll lose the grants that they seek for themselves.    1230
If the world's servant should come, received he prospers;
  If Christ's servant, no one attends to him.

If a poor man come, attended by Homer's muse*
  But brings nothing, he goes back just as poor.
If a new Augustine petitions there without
  Giving a gift first, he'll leave a vagrant.
A layman dressed in gold construes, reads, and chants well;
  If he can pay, whate'er he does is fine.
See for yourselves what sort of piety this is
  Or if justice will thus maintain the laws.    1240
If the Church stumbles, falling perchance through such men,*
  May the Most High in his mercy raise it,
And may he, confounding heresies, end schisms
  Lest anyone might lose his Christian sheep.
In thy mercy, Redeemer, let return to you
  Those whom peace, piety, and one faith bind.*
The Antichrist will do things contrary to Christ,*
  Subverting morals and fostering sins.
I don't know but perhaps he's come now to the world,
  For nowadays I see his many signs.    1250
The ship of Peter, which founders, first raise O Christ;
  Let Pride not swallow it before it sinks.

## Chapter 15

**Here he tells how, according to public opinion, many desire the honors but not the burdens of the prelacy, so that virtues disappear and vices multiply rapidly in the Church.**

  O God, each heart's open and wants to talk to you,
   And no secrets lie hidden from your light.
You know, Lord, that as far as it is from sunrise
  To sunset, the *Regula Prima* has fled.*
That working faith you wanted to construct, clergy
  These days, so to speak, have built crookedly.
The world illegally annuls what was Christ's law
  And claims the new prelates all for its own.    1260
For the name of saint makes not a saint; nay, rather
  Whom God himself approves becomes a saint.
But if we are honored by the folk with the name

And if the world praises, that's praise enough.
Thus disguised faces deceive the Father's order,
   Where honor, stolen, has shed its burdens.

The people's voice accords with God's voice, so that it*
   Should be feared in doubtful circumstances.
The common talk taught me these things that I will say
   And my words don't contain anything new.                     1270
Pharisees climb now into the chair of Moses*
   And scribes write dogma that they don't observe.
Who were constant, humble, generous, pure and modest,
   In whose churches holy orders were kept,
Have now been replaced in their positions by men
   Greedy, arrogant, wanton, and grasping.
Wrath has overcome the peaceful and Pride, the meek;
   Coin owns the just and Venus, the holy.
Thus Justice does not rule cases, nay, rather Will,
   Darkened by evils that lack all reason.                        1280
Thus earth worships gods these days and is rent by them,
   While the clergy's law knows nothing of God's.
Now vain men explicate your laws with empty words
   And do little or naught by the law's weight.
They rarely follow you by example, O Christ,
   And think your law's perfection is empty.
What your precepts put on, they put off from their own*
   And order me to bear on my shoulders.
But any distinction that the precepts propose
   They take from me and want to make their own.         1290
They don't care about a foundation, but assume
   A column's shape and call themselves churches.

Heaven was once seditious and so the Proud One
   Fell from on high and, fallen, keeps the depths.
And for his sin thus Adam fell from paradise
   And Judas thus lost his high position.
Status or place don't cause a man to be blessed;
   Indeed, they confound those who would excel.
O God, just as you've made your Church holy to you,
   Make likewise thence your prelates holy men.           1300
Correct such now by your mercy, I pray, O God,
   Since you bid us bow our necks to such saints.
Those whom you've established our leaders by your law
   Make better that the right path may guide them.

And although their conduct is vain and unstable,
   Grant that the people's faith stay always firm.
Grant the clergy, too, O God, that in word and deed
   They expel evil and aid us on earth.
The longed-for sweet medicine for our griefs at last*
   Let come; though late, it's wont to be welcome.       1310
If there should be good men of the clergy, then we'll
   Be better and God's glory thus greater.

## Chapter 16

**After he has spoken about those in the status of the prelacy who err, it is necessary to speak about the error of curates, who, appointed beneath prelates, carelessly neglect the cure of souls in their parishes, putting them in danger. First he intends to speak about those curates who, neglecting their parishes, cling to courts in order to serve magnates.**

I wrote the heedless prelate's faults just as I heard*
   Them from the voice and there my pen leaves off.
But there are other rectors not without fraud's stain
   Who serve the laws in the cures of the soul.
Where that group is trending now, I intend to write,
   Whether to the world or instead to God.
Reviewing the deeds of rectors at the present,
   I find that what should be God's is the world's.       1320
Because the prelate errs, who is the head of cures,
   The curate errs, who is the prelate's hand.
Without a prebend created in Simon's way,
   He thinks a church no good whatsoever.
But this prebend feeds not the poor man but harlots
   And so it serves not God but a goddess.
Such do not care to live chastely nor prudently,
   Of whom these days are many instances.
Their garb's pompous; their food, full of delicacies;
   And their couch proclaims it has been defiled.       1330
There was a time, you could learn from the words of Christ,*
   That his disciples didn't have two robes.
But since these are not his disciples, they don't want
   To keep the required manner in such things.
They double up not just on clothes but livings, too,
   Which the rule views as sinful above all.

## Vox Clamantis by John Gower: 'The Voice of One Crying'

And gold arrives to gird about their unchaste loins
   So that empty elegance marks them vain.
We see them degenerate in ostentation,
   Looking like knights, lacking only the spurs.                 1340

Whose is the honor, let be the burden; who wants*
   To share the profit, let him share the loss.
Thus a just faith commands, thus law decreed to all,
   But now those who cure deny these statutes.
They receive fat curacies and accept rich things,
   But they don't want to bear the weight of cure.
If a curate can't live in his sins in one post,
   He seeks then to have another new one.
After infecting the first, he fouls the second,
   Thus changes his places and not his ways.                  1350
The prelate's purchased letter exempts the curate
   And thus the curate abandons his cure.
He retains for himself a substitute lay priest
   When a baronial court will retain him.
He's busy as a bee while seeking honors there,
   But, idle, he does nothing in his cure.

Whatever the world's fashion is, he accepts, too,
   So that a court can believe him worthy.
He'll render fawning words and no dog trained to bow
   Will bend so low with such a humble face.                 1360
He supplants his comrades like a second Jacob*
   And does all he can to grasp the world's wealth.
But he can't undertake a thing without the help
   Of skillful Simon, who'll be his agent.
If the gates have been shut, he enters the sheepfold*
   Some other way and, greedy, picks his path.
He cares nothing for the cure of souls while he tends
   The earthly magnate's court for his profits.
The body's deed, not the soul's merit, works for him;
   His gifts, not his merit, get him a place.                  1370
Who's nothing in himself, has not the means to rise,*
   Succeeds when raised up by another's wealth.
But it's absurd when anyone through another
   Swells up more than it is appropriate.

When a royal letter supplicates papal ears*
   And Simon is the means to grease a palm,
Lo! our layman becomes a cleric fit to climb,

With Simon's aid, all the ranks upon earth.
He who'd been poor yesterday, nigh naked without
   Distinction, even the title father,                                               1380
Whose robe was wretched, not amply full but too tight,
   Which scarce his knee reached in its scantiness,
These days a damasked garment wraps him 'round, and its
   Fringe, playing with his feet, fondles the ground.*
A coat that didn't know the middle of his knee
   Now tends his ankles, kissing on his feet.*
If you were to scan his cloak in the world's mirror,
   You'd see the rector's many vanities.

If he's unable to ascend a prelate's rank,
   He gets similar garments anyhow.                                                   1390
Who had but recently a single household pup
   Lo! now it's like the whole earth follows him.
Whose palfrey was lately a walking stick, with reins
   In the saddle now curbs a noble steed.
So he gets rich in cures, but devoid of morals
   Governs his wealth foolishly and grows poor.
Adding up his worldly things, he worries that he
   Won't have enough to give his lord his due.
But let him account to Christ for his cures of souls;
   Foul, without gain, his talents lie hidden.*                      1400
A worldly court thus seizes the client of Christ,
   Who, thirsting for profit, comes to the snare.

## Chapter 17

**Here he talks about those rectors who, the bishop's licentiates, make up a reason to attend the schools so that, in the name of virtue, they might frequent sins of the flesh.**

There's another rector who contrives a reason*
   Why he should attend university.
The bishop, won by gold and silver, gives him leave
   To study with the masters he adores.
Thus the roving rector gets, under virtue's guise,
   Permission to duly study the sins.
Decretals don't please him, nor sacred theology;
   Nay, rather Nature's art suffices him.*                         1410
That mistress teaches many things and he learns them,

And by night scribes what he's studied by day.
Finally, because of its rank, he seeks a chair,
   First paying much that he be brought to this.
That's how a curate is placed in a doctor's chair
   And teaches the required mystic law.

"Woe to the man alone," we read in Solomon,\*
   For no one looks after a single man.
So it's the custom that one learned in his way
   Ought to study with a learned woman.           1420
God himself made the world's first female companion
   And he made her that she might help a man.
The masculine was made first and the feminine
   Second, that through them God would make the race.
And these needful beginnings the discreet rector
   Pursues, offering devotions piously.
What man would not want the rib he senses missing
   From his side, by which he'd be made complete?
The first woman was made from a rib of the man;
   Therefore, the rector wants to have his rib.           1430
For God ordered the human race to be fruitful;\*
   By his commandment man shall multiply.
So multiplies the rector, since his seed abounds,
   That he won't run afoul of God's mandate.
The rector proves, through suchlike pretexts and reasons,
   He can have partners in the school of arts.
Chiefly he studies the act of conception and,
   That offspring come, repeats it many times.
That's how he reads a text and the gloss upon it
   That the lecture be clear to his students.           1440
Reigning over his class, he beats students often
   So that, his rod up, the school is alert.
The more attention he pays to form in "reading,"
   So much less are his material needs.
The work doesn't keep him from teaching day and night
   Until his care leaves him empty-headed.
For the investigation he conducts is deep,
   Discerns and stirs deep matters in a case.
His respondent will respond "Why?" to everything,
   Allows nothing to escape his logic.           1450
And frequently it's over for the doctor and,
   Dumbfounded, he's left sitting in his chair.

*Book III*

The text he chooses harms, repeated harms ten-fold;
   The more he "reads" the more his sense is dulled.
Thus "ars" renders our curate apathetic and,*
   After long effort, he takes nothing home.
He goes there a fool, but, more a fool, he goes back,
   Still frequently returning to the schools.

This is that school in which the clergy studies to
   Scribe nature's deepest laws in its own way.               1460
Its practice suits well both the student and master
   That they construe their own theologies.
This is that school catering to the lapse by which
   A fellow enjoys having his girlfriend.
But yet that school, when it is in league with females,
   Will give a guilty fellow cause to rue.
Thus a school with girls sets a student in such ways
   That he'll be a layman when a master.
Alas! a girl's a weight, as is a school with girls;
   One consumes the body, the other, wealth.              1470
It's shameful to God and astounding to the folk
   When the same man is both master and rogue.

His bride, the Church, goes naked, but his girl is clothed;
   His bride, forsaken, dies; his darling thrives.
So charging that the promised troth has been broken,
   Now comes the Church petitioning her rights.
But since light has disappeared, hence law dies, and so
   The curate's bride is left standing, a waif.
The rector, suiting study to sins, not morals,
   Gives to Venus the tithe that should be God's.          1480
Thus the curate begets his like so that he might
   Fulfill for Nature customary "*ars*."
So the curate thrives like a layman, studying
   The body as he multiplies his kind.
So the school, which once was the mother of morals,
   Is made a foolish stepdame by his sins.

*Vox Clamantis* by John Gower: 'The Voice of One Crying'

## Chapter 18

**Here he talks about those rectors who reside in their curacies, but nevertheless neglect their cures and occupy their thoughts primarily with hunting and pleasure.**

There's a third rector who aims his mind at the world*
   While he stays home residing in his cure.
The bare foliage of his parish grows without fruit*
   Since the fool running it blocks out the light.     1490
He doesn't preach to save souls, visit the wretched,
   Or, touched by love, render aid to the poor.
His steed is stout, although his learning remains lean;
   He sports a fine saddle and a coarse mind.
At his side he bears a hunting horn, whence echoes
   Mountain and glade, whence flees the wary hare.
But the sound of his voice is muted in the church
   And he won't drive his flock's foul hearts from sin.
His dog, who bays with faithful voice upon the hunt,
   Will surely have whatever it might want.     1500
But the beggar who bays at his gate and wants food,
   Alas! is given not a crumb or drop.
O God, how much of your praise merits such a one
   Who gives a dog the food he won't a man?

The sacred feast or fasting days are scarcely past
   But that he takes the field amidst his hounds.
The clamor in the hounds' mouths, when they bay as one,
   Is his church bell whence hymns are sent to God.
His Mass is short and his worship in the fields long,
   Where he designates his hounds his cantors.     1510
Thus the fox and the hare are more what he requires;
   While his tongue says "God," his mind's on the hare.
Thus a fox pursues a fox and like after like
   Chases while he devours the youthful flock.
For the rover seeks where there are pretty women,
   Tender of age – on such he feeds his hunger.
For such a rector lies in wait for the women,
   Encircling like a wolf the enclosed sheep.
When he espies an old husband and a young wife,
   To such in his cure he pays a visit.     1520
There the rector fulfills the husband's duty and

Pays his due debt to the beautiful bride.
Thus the rector takes the fair bodies in his cure
And leaves their souls to wander, filthy waifs.

# Chapter 19

**Here he talks about rectors resident in curacies who nonetheless, neglecting the cures of souls, like worldly merchants buying and selling temporal goods from day to day, acquire the riches of the world.**

 Yet a fourth resident rector betrays his cure;
  Really a merchant, he runs with all sorts.
 Mass done, he plans his market, and then – the tavern.
  Seeking profit at his fellow's expense,
 He gains his gold, but loses the Church's reward;
  That he might have the world, he forsakes God.      1530
 He thinks a day wasted in which he doesn't get
  A profit or some flashy new bauble.
 His watchman is avarice, to keep some poor man
  From having a portion of his riches.
 In no circumstance does a poor man get a share,
  For his chest resists with a double lock.
 But he is plenty charitable to women;
  When Venus commands, then his hand's lavish.
 His golden chest displayed upon his splayed-out knees,
  A girl who comes his way will get his key.      1540
 He's harder than iron, which nothing will soften,
  But soft feminine flesh overcomes him.
 Thus swapping this for that the rector shows his wares
  For a price, idling in his shameful gains.
 All that his one hand gathers, the other scatters,
  The while the fool puts his balm in a sieve.*
 Thus fool preys on fool, so at the end of his days
  A shaven beard is all that he'll have left.*

 Oh! if their sons were able to succeed curates
  And have paternal rights to their title,      1550
 Then those who go to Rome hoping for someone's death*
  Would, I think, achieve little or nothing.
 Such is the devotion affected in the Church
  By our curates now; may God be their judge.

## Chapter 20

**After he has spoken about the error of those in the Church who are beneficed, now he must speak about stipendiary priests, at least those who seek and assume the rank of priest not for the moral purity and decency of holy orders but for the idleness of the world.**

If I shall speak of priests who have no curacy,*
   We see they equal others in their sin.
If this priest does not obtain a church, however,
   His annuities will be just as good.
One now demands to have more than three formerly,
   Since bound by avarice he desires more.           1560
Like tradesmen I see them walking through the cities,
   Led like asses to market for a price.
And yet every worker is worthy of his hire*
   In accordance with the pay that job asks.
Still, no one is allowed to sell divine matters;
   Therefore, the Mass cannot be sold by you.
We think Christ, consecrate on the holy altar,
   Sold once, wishes not to be sold again.*
He gives himself free, who bade sacred things be free;
   Why then, priest, do you seek gain for yourself?      1570
Your clothes and sustenance are adequate enough
   So you can live for God; why look for more?
If you get more profit, it won't satisfy you
   Because illicit income knows no bounds.
With Simon's gold, you'll go to the market at Rome —*
   Which offers you preferment and then takes
The silver you collected earlier so that
   It profits by that which your Mass earned you —
Or a prostitute giving you pleasure will suck
   And render swiftly empty your full purse.         1580

What the Church gives, the harlot and the tavern take;
   These three together do many foul things.
I would think this was a new portent in the world
   If it were but rarely that we spied it.
But since I can see every day what I've mentioned,
   I'm no longer surprised by what I see.
The cormorant often dips its limbs in the stream*
   And secretly breeds in long dalliances.
This signifies those whom fleeting sensual desire
   Utterly occupies and overwhelms.               1590

*Book III*

Among the ancients, priests could be called he [*hic*] and *she* [*haec*],
    But now we can talk of girls [*has*] and boys [*eos*].
For now they replenish the world with their offspring;
    If that's piety, they're pretty pious.
Night, love, and wine urge nothing in moderation,*
    Three things now known supremely well to priests.
The course of his prayers will be brief when he desires
    Kisses bestowed firmly in long dalliance,
While she says, "O my priest, how long the time until
    Your arms are wrapped around my neck again?"    1600

He who desires nowadays to have his wife chaste*
    And wishes to keep his chambers tidy
Should keep from his rooms both the pigeon and the priest:
    One leaves its droppings, the other his shame.
Sober from the table or chaste from his mattress,
    But rarely does the priest rise up for God.
In the taverns he sings *in excelsis* quite loud,
    But in the churches he is all too still.
Well-versed in wine, he goes to the brothel and there
    He spends a long time praying on both knees.    1610
Thus he purges the old ferment while he sprays new,*
    So the priest nowadays desires at Baal's altar
To lay incense that fouls the living God's.
    One woman is enough for me, but twice six him;
Like a young cock, I see him strut these days.
    Thus priests celebrate the sacred rites of Bacchus
And what's sanctified is their drunkenness.
    The old Gentile rite begins to be the modern
And Christ's law is nearly destroyed by such.    1620
    Thus these days priests are tenders of temples and gods,
In whose esteem stands goddess Venus chief.

## Chapter 21

**Here he talks about the habitual sensuality of priests, and how, exacting stipends by a covenant with the folk, they acquit themselves by praying impiously for the dead, not, as obligated, for intercession on their behalf.**

A greedy blaze consumes the earth and its offspring;*
    Where its onslaught rages, it razes all.
That's how, by the unchaste example of the priests,

Fetid lust harms the untaught laity.
Lechery has nothing in common with reason;
   Indeed, lust fuels their physical senses.
Like punishments will befall those whom its mark stains:
   Sulphur and flame shall be their punishments.                  1630
But custom has a way of diminishing shame*
   And renders bold whom long dalliance attracts.
Priests don't believe they sin because they often kiss,
   For kisses used to furnish signs of peace.*
And it's a worthy cause to furnish godly peace,
   For without peace love of piety won't last.
That's how love has been begotten among the priests,
   For it's their custom to kiss frequently.
Habitual practice is thought second nature
   And over time custom becomes the law.*                       1640
And if we should speak about the law of nature,
   It shines forth everywhere among the priests.
And if that's how laws are supposed to be fashioned,
   If long-held practice has the force of law,
Then I think priests establish laws by their practice
   When in their love they kiss incessantly.

The priesthood signifies the bosom of the Church,
   Where by rights decent souls should be cherished.
But how shall they cure others who will not cure their*
   Own? That simply doesn't make any sense.                 1650
I don't know what good such people could do for me,*
   Who lack suitable qualities themselves.
For it is known that God won't listen to sinners
   Since in a wicked mouth his praise is feigned.
Who offers to God undevout words in his prayers
   Begs future damages at his own trial.
Who causes a wrong is seen to have done the wrong;*
   He sins who doesn't act to prevent it.
He inflicts death upon the sick who can but won't
   Prevent disease and allows it to be.                           1660
A prelate who ordains laymen brings more scandals
   When they're not worthy of holy orders.
He who pays good money for them will be cheated*
   Or, God himself knows, doom himself by them.
I do know that they who break bread with the hungry,
   Whose need is clearly without fraudulence,
Who clothe those who are naked and visit the sick,

They are owed just deserts for their goodness.
That prelate errs who ordains those who brashly scheme,*
   Under the false cover of the priesthood,                                           1670
To have worldly leisure, and by endowing them,
   I think, loses his rights of presentment.*

## Chapter 22

**Here he treats the reason why it is that laymen, as friends of justice, abhor the priests' habit of lust, castigate it repeatedly, and assail it mightily.**

The clergy say this, that however criminous
   They are, it's not for laymen to charge them.
One priest forgives another's sins as a favor
   Because, lawlessly, he's guilty of them.
They do not want to be reproached by laymen, but
   Fault them and seek a free rein for themselves.
The sins which please the clergy thus go unpunished
   Unless the layman's justice is applied.                                     1680
An ignorant priest makes an ignorant people;
   He does much evil who knows little good.
A lawless clergy creates a lawless people,
   And thus the priest himself makes his own case.
For since the layman lacks the law, he does not know
   Priests whose guilt he sees are outside the law.
If the clergy were wise, they would accept the folk's
   Wisdom and both alike exist by law.
But since the foolish clergy's folly is now clear,
   Their foolish life is scorned accordingly.                            1690

Nature helps our reason, with many examples,
   To govern its judgment rationally.
So it is that the skulking owl detests dawn's light,*
   Seeks its food in the night, and avoids birds.
If perchance flocks of birds should lay their eyes on it,
   They fly about screeching and slash at it.
This denotes guilty priests, who are corrupt in flesh
   And secretly indulge their filthy lusts.
Laymen, like the birds of light, seek to restrain them,
   Aglow with zeal for law and love of God.                            1700
For Judas, having sinned, was thereby no longer

Worthy of being the servant of Christ.
When a priest endures lust's yoke, let him understand
  If laymen should then lash out against him.

When judgment's just, law asks justice's abuser
  To lose for his lapse what the laws gave him.
We are all of us brothers of the Church in Christ*
  And one always needs help from another.
But the law says this, that if your brother should err,*
  Rebuke and make him thus come back to God.   1710
If he doesn't hear you, speak to the Church, but if
  He won't hear her and will pay her no heed,
He must be considered fully heathen to you,
  Whereby no one has to free him from sin.
A priest persisting in his daily sins, therefore,*
  Ought to have no benefit of office.
He shan't be absolved; it's not justice to honor
  Someone who doesn't reverence the laws.
Who's dared to practice what's prohibited by law
  Should lose the benefits conferred by law.   1720
All that lies hidden will be revealed in the end;*
  Neither holy orders nor rank absolves.
Tell me, what then availed Adam his false excuse
  When he hid himself, sinful, with fig leaves?*
Or what avails it a priest if, helped by office,
  He hides his carnal sin in the shadows?

CHAPTER 23

**Here he writes against that which some priests say, how in committing lust of the flesh they offend God no worse than laymen.**

The priests say that they do not sin more than you do*
  When their flesh succumbs to sins of the flesh.
Just like others, they were created weak of flesh;
  One says that's why he has his own members.   1730
"I am just like another man," he says, "why then
  Shouldn't I have my women like others?"
So he concocts arguments for his transgression,
  As free to sin, he says, as any man.
But here, I think, he dissembles against the truth,
  For his status is sacred above all.

## Book III

He can readily assume another order
   Where there's less blame if he should fall guilty.
And, indeed, holy orders can't be suddenly
   Assumed; rather, they're seen to have stages.        1740
First one ascends through five degrees and is tested,*
   So he previews his status in all ways.
Then each degree is sanctified by a bishop,
   Who is holier than he, and no other.
The priest is anointed with oil on head and hand
   So he's worthier on earth than others.
And, accepting the yoke, he vows his chastity,*
   Whereby, purer, he might make his deeds pure.
And since he takes his vow with open eyes, his sin,
   When he breaks it, causes the greater harm.        1750
Leaders, who should be models of virtue, but sin,
   To my mind err more than those who are led.
For these reasons, which I've considered one by one,
   I think that priests are more at fault than you.

Though the priest is clever enough with his excuse,
   That's not helpful to the state of his mind.
Nay rather, unmindful of his holy orders,
   He looks for the temptations in his world.
I don't think cobbler and priest have the same status,*
   Nor does their sin weigh the same on the scales.        1760
A priest and a layman are not alike shepherd,
   Nor does their wickedness have the same weight.
One swore to be pure when his head was anointed
   And each faithful man is bound by his vow.
He wouldn't have been gifted with such great office
   If he didn't have a greater burden.
For a king, who's greater in the world, cannot do
   What the priest, who's lesser, can do in Christ.
Thus, since by law his office gives him preference,
   The law's force smites his sin more grievously.        1770
Alas! that a wicked hand, fouled by women's loins,
   Should touch the sacred things on God's altar.
Christ abhors his work who handles the Lord's body
   And does shameful business with prostitutes.
When those who should be Christ's servants are the devil's
   Ministers, alas! who'll restore our strength?

## Chapter 24

**Here he describes how each and every thing that concerns the office of the priesthood designates mysteries of great power, and first he will talk about priestly robes properly arrayed according to either Law.**

    Oh! if the priest would but consider well his rights,
        What the honor, what the burden, the task,
    Weigh each one justly and urge each one equally,
        I'd be amazed if he performed poorly.        1780
    All that his status lays claim to is considered
        Sacred, that its men be then more saintly.
    There is nothing so small that pertains to the Mass
        That ought not be sacred by the priests' law.
    The different garments of which the priest makes use
        Bear mystic signs of different powers.
    The ephod is a shirt, called otherwise the alb,
        Which covers the priest's body to his feet.
    As it is white without, let the priest be whiter
        Within, that he wear good morals on earth.        1790
    In his ephod, Samuel strove to be God's servant;*
        His mother, Hannah, wove his little shirt.
    The thin shirt signifies the doctrine of the Faith,
        With whose Grace his mother garbed his frail spirit.
    The ephod's linen symbolizes bodily
        Chastity, since a priest wears purity.

    There is a girdle, too, which chastely binds the shirt*
        Lest the loins through lust should know shameful deeds.
    That he might bear our wretched souls to better things*
        The priest wears a seemly stiffened amice.        1800
    And a wise priest also ties a band on his head,*
        Lest he let his mind's attentions wander.
    A chasuble beset garbs him, shining with gold,
        Which by its power rules all the metals.*
    And in a like way the priest shines with his power
        When he keeps the state of holy orders.
    A holy man wears a gold robe since God's wisdom,*
        Gleaming bright, shines in him above the rest.
    Lest the robe be easily threatened with a breach,*
        Silver shines in its noble weave's gyre.        1810
    Let the good priest not distract himself in the world,

*Book III*

    Lest any chink of sin be seen in him.
Girt with this purity, the priest dresses himself*
    That the world hold his sacred duties pure.

Clothes are woven for Aaron and his elect that*
    Each might fulfill the office of the priest.
So nowadays the priests, whether high or minor,
    Effect Christ's body and consecrate it.
When we consecrate wine and bread on the altar,*
    It becomes the true flesh and blood alike.            1820
He who made the flesh of Christ in his mother's womb*
    Makes his body sacred on the altar.
The altar's appearance is square, that in the world's*
    Four parts the Church's faith should be stable.
Who's dressed in vestments thus, and lives worthy with good
    Morals, not otherwise, shall be ordained.
Those whom such vestments, those whom such glory adorns,
    Their case requires that they be more like saints.
The prelate who, against the law, gives to laymen
    Such items for priests disgraces the Church.            1830
May the Church know which ones it takes to its bosom*
    Are apt for God and reject the others!

## Chapter 25

**Here he tells how the sacrifices upon the altar required by the Old Law figured the priests of the New Law now; in addition, he tells how, according to either Law, those offering sacrifices on the altar ought to be without blemish.***

    The Old Law ordained animals from which the folk
        Once made God offerings on the altar.
    And always from the slaughter of an entire beast
        A certain portion was owed to the priest.
    However, by a hidden meaning this denotes
        For priests mystic rights in the law of Christ.
    That part of the sacrifice that goes to the priest
        Should be remembered well by our curates.           1840
    The priest's portions are, by order of sacred law,*
        The breast and the severed right forequarter.
    The breast is the site of doctrine, for every priest
        Should teach righteousness to those in his charge.

The right arm is mightier and this signifies
  His conduct be steadfast, not sinister.
The severed forequarter means the priest in his life
  Withdraws from folk, behaving unlike them.
There's nothing ordinary in holy orders;
  Indeed, there is a great weight of office.                 1850
For both the Old Law and the New alike make clear
  That it behooves the priests to be holy.
Peter wrote in *Aurora* what I will write, and*
  He'll be true witness and authority.

The Old Law orders, and the New confirms, that those
  Who sacrifice on altars be unstained.
Let their physical conduct be without blemish
  Or any filth, whence it may displease God.
Let them have no blemish nor be charged with coitus,*
  Lest a perverse act stain their pure goodness.             1860
I'll name those faults said to be in holy orders
  That my priest reader be more mindful thence.
He's said to be blind who, covered up with earth's dust,*
  Can't pick out the way to the light of life.
His eye's inflamed whose mind shines within by nature
  But whose carnality obscures his work.
Cataracts blind the eyes and designate that man
  Who swells, ascribing pure deeds to himself.
He is snub-nosed who's not able to see small things
  And performs without grace that which he does.             1870
His nose is too big who doesn't understand what
  He reads and yet acts as if he's learned.
His nose is crooked who maintains that bitter's sweet
  And judges that wicked acts are holy.
He is lame who knows the way, but slow to hasten
  Sticks to this world, his foot bound by the flesh.
He's said to have a broken foot and broken hand
  Who worse than lame comes late to every good.
He's hunchbacked whom the world bows down with its burdens
  And won't let his eyes see his spirit's height.            1880
Scabies reveal the body's burning lust,
  Which causes much decadence by its sin.

If one thinks himself grieved by the aforesaid faults,
  The law commands he not bless bread to God.
Stretching forth his hand, Uzzah meant to lift the ark,*

*Book III*

    But death rewarded his audacious hand.
They say he earned his death because during the night
    He had committed coitus with his wife.
By this it's said he who approaches the altar
    Defiled shall be deserving of death's blow.          1890
Experience teaches a foul hand's unable*
    To cleanse away filth while it's holding mud.
The priest is said to show others the way and if
    He strays then they stray whom he thinks to lead.
This means if a bad priest offers the sacraments*
    Or teaches, then we others are worse off.
Whoever has professed in holy orders' work
    Is not without care if he serves his task.
If you who would be elevated should ascend,
    See first you do what holy orders bid.            1900
See not just to appearance but morals and means
    By which you may make progress in your cures.

## Chapter 26

**Here he says that sufficient age is required in a man before he assume the rank of priest. He also talks about the shaving of his hairs, and says that such things are especially appropriate as a sign of the purity and holiness of the priest. He says further that priests should not be idle in good works.**

    Before the priest assumes his office, he requires
    Mature age that he might govern fully.
For youth's blossom is more to our tempting foe's taste;*
    The passions of both flesh and that age seethe.
Those whom the wicked lusts of youthful flesh still vex
    Aren't suited to be pastors of the flock.
Their shaven crown proclaims that they govern for God*
    And that they accomplish more noble works.      1910
Shaving does not extirpate the roots of the hairs,*
    For shaved they grow in greater profusion.
Thus, although you'd totally banish all passions
    From your mind, you can't put them all to flight.
You won't stay shaved, for the flesh battles constantly;
    You must always wage war with what's within.

Even if you would flee the world, you cannot be*
    Altogether undefiled by its dust.

For although you'd shine with the highest virtues, you*
   Cannot remove all the sins from your mind.                1920
You will, however, retain some minimal fault
   So that your mind won't swell with your good works.
Thus, you can obtain absolution from such sin
   If you're truly remorseful for its slip.
A just man often falls, since every man is frail,*
   Lest vainglory exalt a man too much.
He who has fallen lightly, if he rise more strong,
   Will have a happy outcome before God.
You are the world's light, but not entirely smokeless,*
   For there's no man that can live without sin.*         1930
Good fruits will often attend upon temptations*
   And battles of the flesh have their reward.

It would indeed be fit to suppress raging flames*
   And to maintain your spirit safe from sin.
Let your eyes not see that by which they might be tried,
   And block your ears lest sin's sound enter there.
It is more prudent and proper to leave in peace*
   Than wage the sort of war that you can't win.
A gladiator's finer, shining whole in arms,*
   Than when his clothes are wet with his own blood.      1940
Shining stainless in God's Masses, the victor priest
   In this way gains as his profit God's peace.
Seek with a nimble mind what it is that you love*
   And remove your neck from the chafing yoke.
A wise man ought to throw off vices at their start,*
   Lest sluggish he will find his strength too late.
Crush while they're new the evil seeds of sudden vice*
   And let your palfrey at the outset pause.
For delay lends strength, delay ripens tender grapes,
   And makes what was a plant a useful crop.          1950
If Venus should approach, let your life be austere;
   A little water puts out a new fire.*
You'll suffer iron and fire to suppress the flesh*
   To the extent it takes to heal your soul.
If you shun idleness, Cupid's bows are broken
   And his flames lie extinguished, without light.

That you not stray, you have to put reins on your sin,
   Fleeing wayward ventures and idleness.
It befits priests to concern themselves about things

*Book III*

Proper to their task or about their prayers. 1960
For Paul made baskets to subdue his idleness*
   Since he would not waste time in any way.
Out of leisure time slinks the fiercest plague of lust,
   Rumor's squire and the devil's wasting gift.
From leisure follows wretched sensuality,
   Spiritual poverty, impious sin.
Stirred by unstable fantasy, spirits revel,
   At least while the flesh ignores virtue's work.
God grants every benefit to the hard-working:
   Work should bring with it weighty recompense. 1970
Prudent caution suits the soul while it takes the steps
   That enable it to tame sensual sins.
Caution aids the body to seek the nourishment
   By which to live on earth in righteous ways.
When the flesh seeks leisure and labor sits banished,
   The road to sin is made the usual way.
The devil loves soft and feminine behavior,*
   When manly virtue denies what's virile.
Leisure without labor does harm among such men,*
   In whose midst a Christian cannot be saved. 1980
Sin indeed puts us far from God, and virtue, near:
   One displeases and one appeases him.

## Chapter 27

**Here he talks about the spiritual worth of priests, and how, if they perform their office well, they accomplish more than others. Otherwise, by their bad example, they furnish instead instances of dereliction.**

The priests' honor is great and their power greater,
   If far from sin they're both pious and good.
In their hands they hold the mysteries of the highest*
   Sacrament, by whose Word flesh joins with God.
In baptism's holy font they remove the sin
   By which our first parents came to such grief.
They celebrate our betrothals by the New Law;
   And take no cash if they invoke the law.* 1990
They also bring pardon for relapses confessed
   And grant an errant man return to God.
They also give us the bread of heaven to take

And at our end their unction awaits us.
They should also preside when the dead are buried
    And render in their masses pious prayers.

They are the earth's salt, which preserves us in the world;*
    Without their savor we would scarce be saved.*
By the salt he hurled in the waters Elisha*
    Cleansed them so that no bitter taste remained.     2000
Salt signifies the just priests' prudent discretion,*
    That they may wisely season their own folk.*
They are the world's light, wherefore if they become dark,*
    Then we remain blind wanderers in the world.
Who places an obstacle before blind people,
    As God has proclaimed, shall be accursed.
Who places an obstacle before blind people*
    Shows, by that cursed deed, the sinner's way.

They are Jacob's ladder, touching heavenly heights,*
    With all the rungs by which the way is shown.     2010
They are the holy mount, upon which every man
    Ought to ascend the peak of the virtues.
They are our counsel, our straight way to what's on high,
    The law's teachers, and our new salvation.*
They bar heaven to the folk and open it wide,
    And when they're good, they subdue everything.
"Multiply," they were told, "and produce many fruits";*
    This statement refers to good behavior.
It tells them, "Fill the earth"; note what that means to you:
    Let your good fruits abound within the Church.     2020

Let no hollow man come before God, for no one*
    Without virtue should be in God's presence.
Let the priest reconcile the righteous and sinful*
    With God and waft prayer's incense to heaven.
Let him pray that the just not fall from justice and
    The corrupt rise early and weep their sins.
How vile when a priest, just like an ass, is untaught*
    In morals and ignorant, without law!
Priests are in number like the stars in the heavens,*
    But scarce two in a thousand shine with light.     2030
They read the Scriptures and don't know them, but, tonsured,
    Keep from the crowd, which they think is enough.
There are such, but there are others in the Church whom

*Book III*

    Lofty virtue adorns, who do much good.
Noah sent out a raven that did not return;*
    He sent a dove and, sent, the dove returned.
Thus there are also ravens and doves in the Church,
    Jaundiced wicked men and unjaundiced good.
"First thing tomorrow," they caw when slow to convert,*
    But often the Last Day takes care of such.                       2040
Such are the slothful, whom the chains of the world bind,
    Who don't care to thirst for God's promised realm.
For the priest who keeps the laws of holy orders,
    Teaching holy dogma by words and deeds,
There is no honor in holy orders too great:
    The people's praise is not enough, but God's.
Of those in the clergy whom lofty virtue proves,
    I say they'll get more mercy than they earned.

## Chapter 28

**After he has talked about the error of those who have assumed their ministry of priest among the lay, he intends now to speak, as it is timely, about the error of scholars, who are called scions of the Church.***

    Under the clergy's name we recognize scholars,
        Whom God himself calls scions of the Church.             2050
    The good schoolman's a plant of the divine garden
        That produces the good fruits of the Church.
    He who strives on behalf of morals, not vices,
        Reckons for himself not the world but God,
    Is therefore considered to be God's clerk and his
        Appointment culminates in a good end.
    The just rule of the best teacher of the virtues
        Fosters by reason responsive students.
    Those who cleave to studies, lift their hearts high, and pierce*
        Into the depths are true offerings to God.                    2060

    But among them now I think that many are called,*
        Few chosen that are upright in the post.
    Once they took time for morals in their strict studies;
        Now their studies wake them to the vices.
    If scarcely one now strives for the proper matter,
        Merely its shadow's form suffices him.
    A clerk used to attend schools with a humble mind;

Now worldly ambition's his instructress,
And gadding about, a wandering, stumbling drunk
  Given to sex, he rambles here and there.                      2070
A fruitful tree will not grow from a sterile shoot,*
  Nor will a fallen tree bring forth good fruits.
Old age often retains whatever its youth held;*
  If bad the boy, scarce is the old man good.
It is the good root that bears the seeds of goodness;
  From a bad root grows everything wicked.
Let each thus set his lads aright, so that the rod
  Drive out the doings of misguided minds.
Let the lad who has a master with virtue's flower
  Piously learn matters of righteousness                         2080
And practice them, for a boy whom a dissolute
  Teacher has instructed rarely bears fruit.

## Chapter 29

**Here he seeks the reason that induces the minds of schoolmen to receive the holy orders of the priesthood. He adduces three causes chiefly. He also discusses a fourth cause, which rarely obtains at the present.**

Some persevere these days in spiritual study,
  But I don't know what their purpose might be.
Whatever men may do, intention judges them;*
  God himself grasps what is within the heart.
That being said, explain to me truly, scholar,
  Tell me the basic reason you study.
When you first present yourself for holy orders,
  When you first intend to become a priest,                2090
Oh! what motive is then uppermost in your mind?
  Is it for love of God or of the world?
If you won't tell me what your motives truly are,
  Then I'll tell you what I know to be true.

"There are several reasons for which holy orders
  Are prized everywhere here on earth, to wit:
The first is that I escape the earthly scourges*
  Of common law, which deals men bitter blows.
Furthermore, I don't have to labor by my sweat*
  And thus can have the leisure that I seek.               2100
The third is that it provides my food and clothing

*Book III*

So I can go on, carefree, as I please.
For all these reasons my devotion is total;
   That's why you see the tonsured pate on me.
That leads to school, which makes me study civil law\*
   And skillfully teaches me its logic.
That allows me to climb the school's highest degrees
   And then I seek to rise in a good church.
If my fame grows, I think my prebend will grow, too,
   And it's a light task to dawdle with books.       2110
Holy orders please me and accord with my clerk's
   Learning, as long as I make fat profits.
Now I've said why holy orders suit a scholar,
   So I suppose I'm guilty of the world,
For I think that nothing suits me more, while I can,
   Than to take the world's pleasures for myself."

But there's yet a better reason than those, for which
   A school delights to have a good student.
It's not in ours, but used to be in the old days;
   It based the work of a school on virtue.       2120
There once were the blessed who despised all the world's
   Pomp and ardently sought the highest good.
And since the schools whetted their minds to be holy,
   They pursued the Scripture's pious study.
Neither ambition nor love of things spurred them on,
   But the morals suitable to study.
Contemplating heaven, they declined earthly goods
   And no sensuous cause led them astray.
They chose neither to be in service to a king
   Nor to be called "rabbi" before the folk.\*       2130
Foolish extravagant clothes did not seduce them,\*
   Not wine's debauchery nor woman's love.
With proven morals, they were models for the young,
   Which a student should have in his studies.
Now, however, virtue is turned into vice and
   What were once morals cover much that's foul.
The writings they now say they study to God's praise\*
   Their hunger for office turns to the world's.
Oh what a marvel! The schoolman reads and studies
   Morals while propagating sinful deeds.       2140
Since the clergy are blind, without a moral lamp,\*
   We laymen wander, nomads, without light.

# NOTES TO BOOK III

### Prologue

ll. 11–13, 17–18: claims in these lines should not be confused with a version of the proverbial "vox populi, vox Dei." Gower clearly did not believe that the grumbling populace spoke for, or with, God. He did believe, however, that the complaints of the people were disregarded at peril – particularly since in ecclesiastical courts the voice of "homines probi" was to be taken seriously, potentially triggering inquisition. His opinion strengthened some years after these lines were written with the Revolt of 1381. The intent here is to underscore the moment's urgency by emphasizing that what he writes is not the opinion of a single man, but of many.

l. 39: cf. John 4: 10–14; also below, ll. 83–106.

ll. 45–6: cf. I Corinthians 13: 13; also the three female representations of Faith, Hope, and Charity painted on the rear wall of Gower's tomb.

l. 61: virtually *verbatim* Ovid, *Ex Ponto*, 4. 14. 41.

l. 64: adapted from Ovid, *Ex Ponto*, 4. 9. 10.

ll. 67–8: virtually *verbatim* Ovid, *Tristia*, 2. 301–2.

ll. 74–7: Gower's version of the formula, traceable to Ovid (*Tristia*, 1. 1) and Boccaccio (*Filocolo*, 2. 376–8) before Chaucer (*Troilus and Criseyde*, V. 1786 ff.), differs characteristically from these in the seriousness of its terms: the one who frees all his servants is clearly Christ; the "mala lingua" is legitimately evil, and harmful.

ll. 81–2 and ll. 105–6: Gower takes up the metaphor of writing as a nautical voyage, one he would have found widely present (e.g., Ovid, Cicero, Statius, Quintilian, Jerome, Prudentius); he echoes the idea that composition/sailing is dangerous, especially for so inexperienced a sailor, and probably has in mind Alain of Lille's *De planctu Naturae*, where "naufragium" – shipwreck – prominently evokes a sinking world.

l. 82: *verbatim* Ovid, *Ex Ponto*, 2. 2. 126.

l. 95: proverbial; cf. *VC* I. Pro. 33–4.

l. 100: the line translates a pun on "mundus" = "world" and "mundus" = "clean, pure."

ll. 105–6: *verbatim* Peter Riga, *Aurora*, Leviticus 23–4.

l. 106: "sacrum pneuma" is here both a favorable wind (extending the nautical metaphor – see above note ll. 81–2) and recalls Genesis 2: 7, God breathing life into Adam, formed from earth.

# Book III

Ch. 1 Intro: cf. Gower's attacks on the clergy, *Mirour de l'Omme*, ll. 18421–20832.

A-Text, B[1]-Text, B[2]-Text: The base text for Macaulay's edition was Oxford, All Souls College MS 98 (S), which he took to represent Gower's final version (hence B[2] here). It differs in several loci, showing emendations over erasures, beginning with these passages. MSS Dublin, Trinity College (T) and Hatfield ($H_2$) contain what appears to have stood originally in S – and since unlike the rest of the extant copies they do not mention the Papal Schism of 1378, they are considered the earliest (hence A-Text here). MSS London, British Library, Cotton Tiberius A.iv (C) Glasgow, University Library, Hunterian T.2.17 (G), London, British Library, Harley 6291 (H), San Marino, Huntington Library, HM 150 (formerly Ecton Hall = E), Oxford, Bodleian Library, Digby 138 (D), Oxford, Bodleian Library, Laud 719 (L), showing what probably stood in S before erasure and over-copying, are considered an intermediate stage of production (hence B[1] here).

ll. B[1] 5–10 (B[2] 3–8): the reference is to the Papal Schism of 1378, sometimes called the Great Schism, or the Western Schism, to distinguish it from the East-West Schism of 1054 that established, respectively, Constantinople and Rome as the capitals of the Eastern Orthodox and Catholic Churches. In 1378 the College of Cardinals elected two popes within six months of each other: Urban VI, who presided in Rome, and Clement VII, whose court was at Avignon, an enclave surrounded by France. The ongoing war between England and France exacerbated the situation, with England supporting Urban and France, Clement; most of the rest of Europe aligned itself with one or the other. The situation was functionally resolved in 1417 (albeit with some localized dissent continuing until 1429) at the Council of Constance, with the resignation of both the Roman and Avignonese popes and the election of Martin V, who re-established Rome as the capital of the Church.

ll. 11–13 (A, B[1], B[2]): the issue of apostolic poverty divided the Church from the early twelfth century, when Pope Paschal II, seeking a solution to the power struggle between kings and popes over investiture of bishops, instituted it for churchmen of all ranks. The doctrine was declared heretical in 1323, but it remained a popular ideal among the general populace (including Gower) throughout the fourteenth century, underlying many of the objections subsequently raised by Wyclif and the lollards against Church practices. It applied to monks, who took a vow of poverty, and to the mendicant orders – although neither in Gower's view practiced it. Cf. Matthew 19: 21, Luke 10: 4; also Nigel of Longchamp, *Speculum Stultorum* ("De religiosis in generali"), which may prompt Gower's discussion here; cf. also *VC* B text 11 "Christus erat pauper" with "Pauper erat Christus," Nigel of Longchamp, *Speculum Stultorum*, ed. Mann, l. 2849, and Mann's note, p. 426.

ll. 39–40: adapted from Ovid, *Fasti*, 5. 31–2.

l. 41: adapted from Ovid, *Amores*, 3. 8. 55.

ll. 43–8, 55–6: the lines incorporate a play on "census" ("wealth/property") and "sensus" ("understanding").

l. 63: *verbatim* Ovid, *Fasti*, 1. 225.

ll. 65–6: adapted from Ovid, *Fasti*, 1. 249–50.

ll. 79–80: "Thomas" = Thomas Becket, Archbishop of Canterbury (CE 1162–70), hence "Thomas's office" refers to the position; cf. "Epistle to Arundel," l. 1. "Martin" = St. Martin of Tours, known for the austerity of his life, charity to the poor, and founder of the abbey of Marmoutier; cf. Jacobus de Voragine, *Legenda Aurea*, for November 11.

ll. 83–4: these lines may continue the allusion to St. Martin who, in his most famous miracle, divided his cape with his sword to share it with a beggar, and always wore a hairshirt; cf. Jacobus de Voragine, *Legenda Aurea*, for November 11.

ll. 85–6: the sense of these lines is very clear from ll. 89–90, 93–4, all of which, including the interpretation, are taken *verbatim* from Peter Riga, *Aurora*, Numeri 215–16, 221–2. Fleshpots ("ollarum carnes") were cauldrons for boiling meat (cf. Exodus 16: 3) but with intentional sexual overtones. Leeks and onions were associated with lechery (cf. Chaucer's Summoner, *CT* GenPro 634); the connection with manna l. 86 identifies a reference to Numbers 11: 5, a passage often conjoined to Exodus 16: 3.

l. 103: cf. Nigel of Longchamp, *Speculum Stultorum*, ed. Mann, l. 1329.

ll. 107–8: cf. Nigel of Longchamp, *Speculum Stultorum*, ed. Mann, ll. 1327–8.

l. 115: adapted from Ovid, *Metamorphoses*, 15. 173.

l. 126: certainly a sexual allusion, in context also likely alluding to the two "horns" of a bishop's mitre.

l. 137: cf. Matthew 6: 24.

## Notes to Book III

ll. 141–2: cf. *Mirour de l'Omme*, ll. 18553–64.

ll. 153–7: *verbatim* Peter Riga, *Aurora*, Leviticus 359, 361–3.

ll. 167–72: *verbatim* Peter Riga, *Aurora*, Exodus 331–6; cf. Exodus 17: 8–16.

l. 173: *verbatim* Nigel of Longchamp, *Speculum Stultorum*, ed. Mann, l. 1167.

ll. 175–7: cf. Luke 15: 3–72.

ll. 177–82: *verbatim* Peter Riga, *Aurora*, Leviticus 435–40.

ll. 195–6: the charge levelled here is that the clergy permit sin in order to profit from the penitent. The image, which Gower also employs in the *Mirour de l'Omme*, ll. 20161–72, and *Confessio Amantis*, Pro. 407–13, is of sheep steered purposely into briars (sin) where their wool (wealth) is torn away for the clergy to pocket. Cf. *Mirour de l'Omme*, ll. 20149–50: "Asses plus fait proufit puteine/ A noster dean que le nonneyne" ("The prostitute makes greater profit/ For our dean than the nun"). See also l. 1990 and note, below.

l. 197: cf. Chaucer's Summoner, *CT*, GenPro 656–8.

ll. 219–20: cf. John 8: 3–11.

Ch. 4 heading: as translated, from S, presumably Gower's final version; LTH$_2$ read: "Hic loquitur quomodo de legibus positiuis quasi cotidie nous instituuntur nobis peccata, quibus tamen priusquam fiant prelati propter lucrum dispensant, et ea fieri libere propter aurum permittunt" ("Here he states that by means of positive laws new sins are established for us almost daily, for which however the prelates offer dispensation for money before they are committed, and they permit them to be committed freely, for gold"). "Positive law" is instituted by the clergy alone; it differs from "natural and/or divine law" conferred by God, in that it is fallible and subject to corruption, as in this context. Pardons and indulgences are flagrant examples. The distinction is made explicit in ll. 261–70, below.

ll. 243–4: *verbatim* Peter Riga, *Aurora*, Deuteronomy 61–2.

ll. 249–50: cf. Acts 8: 9–24, *Mirour de l'Omme*, ll. 18997–9; however, Simon Magus flying is extra-biblical, found in the apocryphal Acts of Peter (31–2) and Pseudo-Clementine (*Homilies*, 2. 22–6), either of which could have provided Gower's image. Gower frequently uses "Simon" synecdochally for the sin of simony (whence its name): cf. *Confessio Amantis*, Pro. 204, 241–2, 438–43.

ll. 251–4: cf. Isaiah 40: 3: "The voice of one crying in the desert: Prepare ye the way of the Lord, make straight in the wilderness the paths of our God" – clearly a passage on Gower's mind when writing the *VC*.

l. 258: cf. Matthew 11: 30.

ll. 265–6: cf. *Mirour de l'Omme*, ll. 18505–16.

l. 275: *verbatim* Peter Riga, *Aurora*, Genesis 9; but see also I Corinthians 15: 40–1.

ll. 283–8: refers to the so-called "Donation of Constantine," said to be the conferral of power over Rome and the western Roman Empire to the popes in perpetuity by the emperor, grateful following the cure of his leprosy through baptism by Pope Sylvester I. Despite widespread condemnation as the beginning of the Church's worldly turn, the "Donation" served successive popes as a cornerstone of papal ambition. In fact, the establishing document, *Constitutum domini Constantini imperatoris*, was an eighth-century forgery, unmasked by Lorenzo Valla ca. 1440. Cf. *Mirour de l'Omme*, ll. 18637–60; *Confessio Amantis*, II. 3480–92; *VC* II. 268, and note, and l. 603, below, and note.

ll. 293–4: church lands, including properties owned by bishops, monasteries, and abbeys, accounted for roughly a third of England in the late fourteenth century.

ll. 303–4: cf. John 18: 36.

ll. 307–12: cf. *Mirour de l'Omme*, ll. 18661–732.

l. 313: cf. Matthew 7: 16, 20.

ll. 317–18: cf. Acts 5: 15.

ll. 319–20: cf. Matthew 14: 28–9; *VC* II. 253–4.

l. 327: cf. Romans 12: 19.

Ch. 6 Intro: for much of Ch. 6, cf. *Mirour de l'Omme*, ll. 18649–732.

ll. 337–8: cf. Matthew 26: 52. The comparison here is of Peter as the first pope, who received Christ's peace (cf. *VC* ll. 329–32), with the present popes who practice war, specifically the so-called "War of the Eight Saints" between Gregory XI and a coalition of Italian city-states led by Florence. The war led directly to the Western Schism; among its figures notable in England was Sir John Hawkwood, leader of the White Company of mercenaries who served Gregory XI against the Florentines, and later against the Milanese of Bernabò Visconti.

ll. 363–4: cf. Psalm 43: 7.

ll. 367–8: these lines are built around a pun apparent in Latin on "archa" ("ark") and "arcus" ("bow").

ll. 369–70: these lines incorporate parts of Peter Riga, *Aurora*, Genesis 645–6.

## Notes to Book III

l. 375: the gloss condemns the "Flanders Crusade," declared in 1383 by the Roman Pope Urban VI and led by Henry Despenser, Bishop of Norwich, ostensibly in support of Ghent in its resistance against the forces of the Avignon Pope Clement VII; the campaign was disastrous for Despenser and the English, and widely criticized by John Wyclif among others.

ll. 403–4: proverbial; cf. *Confessio Amantis*, V. 7817–20, V. 2383; cf. Walz, 4c; Matthew 10: 26, I Corinthians 4: 5.

ll. 407–10: a string of proverbial wisdom: cf. Walz, 224, 89.

ll. 421–2: *verbatim* Peter Riga, *Aurora*, Josue 29–30.

ll. 423–4: *verbatim* Peter Riga, *Aurora*, Deuteronomy 197–8.

ll. 425–32: *verbatim* Peter Riga, *Aurora*, Secundus Regem 125–32; cf. I Paralipomenon 22: 7–8.

ll. 433–4: *verbatim* Peter Riga, *Aurora*, Deuteronomy 73–4.

ll. 437–8: cf. Ezekiel 18: 23.

ll. 449–50: cf. Psalm 36: 1–9.

ll. 451–8: probably an expansion of 1 John 4: 20.

ll. 461–2: *verbatim* Peter Riga, *Aurora*, Genesis 991–2.

l. 463: cf. Psalm 110: 10.

l. 497: "si pro mundo fiat": Gower's intent is ambiguous here. He could have meant "for the sake of the world," as Stockton takes it; but that's less self-interested than the context ("cupido," in l. 492 and "avari" in l. 499) would seem to allow. "si pro mundo fiat" could no less easily mean "for all the world's wealth."

ll. 507–8: adapted from Nigel of Longchamp, *Speculum Stultorum*, ed. Mann, ll. 1479–80.

ll. 509–10: virtually *verbatim* Nigel of Longchamp, *Speculum Stultorum*, ed. Mann. ll. 1481–2.

l. 513: virtually *verbatim* Nigel of Longchamp, *Speculum Stultorum*, ed. Mann, l. 1483.

ll. 521–2: virtually *verbatim* Nigel of Longchamp, *Speculum Stultorum*, ed. Mann, ll. 463–4.

ll. 531–2: *verbatim* Peter Riga, *Aurora*, Numeri 493–4.

l. 535: *verbatim* Nigel of Longchamp, *Speculum Stultorum*, ed. Mann, l. 1251.

ll. 537–8: *verbatim* Nigel of Longchamp, *Speculum Stultorum*, ed. Mann, ll. 1253–4.

ll. 539–40: virtually *verbatim* Nigel of Longchamp, *Speculum Stultorum*, ed. Mann, ll. 285–6.

l. 541: *verbatim* Nigel of Longchamp, *Speculum Stultorum*, ed. Mann, l. 293.

ll. 541–2: the expression is proverbial – cf. Walz, 7c; *Confessio Amantis*, Pro. 650, III. 1680; the reference to Cato's *Distichs* lacks substance.

l. 543: *verbatim* Nigel of Longchamp, *Speculum Stultorum*, ed. Mann, l. 287.

l. 551: adapted from Nigel of Longchamp, *Speculum Stultorum*, ed. Mann, l. 309.

l. 557: *verbatim* Nigel of Longchamp, *Speculum Stultorum*, ed. Mann, l. 311.

ll. 559–60: *verbatim* Nigel of Longchamp, *Speculum Stultorum*, ed. Mann, ll. 827–8.

ll. 561–4: virtually *verbatim* Nigel of Longchamp, *Speculum Stultorum*, ed. Mann, ll. 487–90.

ll. 565–7: *verbatim* Nigel of Longchamp, *Speculum Stultorum*, ed. Mann, ll. 485–6.

ll. 573–4: cf. Matthew 12: 30, Luke 11: 23.

l. 579, and ff.: as stated here, "Caesar" should be understood to mean "worldly power" generally. Underlying the usage is the directive "Render unto Caesar" from the synoptic gospels; cf. Matthew 22: 21, Mark 12: 17, Luke 20: 25; and *VC* ll. 599–600.

ll. 593–8: Christ's promise to Peter, the first pope: cf. Matthew 16: 19.

ll. 599–600: see note for l. 579, above.

l. 603: according to the "Donation of Constantine," believed legitimate in the fourteenth century, the papal state was excluded from temporal control, and placed solely under the power of the popes. Cf. Book III, ll. 283–8, above, and note.

l. 614: *verbatim* Nigel of Longchamp, *Speculum Stultorum*, ed. Mann, l. 854.

ll. 619–20: *verbatim* Ovid, *Ex Ponto*, 2. 5. 61–2.

ll. 623–4: *verbatim* Ovid, *Ex Ponto*, 2. 6. 21–2.

l. 628: "Gethis": Ovid's Getae (cf. *Ex Ponto*), ethnically distinct from the Goths but presented as one people in late Roman and early medieval sources, e.g., Claudian, Orosius, Procopius, Isidore of Seville, and probably Gower, from Isidore.

## Notes to Book III

l. 641: virtually *verbatim* Ovid, *Ars Amatoria*, 2. 417.

l. 651: for genealogies of Jesus see Matthew 1: 1, 16; Luke 3: 23–38. Both show Jesus' descent from David and Jacob; however, the accounts differ, relevant here in that Matthew traces Jesus through Joseph, Luke through Mary (daughter of Heli: cf. Matthew 1: 16, Luke 3: 23). Gower seems to have Luke in mind here.

l. 665: "unda renatos" that is, the water of baptism indicates rebirth in Christ.

ll. 667–8: cf. Matthew 10: 5–10.

ll. 681–2: "princeps huius mundi": cf. John 12: 13, 14: 30, 16: 11; also Ephesians 2: 2 and II Corinthians 4: 4.

ll. 691–4: cf. John 8: 3–11.

l. 695: cf. Matthew 16: 19. The keys of Peter, the first pope, remain central to the papal arms.

ll. 717–18: the lines contain word-play on "capitale" (= capital, or "deadly," sin) and "caput" ("head"). The image of the devil's "ers" as a place of particular punishment is common in both literary and visual art (cf. e.g., Chaucer, "The Summoner's Tale," *CT* III. 1665–708; Giotto, *Last Judgment*, Padua), and parodies a widely known positive story of members of various religious orders sheltered under the Virgin's cloak in heaven, traceable to (at least) Caesarius of Heisterbach's *Dialogus Miraculorum* (VII. 59), ca. 1220.

l. 721: adapted from Nigel of Longchamp, *Speculum Stultorum*, ed. Mann, l. 2213.

ll. 721–4: cf. Matthew 11: 28–30.

l. 738: cf. Isaiah 1: 5.

ll. 753–6: cf. Acts 3: 1–8.

l. 762: "Floriger et veris floribus": word-play takes precedence over sense here; what's meant is that rhetorical flourish (i.e., "flowery rhetoric") too often lacks virtue.

ll. 777–8: cf. Matthew 18: 21–2.

ll. 781–2: cf. Jeremiah 31: 15, Matthew 2: 18.

l. 788: for the play on "cauda" and "caput," see note to ll. 717–18, above.

ll. 795–6: adapted from Godfrey of Viterbo, *Pantheon*, col. 268.

l. 800: cf. Matthew 7: 12, Luke 6: 31; but the "Golden Rule" as a philosophical ideal needed no particular scriptural reference.

ll. 801–4: virtually *verbatim* Peter Riga, *Aurora*, Deuteronomy 37–40; ll. 801–2: cf. Luke 10: 27, Mark 12: 30–1; also Matthew 22: 37–9.

l. 819: cf. *Confessio Amantis*, Pro. 261.

l. 835: *verbatim* Ovid, *Fasti*, 5. 209.

l. 843: *verbatim* Peter Riga, *Aurora*, I Kings 415.

ll. 861–2: cf. Matthew 4: 8–10, Luke 4: 5–8.

ll. 867–8: see note to ll. 721–4, above.

ll. 877–8: cf. Mark 9: 33–7.

l. 901: cf. Luke 14: 5.

l. 903: cf. Acts 11: 28–30.

l. 904: the reference is to Paul's "Jerusalem Collections," to bring relief to the famine-stricken believers of that city: cf. Romans 15: 26–7, I Corinthians 16: 1–4, II Corinthians 8–9.

ll. 911–12: *Qur'an*, 5: 33–4 proscribes "waging war against Allah and his Messenger," on pain of death, crucifixion, or excision of a hand and a foot on opposite sides of the body. Certain *hadiths* also claim death as proper punishment for blasphemy. Such punishments are not universally credited in Islam, however, and it seems clear that behind these lines lies only a general idea (if not a misunderstanding) probably current in fourteenth-century Europe.

l. 915: "Caesar" here denotes worldly clerics, wealthy (but spiritually bankrupt) monastics and bishops especially who ruled their lands like feudal lords, ignoring parish and diocesan responsibilities. Wyclif termed them "Caesarean clergy" – an opinion Gower echoes. See also note to l. 579, above.

l. 919: cf. Matthew 10: 34.

ll. 923–4: in Roman myth, a prophecy decreed Saturn would be overthrown by one of his children. To avoid this, he ate five of his progeny as they were born to Ops, one of his two wives. The sixth child, Jupiter, Ops replaced with a stone which, passing through Saturn's system, liberated the other five gods. Cf. *VC* II. 221 and *Confessio Amantis*, VII. 935–46.

ll. 925–6: cf. Ezekiel 34.

l. 927: alludes to "trial by fire," one of several "Ordeals of God" from which participation by clergy was prohibited (Canon 18) during the Fourth Lateran Council of 1215, and practiced elsewhere in Europe but not in fourteenth-century England.

ll. 933–4: cf. Joel 3: 10.

l. 940: "lex positiva": see Ch. 4 heading, note.

ll. 949–50: cf. John 18: 10–11, Luke 22: 50–1, Matthew 26: 51–2, Mark 14: 47.

ll. 955–6: the lines are built around a pun on "clemens" ("merciful") and "inclemens" ("harsh"), and criticize anti-Pope Clement VII of Avignon, i.e., "Clement" should be "Inclement," lacking compassion.

ll. 957–60: cf. Apocalypse 22: 8–9; *Mirour de l'Omme*, ll. 18733–44.

ll. 963–4: cf. Luke 7: 44–5.

ll. 965–6: cf. Matthew 23: 9.

ll. 973–4: cf. Matthew 16: 19.

l. 985: "commune sit omne": For Augustine, ownership of property was the direct result of the Fall of Man. Wyclif elaborated on this to argue against ecclesiastical ownership of any property, and for the king to take possession of church lands. Gower seems to approximate both positions. Cf. Acts 2: 44, 4: 32; *Confessio Amantis*, V. 1–5, VII. 1991–2002.

ll. 989–90: "veteri lege": by the "Old Law," Gower seems to have in mind Hebrew scriptures (cf. Bereshith 14: 22–3) since, in contrast, the Old Testament seems to allow consecration of battle spoils (cf. 1 Paralipomenon 26: 26–7).

ll. 997–8: these lines are built around a pun on "libras" ("pounds sterling") and "libros" ("books"), the latter being the proper study of clergy. A mark in Gower's London was worth two-thirds of a pound – 13s. 4d. – the point here being a devaluation of Mark, i.e., biblical study.

l. 999: "summa" = "summae," theological treatises, e.g., Thomas Aquinas's *Summa Theologiae*.

ll. 1003–4: the lines are built around wordplay "honor" and "onere" ("load, burden," hence – as here – "responsibility"), the idea being that officials' duties convey the honor, earned through effort; cf. *VC* V. 166 below, and note.

Ch. 12: most of the verses in this chapter are Leonine couplets, constituting a metrical shift from what has gone before.

ll. 1005–6: cf. John 10: 1.

ll. 1009–14: "fiscus" = public treasury (exchequer) or king's purse. See note to l. 985, above.

ll. 1017–20: Wyclif's concept of *dominium* excluded the clergy from judicial authority as well as property ownership. Gower's position here is, if not identical, then certainly quite close. "Legis...novitiate" = lex positiva.

l. 1027: cf. Ephesians 4: 5.

ll. 1037–8 and ff.: underlying these lines, cf. I Corinthians 9: 14.

ll. 1045–6: cf. Matthew 5: 38–40.

ll. 1055–6: the plow as a metaphor for the Church was common in the fourteenth century, strongly underlying of course *Piers Plowman*; the origin is scriptural: cf. Luke 9: 62 and I Corinthians 9: 10.

ll. 1063–4: cf. Matthew 15: 14, Luke 6: 39.

ll. 1065–74: these lines are an extended trope on John 12: 35.

ll. 1077–80: *verbatim* Peter Riga, *Aurora*, Exodus 789–92.

ll. 1085–6: honey as a metaphor for the holy word is common: cf., e.g. (esp. related to ministry), Psalm 19: 10–12, Proverbs 24: 11–14.

ll. 1095–6: adapted from Ovid, *Ex Ponto*, 3. 5. 17–18.

ll. 1099–100: cf. Matthew 25: 14–30; cf. also l. 1400, below.

l. 1106: cf. Matthew 5: 6.

ll. 1113–14: *verbatim* Ovid, *Ars Amatoria*, 3. 595–6.

ll. 1118–20: *verbatim* Peter Riga, *Aurora*, Genesis 972–4.

ll. 1121–4: virtually *verbatim* Peter Riga, *Aurora*, Genesis 979–82.

ll. 1129–34: the subject of criticism here is lollardy.

ll. 1137–8: virtually *verbatim* Peter Riga, *Aurora*, Leviticus 329–30.

ll. 1141–2: not to be confused with Wyclif's concern that a sinful priest cannot administer the sacraments; here the idea is that the rebukes of a proud or ignorant priest are recognizably empty.

ll. 1145–50: virtually *verbatim* Peter Riga, *Aurora*, I Kings 129–34; cf. *Mirour de l'Omme*, ll. 19117–22.

ll. 1151–2: cf. Ecclesiastes 7: 17–18.

ll. 1166: proverbial.

ll. 1171–2: adapted from Peter Riga, *Aurora*, Exodus 783–4.

ll. 1177–8: virtually *verbatim* Peter Riga, *Aurora*, Leviticus 313–14.

ll. 1183–6: *verbatim* Peter Riga, *Aurora*, Exodus 785–8.

ll. 1187–8: *verbatim* Peter Riga, *Aurora*, Exodus 1113–14; for "unguine leticie" cf. Isaiah 61: 3.

## Notes to Book III

ll. 1189–92: *verbatim* Peter Riga, *Aurora*, Exodus 1119–22.

l. 1199: cf. Acts 10: 34.

l. 1212: a pointed parody of a clutch of biblical passages: cf. e.g., Hosea 8: 7; Proverbs 11: 18, 22: 8; Job 4: 8; II Corinthians 9: 6; Galatians 6: 7–8; and see also Psalm 125: 5 (Vulgate); cf. also *Mirour de l'Omme*, ll. 7567–9, where the attribution to "l'apostre" suggests at that time at least the reference was to Luke 19: 21; Walz, 257b.

l. 1213: virtually *verbatim* Ovid, *Ars Amatoria*, 3. 655.

ll. 1215–16: adapted from Ovid, *Ars Amatoria*, 3. 653–4.

l. 1217: "Simon" = simony, but see also note to ll. 249–50, above.

ll. 1219–20: cf. John 4: 13–14.

ll. 1233–4: adapted from Ovid, *Ars Amatoria*, 2. 279–80.

ll. 1241–3: virtually *verbatim* Peter Riga, *Aurora*, Genesis 745–7.

l. 1246: *verbatim* Peter Riga, *Aurora*, Genesis 748.

ll. 1247–52: cf. *Mirour de l'Omme*, ll. 18793–804.

l. 1256: Regula Prima: probably to follow the gospel of Christ, to live in obedience, without possessions, and in chastity. Possibly Gower had in mind the "First Rule" of Francis of Assisi, given to the Friars Minor and approved orally by Innocent III in 1209, although the elements are generally applicable to the clerical life properly pursued. Gower's strong disapproval of friars, notably, is because they have strayed from this rule.

l. 1267: vox populi, vox dei: proverbial, and often relied on, e.g., cf. Alcuin to Charlemagne letter 164 (CE 798); William of Malmesbury, on Archbishop Walter Reynolds's sermon on the text "Vox populi, vox Dei," denouncing Edward II (1327).

ll. 1271–92: the extended passage derives from Matthew 23.

ll. 1271–2: cf. Matthew 23: 1; cf. *Mirour de l'Omme*, ll. 18805–16; *Confessio Amantis*, Pro. 304–9.

ll. 1287–8: cf. Matthew 23: 4.

ll. 1309–10: *verbatim* Nigel of Longchamp, *Speculum Stultorum*, ed. Mann, ll. 1471–2.

ll. 1313–486: cf. *Mirour de l'Omme*, ll. 20209–784; *Confessio Amantis*, V. 1860–99.

ll. 1331–2: cf. Matthew 10: 9–10; Mark 6: 8–9; Luke 9: 3; also Luke 3: 11.

ll. 1341–6: cf. *Mirour de l'Omme*, ll. 18889–900.

ll. 1361–2: cf. Genesis 27: 1–36; also 25: 28–34.

ll. 1365–6: cf. John 10: 1.

ll. 1371–4: *verbatim* Nigel of Longchamp, *Speculum Stultorum*, ed. Mann, ll. 49–52.

ll. 1375–8: cf. *Mirour de l'Omme*, ll. 20287–93.

l. 1384: *verbatim* Peter Riga, *Aurora*, Genesis 1086.

l. 1386: loosely derived from Peter Riga, *Aurora*, Genesis 1242.

l. 1400: cf. Matthew 25: 14–30; cf. also ll. 1099–100, above.

ll. 1403–8: cf. *Mirour de l'Omme*, ll. 20221–44.

ll. 1410–12: probably a sexual double-entendre here, around "ars" (arse) and wielding a pen at night; cf. l. 1455, below.

l. 1417: "Ve soli" quoted from Ecclesiastes 4: 10. Its use here is deeply ironic, as is the succeeding passage.

ll. 1431–2: cf. Genesis 1: 28; see ll. 2017–20, below; *Confessio Amantis*, V. 6421–3, VIII. 26–9. The sense here resembles "Wife of Bath's Tale," *CT* III. (D) 26–9.

l. 1455: "ars" cf. ll. 1410–12, above.

ll. 1487–524: for the full passage, cf. *Mirour de l'Omme*, ll. 20305–16.

ll. 1489–90: cf. John 15: 1–6, and possibly Matthew 7: 18.

l. 1546: cf. *Mirour de l'Omme*, ll. 17655–8; *Confessio Amantis*, III. 431–4.

l. 1548: possibly a reference to burial practices, and/or probably to Leviticus 21: 1–6.

ll. 1551–2: i.e., when a cure (especially one well endowed) becomes vacant by the death of the incumbent, the pope and curia were petitioned to secure it for the petitioner presenting gifts, preferably in person.

ll. 1555–66: clergy without a benefice/prebend – that is, a church position with an income – supported themselves as they could, some becoming (as here, and especially in Ch. 21) "annuelers" who were paid, either in the will or by the family, to sing masses for the deceased on the anniversaries of his/her death. Fees varied, but having more than one such task obviously raised income; and how faithfully they carried out their task was ever a concern. Cf. ll. 1651–4 below; *Mirour de l'Omme*, ll. 20497–508.

ll. 1563–4: cf. Luke 10: 7; Matthew 10: 10.

l. 1568: cf. Matthew 26: 15; Judas' thirty pieces of silver are recalled in l. 1577, below.

ll. 1575–7: cf. note to ll. 1551–2, above.

l. 1587–90: *verbatim* Peter Riga, *Aurora*, Leviticus 695–8. Cf. also Deuteronomy 14: 17. Cormorants clearly maintained a negative image: cf. Milton, *Paradise Lost*, IV. 194–200, at 196 (Satan "sat like a Cormorant" on the Tree of Life).

l. 1595: virtually *verbatim* Ovid, *Amores*, 1. 6. 59.

ll. 1601–4: proverbial in English and French – cf. Smith and Heseltine, "Pigeons and priests"; not present in *Mirour de l'Omme*.

ll. 1611–12: cf. I Corinthians 5: 7; with a pun on "expurgate [vetus] fermentum" (i.e., "purge the [old] leaven"/"vomit beer").

l. 1623: *verbatim* Peter Riga, *Aurora*, Deuteronomy 161.

ll. 1631–2: virtually *verbatim* Nigel of Longchamp, *Speculum Stultorum*, ed. Mann, ll. 55–6.

ll. 1634–5: the "kiss of peace" was a Christian adaptation of an ancient mouth-to-mouth greeting between baptized men, and particularly adopted by Paul: cf. Romans 16: 16; I Corinthians 16: 20; II Corinthians 13: 12; Thessalonians 5: 26; 1 Peter 5: 14; Gower knew it in the fourteenth century in its legitimate place as a part of the Eucharistic liturgy, in the Roman rite situated following the Pater Noster, immediately preceding the breaking of the bread. Cf. also Psalm 84: 11 (Vulgate), the "Four Daughters of God." Gower's intention here is to call out a salacious corruption of the practice, however.

l. 1640: proverbial – cf. Smith and Heseltine, "custom."

ll. 1649–50: possibly an ironically pointed reversal of Matthew 27: 42; cf. also Mark 15: 31; Luke 23: 35.

ll. 1651–4: for Gower the concern over corrupt annuelers was real: he left money in his will for yearly masses sung for him on the feast of St. John. Cf. also ll. 1663–4, below.

ll. 1657–60: cf. James 4: 17.

ll. 1663–4: see note to ll. 1651–4, above.

ll. 1668–71: "de merito...dona...": i.e., "ius patronatus" in canon law which empowers the bishop to award a benefice; in common law, the equivalent is the advowson, permitting a landowner on whose property a church becomes vacant to present a clerical candidate to the bishop for endowment. Gower's point is that bishops who abet candidates seeking offices in the church only to acquire power and/or wealth should forfeit their right to confer ecclesiastical appointments.

ll. 1671–80: cf. Wyclif, *De civili dominio*, argued against the Church's right to secular authority and/or to own property – views clearly shared by Gower. Cf. ll. 1715–20, below.

ll. 1693–700: virtually *verbatim* Peter Riga, *Aurora*, Leviticus 687–94; cf. *Confessio Amantis*, I. 1727–8.

l. 1707: that all believers are brothers in Christ is particularly a Pauline locution, and commonly found in the Epistles, e.g., I Corinthians 12: 1; Galatians 1: 2.

ll. 1709–14: cf. Matthew 18: 15–17; Luke 17: 3–4.

ll. 1715–20: see note to ll. 1671–80, above.

ll. 1721–2: cf. Luke 8: 17, 12: 2; Mark 4: 22; also proverbial.

l. 1724: virtually *verbatim* Peter Riga, *Aurora*, Numeri 462.

ll. 1727–30: cf. *Mirour de l'Omme*, ll. 20713–24.

ll. 1741–4: that is, the five minor ecclesiastical orders following tonsure (in ascending order: ostiary, cantor, lector, exorcist, and acolyte) and the four major orders (subdeacon, deacon, priest, and bishop).

ll. 1747–50: the First Lateran Council (CE 1123) forbade subdeacons, deacons, priests, and monks either to marry or have concubines, insisting on chastity, defined as abstention. See notes to ll. 1859–60, 1895–6, below.

ll. 1759–64: cf. *Mirour de l'Omme*, ll. 20725–36.

ll. 1791–5: virtually *verbatim* Peter Riga, *Aurora*, I Kings 121–5 (Vulgate).

l. 1797: virtually *verbatim* Peter Riga, *Aurora*, Exodus 899.

l. 1799: composite from Peter Riga, *Aurora*, Exodus 827 and section heading.

ll. 1801–2: composite from Peter Riga, *Aurora*, Exodus 877–8 (l. 1802 *verbatim*).

l. 1804: "cuncta metalla regit": in alchemy, gold was considered the purest of the seven metals (in descending order gold, silver, mercury, copper, lead, iron, tin) and the perfect substance – hence it "rules" the others. Cf. *Confessio Amantis*, IV. 2451–530.

ll. 1807–8: virtually *verbatim* Peter Riga, *Aurora*, Exodus 807–8.

ll. 1809–11: virtually *verbatim* Peter Riga, *Aurora*, Exodus 879–81.

ll. 1813–14: virtually *verbatim* Peter Riga, *Aurora*, Exodus 905–6.

ll. 1815–18: virtually *verbatim* Peter Riga, *Aurora*, Exodus 801–4.

## Notes to Book III

ll. 1819–20: virtually *verbatim* Peter Riga, *Aurora*, Exodus 1023–4.

ll. 1821–2: *verbatim* Peter Riga, *Aurora*, Exodus 1027–8.

ll. 1823–4: *verbatim* Peter Riga, *Aurora*, Exodus 715–16.

l. 1824-25: "ut quatuor orbis/ Partibus": four-part division of the world prior to the discovery of the Americas is unusual. Medieval maps generally divided it into three, not four, parts, (e.g., Isidore of Seville's T/O map), each part given post-diluvially to the three sons of Noah : Europe (Japhet), Asia (Shem), and Africa (Ham). Gower follows this pattern, Confessio Amantis VII. 521-620, and also in the image of the archer at the beginning of MSS Glasgow. University of Glasgow, Hunter 59 (T.2.17) and London, British Library, Cotton Tiberius A.iv, both of which presumably Gower had approved. It is possible for the fourth part mentioned here Gower had in mind either Paradise (cf. Confessio VII. 570-71), or more likely "the gret Occeane" (cf. Confessio VII. 591-600) which surrounds all three continents.

ll. 1831–2: virtually *verbatim* Peter Riga, *Aurora*, Leviticus 103–4.

Ch. 25 heading: "veteri lege" = Old Testament; "nove legis" = New Testament.

ll. 1841–8: virtually *verbatim* Peter Riga, *Aurora*, Leviticus 573–80.

l. 1853: that is, Peter Riga, the *Aurora*.

ll. 1859–60: *verbatim* Peter Riga, *Aurora*, Leviticus 169–70; see also note to ll. 1747–50, above.

ll. 1863–84: virtually *verbatim* Peter Riga, *Aurora*, Leviticus 777–804, rearranged as follows: 777–8, 793–6, 783–8, 779–80, 789–92, 797–8, 803–4 (781–2, 790–802 omitted).

ll. 1885–90: virtually *verbatim* Peter Riga, *Aurora*, II Kings 115–20; cf. *Mirour de l'Omme*, ll. 20737–48.

ll. 1891–2: virtually *verbatim* Peter Riga, *Aurora*, II Kings 133–4; cf. *Confessio Amantis*, II. 574–5.

ll. 1895–6: see note to ll. 1747–50, above.

ll. 1905–8: virtually *verbatim* Peter Riga, *Aurora*, Numeri 143–4, 149–50.

ll. 1909–10: cf. *Mirour de l'Omme*, ll. 20749–72.

ll. 1911–16: virtually *verbatim* Peter Riga, *Aurora*, Numeri 127–32.

ll. 1917–18: virtually *verbatim* Peter Riga, *Aurora*, Deuteronomy 189–90.

ll. 1919–23: virtually *verbatim* Peter Riga, *Aurora*, Josue 251–5.

ll. 1925–8: cf. Proverbs 24: 16.

l. 1929: "Lux estis mundi": cf. Matthew 5: 14 (Vulgate): "Vos estis lux mundo"; note to l. 2003, below.

l. 1930: cf. John 8: 7; III Kings 8: 46 (Vulgate).

ll. 1931–2: loosely based on Peter Riga, *Aurora*, Numeri 397–8.

ll. 1933–4: adapted from Ovid, *Remedia Amoris*, 53–4.

l. 1937: *verbatim* Ovid, *Remedia Amoris*, 669.

ll. 1939–40: virtually *verbatim* Ovid, *Tristia*, 4. 6. 33–4.

ll. 1943–4: *verbatim* Ovid, *Remedia Amoris*, 89–90.

ll. 1945–6: *verbatim* Ovid, *Remedia Amoris*, 115–16.

ll. 1947–50: *verbatim* Ovid, *Remedia Amoris*, 81–4.

l. 1952: adapted from Ovid, *Heroides*, 17. 190.

l. 1953: *verbatim* Ovid, *Remedia Amoris*, 229.

ll. 1961–2: "fecit enim sportas": A rather curious statement, in that St. Paul of Tarsus was a tentmaker (cf. Acts 18: 3) not a maker of baskets. Possibly a confusion of St. Paul of Tarsus with Paul of Thebes (St. Paul the Hermit), who serves as patron saint of basket-makers; relevant also might be Paul of Tarsus' escape from Damascus when his disciples lowered him from a window in a basket, thwarting a murder plot (cf. I Corinthians 11: 33, Acts 9: 25). Paul's basket-making seems to have had some currency in fourteenth-century England. Gower shares this story with Langland (*Piers Plowman* B-text Passus 15, 285; C-text Passus 18, 17–18) and Chaucer (*CT* VI. [C], 445 [Pardoner's Prologue]).

l. 1977: *verbatim* Peter Riga, *Aurora*, Exodus 21.

l. 1979: loosely based on Peter Riga, *Aurora*, Genesis 271.

ll. 1985–6: i.e., the Eucharist; see also l. 1993, below.

l. 1990: i.e., when true priests assign penance for violation of God's law, they don't take bribes. Cf. ll. 195–6 and note, above; also Chaucer's Friar and Summoner.

l. 1997: cf. Matthew 5: 13.

l. 1998: cf. Luke 14: 34.

ll. 1999–2000: virtually *verbatim* Peter Riga, *Aurora*, IV Kings 81–2.

l. 2001: *verbatim* Peter Riga, *Aurora*, Leviticus 389.

l. 2002: *verbatim* Peter Riga, *Aurora*, Leviticus 392.

l. 2003: cf. Matthew 5: 14; and note to l. 1929, above.

ll. 2007–8: virtually *verbatim* Peter Riga, *Aurora*, Leviticus 761–2.

l. 2009: virtually *verbatim* Peter Riga, *Aurora*, Genesis 939.

l. 2014: "nova nostra salus": cf. John 3: 3–6.

ll. 2017–20: *verbatim* Peter Riga, *Aurora*, Genesis 163–6.

ll. 2021–2: *verbatim* Peter Riga, *Aurora*, Exodus 1285–6.

ll. 2023–6: *verbatim* Peter Riga, *Aurora*, Numeri 253–6.

ll. 2027–8: probable allusion to Brunellus the Ass: cf. Nigel of Longchamp, *Speculum Stultorum*, *passim*.

l. 2029: cf. Jeremiah 33: 22.

ll. 2035–8: *verbatim* Peter Riga, *Aurora*, Genesis 625–8.

ll. 2039–40: virtually *verbatim* Peter Riga, *Aurora*, Genesis 631–2.

Ch. 28: cf. *Mirour de l'Omme*, ll. 20785–832.

ll. 2059–60: *verbatim* Peter Riga, *Aurora*, Leviticus 61–2.

ll. 2061–2: cf. Matthew 22: 14.

ll. 2071–2: cf. Matthew 7: 17–18; Luke 6: 43–4.

ll. 2073–4: proverbial – cf. Walz, 137, 255a, b; *Mirour de l'Omme*, ll. 20827–9.

l. 2085: in English law, a crime must combine guilty intent ("mens rea") with a guilty act ("actus reus").

ll. 2097–8: a reference to *priveligium clericale* ("benefit of clergy"), exempting clergy from trial and corporal punishment under common law statutes in secular courts, trying them only in ecclesiastical courts under canon law, which excluded most bodily punishment. Cf. Psalm 72: 5 (Vulgate).

l. 2099: cf. Psalm 72: 5 (Vulgate).

ll. 2105–10: "civilia iura": Medieval universities taught two types of law – canon and civil (or Roman), taken together as the "ius commune" – not to be confused with English common law. Clergy hoping for an extra-clerical career, or advancement to high office within the Church (e.g., the "Caesarian clergy" attacked by Wyclif) studied both. Cf. ll. 2137–8, below.

l. 2130: cf. Matthew 23: 7–8, although the full chapter, in which Jesus castigates hypocritical scribes and Pharisees, is relevant to Gower's passage here.

ll. 2137–8: see note to ll. 2105–10, above.

ll. 2141–2: cf. John 12: 35.

# BOOK IV

Book IV takes to task the regular clergy, who indulge in a gluttonous lifestyle, acquisition of wealth, and sexual misconduct, all in flagrant violation of the precepts of poverty and chastity to which they have vowed obedience. Gower's first topic is monks and canons; his concern, the disparity between the requirements of the way of life they've sworn to live and their behavior. He sees extraordinary misbehavior among the members of the cloistered orders, the most of whom live hypocritically worldly lives while professing an ascetic rejection of the world's delights. Their commitment to gastronomic excess in food and drink is richly described within a harsh account of a monastic life characterized by ambition, backstabbing, angry misbehavior, and a general disregard of moral values. Remarking the notorious sensual excesses of many religious houses, Gower condemns especially the presence of women and advises monks to keep "she-wolves" far from the cloister (ll. 431–68).

Women who live in cloistered communities come in for somewhat different judgment, based upon an assumed lesser intelligence and a fragile nature, both to be taken into account when critiquing their weaknesses. Incapable of understanding Scripture properly and naturally weak, they can't be held to the same standard as men, but those among them who uphold chastity will nevertheless be rewarded with a special status in paradise because of the high valuation God places upon virginity. A coarse and bawdy prejudice is apparent in some of Gower's observations, when, for instance, he remarks that women in convents are prone to sin in matters of food and the flesh, both of which leave them with uncomfortable and shameful lumps in their stomachs. Because of feminine frailty, a wise convent will, like a wise farmer, accordingly grow a high hedge around its wheat field. Bishops visit the convent to administer naked instruction and are not hesitant to "stone" the nuns in ways that leave not bruises but offspring. Venus' priest Genius appears, in the guise of the visiting bishop, to administer vigorously Venus' law rather than the Church's. The relationship of this Genius to the same-named figure in the *Confessio Amantis* poses an interesting possibility for the interpretation of both poems, but whether the two can be profitably compared remains an open question.

Gower devotes almost half of Book IV to an especially harsh rebuke of the friars. After assuring those few who do fulfill their vows that a good end awaits them, he lashes out at the bulk of the brothers who, living in the world, encounter and succumb to the temptations of the flesh on a regular basis. Some of Gower's critique echoes standard anti-fraternalism of the period. Unfettered by either cloister or parish, but roaming freely, like a vast flood that has ebbed and lost its force, the friars have spread in their own version of a diaspora, usurping some powers and functions of the secular clergy and causing chaos everywhere. Since Innocent III granted friars their special status, absolving them of accountability to ecclesiastical authority other than the pope himself, they have insinuated themselves into the world by preaching and hearing confessions to their own financial, rather than the spiritual, profit of those to whom they minister. They then use their gains to construct lavishly appointed friaries where they live in luxury and scheme to perpetuate themselves. Viewing the problem of the friars from a legal perspective, Gower questions their very right to exist, seeing their origin in the clever manipulation of a pope who was persuaded to take what rightfully belonged to other religious, specifically preaching and confessing, and bestow it upon the friars, who were quick to exploit their grant to their own profit and the detriment of the Christian world in general. If such a theft had occurred in the secular world, Gower says, justice would have been available to the clergy whose authority and income have been stolen by the friars.

A fair amount of Gower's criticism of the clergy would seem to be class-based. He laments that the freeborn rarely join the regular orders of clergy, with the result that their houses are filled with coarse peasants unworthy of the freeborn status that comes with entry into an order (ll. 237–8). The fathers of today's monks, he notes, bore their burdens on their shoulders, while the monks themselves now bear their loads (of food and wine) in their guts (ll. 57–60). He remarks about cloistered women that their past sexual exploits can't be held against them once they embrace sacred virginity, hinting perhaps that some nuns had once been prostitutes, or at the least guilty of sexual misconduct (ll. 665–70). Friars, recruited as youths from the peasantry and serving no purpose in the Church, should be returned to the plow to alleviate the current shortage of agricultural workers (ll. 957–8).

Gower's account of the friars' sexual exploits and his bawdy solution to the problem are worthy of note as another of the poem's comic high points. Like bees pollinating flowers, the friars circulate around the countryside, impregnating the local women. Arguing like a canon lawyer, the poet begins his account with the phrase *notandum esse* (it should be noted), the inevitable beginning of a minor canon law genre called a *notabilium*, typically a learned comment on a passage in a decretal. Gower's legal point is that the bee who inserts his stinger is condemned to lose it and, accordingly, by the principle of *in consimili casu* (in a like case) the friar, too, should lose his "stinger" for his inappropriate behavior. This will not only render him harmless to the local women, but also incline him to stay home in his "hive," like a drone, and attend to his domestic duties. However, the precepts of Burnellus, the ass of Nigel of Longchamp's famous satire, are all the vogue in the cloister and Burnellus, not Benedict nor Bernard, is the preferred prior.

*Vox Clamantis by John Gower: 'The Voice of One Crying'*

# HERE BEGINS THE FOURTH BOOK

## CHAPTER 1

**Since he has discussed the error of the clergy, to whom pertains especially the guidance of our souls, now he intends to discuss the error of the men of the religious orders. First he will speak about monks and others who acquire possession of temporal goods. Commending, to be sure, the sanctity of their order, he rebukes chiefly those who act to the contrary.**

There are also the cloistered men of diverse sort,
   Of whom I'll write a few things that I know.
As their behavior proves, property defines some,
   Poverty others, although it's much feigned.
A religious order is good in itself, but
   We say those who betray it are wicked.
I think those who live true in the cloister are blessed,
   Those who aren't guilty of love of the world.
Those who put their hand to the plow, not looking back,\*
   The order will designate holy men.                   10
God's among these monks and they're heaven's fellowship,
   Who wish to be cloistered, without the world.
But when you try to love opposites equally,\*
   The one love saps the strength of the other.
Thus they who think to hide their face in the order's
   Shade and beneath it commit the world's sins,
To such I address my writings and others won't
   Be harmed by them; let each bear his own load.\*
Nothing I write is my own, for I shall relate\*
   Things borne to me by the *vox populi*.                     20

Indeed there are monks who've title to property,\*
   Whom an order cannot tie down by rules.
For some landowners seek out an order's leisure
   So that they won't suffer any hardships.
They forbear to bear hunger and drown thirst with wine\*
   And flee from all cold with warm mistresses.
A full stomach does not arise in the nighttime,
   Nor a voice hoarse from drink chime in the choir.
If one such can't gulp many platters at table
   And empty many cups in his drinking,                  30
He thinks he's fallen ill, hence demands that he be

*Book IV*

    Restored and then idles about in play.
For he who's sworn is scarce worn by all his drinking:*
    The Domnus wants to draw nigh God with wine,*
But when you will have wine, it brings the women in;
    These days the wanton cloisters offer both.
If he can gain heaven in his comfy clothing
    And gluttony is rife 'mongst those above,
Then I think the monk distinguished on either count
    Shall be Peter's fellow in heaven's vault.     40

## Chapter 2

**Here he speaks about those monks who, forsaking the virtue of abstinence against the statutes of the first order, enjoy the delights of the flesh in many ways.***

    There's no way the dead belong among the living:*
        Who renounces the world gives up its ways.
Neither the tonsure nor the plainest garb avails*
    If one's a wolf, although he seem a sheep.
Men are able to deceive, though no one's able
    To deceive our Christ, who deceives no one.
Indeed, he condemns the deceit of religious
    Pretense and thinks it amounts to nothing.
But now the monk departs the world in dress only*
    And thinks an order's manner is enough.     50
He cares only for his order's material wealth:
    Clothes make the monk; his mind wanders the world.
For such a monk, because he knows the belly's flesh
    Seldom thrives on the order's meager fare,*
Seeks the gullet's plenty and consumes foods he craves
    To fulfill his gut's joys in his gullet.
Unlike his father, whose shoulders bore his burdens,
    The monk bears the best wine in his belly.
He pours Bacchus in his stomach as if it's a jug;
    There's no empty spot in his swollen gut.     60

For a host of reasons, a monk should steer clear of
    Bacchus, for one, lest his flesh seek out shame.
The man ought not waste his fellows' goods, sit about
    Drunkenly, nor behave feverishly.
Yet he cares for nothing but stuffing his foolish

## Vox Clamantis by John Gower: 'The Voice of One Crying'

Flesh, while every day starving his poor soul.
Nowadays the monk's snow-white bread, exquisite wine,
   And roasted meats provide a daily feast.
These days, behold! the cook roasts, broils, thickens and thins,
   Rubs, plucks, decorates, and tastes what he makes.     70
If the gluttonous monk can fatten up his guts,
   He thinks Sacred Writ doesn't enjoin work.
Despising manna, this sort wants blackened cook pots
   And puts his vices before his morals.
Lest hunger weaken the stout fellow, lo! his gut's
   Friend Gluttony packs his languid stomach.
He does not know about honors; blessed bellies,
   Monks say, are the way, life, and salvation.*
Rushing swiftly, he runs when the dinner bell rings;*
   Not one crumb from the table escapes him.     80
But rising with sluggish foot from his cot by night,*
   He seeks to be last when he comes to Lauds.

Houses for the order's monks were but caves at first;
   Now they're furnished with grand halls of marble.
There was no steamy kitchen nor did any cook
   Serve them by the fire tasty stews or roasts.
No steamed dishes nor platters piled up high with meat*
   Gave the monks rich fare in the early days.
The body's gluttony did not weigh down their minds;
   Their fervid flesh sought no hot debaucheries.     90
Those who these days cover themselves with softest wool*
   Covered their bare flesh with animal hides.
The pasture provided food; the spring, drink; a foul
   Hair shirt, clothes, but there was no grumbling then.
There was no envy or pomp in the cloister then;
   Who was greater served just like the lesser.
There was no weight of silver nor a chain of gold*
   That could then violate their holy state.
Coins didn't touch their pockets nor wine their palates;
   Carnal flames didn't run wild in their loins.     100
They had a holy mind that served their purpose well,
   Persisting in the work they'd well begun.

They had been righteous men, fugitives from the world,
   Those men whom no love of the sins weighed down.
The world did not drag them from off the righteous path*

Nor fetid flesh beckon them to evil.
They put aside all the vanities the world serves
   And longed only for the God of heaven.
There was no shame then to take rest upon the straw*
   Nor to lay down some hay beneath one's head.         110
Woods were their house; plants, their food; boughs, their bed chamber,*
   Which the earth provided without effort.*
The highly valued hazel flourished among them
   And sturdy oaks provided great riches.*
They gathered madrone fruit and mountain strawberries,*
   Which were preserved with neither salt nor spice.
If any acorns fell from the broad tree of Jove,*
   They gleaned them and remained strong with these foods.
Content with simple produce from willing Nature,*
   They loosed their humble prayers to God on high.         120
Perfect sowers of the seeds of justice then, they
   Now reap, endlessly, fruits a hundred-fold.
But the salvation of souls that was religion,
   Weakened, dies out, overwhelmed by the flesh.

## Chapter 3

**Here he tells how the manner and rule originally established in orders by their founders have lately been subverted among many by sinful practices.**

   The spirit is oft drawn to new fashions and here
      The monk's altered rule will be my witness.
   These days the monks' first rule [regula] has been shortened,
      For re subtracted, just gluttony [gula] remains.
   Drinking lavish wines by the tun is all the mode*
      With monks, who gulp without moderation.         130
   That a wagging tongue can't disturb their greedy jaws,*
      The order commands silence at mealtime.
   Lest a foot weighed down by a heavy paunch give way,
      The monk first takes a seat before he drinks.
   It helps, too, that the rotund monk's head is tonsured,*
      Lest flowing hair get in the way of drink.
   Monks contract mutual pacts that if one of them
      Makes a toast he'll leave naught in the bottom.
   So they empty full vessels and refill empties,

## Vox Clamantis by John Gower: 'The Voice of One Crying'

That their houses make Bacchus proper feasts. 140
A roomy robe is thus helpful to our stuffed monk,
   Lest the sight of his paunch should be exposed.

Love of eating always rages in such a monk;
   Food and sleep provide what he most desires.
What sea, what land provide, and what the air brings forth*
   The greedy man devours with greedy maw.
Just as the sea receives rivers from all the earth*
   And yet ocean's great thirst always wants more,
And just as a deep pit receives wandering streams*
   Yet is unsated no matter how much flows, 150
And just as the heat of a fire burns up timber*
   Yet the more that there is the more it wants,
Just so the monk's gullet gulps with his profane mouth,
   For love of his belly, his diverse feasts.
So he bears a gut heavy with a ripe burden
   And his mind, light and empty, turns from Christ.
Laden with drink, the holy man is immobile,
   Stays fixed and heavy in the place he took.
When he drinks wine, the monk's empty mind grows sluggish,
   Relinquishes the cloister's heavy weight. 160
So his full pious guts rejoice when they're infused
   With the flowing wine his spirit favors.
So soporifics fashion the saint's lengthy sleeps*
   And too much wine consumed causes slumber.
I don't know how a wine drinker can be chaste, for*
   Venus rages in wine like flame in fire.
Thus Venus, lurking snugly beneath a hair shirt,
   Does wicked deeds and joys in sacred guise.

Envy murmurs in the cavern of the monk's breast;
   His mouth dumb without, his mind spins within.* 170
And since his tongue is still, his hand, privy to signs,
   Tells more than enough filth with its fingers.
So the loquacious digit speaks, redeems the word's*
   Silence, and rages in spats like a whore.
His face swells with his wrath, his veins blacken with blood,*
   His excited eyes flash brighter than fires.*
His raging anger will lend color to his eyes,*
   In which the other's demise can be seen.
The pride that shows perniciously in such a face*
   Would gladly commit murder with a sword. 180

*Book IV*

Although the order forbids him to war with words,
   He fights and in his mind he severs heads.
Although he can't speak, his heart mutters secretly\*
   And grows hoarse with envy of his brother.
His face enraged, his muttering passes for words
   And in his mind he kills whom his hand can't.
His pale face, heaving breast, and frightful demeanor
   Are the messengers of his disturbed mind.
For whatever a man undergoes, his features
   Reveal the symptoms of his inner strife.           190

The face reveals the mind's emotion and remarks\*
   The anger of a heart fired by grievance.
For no index of the mind, when it voiceless speaks,
   Can be more reliable than the face.
No matter how severe their simple garment is,
   Their behavior teaches what lies within.
The monks put their superior far from their love
   And hate those they're unable to follow.
They flock together at the ringing of the bell,
   But hold the service emptily, by form.           200
Their voices sing as one, their minds mutter within;
   Their mouths seek heaven's place; their minds, the earth's.
They serve the form of the order, not its substance,
   Soothe their worthless flesh with the fruits they've plucked.
Thus they manifest work and wisdom without, but
   They behave much more stupidly within.

## Chapter 4

**Here he talks about those monks who, against their order's founding rules, dare secretly, without the knowledge of their superiors, to appropriate the world's wealth for wicked purposes.**

It is more helpful not to take than to break vows,
   For no praise should be given a liar.
Brotherly love, indeed, ought to be mutual,\*
   At least for those a pious order binds.           210
The modern day, however, doesn't suffer this,
   For spite turns to anger what love there was.
Like a grazing ox endlessly chewing its cud,
   The devil's 'prentice gossips in cloisters.

## Vox Clamantis by John Gower: 'The Voice of One Crying'

If you would not be chewed up, take no corrody\*
   In the midst of those where good faith is rare.
When they want what is yours, then they will worship you,
   But they don't intend to stay grateful long.
Their first endowment conferred nothing upon them\*
   Beyond the daily income that they seek.                         220
Reason denies, as does the order, that a man
   Can be both an owner and a beggar.
But nothing in the world now sates these idle monks,
   Who always have a hunger and a thirst.
We read about Jerome and likewise Benedict\*
   That we better follow their examples.
They sold the ornaments from their altars and gave
   The poor the proceeds as nutritious foods.
To the poor belong Church's goods, which religious
   Are not allowed to keep when they see need.                 230

If you'd give to a monk, he'll grab all you offer,
   But he's got nothing if you beg from him.
They're all alike, because it's in this same spirit
   That each one wants what's his all to himself.
So whatever rules the old order first cherished\*
   The new order corrupts with its changed ways.
We rarely see the freeborn become monks; therefore,\*
   There are more crude peasants in the order.
Yet those holy men, sworn by a holy order,
   Are by their office free and worthy men.                     240
But what shall I say to those who are not worthy
   By their birth or order? They waste their time.
Even if Benedict has confirmed those who are\*
   Accursed, God for his part does not bless them.
My writings accuse those whom the world attracts more
   Than Christ and who look backward from the plow.\*

Why, I ask, does he want aught who's forsaken all?
   Why would he do evil who's vowed good deeds?
You who seek to have the heavens should scorn the earth;
   If you seek lasting things, flee the fleeting.                250
Do those made monks rightly have their own property?
   I don't know about right, but watch their acts!
If a shrine's guard, when he has a chance to take some,
   Wants coins for himself, he'll be my witness.
When a monk in the performance of his duties

*Book IV*

    Keeps some for himself, his ends prove his means.
For when he has gathered enough, he will enrich
    His nephews and thus endow new cloisters.
And often he calls nephews those whom he has sired
    In praise of Venus, whom he, pious, serves.             260
Indeed, his children are turned out under false names
    So that charity, blinded, will help them.

So false almsgiving abounds in corrupt cloisters
    When a monk gives his gifts to his children.
Secret monkish piety flowers in the world
    When one pretends to take gifts for God's love.
When theft becomes legal, then I'm able to say
    It's legal to bring God things from such gifts.
But who thus turns what's common to his own uses*
    Bears God's curse to the value of the gift.          270
Cloisters collapse into ruins by gifts of such sort
    When their storehouses groan with such a grain.
A hundred monks grow gaunt while they stand their duties
    So that two or three may have their fat lips.
"All things are ours," they say, but the scale's pans don't hang
    Level when one takes himself more than three.

## Chapter 5

**Here he tells how monks ought not wander outside the cloister.**

    The sea is the proper habitat for live fish*
    And the cloister is the fit home for monks.
Just as the sea will decline to keep its dead fish,
    So the cloister thence spews out its bad monks.       280
Let a monk be in cloister, a fish in water,
    Or else order has been turned upside down.
Should a fish, forsaking the waves of the ocean,
    Seek to take its sustenance from the land,
The name of fish is no longer appropriate
    And it should be considered a portent.
I would say to the cloisterer who hungers for
    The world's pleasures and then deserts his cell,
He won't be a monk but by rights called apostate,
    What God's wrath calls "monster of the temple."*       290
And they who stay in cloister but wandering in mind

Look to the world with new love in their heart,
Their transgression befouls them in the sight of God,
   Whence they lose their cloister's worthy rewards.
He is not wise who gathers good things for many
   Years and dissipates them all in one day.
The monk who runs around the towns and countryside
   Often meets something which makes him sinful.
But there are few at present who in thought or deed
   Won't give their wandering hearts to their pleasures.        300
Solomon said the very clothing that a man*
   Wore on the outside taught what was inside.
But though a monk fancy himself in humble clothes,
   You'll now see many proud things on his back.

## Chapter 6

**Here he talks about those monks who take upon themselves the habit of an order, not for divine service, but rather for the honor and pleasure of this world.**

The crow's a black bird and a corpse robber, whom blind*
   Lust colors black to signify evil.
With this species of bird the Lawgiver marked those
   Whom worldly love cloaks in religion.
He also intends one whom religious garments
   Disguise so he'll sooner bask in honor.        310
A monstrous beast is ugly, a grassless pasture,*
   A bush without leaves and a hairless head.
Yet more shameful is a monk who dons the order's
   Habit and doesn't have a monk's nature.

Since the monks' ancient rule commands they flee the world,
   They say they do but flight becomes pursuit.
The poor man who was born by serf's lineage to plow*
   Would, though base, be prior to the Prior.
Whom the world has granted no honor pursues it
   In the cloister, forgetting his old state.        320
Those whom Nature made lowly by patrimony
   The order raises high when they're made monks.
But they want to be called My Lord and not Abbot*
   And they make wide what was a narrow way.*
They have no burdens and they think they can't be tasked;
   Therefore they don't know how to pray to God.

Book IV

## Chapter 7*

**Here he tells how patience and other virtues, the vices having supervened, have departed from certain cloisters.**

>Domnus Patience is dead and the monk Mutterer*
>  Lives on, but there's no peace in his cloisters.
>Domnus Chastity is also dead now and Lust*
>  Succeeds him and devastates the houses. 330
>And Domnus Inconstant denies Constant cloisters*
>  That resident tenant Hatred has claimed.
>And Domnus Hypocrisy joins Domnus Deceit,*
>  While Fraud conspires to have a high status.
>The old monks not long ago planted fruits of love;
>  The new order now bears those of hatred.
>
>The rule of Saint Bernard or Maure no longer suits,*
>  But now displeases our new fellow monks.
>Greedy, proud, and envious, they stand against it
>  And now decline to bear the order's rule. 340
>So Slander banished Benedict from the cloisters;
>  So Gluttony, Temperance; and Falsehood, Faith.
>Abbot Easy's there, whom pliant cloisters follow,
>  So the order's weak shadow cloaks weak men.
>That which was spirit is now only worthless flesh,
>  And Domnus World attends to every need.*

## Chapter 8*

**Here he says that errant canons as well as monks should be censured for their excesses.**

>Just as decretals state, in similar cases*
>  You should logically give the same judgment.
>All those designated religious in the Church,
>  Possessors as well, are reckoned the same.* 350
>Just as sinful as monks in a similar case,
>  Therefore, are canons whom error misleads.
>But now, as it happens, many prune back their rules,
>  Which, trimmed, fall almost still by their new law.
>That rigorous text that their founder had written
>  They nowadays weaken in their glosses.

*Vox Clamantis by John Gower: 'The Voice of One Crying'*

They think it enough to have a holy order's
  Name, but do little that the order asks.

If the name of canons is derived from "canon,"*
  You couldn't prove it by their behavior.                     360
When people are watching, they pretend that they are
  Saints, but often their rule settles for less.
Underneath they wear white clothes, but on top of them
  Black outer garments cover up the white.*
But their deeds will show that they are the opposite;
  Without, they feign white, but, within, act black.
I'm not speaking about those who keep their cloisters
  In order to meditate without show.
Nay, I speak of those who on the inside search out
  The world while outside they bear heaven's badge.        370

## CHAPTER 9*

**Here he tells how the religious living in wickedness are the most wretched among all men whatsoever.**

I think monks are born in less felicitous hours*
  Than others unless they're perchance good men.
For while alive a professed monk dies to the world
  Since he's not able, like another man,
To enjoy outside pleasures; but should he, within,
  Desire the world, he'll lose heaven's rewards.
To have neither a present nor a future life
  He thus stands, whereby he is twice wretched.
He dies dead to this life, then by his second death*
  He may learn that he's lost his other chance.                 380
So he dies to the world – for by the order's rule
  He gets no joys from it while he's alive –
And unless he contemplate but God in his heart
  And is joyous, he'll not have heaven's place.
I don't know what fool is more stupid than the monk
  Who denies himself his reward in both.
He simply wastes his time whose present life denies
  Joy and whose afterlife holds no heaven.

# Book IV

## Chapter 10

**Here he tells how each one who wishes to enter upon the profession of religion is obligated deep within to forsake all the vices of the world and to acquire and observe the virtues of the soul.**

O comrades who have sworn to a cloistered order,
    I'll sum in brief what your task is and why.      390
Having been taught, I have pondered the saints' writings,
    Which your teachers ought to keep more in mind.
Saintly words avail most when they're plainly revealed;
    Therefore, you monks, you must behold what's there.
You have vowed, brothers, you have vowed; maintain your vows*
    And fulfill the work that you have promised.
You have vowed to the Lord that you will change your ways;*
    Since God's chosen you, abide in God's love.
Monks ought to maintain a rigorous way of life,
    Not grieve to bear hardships in their season.      400
The work is menial, but the work's reward is great;*
    It goes quickly; the rewards are endless.
Hence holy monks, committed totally in mind,*
    Should cleanse their sins with weeping and wailing.*

Now let live humble who before had dwelt in pride,
    Whoever had been lustful let be pure.
Let every man who sought wealth, strove for high office,
    Find every useless honor henceforth vile.
To one who joyed in feasts and in the board's riches
    A sober dinner now shall give scant food.      410
He shall shun the world's delicacies, though they please,
    For sweet things certainly will ruin his taste.
Who used to be gay in his extravagances,
    Now let him wash his sins away with tears.
Let the chatterbox be still, the hothead cool down,
    The jealous spew out envy's dire venom.
Whom the sword and rapine have previously pleased
    Shall now be merciful and love mild peace.
Whosoever swelled up, flattered by windy praise,
    Let now consider men's praises nothing,      420
And who always used to harm others savagely,
    Let learn to suffer bitter injuries.
He who was quick to trials, headlong to quarrels,

Let bravely bear another's reproaches.
Let bill and coo nowadays the doves who have fought,*
  Their former anger no longer prevail.
Let your brief angers be sinless, that rage won't know
  At all the doings of your inner mind.
This true conversion, brothers, merits forgiveness;
  It works to appease an offended God. 430

## Chapter 11

**Here he tells how religious ought especially to avoid the companionship of women.**

Shun the discourse of females, holy man, beware*
  Lest you entrust yourself to raging fire.
A mind captured by the love of women is bound*
  And cannot reach the peak of the virtues.*
What can you possibly gain from talking with them?
  You'll come a monk, leave an adulterer.
Therefore, unless you've fled the poisonous serpent,
  You'll be bitten when least you expect it.
Each and every woman kindles the fire of lust;*
  If one should touch her, he is burnt at once. 440
Ponder patristic works and the books of ancients*
  And grieve that holy men have fallen thus.
Did not woman get man outlawed from the blessed*
  Abode and become the source of our death?
Let thus the good shepherd keep watch and everywhere*
  Drive ravening she-wolves from the cloisters.

Preserve the faith: how do your responses help you,
  Shepherd, who cede the swift she-wolf the fold?
Checked by a voice, she often stops chasing a lamb,*
  Which when the shepherd's voice falls still is lost. 450
The she-wolf assails many sheep and by her wiles*
  Will lay the fold waste when the shepherd lags.
Just as, driven by hunger and eager for blood,*
  The greedy wolf snatches the unwatched fold,
The old serpent who violated paradise
  Wants to violate the holy cloisters.
Let shepherds drive the she-wolves off, lest the flock fall
  Into their maws, which are never sated.
Shepherds, look to preserve the fold; beware she-wolves,

Lest they stain the cloisters with your flock's blood. 460
They strike down souls and they dispatch many to hell;*
  No plague is more to be feared by the monks.

Woman, the death of the soul, should never come near
  To monks; keep her far from the sacred choir.
Let a woman be kept far from a troop of saints;
  Even if she can't win, she'll start a war.
Therefore, O monks, beware lest the sins of the flesh
  Erode in dalliances the soul's virtues.
Why does someone blush if I see he acts badly*
  When he should blush all the more since God sees? 470
If the shire judge should know what he's done, he would fear;
  Why is he not afraid that the Lord knows?
So when the foe prompts deadly evil in the monk
  And tries a thousand ways to deceive him,
Let him believe God's always present everywhere;
  He can't think that he can hide if he sins.
God knows and sees everything; nothing gets past him;
  All things are always revealed to his eyes.
If he's still and defers and does not punish yet,
  He will, and be the Just Judge of merit. 480
Therefore, let brief and empty pleasure not concern
  Monks; rather, let them cultivate God's law.
Let them do that for which they've come, fulfill their vows,
  Lest the foe have a place in the cloister.
Let them read, work, and pray in their separate turns,*
  Never be away from sacred studies,*
Be always zealous in useful, worthy matters,
  For sloth is a most pernicious danger.
The tinder of lust, the occasion of evils,
  It readies a wicked place for their souls. 490

## Chapter 12

**Here he treats those matters in the profession of religion which in the end must be strictly observed according to the inviolable rules of the founders.**

Who stores up the saints' ancient teachings in the heart's
  Vault and vows the order's rules at the start
Knows well that in the cloister he must shun the world,

In which he now, nonetheless, claims a place.
O good cloisterer, who quits the world, don't return
  To it again; nay, flee what it teaches.
Do not seek a soft couch where the flesh is pampered;
  Let cloister be luxury; the book, joy.
Your heart let grieve; your hand, be free; your fast, frequent;
  Your love be not unchaste, nor honor vain.     500
Let water be your drink; food, meager; clothing, coarse,*
  Let your back be scourged; sleep, brief; rest, cut short.
Bend your knee, beat your breast, pray ever with head bared,
  Seek God, spurn the world, and flee from evil.
Face to earth, let your mind cling to heaven, your tongue
  Speak from humble heart and sound humble words.
He who sows words with prayers and lacks a faithful heart
  Tills barren shores, for they'll be profitless.
Not the voice but the prayer, not the chord but the heart,
  Not asking but loving sings in God's ear.     510

Let humble mind, open eye, chaste flesh, pious heart,
  Upright faith, and firm hope show you the way.
If you desire to taste heaven's sweet vintages,
  It's needful that you first drink the world's myrrh.*
Subject yourself to the Prior with humble heart,
  Be peaceful in the order without plaint.
To obey the Prior is the monk's highest virtue,
  To bear the rule's yoke and deny himself.
Do not let your vile clothes, your lowly place vex you;
  Often these things stir up your order's fools.     520
Who debases and considers himself lowly,
  Both fears and flees from a fleeting world's heights,
He is both wise and the one closest to heaven,
  And bears not, empty, a hollow monk's name.

The Lord's law be your rest; the flesh, your gift; the world,
  Your exile; heaven, your home; God, your life.
Bear irksome orders given, take and willing do,
  Be thus in the Lord a religious man.
What the Abbot urges you, though a chore, perform
  Nonetheless patiently if it's lawful.     530
Don't think it base, though it is, and be satisfied
  Because your spirit will be pure in Christ.
Since youngsters come under an old Prior's commands*
  And can't act against the rule's authority,

*Book IV*

Let Priors manage boys gently, in lawful ways,
   And with a humble heart win a bad lad.
Observe that the first yoke chafes a ladened bullock*
   And a new saddle irks a fleet stallion.
Thus a harsh rector aggrieves a youngster and gives
   A reason constant grumbling stirs his breast.   540
Hold these texts in your mind's chambers, O monk, and, chaste,
   Be dead to the world and alive to God.
Earn your perpetual rest with a little labor
   And summon lasting joys with a few tears.
For if the flesh's grief is nothing to you now,
   There'll be peace and rest ever without end.

## Chapter 13

**Here he talks about women in a nun's habit who receive the profession of their order under the veil of a sacred community, but do not observe continence.**

I've finished writing the sins of the errant monk
   And I'll sing you women veiled in the Church.
An order suits men, when properly recruited,
   To be secluded and seek heaven's realm.   550
It is likewise appropriate for pure women
   Beneath the veil to keep chaste vows to God.
As a sacred order binds monks, it binds, too, nuns
   And both shine by their merits before God.
But if frail women should go astray in cloisters,
   They contend with sins unworthy of men.
For a female foot can't stand like a manly foot
   Nor coordinate its own steady steps.
Neither learning nor sense, constancy nor virtue,
   Flourish in women as they do in men,   560
But, whether for their fragile substance or nature,
   You see female morals are unstable.
Those whom an order thinks are wise we see often
   That they are pregnant by their foolish acts.
And they who know Scripture fall most often of all
   By the ignorant sin of a layman.
Since they read the text simply and ignore the gloss,
   They think they do what the Scripture allows.
Scripture's lesson teaches them to try everything;*

Thus, since they read all, they want to try all. 570
To wax and multiply are the laws of Nature,*
  Which God wrote with his tongue at creation.
This Scripture of God's they wish to keep, to render
  Nature's usual laws with pious mind.

Women strive after forbidden things, but rarely*
  Do what's allowed without grumbling inside.
But nuns are more accomplished with certain Scriptures
  And patiently do what these bid them do.
It is written that seeds which good earth doesn't take*
  Do not bring forth fruit but wither away. 580
But a nun also is such earth as lies open,*
  For Ceres there is multiplied tenfold.
And so, since frail women take on onerous weight,
  Sometimes they reasonably seek leisure.
It happens therefore that on Venus' day they take*
  Meats because they have a fussy stomach.
For Venus trusts to Genius[2] her freeborn pupils'*
  Platters, since he'd himself cook for her nymphs.
But a gullet oft sated grows heavy and swells;
  Then, oppressed by the weight of food, it hurts. 590
The venomous lump that toxifies the belly
  Is so heavy it instils fear of death.
But the dish that's taken secretly, where there's no
  Light, often harms and causes grave distress.

## CHAPTER 14

**Here he tells how bishops by their visitations, during which they say they correct them, often make veiled religious women weaker.***

Venus and Genius now teach the cells they govern
  To keep the flesh's laws, not the cloister's.
Genius is the convent's warden and confessor
  And sometimes holds a prelate's position.
Under guise of law, he visits those whom he rules
  In cloister, lawlessly coming to beds. 600
Although in a furred cape when he gives instruction,

---

[2] A marginal comment occurs in CG: "Note that, according to Ovid, Genius is called the priest of Venus." S cites less specifically: "according to the poets."

## Book IV

He vigorously serves them naked law.
By Genius's judgment they are stoned for their sins,\*
  But no fatal stroke is pressed upon them.
Oh! the cleric's virtue when he's keeper of souls;
  How many blessed priestly deeds we see!
Just like another God, he makes whole those he smites,
  Lest a report should fly forth from the cell.
The father holy, so is mother, but the babe
  Is holier since to the cloister born.                         610
I should think this type of sin is most damnable
  Were it not that a woman lightly falls.
You shall not try her strength, therefore, because you know
  That a slight cause can break a fragile thing.\*
For unless a young woman is always guarded,
  She's frail as Nature teaches her to be.
When a new branch begins to grow in the green bark,\*
  Any brisk breeze will snap the tender thing.
In cloisters where wise discretion is the watchman,
  The wheat field is enclosed by high hedges.\*             620
The first instance of this frail flesh was made of mud;\*
  Its spirit came from the mansions on high.
The spirit is willing, the flesh weak; therefore, don't\*
  Seek to be alone with a lone woman.
A virgin should not stay alone with a lone man;
  Though she's not touched, rumor reports a sin.
As in the cloisters, let a guard be in the fields;
  Let the play be proper and the work apt.
Let nuns be allowed without shame the diversions
  Which modesty, laws, and their rule allow.               630
Let thus waywardness not corrupt frail veiled women
  And gentle reins aid them with guiding hand.

What's it to me if a wife by guile fool her man,
  Who knows naught of his wife nor sees her deeds?
But I am amazed at her guile who deceives him
  In whose sight all the ages are revealed.
If men's brides be sacred, the more the brides of Christ
  Should stay by sacred custom pure for God.
A girl is dressed in black garments, her hair cut off,\*
  When at the start she first becomes a nun.              640
Her flesh wears mourning outside so her soul within
  Be lovely and grow white, full of God's love.
Since she's black on the outside, she'll become scorned filth,

And not God's own, if she's blacker within.
But all her external blackness, when she stays pure,
   Is a sign that her character is white.

## Chapter 15

**Here he talks about the praise of chastity, which greatly suits women professed in a religious order.**

   Oh! how beyond all praise virginity does shine,\*
      Which trails the lamb through all of heaven's fields.
   Wedded to Godhead, it shines on earth, forsaking
      The bodily acts that Nature teaches.               650
   An impure woman reeks, a chaste one smells faultless;
      The one clings to God; the other, a corpse.
   Heaped three-fold with a hundred blooms, flowered garlands
      Adorn the virgin's head in God's presence.\*
   The virgin's order transcends the angelic troops,
      Counts more in heaven than a three-fold crown.\*
   By John's witness, a virgin's mind soars before God\*
      Higher, eager like an eagle for heights.
   As a rose growing out of thorns surpasses them,
      So the virgin's status exceeds the rest.             660
   Just as a more precious white pearl pleases the more,
      So, too, the cloistered virgin sworn to God.
   For such a nun is worthier of the cloister
      And holier when she maintains her vows.
   But anyone who seeks cloisters beneath a veil
      Shall be sanctified by the rule she serves.
   If she's been a good woman, it makes her better,
      And ever adds good morals to her ways.
   Although defiled before she's veiled, who chastely lives
      From that point on will have no prior sin.          670
   Thus men aren't allowed to violate hallowed nuns,
      For a sacred veil bears chastity's sign.
   Presuming to defile the bride of another,
      How serious a judgment there will be!
   But know: who violates cloisters sins more gravely,
      Presuming to defile the bride of God.

*Book IV*

## Chapter 16

**After he has dealt with those in a possessory order who offend against their vows, he must talk about those who wander about in the order of mendicant friars. He talks first about those who, aspiring to worldly gain under the pretense of poverty, have taken ownership of almost all the earth.\***

    When he was upon earth, not all whom Christ gathered
        To him were true to God's transforming law.
    But it's not right that the sin of the apostate
        Should afflict those who worship the true faith.        680
    There is no place so fruitless that there's no useful\*
        Plant mixed in with the undesired weeds.
    Nor is some place so fruitful there's no unwanted
        Noxious plant amidst the good and useful.
    Just so, there's no broad assemblage of the righteous
        In which there's no mingling of unrighteous.
    Likewise, their deeds show those friars who are called saints
        And those who will have to be forgiven.
    I don't want to blame all for the sins of a few,
        Nay, let each one be seen for his merits.        690
    But I, messenger to those driven by error,\*
        Bear words the voice gave me that need be said.
    As a shepherd parts sheep from goats, an order parts\*
        Those it thinks are righteous from the wicked.
    This voice's message has more that I'll write for those
        Whom the order designates transgressors.
    I don't wish to put on Peter crimes which Judas
        Committed; let each bear his own burden.\*
    I say an order's duties were saintly at first
        And its initial founders, pious men.        700
    That friar remains blessed who imitates them,
        Who, renouncing the world, seeks to have God,
    Who takes the cloister's poverty and goes beyond\*
        It, patiently bearing the order's rule.
    Such a man is praiseworthy for his high merits
        Because the earth is renewed by his prayers.
    But who hides in the order, form without content,
        Who exhales sermons and breathes in riches,
    To such modern-day men this book proffers its words,
        Just as the people's voice provided them.        710

## Vox Clamantis by John Gower: 'The Voice of One Crying'

The throng of friars overflows with mendicants,
   From whom, ebbing, *Regula Prima* flees.\*
That sort grow soft who used to bear by order's vow
   The hard things necessary to please God.
First they give themselves a name that claims they're "headless,"\*
   And say they're paupers, to whom all bring wealth.
The friars swear that they're the disciples of Christ
   And follow his example's every law.
Their mendacious oath says this, but that's just what suits\*
   Them, as they say who know Sacred Scripture.     720
Now they are like men who own nothing of their own\*
   And yet, in pauper's guise, hold everything.
If there will be grace or damnation for these friars
   I don't know, but all the world teems with them.
The pope is in their hand, who eases their order's
   Rigors and opts to allow many things.
And if the pope's power itself denies their suits,
   Their perverse order slyly approves them.
There's neither king nor prince nor magnate in the world\*
   Who does not confess his secrets to them.     730

And so mendicants outrank lords and from the world
   They take, silent, what their rule flat forbids.
I'd say that these aren't disciples but rather gods,\*
   Whom both life and death bring guaranteed gains.
For each wants the interred dead bodies of worthies\*
   To whom he clung, confessor, here on earth.
But if a corpse is indigent, he won't claim it;
   His piety knows naught without profits.
They don't want to do baptisms, for they won't till\*
   Or tend without a profit in their hands.\*     740
Just as a merchant will buy every sort of goods
   That he can take much profit from them all,
So a greedy friar embraces all the world's
   Affairs to joy in various profits.
They're those whom the grasping world does not abhor but
   Loves and it's handed their status to them.
It's obvious that they are more corrupters than\*
   Reformers; their true name is in their deeds.
A pharisaical scion's grafted on the vine\*
   And its fruit is most bitter to the taste.     750

*Book IV*

## Chapter 17

**Here he talks about those friars who, hypocritically rebuking the people's sins when preaching in public, nevertheless are devoted in private to pleasures and delights.**

    A friar's devout hypocrisy sows sermons
        So that on earth his crop of profits grows.
    He roars frightful words when he damns sinful practice
        In the town square, as if he's God's servant,
    And, like Satan's servant, he glosses and remits
        Those sins when he tarries in private beds.
    And those whom his deep resounding voice first aroused
        His sweet nothings later oil in their ear.
    And thus a sinner ministers sins to others
        And then takes profits for fostering vice.        760
    The friar knows well that when sin withers away
        His profit dries up for eternity.
    Say where a friar comes thrice without taking gain;
        He won't return a way he's had bad luck.
    If you take the sins from the friars' foundations,
        Their lofty house will topple by itself.

    Oh! how the words of the prophet Hosea are*
        Come true, who speaking truly once said this:
    "A certain tribe will arise in the lands who'll eat
        The people's sins and know many evils."        770
    We see in our days that this prophecy has been
        Fulfilled and by it are meant the friars.
    Whatsoever's been necessary for their food,
        Fate ministers it all to them from sin.
    There are no tender morsels that ever refuse
        Friars a bite if they are confessors.
    You see that doves are wont to come to spotless roofs;*
        A dirty tower doesn't get such birds.
    No courts but those of magnates give hospice quarters*
        To friars these days where they wish to stay.        780
    Ants never make their way to empty granaries*
        Nor wandering friars to a wealthless place.*
    Forgetful of the blooms it previously bore,
        They scorn the thorn when the roses are gone.*
    So, too, friars spurn the benefits of friendship
        With one once rich when he can give no more.

Many are friars in name, but few by the rule;
   As some say, Pseudo preaches in that case.*
Their clothing looks poor, but their money box is rich;
   Beneath their holy words they hide vile deeds.     790
Thus poor without poverty, saintly without Christ,
   There are now good men lacking in goodness.
They shout "God" with their mouth and in their hearts adore
   Gold, whose ways everywhere they want to know.
The devil has subjected all beneath their feet;
   They claim hypocritically they keep naught.
So he who preaches "spurn the world" owns worldly things,
   Whilst sheep's clothing conceals the fearsome wolf.
And thus the plebs, enchanted by fictions, will find
   Outwardly holy whom guile grasps within.     800
There's scarcely one who reproaches the other's fraud,
   But each promotes yet more beguiling schemes.
So corrupted by the same vice they're driven more
   And with their frauds they infect the whole earth.
At the least, may the Lord repress those whom he's known
   These days to sin against the age-old faith.
I don't ask they perish but, broken, be mended
   And live up to the role the order grants.

## Chapter 18

**Here he talks about those friars who, as if exempt from the yoke of their order, zealously seek the highest chairs in the university, for the reputation of this world and in order that they become more entitled to hear confessions.**

Let he who is the leader become the servant,
   An example of which Christ provided.     810
But when he who calls himself Christ's disciple earns
   High status, he does not behave that way.
Though he keeps the signs of the poor mendicant, lo!
   The friar aims at a place of honor.
He longs to take the name of Master in the schools,
   Where, exempt, no *regula* restrains him.
He has a room alone, makes what's common his own,*
   And then thinks no cloisterer his equal.
Since cloisterers owe their masters veneration
   And ought to bend their necks down to their feet,     820

## Book IV

Pride and arrogance hide beneath theology
   When an order tends to lead not be led.
Then they penetrate the most eminent chambers;
   There is no court whose gate is closed to them.
Seeing multi-colored displays, the chameleon\*
   Changes and acquires its many colors.
Like it, the friar, pondering what men desire,
   Wishes to become a peer among peers.
Since a court senses the friar is like itself,
   The prelate's rules vanish when he arrives.      830
He wanders around outside and ransacks within,
   No work nor place is unbeknownst to him.
Now doctor, now confessor, now a go-between,
   He puts his hand to all things high and low.
Like the Lord's spirit, the friar wafts everywhere
   And comes to beds when husbands are not home.
Thus, the man away, the impious false friar
   Enters and claims himself the other's role.
So he comes, enticed, to the bedecked bed's chamber,
   And oft he'll be there for the first pickings.      840
So Solomon was born of her who wed Uriah\*
   When a pious intruder took his place.
The friar's devotion fills in for the husband
   And, swelling the family, he fills the halls.
The one beats the bushes, the other gets the bird;\*
   One sows the ground, the other reaps the field.
They both run in the race, but who was far behind\*
   Is the one who unfairly takes the prize.
So the husband often takes in others' labors,
   Though the end's not profit but delusion.      850
The husband believes and joys that he's had offspring,
   But not one fingernail belongs to him.
The hypocrite prays sacred verses with the man
   As if God rose with the words from his mouth.
With the wife he sings Venus' praises and fulfills
   His office in the goddess's high honor.
Thus his labors down low craft a structure up high,
   Whose wretched fabrication needs night's help.

Oh! the friar's compassion aids and entwines all
   And bears another's burden patiently.      860
See, he has come to sanctify not just our souls
   But our bodies also with his labors.

*Vox Clamantis by John Gower: 'The Voice of One Crying'*

He is not the lord's confessor but the ladies',
    Who beguiles them more than Titivillus.*
He's a confessor like the thief gallows display,
    Since he snatches our rights from a woman.*
He's a confessor who turns a bad thing to worse,
    For, washing them, he dirties matters more.
Skin for skin, a friar will give all that he owns,*
    Himself and his property, for our wives.            870
Oh! who shall render due reward to such a man,
    God or the devil? Last words are binding.*
For the end of sin fetches the wages of death*
    When an old sin is filled with a new shame.*
Of those who living perform so many wonders,
    The names are written in the book of death.

Nature has decreed something among bees I feel
    Worth remark, with which friars should be marked.
For if a bee stings, he must pay for his offense
    Since he will no longer have his stinger.            880
Then he stays home in his hive and flies forth no more
    To make some honey from the field's flowers.
O God, if the adulterous friar likewise
    Would lose his bloated pricker when he stings,
That he could no longer harvest blooms in women
    Nor wander from his house into the world!
Because, free from the cause, he would then be free from
    The effect, in which many dangers lurk.

## Chapter 19

**Here he tells how those friars living extravagantly are not in any way necessary to the operation of the Church of Christ.**

When I think about it, I find myself wondering
    For what purpose or reason it happened.            890
Before there was an order of friars, it's said
    The Church contained the ranks that suited it.
The pope was the prince who appointed the others,
    Provided laws so they could rule the folk.
The prelate holds his court; under him the curate,
    Assuming cures, tends the people's burdens.

## Book IV

The prelate's the proprietary who bestows
    The benefice, where the curate holds sway.
The curate then swears that, in the prelate's place, he'll
    Perform assigned tasks at the time adjudged.      900
What seems to you, therefore, the reason or the cause
    The friar holds the place of another?
To bide among white birds is forbidden ravens,*
    Which every flock considers unwelcome,
And all laws forbid the friar who shuns his work
    To bide among the church's citizens.

One must act more cautiously in matters of doubt
    And a case in the world is not like God's.
Should one usurp worldly rights, the force of the law
    Reins him in, does not let him go astray.      910
If another should take my worldly possessions,
    The law will then consider him unjust.
Impartial law does not allow inequity,
    So that one can usurp another's place.
One cannot seize what are another's physical
    Goods unless he deny law's basic rights.
But by some law the friar justifies the deed
    When stealing another's spiritual goods.
If he claims papal dispensation, let us see
    If it was prompted or freely offered.      920
We know that popes never conceded on a whim
    Such things, though an order often begs them.
The pope can be deceived, but He Who Sees Within
    Knows whether it's for love of gain or God.
His tongue solicits cures of souls, his mind wants gold,
    So with both hands the friar grabs our things.
Defrauding our souls, he kidnaps our salvation,
    And beyond that he tries to take our wealth.
That's not what Francis sought, for, abandoning all,
    He openly bore the world's poverty.      930
The earth bears thorns when tillers slacken in the fields,
    So Ceres brings less profit to harvests.
The Church is pierced, stabbed on all sides by envy's goads,
    Which it feels, come untimely from friars.
Thus every good plowman should uproot the thistles
    Lest pharisaical plant foul sacred site.*

*Vox Clamantis by John Gower: 'The Voice of One Crying'*

## Chapter 20

**Here he tells how those friars who live immoderately are not useful in any way to the common good.**

Adam's toil is not for friars, that they gain heaven
   Tending their own or others' vines or fields.
Nay, they already enjoy the physical rest
   They seek and no earthly burdens irk them.                 940
Nor do they perform conspicuous acts of arms
   By which they stoutly serve the public weal.
Thus they belong neither to the knights nor farmers*
   Although both classes grant their wanderings.
Nor are friars clergy, though they try to usurp
   The status, which the school's aegis permits.
Friars take the clergy's honor, not its burden,
   By which they seek to have the foremost chair.
They don't cure the people's souls nor feed their bodies,
   So how do they avail the common good?               950
As you can't count the acorns on a broad oak tree,*
   You can't count the numbers of the friars.
Nay, as a river floods, swollen by waves of rain*
   Or with snow melted by warming Zephyr,
The cowled order has overflowed, but lost its force
   And ceases to go its initial ways.
If things made sense, the dearth of workers demands that*
   Such a lot should have furrows of their own.

David affirms they are not involved in men's toils*
   Nor suffer the lash of positive law.                 960
Neither royal law nor bishop's decrees succeed,
   Seeking to abate the friars' excess.
The world loves those things which are its own and therefore
   Brings its beloved friars prosperity.
They do not plow, weave, reap, nor store up crops in barns;*
   The world feeds them no less on that account.
So their hearts rejoice and aren't wearied with sorrow
   Since they consider the earth heaven's van.
Thus the friar succumbs to his heart's desires and*
   What he seeks fulfills his course in the world.         970
What honor would Hector's son have had, forsook he*
   Arms and boasted, foolish, his father's deeds?
What is Friar Apostate worth if he acclaims

*Book IV*

    Saint Francis, whom he declines to follow?
With their false words the friars obscure the world's sense
    And without light conceal their cursed ways.
There's error in the disorderly order's shade;
    The new sacred order is nigh possessed.
But honor's due to those in a proper order
    Who keep Francis's required mandates.                 980

## Chapter 21

**Here he talks about those friars who frequently entrap into professing their order, by the enticement of misleading recruitments, incautious lads of an age that lacks discretion.**

    I suspect that none of the friars is an adult\*
        When he takes his vows in the beginning.
Yet it's not as if Francis was in his childhood
        When he was drawn to take his order's vows.
Pliant youngsters, taken by a smooth tongue's stories,
        Were not the first ones to venerate him.
I think Francis had arrived at his adulthood\*
        When he took up his task with knowing heart.
And I think his order gave God like followers
        By his eager teaching, not plea nor price.              990
But the old use is gone, for skillful deception
        Now attracts children, who know nothing then.
A youthful order asks soft things from youthful lads;
        Like a stepmother, it's but a semblance.

    As bird calls from a fowler lure birds to his snares,
        So sound from a friar's mouth draws children.
As a bird is caught, unaware of the trap's fraud,
        So boys fall for the friar's sly deceit.
And since the old friar could thus ensnare the boy,
        The brother should have the name of father.           1000
So born from guile the offspring follow the father
        And add their own to the paternal wiles.
And so by itself one root infects a hundred
        Branches, which bear the world the fruits of fraud.
For a boy beguiled by an old friar beguiles,
        By that same example, when he's grown old.
So later they deceive who first had been deceived

And fraud flourishes, multiplied by fraud.
The friars' numbers wax large, but their order wanes
   When a wretch rejoices in wretched peers.*           1010
"Woe unto you who have traversed the earth to make*
   One man convert," God himself has declared.
That was said of Pharisees, but these days I can
   Say it about friars with their new law.

## Chapter 22

**Here he talks about the apostasy of the order of mendicant friars, especially those who undermine the courts of virtually all magnates with the feigned simplicity of their hypocrisy, and very often cause incalculable errors by their fabrications.**

As much good follows everywhere the good friar,
   It happens that much bad follows the bad.
For there are three masters, one of whom each man serves,
   By whom he desires himself to be ruled:
God, the world, and the apostate devil, whose load
   The friars bear, having joined his order.            1020
For God's rule doesn't know him, nor does any free
   Knightly service give him worldly status.
He doesn't have God nor can he possess the world;
   Thus, Satan's own, he submits to his yoke.
Each apostate, the flawed agent or abettor
   Of sin, nourishes what evil he sees.
Solomon is witness that such men are harmful*
   And commit vile sins of their own devise.
Where such a one goes in the world, by art or skill
   He accomplishes much that should be feared.         1030
No wall hinders, no enclosures can withstand him,
   And each dead end is a throughway to him.
He encircles the entire earth by sea and land
   To find everything that can please him most.

He labors in frauds, composes guileful sermons,
   Piles up, expands, and multiplies his tricks.
He plots lawsuits, inflames quarrels into anger,
   Nourishes grudges, and fosters envy.
He bursts the bonds of peace, disturbs the agreements
   Of fellowship, and rips apart good faith.           1040
He promotes unchastity, urges loss of shame,

## Book IV

Wedlock's break-up, stains on the marriage bed.
Pretending good faith, he puts on an honest face
   All the more carefully to cloak his fraud.
But promising good faith, he causes damages
   And if he gives out gifts, it's to deceive.
Under his coarse wool, he wears finely spun linen;*
   His face's candor hides his guileful heart.
When his tongue and venomous lips disguise their words,
   He makes honey venom, venom, honey.              1050
As sinners' acts hide beneath virtuous men's guise,
   So also a man becomes a foul ape.*
Swelling with pride, he often feigns a humble show,
   He whom God's spirit has privately fled.
Whatever honest virtue is in the order
   Francis founded, this one's eager to ruin.
He paints over all things and with his made-up face
   Deceives while his guileful heart lurks within.

You will find written that the ostrich wears feathers*
   Equal to the plumes of heron and hawk.           1060
But its wing is not capable of such swift flight
   And marks it a fraud that pretends to fly.
The hypocrite, too, simulates gold deeds without;
   Within, his wicked mind makes leaden vows.
Indeed there are many such who color their words,*
   Who gratify our ears, sound golden words.
They're leafy with words, but there's no fruit in their deeds;
   They convince simple minds with sweet talking.
But the temple of the Lord excludes such, abhors
   And shuns the polished trappings of their words.    1070
Their tongue declaims the golden words of the poets,*
   Which painted language gilds – but beware them.
The word of faith is plain and earns good men merit;*
   A shifty word preaches against God's plan.
God scorns all eloquence, when a polished surface
   Disguises poison with honeyed language.*
Who sows good words, but acts badly, sins shamefully,
   For performance should follow holy words.*
They whom higher learning nurtures sow obstacles
   Colored with words in subtle polished tones.       1080

Often profit, or empty honor's attainment,
   Makes the friars' sermons more culpable.
Under the guise of wheat, they often pour out tares

When prideful teaching strives for love of praise.
The zealous minds of these skilled men ascribe results
   To their own merits and beget schisms.
Python or Magus is schismatic, since he roils*
   The truth you believe and urges falsehoods.
But wisely stop your ears up against the voices
   Of enchanters, lest your heart cleave to them.            1090
They're not proper friars nor faithful in their love
   For the Church of Christ, as it's kept by them.
The defective Synagogue, which does not instruct
   The full truth, symbolizes their teaching.
That's why that prideful multitude of volumes which
   The Synagogue holds often harms others.*
They are not the true citizens of the Church; nay,
   Handmaid Hagar, treacherous mother, bore them.
Let Hagar thus withdraw, Sarah beget Church's*
   True clergy, and the Synagogue depart.                1100
Piety and Love planted the seeds of the friars,
   Whom ambitious Frenzy at present tends.
Friar Hatred is there, who loathes the bonds of peace,
   Whose lineage has taken the road from hell.
For this professed man has broken his cloister vows
   And won't allow his peers to be at peace.
But to the friar who perceives himself in sin
   And does not stop, to such I say these words:
"The bad man's sin should not erase the just man's praise,
   For light shines with more glory in shadows.         1110
Let each one bear his own burden; let wicked men*
   Take blame for their actions; the good man, praise."

## CHAPTER 23*

**Here he tells how these mendicant friars give themselves over to wandering the world from place to place, seeking in their idleness more sumptuous delicacies. He also talks about their unnecessary structures, which are built in an extravagant manner as if by the powerful men of this world.**

Dispersed Jews figure the friars' diaspora,*
   Whom random wandering drives through the world.
Neither one stays fixed in place, but constantly moves
   Around and changes places everywhere.

## Book IV

Thus the impious friar treks all through the world,
   Nor is there a house where he won't seek place.
In guise of a pauper, he takes alms as plunder
   And with a sheep's fleece hides his wolf's muzzle.          1120
No one deserves goods without labor, and therefore*
   Friars roam all lands in expiation.
Perhaps because heaven has closed its lofty gates,
   They travel seas, rivers, and all the earth.
This I read, that a plant frequently moved rarely*
   Thrives but often suffers a barren fate.
But no rule on the earth lacks for an exception,*
   For the friar's motion makes him prosper.
Wheresoever he guides his steps through desert wastes,
   The world follows him and does him service.            1130
As a packed snowball typically grows bigger when
   Rolled, and in a short time is much enlarged,
The world enriches the friar when he travels
   And what he touches sticks fast to his hand.
Friars likewise strike their wicked deals with the world
   In such a way they're most always secret.

There can appear to be some virtue in many
   Who possess neither virtue nor goodness.
They'll voice suchlike, but the sense will be unseemly
   And much that's unwholesome satisfies them.           1140
They contrive devotion to ornament the Church
   As if such things hold signs of salvation.
A friary built for them rises above all,
   As they pile up stones and cherish carved woods.
It has double doors, fancy porches, halls, such and*
   So many rooms you'd think it the labyrinth.
With many doorways, a thousand different windows,
   A thousand marble columns prop it up.
Their house will be built high and wide, with walls adorned,
   Agleam with many paintings and designs.             1150
Indeed, each cell gleams in which useless friars live,
   Adorned with a carving's painted beauty.
Doorposts have carved symbols that will endure ages,
   With which they think to bind the people's hearts.
Pretending to be Christ, they seek the world, pursue
   It and aspire, secretly, to its praise.
Their holy devotion, disguised in such a form,
   Is feigned and their house is witness to it.

*Vox Clamantis by John Gower: 'The Voice of One Crying'*

But he who sees all and probes the depths of the heart
  Knows that such work is prepared for the world.     1160
Yet Parisian history teaches, by example,*
  A man should be content with less a house.

No officer of the king has homes of his own
  More splendid than the chambers of the friars.
Their garments' plainness will not characterize them
  So much as their house's pomp shall brand them.
Their house holds vigil in its pursuit of building
  A church, eager in flesh, dull in spirit.
Thus the friars' holy devotion shows outside,
  But inside hides a heart's empty likeness.     1170
Such fruitless men, in whom is much impiety*
  But little faith, are like unto the elm.
Say, friar, with your foul heart, what's it profit you
  That you have built so many fine houses?
Be the Lord's house, adorn it with sacred morals,*
  Be religion's tiller, and love virtue.
All's clear in the end; feigning the outside won't work*
  And you'll get no inner rewards from it.
If the fleeting praise of the world should last your days,
  That praise will be shame when you lose heaven.     1180
You belong to the order; let its rule be yours;
  Leave and what you do henceforth is in vain.

## Chapter 24

**Here he tells how those things which used to be virtuous have been generally subverted by sinful men, not only in the order of the mendicant friars, but also in all the degrees of the clergy. In fact, he says that the manner and rule, especially these days, are privately observed according to certain notions of Burnel.**

Only in their clothing are friars different;
  Otherwise, in their manner they're alike.
None of the rules remain that had been made before,*
  For the new order has newfangled laws.
And just as the friars' order is now set loose,
  The standards of the Church become like new.
Yet the sacred order which Friar Burnel once*
  Ordained abides and it is resurgent.     1190

*Book IV*

Now I won't disclose, nor do I wish to disclose,
    All the decrees that Burnel determined.
But I'll speak now in turn of two that he ordained
    And they are at the present time like laws.

The first mandate confers on you every delight;
    Whatever on earth pleases, it allows.
If you'd buy and sell, you can be a merchant, but
    If you'd fornicate, you can fornicate.
Whatever more that the flesh desires are the rights
    Owed nowadays to our blessed friar.    1200
Enjoining further, he bade by the second law
    What's harmful to the flesh be kept afar.
All that is spiritual in turn is held vile
    And flesh ought to have its delicacies.
Let loose your heart, for, indeed, no one shall bind you;
    Go forth your ways wheresoever you will.
Decked in blandishments, Burnel's newfangled order
    Is held worthy since it wants what men want.
Never mind about Bernard, or, for that matter,\*
    Benedict, but let Burnel be my Prior,    1210
Where physical repose thrives, where the worshipper's
    Tongue, slothful in prayer, is almost silent.
So when the order wants to help us with its prayers,
    I leave croaking to frogs and that is that.\*
Should evil come upon us, I believe that these
    Men of the clergy are the greatest cause.
For, indeed, who is able to bring us good times
    When God's order dies among the cloistered
And heavenly devotion flees other clergy?
    That's why salvation flees us everywhere.    1220

## A-Text

Now because the clergy's lot strays from Christ's order,\*    1221
    The world prescribes what God himself forbids.

Because your school, Burnel, is common in the world,
    Everyone there's deceived from head to foot.
But when blessed Gregory's school shone upon earth,\*
    The true faith thrived and bore all fruits in peace.
But now there's a new Arius, like Jovinian,\*

### Vox Clamantis by John Gower: 'The Voice of One Crying'

A Doctor urging schism in church schools.
Where there's light, there's darkness; where a rule of life should
   Teach peoples to take the straight way, there's death.*       1230
So let every good man, gentryman or yeoman,
   Pray for the clergy and send God his prayers.


## B-Text

Since our intercessors discordantly deceive,                            1221
   We people stand, untaught, lost in the world.
What good a body by itself without a soul?
   What good pious clergy that don't help us?
But he who'd sort out the clerics' kind or species
   Shall scarce spot a good man from the top down.
So there's darkness for light, death where the rule of life
   Should teach people the safe road to travel.
I've said about the clergy as others have said:
   It's caused the world more sin than all the rest.           1230
Without a shepherd, the flock is scattered, and lo!
   It seeks out, on all sides, new fields of sin.

# NOTES TO BOOK IV

On Book IV generally, cf. *Mirour de l'Omme*, ll. 20833–1780.

ll. 9–10: cf. Luke 9: 62, I Corinthians 9: 10; also Book III, ll. 1055–6, and note.

ll. 13–14: cf. Matthew 6: 24; also Book III, l. 137.

l. 18: cf. Galatians 6: 5; also ll. 698, 1111, below.

ll. 19–20: cf. Book III, Pro., ll. 11–13, 17–18, and note.

ll. 21–2: probably a reference to Benedict's Rule 33, forbidding private property, unless excepted by the abbot. Monks should own nothing; all things should be held in common. Cf. ll. 235–6, below.

ll. 25–8: cf. *Mirour de l'Omme*, ll. 20857–68.

l. 33: built around a pun on "fessus" (wearied, worn out) and "professus" (one who's taken religious vows).

l. 34: "Domnus/dompnus": an especially monastic form of "Dominus," properly a ranking dignitary in the Church; see also l. 323 and note, and ll. 327, 329, 331, 333, below.

Ch. 2 prologue: "primi ordinis statuta": i.e., the Rule of St. Benedict of Nursia, acknowledged father of monasticism.

l. 41: a final step in becoming a monk was the ritualistic "death of the self," signifying an end to worldly desires, variously celebrated liturgically and symbolically depending on the order (e.g., the Benedictine practice of covering the newly professed with a funeral pall). Cf. ll. 379–88, 639–41, below.

ll. 43–8: cf. Alexander Neckam, *De Vita Monachorum*, ed. Wright, II. 175, ll. 15–16.

l. 49: see note to l. 41, above.

l. 54: "tenui victu": "meagre fare": In principle, monastic meals provided "enough, but no more." Benedict's Rule, e.g., chapters 39–40 allowed two daily meals with a pound of bread, two cooked dishes, and a quarter-liter of wine allotted each monk per meal. Only the sick were permitted meat other than fish.

## Vox Clamantis by John Gower: 'The Voice of One Crying'

l. 78: cf. John 14: 6.

ll. 79–82: adapted from Nigel of Longchamp, *Speculum Stultorum*, ed. Mann, ll. 881–4.

ll. 81–2: required communal prayers are sung at each of the seven (or eight) canonical hours: prime (6 AM), terce (9 AM), sext (noon), none (3 PM), vespers (sunset), compline (bedtime), matins (2 AM), and lauds (sunrise, earlier in summer, later in winter); the latter two are often counted as a single hour, according to season (cf. Benedict's Rule Chapter 8). Benedict's Rule Chapter 22 required monks to sleep in their habits, to be prepared to rise for prayers at matins and lauds.

l. 87: cf. Godfrey of Viterbo, *Pantheon*, col. 88.

l. 91: cf. Godfrey of Viterbo, *Pantheon*, col. 88.

l. 97: cf. Godfrey of Viterbo, *Pantheon*, col. 88.

ll. 105–6: virtually *verbatim* Peter Riga, *Aurora*, I Kings 225–6.

ll. 109–10 virtually *verbatim*, Ovid, *Fasti*, 1. 205–6.

l. 111: virtually *verbatim* Ovid, *Ars Amatoria*, 2. 475.

l. 112: virtually *verbatim* Ovid, *Fasti*, 4. 396.

l. 114: virtually *verbatim* Ovid, *Fasti*, 4. 400.

l. 115: *verbatim* Ovid, *Metamorphoses*, 1. 104.

l. 117: virtually *verbatim* Ovid, *Metamorphoses*, 1. 106.

l. 119: partially from Ovid, *Metamorphoses*, 1. 103.

ll. 129–30: verbal play on "modus" (tun), "modus" (moderation), and "absque modo" (immoderately).

ll. 131–2: Benedict's Rule Chapter 38 requires silence at mealtime in order to hear the scriptural readings which accompanied all meals.

ll. 135–6: tonsure was required of clerics in minor and major orders, as a sign of humility and obedience.

l. 145: virtually *verbatim*, Ovid, *Metamorphoses*, 8. 830.

l. 147: *verbatim* Ovid, *Metamorphoses*, 8. 835.

ll. 149–50: adapted from Ovid, *Metamorphoses*, 8. 836–7.

ll. 151–3: adapted from Ovid, *Metamorphoses*, 8. 837–40.

l. 163: adapted from Ovid, *Ars Amatoria*, 3. 647; Benedict's Rule Chapter 22 requires monks to be ever ready to rise to do the work of God, and pre-

## Notes to Book IV

scribes "no excuse for the drowsy." Cf. also Chapter 43, listing punishments for late-comers to prayers and meals.

ll. 165–6: cf. *Confessio Amantis*, Pro. 474–8. The image of Venus beneath the hair shirt may also owe something to the *Vers de la Mort* of Hélinand de Froidmont: cf. *Mirour de l'Omme*, ll. 11401–12.

ll. 170–2: Benedict's Rule Chapter 38 prescribes sign language for use during meals to avoid interrupting readings.

l. 173: *verbatim* Nigel of Longchamp, *Speculum Stultorum*, ed. Mann, l. 1167.

l. 175: *verbatim* Ovid, *Ars Amatoria*, 3. 503.

l. 176: virtually *verbatim* Ovid, *Ars Amatoria*, 3. 504.

l. 177: virtually *verbatim* Ovid, *Metamorphoses*, 8. 466.

l. 179: virtually *verbatim* Ovid, *Ars Amatoria*, 3. 509.

ll. 183–6: Benedict's Rule Chapter 5 notes that a monk of ill will who murmurs in his heart will not be pleasing to God.

l. 191: proverbial.

ll. 209–10: cf. Benedict's Rule Chapter 7, on respect between monks; cf. also *VC* III. 451–60 and note, above.

ll. 215–16: "corrode," "corrodia": a play on forms of "corrodo, -ere" (to gnaw to pieces, wear away), and "corrody," in Gower's day a provision of food and lodging by a religious house for an individual who could be a lay person.

ll. 219–20: "fundacio prima" = daily allotment of food, lodging, and clothing of a monk,

ll. 225–8: the combination of St. Jerome (September 30) and St. Benedict (March 21) in this context is somewhat puzzling. Both are presented as ascetics in the *Legenda Aurea*, mortifying their flesh with extreme fasts and bodily laceration – in that sense they offer stark contrast to the self-indulgent. On the other hand, only Benedict gave to the poor, stripping his monastery during a famine.

ll. 235–6: cf. ll. 21–2 above, and note; also Benedict's Rule Chapter 38, on commonality of goods (citing Acts 4: 32).

ll. 237–8: cf. Benedict's Rule Chapter 59, on the sons of nobles and of the poor.

ll. 243–6: cf. *Mirour de l'Omme*, ll. 16123–8.

l. 246: cf. Luke 9: 62.

ll. 269–70: cf. Benedict's Rule Chapter 38.

ll. 277–8: cf. *Mirour de l'Omme*, ll. 20845–6; Chaucer, *CT* GenPro 179–81.

l. 290: "monstrum templi": An alternative translation would be "abomination of the temple": cf. Daniel 9: 27; Matthew 14: 15.

ll. 301–2: cf. Ecclesiasticus 19: 27; *Confessio Amantis*, I. 2705–7, and Latin marginal note.

ll. 305–6: virtually *verbatim* Peter Riga, *Aurora*, Leviticus 659–60.

ll. 307–10: virtually *verbatim* Peter Riga, *Aurora*, Leviticus 663–6.

ll. 311–12: virtually *verbatim* Ovid, *Ars Amatoria*, 3. 249–50; 311–13: with a play on "turpis" (ugly/shameful).

ll. 317–18: Benedict's Rule Chapter 59 allowed for the admission of the children of "those who have nothing" – hence plowmen, etc.

l. 323: a play on "dompni" and "domini," monk and lord respectively.

l. 324: cf. Matthew 7: 13–14; also *VC* III. 251–4, above.

Ch. 7: cf. *Mirour de l'Omme*, ll. 21133–80.

ll. 327, 329, 331, 333: "Dompnus": see notes to ll. 34, 323, above.

ll. 337–8: Saint Bernard = Bernard of Clairvaux, a founder of the Cistercian Order (or Bernardines), originally an offshoot of the Benedictines which resisted attempts at reforms, among them the cessation of manual labor, a central element in Cistercian life. Bernard was known for his extreme abstinence: cf. *Legenda Aurea* (August 20). St. Maurus (French Maur), founder of Glanfeuil Abbey (later St. Maur sur Loire), the first Benedictine house in Gaul, was chosen by Benedict to establish the Benedictine Order in France.

l. 346: "Domnus": see notes to l. 34, 323, 327, 329, 331, 333, above.

Ch. 8: canons were unbeneficed priests who lived together in proximity to, or within the close of, a cathedral; unlike monks, they were not cloistered and could perform mass on demand at diocesan parishes. Augustinian canons, or canons regular, abjured private wealth, in accord with the Rule of St. Augustine, though not all canons did this: these latter are "secular canons." The priory of St. Mary Overey in Southwark was a house of Augustinian canons.

l. 347: "decreta" (decretals) = Papal letters, replies (with the weight of decrees) to curial questions.

l. 350: "possessores" = secular canons.

ll. 359–70: cf. *Mirour de l'Omme*, ll. 21157–80.

ll. 359–60: "Canonici/canone": canon law derives from "canon"; hence a lawless canon is a verbal contradiction.

l. 364: Augustinian canons' habits were black, with a black scapular – hence the name "Black Canons"; in contrast to Premonstratensian canons who wore white – hence "White Canons."

Ch. 9, ll. 371–88: cf. *Mirour de l'Omme*, ll. 21061–72.

ll. 379–88: see l. 41 above, and note; also ll. 639–41, below.

l. 395: adapted from Alexander Neckam, *De Vita monachorum*, ed. Wright, II. 175. 21.

l. 397: *verbatim* Alexander Neckam, *De Vita monachorum*, ed. Wright, II. 176. 3.

ll. 401–2: *verbatim* Alexander Neckam, *De Vita monachorum*, ed. Wright, II. 178. 25–6.

ll. 403–4: virtually *verbatim* Alexander Neckam, *De Vita monachorum*, ed. Wright, II. 177. 29–30.

ll. 405–30: virtually *verbatim* Alexander Neckam, *De Vita monachorum*, ed. Wright, II. 176. 5–30.

l. 425: *verbatim* Ovid, *Ars Amatoria*, 2. 465.

l. 431: *verbatim* Alexander Neckam, *De Vita monachorum*, ed. Wright, II. 187. 19.

l. 433: *verbatim* Alexander Neckam, *De Vita monachorum*, ed. Wright, II. 187. 21.

ll. 434–7: virtually *verbatim* Alexander Neckam, *De Vita monachorum*, ed. Wright, II. 187. 23–5.

l. 439: *verbatim* Alexander Neckam, *De Vita monachorum*, ed. Wright, II. 187. 28.

ll. 441–2: virtually *verbatim* Alexander Neckam, *De Vita monachorum*, ed. Wright, II. 188. 1–8.

ll. 443–4: *verbatim* Alexander Neckam, *De Vita monachorum*, ed. Wright, II. 188. 7–8.

ll. 445–6: adapted from Alexander Neckam, *De Vita monachorum*, ed. Wright, II. 188. 23–4.

l. 449: cf. Ovid, *Fasti*, 3. 85, with reversal of lamb and wolf, making woman the latter.

l. 451: adapted from Ovid, *Ars Amatoria*, 3. 419.

ll. 453–4: *verbatim* Ovid, *Tristia*, 1. 6. 9.

ll. 461–6: virtually *verbatim* Alexander Neckam, *De Vita monachorum*, ed. Wright, II. 188. 25–30.

ll. 469–80: virtually *verbatim* Alexander Neckam, *De Vita monachorum*, ed. Wright, II. 178. 5–18 (lines slightly rearranged).

l. 485: Benedictines were enjoined to pass their day in prayer, manual labor, and reading.

l. 486: *verbatim* Alexander Neckam, *De Vita monachorum*, ed. Wright, II. 177. 32.

l. 501: adapted from Nigel of Longchamp, *Speculum Stultorum*, ed. Mann, l. 677.

l. 514: "mirra" = myrrh (from Arabic "murr," bitter); Christ refused wine mixed with myrrh at his crucifixion; cf. Mark 15: 23.

ll. 533–40: Gower differs from Benedict's Rule Chapter 30, preferring gentle treatment rather than enforced fasts and beatings to correct errant boys.

ll. 537–8: virtually *verbatim* Ovid, *Remedia Amoris*, 235–6.

ll. 569–70: built around a play on "probare" ("approve"/"test, prove"); cf. I Thessalonians 5: 21.

l. 571: cf. Genesis 5: 28, frequently mis-applied: cf. Wife of Bath, Chaucer, *CT* III. (D) 28.

l. 575: adapted from Ovid, *Amores*, 3. 4. 17.

ll. 579–80: cf. Matthew 13: 3–8; Mark 4: 3–8; Luke 8: 5–8.

ll. 581–94: the underlying meaning here is that the nuns are pregnant. This is carried forward throughout Ch. 14, below.

l. 585: "Veneris...diebus" = Fridays.

l. 587: Genius here and throughout Ch. 14, following, clearly derives from the *Roman de la Rose*: cf. ed. Lecoy, ll. 19398 ff.

Ch. 14 heading: "ordinarii" = strictly speaking, bishops (sing. "ordinarius"). In canon law, an "ordinarius" is one holding power directly (e.g., the pope) or a delegated agent, i.e., a priest or other official wielding vicarious power given by the bishop: here, to take confession in nunneries. Gower's criticism covers both.

ll. 603–4: cf. John 8: 3–8, and a play on "stone" = rock, also testicle.

## Notes to Book IV

l. 614: *verbatim*, with minor word-order reversal, Nigel of Longchamp, *Speculum Stultorum*, ed. Mann, l. 854.

ll. 617–18: virtually *verbatim* Ovid, *Ars Amatoria*, 2. 649–50.

l. 620: virtually *verbatim* Ovid, *Ars Amatoria*, 3. 562.

ll. 621–2: cf. Genesis 2: 7.

l. 623: cf. Matthew 26: 41; Mark 14: 38; cf. *Mirour de l'Omme*, ll. 14161–72.

ll. 639–41: cf. l. 41, and note; also ll. 379–88, above.

ll. 647–8: cf. Apocalypse 14: 4 (Vulgate).

l. 654: "florida serta" from Ovid, *Fasti*, 6. 312.

l. 656: "trina corona" = papal tiara, with three crowns symbolizing Father of kings, ruler of the world, and vicar of Christ on earth.

ll. 657–8: cf. Apocalypse 12: 14 (Vulgate).

Ch. 16 heading: "ordine fratrum mendicancium" = mendicant friars, of which the four major orders in the fourteenth century were the Franciscans (Friars Minor), Carmelites (Calced and Discalced), Dominicans (Friars Preachers), and Augustinians (Hermits). Gower's general source for his attack on the friars from here to the end of Book IV is William of Saint-Amour's *De periculis novissimorum temporum* (1256), on which most subsequent anti-Fraternal criticism was also based.

ll. 681–2: virtually *verbatim* Ovid, *Ex Ponto*, 4. 4. 3–4.

ll. 691–2: cf. Book III, Pro. 11–13 and note; also ll. 19–20 above and 709–10 below.

l. 693: cf. Matthew 25: 32–3.

l. 698: cf. Galatians 6: 5; cf. also ll. 18 above and 1111 below.

ll. 703–4: friars, like monks, were to own nothing of their own, but as originally conceived by Francis were to live a more austere life, having no monastic home and begging their food.

l. 712: "Regula Prima": probably a reference to the "Regula Primitiva," the only rule given by Francis to his followers: live in accord with Christ's teaching and walk in his footsteps.

l. 715: "Acephalum" (headless): Friars, by decree of Innocent III, owed obedience only to the pope; no bishop had authority over them.

ll. 719–20: cf. II Timothy 4: 3–4.

l. 721: adapted from Nigel of Longchamp, *Speculum Stultorum*, ed. Mann, l. 2213.

ll. 729–30: possibly an allusion to the controversial Dominican Thomas Rushook, confessor to Richard II; however, Richard was merely following in a tradition of friars as royal confessors that included Edward II, his wife Isabella of Valois, and Edward III. Criticism in France of friars as royal confessors dates to William IX, with much bitterly satiric verse produced, some of which Gower may have known. See also ll. 779–80, below.

l. 733: "discipulos": Francis of Assisi took eleven followers with him to gain the approval of Pope Innocent III for his new order in 1209; unsurprisingly, these became known as his disciples. Cf. also "disciples," *Mirour de l'Omme*, l. 21481.

ll. 735–40: cf. *Mirour de l'Omme*, ll. 21469–80.

l. 739: unlike masses for the dead, there was no fee for performing baptisms.

l. 740: "Non erit in manibus culta": possibly an intended contrast with Benedict's Rule, prescribing manual labor for monks.

ll. 747–8: virtually *verbatim* Nigel of Longchamp, *Speculum Stultorum*, ed. Mann, ll. 977–8.

l. 749: "pharisea": The Pharisees were a conservative Jewish sect known especially for their sanctimoniousness. Cf. Matthew 23: 5–7; also 936, 1011–13, below.

ll. 767–70: cf. Osee 4: 8 (Vulgate); cf. *Mirour de l'Omme*, l. 21397, there attributed to Zephaniah.

ll. 777–8: virtually *verbatim* Ovid, *Tristia*, 1. 9. 7–8.

ll. 779–80: cf. 729–30 above, and note.

l. 781: virtually *verbatim* Ovid, *Tristia*, 1. 9. 9.

l. 782: adapted from Ovid, *Tristia*, 1. 9. 10.

l. 784: virtually *verbatim* Ovid, *Fasti*, 5. 354.

ll. 788–800: cf. *Mirour de l'Omme*, ll. 21625–48; cf. also *Confessio Amantis*, V. 1874–83, where "Pseudo" is applied to lollards, not friars.

l. 817: having a room = rejection of vow of mendicancy.

ll. 825–6: cf. *Confessio Amantis*, I. 2698–702; *Cinkante Balades*, XVI. 1–2.

ll. 841–2: cf. II Kings 11: 27 (Vulgate). David "intrudes" on Bathsheba after Uriah is killed; for Solomon, cf. II Kings 12: 24 (Vulgate).

l. 845: proverbial, cf. Walz, 85a; *Confessio Amantis*, II. 2355–6; *Mirour de l'Omme*, ll. 8898–901.

ll. 847–8: cf. I Corinthians 9: 24; *Mirour de l'Omme*, ll. 14365–7.

l. 864: "Titivillus" = a demon, reputedly the nemesis of scribes.

l. 866: "rapit" = "seizes/snatches," but also with the overtone of "rapes."

l. 869: cf. Job 2: 4.

l. 872: "ultimo verba ligant": "last words are binding," so here "demon" is intended; proverbial.

l. 873: cf. Romans 6: 23.

l. 874: proverbial, cf. Walz, 31a, b, c; also *Confessio Amantis*, VII. 5115.

l. 903: *verbatim* Ovid, *Metamorphoses*, 2. 632.

l. 936: "pharisea": cf. l. 749 above, and note; and 1011–13, below.

ll. 943–8: the reference is to the traditional "three kl," into which medieval political thought divided society – clergy, knights, farmers.

l. 951: *verbatim* Ovid, *Ars Amatoria*, 3. 149.

ll. 953–4: *verbatim* Ovid, *Fasti*, 2. 219–20.

ll. 957–8: alludes to the plague-induced labor shortage, particularly of field workers, beginning 1348–9; Edward III's Ordinance of Laborers (1349) and parliament's Statute of Laborers (1351) were the result, requiring all under sixty years of age to work, no wages above pre-plague levels, restrained food prices, and making it a crime to poach anyone's servant, or give alms to able-bodied beggars.

ll. 959–60: cf. Psalm 72: 5 (Vulgate); also Book III. 2097–8, and note.

ll. 965–6: cf. Matthew 6: 26–8.

l. 969: cf. Psalm 72: 7.

ll. 971–4: cf. *Mirour de l'Omme*, ll. 21517–28; Hector's son = Astyanax.

ll. 981–90: cf. *Mirour de l'Omme*, ll. 21553–64.

l. 987: St. Francis was probably in his early twenties when he founded his order.

l. 1010: e.g., "Misery loves company"; proverbial, cf. Walz, 222; also *Confessio Amantis*, II. 261–3.

ll. 1011–13: cf. Matthew 23: 15; also above 749 and note to 936.

ll. 1027–8: cf. III Kings 11: 1–11 (Vulgate), Solomon here taken as an example of apostasy, in his case the result of his predilection for women.

ll. 1047–8: *verbatim* Peter Riga, *Aurora*, Deuteronomy 89–90.

l. 1052: "turpis Simea": the ape, generally presented as an image of degenerate man, given particularly to usury and lust.

ll. 1059–64: *verbatim* Peter Riga, *Aurora*, Leviticus 667–72.

ll. 1065–70: virtually *verbatim* Peter Riga, *Aurora*, Deuteronomy 29–34.

ll. 1071–2: *verbatim* Peter Riga, *Aurora*, Josue 99–100.

l. 1073: virtually *verbatim* Peter Riga, *Aurora*, Deuteronomy 35.

l. 1076: virtually *verbatim* Peter Riga, *Aurora*, Deuteronomy 36.

l. 1078: *verbatim* Peter Riga, *Aurora*, Genesis 862.

ll. 1087–90: virtually *verbatim* Peter Riga, *Aurora*, Numeri 445–8.

l. 1096: *verbatim* Peter Riga, *Aurora*, Genesis 1042.

ll. 1099–100: adapted from Peter Riga, *Aurora*, Genesis 841–2.

l. 1111: cf. 18 and 698 above.

Ch. 23 heading: cf. *Mirour de l'Omme*, ll. 21181–780.

ll. 1113–14: *verbatim* Peter Riga, *Aurora*, Genesis 1403–4.

l. 1121: proverbial; cf. Walz, 78.

l. 1125: proverbial.

l. 1127: proverbial; cf. Smith and Heseltine, "Rule without exceptions."

ll. 1145–8: virtually *verbatim* Alexander Neckam, *De Vita Monachorum*, ed. Wright, II. 192. 21–2.

ll. 1161–2: the couplet seems to have some currency: it appears *verbatim* in Thomas of Eccleston's *De adventu fratrum minorum in Angliam*, col. X.

l. 1171: "ulno": presents a problem, in that, if translated as transcribed by Macaulay, the word hardly fits the context ("ulnus" = "a measure of land"). Stockton suggests reading "ulmo" = "elm," and cites as proverbial; cf. Smith and Heseltine, "To ask pears of an elm"; and further Ovid, *Metamorphoses*, 14. 661–4. For the whole passage ll. 1170–4, Gower may also have had in mind Matthew 6: 30–4.

ll. 1175–6: *verbatim* Alexander Neckam, *De Vita Monachorum*, ed. Wright, II. 193. 1–2.

## Notes to Book IV

l. 1177: cf. Luke 8: 17.

l. 1185: "Regula nulla manet": i.e., Francis's expectation of poverty, piety, mendicancy.

ll. 1189–212: cf. Nigel of Longchamp, *Speculum Stultorum*, ed. Mann, *passim*. Burnell (or Brunellus) the Ass decides to found his own new religious order, combining all of the permissive rules he has liked in all the orders. As Macaulay noted, "What is said here...expresses the spirit of these rules rather than the letter."

l. 1209: "Bernardus" = Bernard of Clairvaux, founder of the Cistercian abbey there and architect of the Cistercian Order; Benedictus = Benedict of Nursia, founder of the Benedictines.

l. 1214: "Linquo coax ranis": cf. the poem of that title by Serlo of Wilton (d. 1181), expressing his disillusionment at the condition of theological study in the Oxford schools.

l. *1225 (A-text): Gregory I ("The Great") was pope CE 590–604.

ll. *1227–8 (A-text): i.e., John Wyclif. The Cyrenaic presbyter Arius (d. CE 336) contended that Christ was subordinate to God the Father, and hence the two were neither consubstantial nor coeternal – a belief ("Arianism") in direct contradiction to Trinitarianism, and declared heretical at the First Council of Nicaea, in CE 325. Jovinian (d. CE 405) rebelled against ascetic monasticism, promoting among other beliefs clerical marriage, and cessation of fasting, prompting Jerome (who called Jovinian the "Epicurus of Christianity") to pen a rebuttal – *Adversus Jovinianum* – a virulently anti-feminist tract in two books, much quoted in the Middle Ages by many, among them Chaucer and Gower. The comparison here of John Wyclif to these two heretics.

# BOOK V

Book V begins as though it will be a critique of knighthood (*milites*), construed initially as the second estate of the three-tier social system Gower set out to analyze. It turns into a discussion of the commons, however, as the poet realizes that the system he has proclaimed will guide his account proves to be no longer useful to a discussion of a society that has outgrown it. The separation of a knightly class from the upper nobility, and the former's consequent interspersion alongside the commons, Gower saw reified by the protocols of parliament, which by at least the Good Parliament of 1376 had become bicameral, the peerage sitting apart from the commons, whose elected speaker reported the results of its deliberations to the upper house. The peerage comprising the House of Lords was restricted to some seventy or so families whose heads traditionally received periodic notification from the king that their counsel was required. The rest of the nobility necessarily came to belong to the House of Commons, represented there along with everybody else by Members of Parliament. If not already belted knights, elected by regional authorities, parliamentary members received the title "Knights of the Shire" for the duration.

Gower's commentary on the *milites* here must accordingly be taken to refer to knights and gentlemen, i.e. the gentry who constitute the rural elite, the shire landholders who were retained by magnates who expected loyal service in their affinities in return for lands. This is Gower's own class, and he chastises it severely, seeing around him contemporaries neglectful of their traditional responsibility to protect the Church, widows and orphans, and the common good. Rather than the contracting of marriages conjoining families to the mutual benefit of both and the buttressing of the social and economic fabric of rural England, such as these committed themselves to sexual dalliance and the pursuit of empty fame. Pursuing gratification with beautiful young women or seeking upward mobility with wealthy dowagers, the gentry fail to seek out useful marriages with women of neighboring estates who will serve their manors as mainstays of rural society and bring forth the next generation to ensure the continuation of the family and its prosperity (ll. 293–332).

Gower's name for his love-besmitten young gentryman, Amans, calls attention to another overlap with the *Confessio Amantis*. Both Amans and Genius, it could be argued, have been imaged in lesser avatars of their later versions by this point in the *Vox Clamantis*. Gower also assails those gentry who seek reputation rather than, or in addition to, sensual pleasure, squandering their wealth and energy on a worldly fame that neither benefits society nor in the end serves their own well-being. Their vain activities won't earn them God's praise, the only true form of renown.

The rise of the gentry, as well as the appearance of wealthy freeborn peasants who comprise the yeomanry, Gower believes, has blurred traditional lines of distinction. Worse, well-to-do serfs, allowed by their masters to accumulate wealth, imitate the freeborn and further complicate the appearance of rural society (noted in 7. 237–8). Some yeomen lead lives so attractive on the surface that their betters imitate *them* and revel in coarse rural delights rather than pursuing ends more suitable both to their stations and to society (7. 239–40). Gower's ire has been stimulated most grievously, however, by his own experience of those bound agricultural laborers who refuse to perform their obligated services, and by the free laborers who hire out their services, demanding wages well in excess of those specified by the Ordinance (1349) and Statute of Laborers (1351) – two failed attempts to maintain an economic status quo in the labor-scarce aftermath of the Plague. Throughout, Gower evinces little sympathy with the working rural poor: they must be kept burdened and suppressed lest their endless insubordination upset the world. His disdain for the oppressed, and his fear of their violent capabilities, most certainly preceded his experience of June 1381.

Gower also takes note of an urban elite, comprised of two classes: the Staplers (merchants who import and export goods), and the Franchisers (shop owners who sell products to those living in the cities that increasingly dominated national life). These two classes collectively comprise the *cives* (economically, and in consequence politically empowered citizens) of the cities. Only they are authorized, by agreements with crown and city, to function as import/export dealers and artisans/shopkeepers. The well-being of cities depends upon a fruitful cooperation of these two categories of citizen, for between them they control government and justice. When they are in accord, the common good will be enhanced; when not, profits will dwindle and the city fail to prosper. The sins Gower attributes to the two types of entrepreneur are Usury and Fraud, the former for the Staplers and the latter for the Franchisers. The Staplers lend money at exorbitant rates, and the Franchisers sell products that don't meet minimum legal standards, a circumstance illustrated by the poet's exposure of the deceits practiced by various crafts. The uncontrolled pursuit of (unjust) profits thus will erode the spiritual well-being of the community.

Among the intriguing parts of Book V is the harsh criticism of an unnamed member of the urban elite who has risen from *minor* to *maior*, from a low position in society to the heights of mayor, a position for which Gower finds him unsuited based on his social status and behavior in office, manipulating the mayoral court over which he presided to pervert justice. This could be John of Northampton, an ambitious populist leader of the drapers throughout the 1370s who became mayor of London, just as Gower was finishing his poem, in the immediate aftermath of the Rising of 1381.

The city's well-being suffers as well from an unspecified "man of tongues" (perhaps Northampton's arch-rival Nicholas Brembre) who roils the political situation by keeping alive residual anger from old, unsettled disputes. Such a man, Gower says, must be extracted like a rotten tooth from the body politic before the poison spreads. Both politicians will come to bad ends. Northampton was exiled in 1385 (but later permitted to return through intervention of Queen Anne and John of Gaunt); Brembre was executed by decree of the Merciless Parliament of 1388 for his perceived role in Richard's misadministration of the realm. The book concludes with an appeal for a rector who will guide the city properly, by the terms of the law and established custom.

*Book V*

# HERE BEGINS THE FIFTH BOOK*

## Chapter 1

**After he has spoken about those in clerical status who ought to govern spiritual affairs, he must now speak about those in knightly status who are obligated to defend and uphold secular affairs.**

I've talked about the clergy and now I'll explain*
   How the ancient system pertains to knights.
From the outset, knighthood was furnished great honor,
   Established at first for three purposes.
Firstly, it ought to defend the rights of the Church
   And, secondly, foster the common good.
Thirdly, it shall support the orphan's feeble right
   And strengthen with its might the widow's cause.
For these reasons the law desires the knight in arms
   To be ever quick to take up its fight.             10
Thus, indeed, the knight conquered his foe long ago,
   Wherefore his fame lives in the world anew.
Nevertheless, the knight took up arms not for fame,
   But waged his deeds for the sake of justice.
The knight who preserves the manner of that system
   Should be rewarded with well-deserved praise.
But if a knight should wage his wars for vainglory,*
   He won't deserve any praise just for that.

Tell me now also: what honor has a victor*
   If love of a woman can vanquish him?              20
I don't know what the world will answer me to that;
   I do know this: it won't bring him Christ's praise.
If one would enjoy honor, let him earn honor,
   And bear the task his burden lays on him.
The one whom Venus shows the way to arms will come
   In the end to naught but well-earned folly.
It's not fitting that lead be mixed with shining gold
   Nor that Venus would know a true knight's deeds.
Whom she has snared, a woman rarely releases,
   But rather wraps yet more in foolish love.          30
A man once free who willingly enslaves himself
   Should be held more foolish than any fool.
It makes sense that a knight should avoid the battles

In which he'll be captured when he can't win.
A wise man enters no fords where he'll surely drown,
  But rather curbs his way at deadly sights.

## Chapter 2

**Here he tells how a knight who blazes with love for a woman, and involves himself in the exercise of arms out of lust, by no means deserves the honor of praise for it. He also describes the weaknesses of such love, whose passions in turn have hugely opposing impulses.**

Oh! if a knight would consider the ways of love,
  So quickly changed, he would not suffer them.
Love is not all one hue, but clashes with itself;
  It moderates with no moderation.                                40
Love lays bare and conceals, disjoins and reunites,
  And often drives happy hearts mad with grief.
Love is a corrupt judge; marrying opposites,
  It makes less noble the natures of things.
Contrast accords in love, knowledge is ignorant,
  Wrath jests, honor soils, indigence is rich,
Delights grieve, praise reproves, despair is full of hope,
  Hope dreads, harms profit, profits are harmful.
Anxiety tastes good in love, bitter is sweet,
  Winter blooms, chills sweat, sickness nourishes.              50
That you beware, O knight, the dangers shown to you,
  Read about the forms that love's disease takes.

Love is sick health, troubled rest, a rightful error,*
  Warlike peace, a sweet wound, charming evil,
An anxious joy, a crooked road, a gloomy light,
  Gentle harshness, an airy lump of lead,
Both blooming winter and a withered bloomless spring,
  A thorny rose, an errant unjust law,
Weeping laughter, laughter weeping, control unbound,
  A hostile comrade and a loyal foe,                            60
A fickle firmness, a contradictory wish,
  Hope hopeless in itself and doubtful faith,
Black whiteness, luminous blackness, bitter honey,
  Savory gall and a charming prison,
Irrational reason, fatuous discernment,
  A wavering judge, an all-knowing fool,

Book V

>Food indigestible and drink that causes thirst,
>>Unsatisfiable mental cravings,
>Living death, dying life, harmonious discord,
>>Blabbering mind, mute speech, hidden fever, 70
>A poor prosperity, prosperous poverty,
>>A servant prince, subject queen, needy king,
>Drunken sobriety, insane mercy, Scylla's
>>Port, a harmful cure, and a safe journey.
>Love is a cuddly snake, a fierce lamb, a meek lion,
>>A timid hawk and a rapacious dove,
>A fatuous school rendering more fatuous
>>A student whose mind is ever eager.

## Chapter 3

**Here he describes the form of a beautiful woman, for the desire of whom the ensnared hearts of knights are very often abandoned by reason's judgment.**

>Our fearful Amans beholds his woman aglow,*
>>In whose face is the redness of the rose, 80
>Her golden tresses, her attractive little ears,
>>The smoothness of her brow, which gleams so white,
>Her youthful cheeks, her eyes that shine just like the sun*
>>And are embellished by her steadfast gaze,
>Her nose so straight, and her daintily flared nostrils,
>>Her honeyed lips – and her mouth's breath is sweet –
>Her even, well-spaced teeth more shining white than milk,
>>The beauty of her finely chiseled chin,
>Her face's luster that makes her ivory neck gleam,*
>>In company with her crystalline throat, 90
>And whiter than snow shines the whiteness of her breast,
>>On which two white fruits, so to speak, are fixed.

>He views her long arms, plump with a touch of roundness,
>>Whose embraces he thinks celestial realms.
>He sees that her hands and adorned fingers glitter
>>And that no soft wool is softer than they.
>And he sees youthful shoulders unused to burdens,
>>In which no bone shows, and he marvels more.
>At her side, he sees her stretch her slender figure
>>And no straight line stands straighter than she does. 100

He sees her approach coming forth to the dances
   And he observes the measure of her step.
The Sirens' singing cannot compare with her voice
   Nor scarce sounds an angelic voice like hers.

He sees that her head glows, encircled with bright gems,
   And that her clothes are splendid and suit her.
Wanting to appear elegant, she's all dressed up
   That Amans might be ravished by wonder.
All of her limbs are seen to be so well-arrayed
   That God on high must have fashioned that work.      110
The part on her head, her wide brow, her milky neck,
   Her mouth, small lips, her glow and bright eyes please.
Resplendent are her pate, brow, eyes, nose, teeth, mouth, cheeks,*
   Chin, neck, hands, breast, and foot, without a flaw.
Not one single blemish has nature bequeathed her:*
   Her beauty sweeps from her head to her feet.
The shape of the girl transcends human appearance:*
   She's like a goddess, beyond humankind.
Above all the others whom grace of form adorns,*
   She is that blessed phoenix without peer.      120
Her clothes will be grand, her head cinched with a blossom,*
   A modest blush surrounding her fair cheeks.
Her shape pleases, her snowy hue and flaxen hair,*
   Her bright elegance fashioned without art.
Any man looking on her would be so taken
   That he would tender, prone on earth, his prayers.
If she should turn her countenance to her Amans,
   The man stands transfixed by her piercing gaze.

When someone sees so sweet, adorned, and elegant
   A feminine sight, but more angelic,      130
He thinks she's a goddess and puts into her hands
   The power of life and death over him.
Then, as he turns her wondrous figure in his mind,
   He can't turn away from her as he leaves.
Except for her his sight captures nothing outward;
   Inward the sting of love pricks through his heart.
Just as a rock unmoving stands, just so he stands
   Nor from the sight, as if entranced, does move.
Thus his mind's eye, by the flesh's darkness blinded,
   Grows weak and to his own downfall he sinks.      140
He knows not what he sees, but is inflamed by it

## Book V

So that he rages blind in his blind love.
Colder than ice, hotter than a consuming fire,
  He freezes thus with fire and burns with cold.
Just like a bird rolling in lime and smeared with it,*
  So he asserts his claim and burns with love.

Thus Love tames all, whatever Nature has brought forth,*
  And yet itself remains untamed by all.
It imprisons and ransoms, binds and loosens bonds,
  Subdues all to it, but is free from all.                    150
It limits, delights, lessens and restores Nature,
  Who laments in love but can't joy without.
Love commands everything, excepts scarce none its rule,
  For it grants oft that saints are sinners too.
There is no one able to escape immune from
  Its laws, but it's immune from everything.
His prudence fails the man whom his valor could not;
  No living man safely withstands Love's laws.
There is no recompense for the wounds that Love gives;
  It wounds mankind but bears no wound itself.               160
Since Love brandishes its wounding dart ere piercing
  Hearts, flee cautiously then farther away.
There are no arms that can win battles against Love
  Nor has anyone firm peace pacts with it.

Love is a trustful state quickly collapsed by grief;*
  Who takes it up can't know how it will end.
The knight is not unconflicted who tells himself,
  "Oh how I know love galls me secretly!"*
The mind of Amans is driven by countless wiles,*
  A rock swept on all sides by coastal seas.                 170
Love submerges nobleness, which, resurfacing,*
  Often won't recognize the noble way.
Always creating uncertainty in the mind,
  Love lays hearts bare and then swirls over them.
And so blind love arouses foolish blind lovers*
  So no lover sees what should be proper.
Say, what won't he dare in the fury of love's charge?
  Longing for embraces, he knows no fear.
He can't see the leaves in the woods, the soft grasses*
  In the fields, the water in full streams.                  180
So rather as if blind he takes gains and losses
  As his impulse constrains his mind to love.

## Vox Clamantis by John Gower: 'The Voice of One Crying'

Not heaven nor earth, Acheron, sea, star and sky*
   Can hinder his undertakings by force.
Often enduring rain loosed from heavenly clouds,*
   He'll just lie freezing upon the bare ground.
Night and winter, long journeys, and bitter sorrows*
   Are the rewards that Love offers to fools.
Love has as many pains as the serfs have complaints,
   Its madness and mercy alike on earth.     190
Amans feels his injuries, yet, burning, persists
   And seeks out the occasion of his pain.

Oh! since Love is not treatable by any herbs,*
   Neither strength nor sense escapes from its woes.
No one's able to avoid this inborn disease;
   Nothing except Grace alone can cure it.
Oh! how burdened is our nature, since it forces
   Us, driven to our own downfall, to love.
Oh! our nature, which nobody can elevate,*
   Which does not excuse the evil it does.     200
Oh! our nature, made of intertwined opposites,
   Both of which it's not allowed to follow.
Sensual pleasure wages war with chastity;
   What the body wants, the spirit forbids.
Oh! our nature, which is fashioned in such a way
   That it can't avoid what it ought not do.
Oh! our nature, which dissolves the power of frail
   Reason and like a beast holds fast to sin.
Our arts don't help, the wound rages incurably;*
   The wiser we are, the more then we rave.     210
And if you should wish to suppress the flame safely,*
   Foresee its manner before you thence fall.
Until the seas calm and Love tempers its practice,*
   You should in the meantime seek a refuge.
You'll conquer if you flee, be conquered if you fight:*
   Be a hare fled, not a lion conquered.
A woman does not flee from flames or warlike bows;
   The frailer she is, the fiercer her fire.
As a woman deceives men, so a man, women,
   When love like a fox sings words like a wolf.     220
Gulling a trusting girl is not a praiseworthy*
   Achievement but a work of fraudulence.
No man's art is subtler than the art of Venus;
   By her art Love seeks rights which last for years.*

Book V

## Chapter 4

**Here he says that, where the pleasure of women's love dominates a knight, it truly extinguishes in him all valorous service.**

    A valiant knight need not fear a bodily wound,
        For which the praise of the world will be his.
    But let him fear wounds of the heart, which blind delight
        Inflicts with incurable fiery darts.
    Physical wounds are treatable, but Galen can't*
        Make that one sound who languishes from love.*          230
    If a knight should keep womanish ways, his honor
        Will depart, an orphan from noble stock.
    When a wise knight takes on the guise of one stupid
        And foolish, reputation deserts him.
    When sensual love holds the spirit in its snare,
        Reason is deprived of its common sense.
    When carnal shade obscures the light of human sense
        And reason's mind withdraws into the flesh,
    Human reason, scorned by the flesh, enters service
        And scarcely maintains a handmaiden's place.          240

    But blind love's scales do not weigh equally for all
        Nor does Love give rewards deservedly.
    For no reason she drives the faithful from office
        And gives their places to the unfaithful.
    Sometimes she denies me a richly deserved grant
        Which she gives you when you're not deserving.
    As if you'd have to discern colors without light,
        So blind love dispenses your rights to you.
    Now, however, it is as if every knight serves
        Love and seeks at her gates to have his fate.          250

## Chapter 5

**Here he talks about those knights, one of whom exercises the labors of arms for woman's love, the other for the world's foolish reputation; however, in the end each of the two perishes in vain, without the reward of divine praise.**

    One part of knighthood seeks the love of a woman,*
        Another, what the world's high praise may say.
    Everywhere knights hope for fresh acclaim and attempt

To win the reward which Fame may hand them.
God knows then by what right a knight would gain respect,
  Whether the world or woman's love gives it.
If he seeks the world's lauds, the wealth of Croesus flows*
  Forth so that high praise ring out for his gifts.
Then he sows gold, garments, jewels, and horses just
  Like seed that he hear a harvest of praise.          260
But if a knight should choose for himself woman's love,*
  It will cost him more than the price he pays.
Everything that Nature or God has brought to him,
  Body, property, soul, his goods, he'll give.
Yet when he has performed the acts of his labor
  And both praise and deceit alike fail him,
When the world's chatty fame has not come to his ear
  Nor chaste love rendered to him love's treasure,
Then, deceived, he says, "Alas how Fortune thwarts me!
  After so long, my efforts are fruitless."          270
He gets it rather late, who thus foolish laments,
  Since no one but himself has cheated him.

The world brings heavy burdens, woman heavier;
  It nudges, she pushes; it strikes, she slays.
When a knight thinks he's conquered a woman's power
  And she grants all his claims with loyal love,
He's more conquered just then, when he thinks he's conquered,
  And the woman, conquered, reconquers him.
Or even if the knight should opt for worldly fame,
  It, too, in a short time passes in vain.          280

Oh! why then does a knight desire the world's honors,
  A world whose honor lacks the praise of God?
Why does a knight find the crowd's vain words an honor
  And seek to have them at the cost of death?
In fact he's heedless, when conquered by a woman,
  How, guilty before God, he's lost honor.
What, therefore, does the bold spirit of the knight want
  In a void that is devoid of reason.
Unless God is its author, praise is sung in vain,
  And honor that rings without God is base.          290
I don't know what praise or honor a knight desires
  When God knows that he's not worthy of it.

Book V

## Chapter 6

**Here he talks for a time about the commendation of a good woman, the proven virtue of whose character transcends all the world's delights; he also talks about the evil woman, whose wiles a wise man scarce withstands.**

    One woman there was through whom heaven's God himself
        Descended, from whose flesh he became flesh,
    In whose honor those women are worthy of praise
        To whom praise's honor is rightly due.
    All things that are good arise from a good woman,
        Whose honest love provides a wealth of love.
    A good woman's price is beyond gold or silver
        And no price is equal to her value.         300
    The tongue cannot tell or the pen describe her worth
        Whose character is marked by total good.
    Her noble husband sits at his gates with honor
        And her household contains every good thing.
    Her servants are dressed in thickly layered clothing,
        Which her hand, busy with useful skills, makes.
    Idleness does not tempt her feelings to run wild;
        Modest, she keeps herself at women's work.
    A good woman should ever get praise for merit,
        Which wicked blabbing tongues can't take away.         310

Yet a woman who has behaved improperly
        Has not defiled those who have remained true.
    The things we say of fools don't concern the upright
        And a thief's crooked schemes, one who's honest.
    Although the name for a whore is harsh, it won't touch
        The woman attended by modesty.
    Although harlots are infamous, a shameful name
        For shameful women won't shame chaste women.
    If one angel is good and another is bad,
        The bad one's sin can't injure the good one.         320
    It is not fitting that the shameful woman's name
        Besmirch the chaste or detract from her praise.
    And while foul useless plants may grow in with a rose,
        The rose is no different than before.
    It always was and will be, when guilt discloses
        Crimes, that those who see such things call them out.

But let what I write here be to the sure honor
   Of those whose beauty observes modesty.
Therefore I say, let blame depict blameworthy wives
   That more praise be given the praiseworthy.            330
It helps to know evil that we better shun it,
   That we beware the slippery way at hand.

Evils are wont to come from an evil woman,
   Who is indeed a second plague to man.
Woman, a sweet evil, sly with her blandishments,*
   Crushes the mind, that masculine glory.
His senses, riches, virtues, strengths, his fame and peace
   She destroys with her various deceits.
She deceives a thousand ways and sets a thousand
   Sly snares that a single man might be caught.            340
For such a woman comes decked out with shining gems,*
   With gold and clothes, so that she might deceive.
Her garments are fitted, her swelling breast restrained,
   Her neck lengthened by a display of chest.
She adorns her head with tinted hair and veils, and
   With golden pomp of gems endows her work.
That she better attract frenzied eyes to herself
   She wears various rings on her fingers.
It's not her work to soften wool by spinning it,*
   But, adorned, to be able to snare men.                350
A comely woman must be seen by the people;
   From out the crowd perhaps there's one she draws.

Ah! how oft a lover's kindled with guileful words*
   When a pretty shape's cunning tongue tempts him!
In its place is charm, if a woman doesn't have*
   Pleasing words with which to coax foolish men.
Clasping her hands, she will dispatch abundant sighs,
   And her words won't lack a weighty promise.
She'll oft sound somewhat throaty, yet laugh pleasingly,*
   Flustered tongue driven by a flustered tone.*         360
What can't art do? She learns to weep becomingly;*
   Whom she can't draw by speech, she gulls with looks.
With grimaces and tears falling down her false face,
   She deceives and pretends she scarce can talk.
The cunning girlfriend will get sick when she has to
   And grieflessly her public face will grieve.
Sirens were sea hazards who with melodious voice*

## Book V

    Held fast whatever ships they encountered.
So he who frequently hears female blandishments
    Can't stir his foot away secure from ruin.     370
Just as a single hand can paint many figures
    And will vary a work with many forms,
So one woman multiplies her many lovers,
    Whom Venus makes believe her foolish charms.
What wise Nature has granted to her she transforms*
    And her sly tongue pleases with its lisping.*
For fluently she twists her many fools around,*
    Pleases while now laughing and now weeping.
She paints all portions of her delicate body
    And adds to the form God himself gave her.     380
I'm loath to bring the accusation of this plaint,
    Which one more adept has brought in the past.
Of course, I refer to poems the seer Ovid wrote
    In his work, whose words don't belong to me.

As a young woman tries to preserve her beauty
    And strives to increase it in different ways,
An old one hopes to refresh the color she's lost,
    A task she will attempt with her lotions.
Just as dread winter acts so that no lilies bloom
    And the thorns left from the lost rose freeze hard,*     390
So old age plunders old women of their beauty
    And leaves a wrinkle where once was a blush.
When age brings another hue, an old woman's skill
    Covers her ancient cheeks with colored tint.
For then it's the mode that a woman should adorn
    Her face so that she might glow with make-up.
With art she draws her eyebrows and with blush her lips;
    That they please more, she mixes in some tint.
She will adorn her grey hair with cosmetic dyes*
    And seek by art a better hue than was.     400
She goes out with hair thickened with that she has bought
    And for some money makes another's hers.
Thus the old maid comes, shoulders hid with golden hair,*
    And craftily puts on a young girl's face.
She often wears yellow, since wrapped in yellow robes*
    Her own coloration does her less harm.
As many blooms as new earth brings forth in warm spring,*
    That loathsome woman has for her own care.
Don't think all pretty women paint themselves one way,

For each one is practiced in her own art. 410
One seeks a blush, another wants snowy beauty,
   One paints her cheeks, another washes them.
Another will fast desperately and let blood*
   And cause herself to be completely pale.
For she who is not pale is thought a peasant girl;
   "This suits, it's a lover's true hue," she says.
A woman assails our minds in a thousand ways;*
   If you don't look to yourself, you'll be lost.
The venom of feminine love destroys your sense
   And by grace alone one escapes its snares. 420
She gives sweet embraces, plants on you soft kisses,*
   But fosters poisons deep in silent heart.
Many men have perished due to women's deceits;
   Nothing frightens women, who think all's fair.
They dare all things that imperious lust commands;
   Both fear and reason ebb and shame itself.
Since beauty will often contend with modesty,*
   There are rarely chaste maids among the fair.

Woe to a man who contracts marriage with folly!*
   His marriage couch won't be without sorrow. 430
She'd have kept her pact had she not been so lovely,
   As this well-known tale so often teaches.
Whom Venus inflames, no guardian can preserve;
   A foolish woman knows no boundaries.
When Venus and woman agree on time and place,
   These two won't fail to get that which they seek.
A woman's watchman will be foiled when she will not
   Watch herself, if he be Cato himself.*
Doves will first undertake to avoid their dovecotes;*
   Beasts, caves; cows, meadows; and sea birds, water, 440
Ere Venus' girl seeks out a foolish lover
   And can't contrive a spot for their doings.
The many shells the shore, the blooms a rose garden,*
   The many sleepy grains the poppy has,
The beasts the woods sustain and the fish in the sea,
   The feathers with which birds flutter the air
Don't add up to a sum that can be called equal
   To the sins a wicked woman contrives.

The world is deceitful, a woman even more,
   For paradise revealed that she is false. 450

Lo! the world is a wolf hiding beneath lamb's fleece;
   Where first it licks you, in the end it gnaws.
But that's at least far off, whereas the snaky dove
   Incites harms at hand in marriage chambers.
For she's indeed a snake, who through a thousand twists
   Deceives and, striking, slays peace-loving hearts.
The strong or wise man who remains unharmed by her
   Is celestial, for earth can't conquer her.
Not Sampson's strength nor David's sword had any worth*
   Against that one, nor Solomon's wisdom.*       460
So why does today's knight try so hard to conquer
   What so many men couldn't overcome?
There's not a man whom past dangers make circumspect,
   For still he falls into the trap he sees.
Who forbids lesser men to take example from
   Greater? But our love doesn't allow that.
The rash warrior goes to war and, forgetful
   Of his old wound, takes up his arms again.

## Chapter 7

**Here he tells how a well-ordered gentry guarantees the advantage of common security to all the other classes.**

   Oh! how in this land a bold distinguished knighthood
      Maintains its proper place when it lives right.
   If he not labor for worldly praise or profit       470
      Nor untamed love subdue his iron heart,
   The knight will then triumph with never-ending praise,
      His name ennobled for eternity.

   If knighthood has been good, then God will stand by it,
      That the knight conquer with unconquered sword.
   If knighthood has been good, its good fame will awake,
      Which now lies flat in bed vanquished by sleep.
   If knighthood has been good, then when peace is revived
      A man has his affairs with his own wife.       480
   If knighthood has been good, then it will scatter wide
      The Church's foe and it will grow in faith.
   If knighthood has been good, then the harsh assessment
      Which sounds in the land will be without note.

If knighthood has been good, then peace will not be slow
  To come and then prosperity returns.

Who's a good knight does not know how to be afraid,*
  Nor bears a feeble spirit's inmost wounds.
Who's a good knight treads down all the pride of the world,
  Fiercely conquers evil with humble heart.          490
Who's a good knight wages war in the name of Christ
  And with his hand protects the commonwealth.
Who's a good knight knows well and proves that in the world
  The start of peace comes from the end of war.
For such a knight is truly worthy of our praise,
  Whatever praise his code has in this world.

## Chapter 8

**Here he tells how the wickedness of the gentry harms and offends all the other degrees of society by its unfitness.**

But if a knight has borne his arms improperly,
  Much fearful wicked damage will ensue.
If knighthood's wicked, its shield and spear are useless;
  Its sword won't gleam with honor in its hand.      500
If the knight is wicked, who'll defend us in arms?
  If he proves soft, it will go hard on us.
If knighthood is wicked, how can priest and plowman
  Manage when war shows up on their doorstep?
If knighthood's wicked, a fierce foe that's been gentled
  Is allowed to renew his misconduct.
Thus the good knight brings good; the bad, fearsome evils,
  Who carries in his hands our protection.
A clean hand confers blows of wondrous gallantry;
  The one stained in its own filth flees the field.  510
Guilty, he pauses when he plans his wicked deeds,
  And the work reels in his unstable mind.
Arms thrive by good morals, else fortune vanishes;
  Neighbor to vice no gallantry endures.

Oh! warrior knight, be thus zealously moral,
  Oppose vice, and support the public weal.
It means nothing if I vanquish all the world's hosts

## Book V

And then, disarmed, lose to a single vice.
And who's not more to blame than a knight slow to arms
   But quick to profit in the assizes?        520
He's a vile knight who's like a hawk to his tenants
   And a quail in the presence of his foes.
He's not worthy of the embraces of Rachel,*
   Whom Mars' renowned arms decline to bless.
The comely girl who confers love on such a man
   Errs and ignores what love's honor should be.
Foul Leah is more suitable for such husbands
   Who subscribe least to the deeds of valor.
Let such go to Leah and wed her to themselves;*
   The timid are Leah's and not Rachel's.        530
No man should be loved who is not worthy of love;
   He who denies its burdens should lack love.
Not without the anxious work of seven years' time*
   Seized by love had Jacob Rachel's embrace.

A knight who takes up arms for the sake of profit
   Will not be valorous in his service.
It is the vulture's nature to seek men's corpses,*
   To follow warring camps to find its food.
They who want war are like that, who follow the camps,
   Who covet profit in hungering for spoils.        540
Birds dread the swift hawk because it preys on neighbors
   And every herd fears the ferocious wolf.
You who prefer your pleasures, knight, and abandon
   Your arms and look to have your peace at home,
And plunder much spoil from the poor like a lion
   And snatch the land's fat to make others starve,
Urged by both languor and the delights of pleasure,
   Should flee the profits of greed and likewise
Undertake the daunting duties of bloody war,
   And then I think vice will show you its back.        550
A knight should put his honor before his profit
   And, offering prayers to God, he'll conquer all.
Alas! I see that honor now comes after gold;
   The world and the flesh are preferred to God.
The gentry increase in number, decline in deeds,
   Their honor and their mission hollowed out.

*Vox Clamantis* by John Gower: *'The Voice of One Crying'*

## CHAPTER 9

**After he has spoken about those in the gentry who ought to preserve the commonwealth inviolate, he must now speak about those who are obligated to endure the tasks of agriculture, necessary to the food and drink required for the sustenance of humankind.**

> Now that you've heard what the gentry are, I shall say
>   More about the rest, how they should be ruled.
> For below gentry there remains a rural class
>   In which peasants tend grainfields and vineyards.          560
> They are those who by the sweat of their hard labor*
>   Grow food for us, as God himself decreed.
> Theirs is rightfully our first father's prescribed way,
>   Adam's, that he received from God on high.
> For God told him, when he fell from Eden's bowers
>   And began his travails upon earth's ways,
> "O sinner, the labor and the sweat of the world
>   Are yours, in which you will consume your bread."
> So if the farmer continues God's arrangement
>   And thus takes cultivation's work in hand,                 570
> Then the fertile field will bear grains as usual
>   In their seasons and grapes will be ample.
> Yet now the husbandman scarce seeks to take that work,*
>   But in his vices loafs on every side.
>
> Among commoners who stray with wicked intent,*
>   I think the furrows' servants most at fault.
> They are slow, they are absent, and they are greedy;
>   For doing the least they seek the most pay.
> The practice has come about that one villein wants
>   More than two sought to ask in former times.              580
> A single one not long ago was more useful
>   Than three are now, as those who know well say.
> For just as the fox, the woods ringing on all sides,
>   Seeks out lair after lair and enters it,
> So now the servants of the furrow lawlessly
>   Seek out place after place in which to hide.
> They want the leisure of magnates, yet they've no way
>   That they can feed themselves unless they serve.
> Both God and Nature have ordained that they should serve,
>   Yet neither he nor she can govern them.                    590

## Book V

All fief holders lament these people in their turn;
   Everyone needs, but none can govern them.
Villeins of old did not scorn God so brazenly*
   Nor pilfered they the world's noble estate.
But God inflicted servile work upon villeins
   In order that it might curb their proud hearts.
And liberty, which ruled the serfs and subdued them
   By its law, remained safe for the freeborn.

Yesterday's experience has made us more informed
   Of the perfidy wicked villeins have.                   600
As nettles reduce grain's yield if they're not controlled,
   Unruly villeins aggrieve honest men.
A villein pricks someone soothed and soothes someone pricked,
   Nor does the old order's prescribed way err.
Let law cut down the noxious nettles of the mob*
   Lest the thistles should ruin the nobler grain.
Unless crushed first, the villein kind crushes that which,
   Noble and worthy, the freemen possess.
Its open deeds teach that the villein class is base
   And disrespects the freemen's decency.                  610
As curved ships heel over, improperly laden,*
   So do crude villeins unless weighted down.

God and our toil convey and grant all things to us;*
   A man will earn no wages without toil.
Let the villein therefore commit his limbs to toil,
   Postponing leisure, as he ought to do.
As a barren field, though seeded, the granaries
   Betrays and no autumnal yield brings home,
So, too, the wretched villein, the more he's seeded
   With love, deceives and drives you into ruin.            620
Serfs don't perform rightful services willingly
   Nor do they have good will toward the law.*
Whatever service their bodies are made to do,
   Their inclination is always wicked.
Miracles happen contrary to nature; God
   Alone can break the powers of Nature.
It's not humanly possible that anyone
   Of the serfs' kind is able to reform.

## Chapter 10

**Here he talks also about the different workers from the rabble who, employed under the rule of others, ought to be subjugated to their various tasks for the common good.**

    And there is another sort allied to villeins,
        Which is common and lacks any status.         630
    They're the ones who decline to hire out by the year;
        A man will scarcely keep them by the month.
    And some of them I hire with contracts by the day,
        Now here, now there, now for me, now for you.
    From a thousand of them, there's scarce one laborer
        Who cares to keep his agreement with you.

    These are the people who act badly in your hall,
        That last as long as your food and your drink.
    When you have hired such a table companion,
        He disapproves of all the usual food.         640
    All salted foods do harm nor will cooked dishes please;
        Unless he gets a roast, he's quick to groan.
    No small beer nor cider is suitable for him;
        Unless you do better, next day he leaves.
    Oh! why should he seek for himself delicious drink,
        Whom spring water has nurtured from his birth?
    Born from the pauper's kind and also poor himself,
        He demands a lord's fare for his belly.
    Ordained law is no help, for there's no rule for such,
        Nor does anyone see to their misdeeds.         650
    This is that sort without reason, like beasts, for they
        Do not love man nor think that God exists.
    Unless there is dire justice meted out to them,
        I think the lords will yield to them shortly.

## Chapter 11

**Because no province by itself alone brings forth all the different kinds of things necessary to human use, merchants are established, among other helpers of the world's citizens, through whom the goods of each region are distributed by turns, whose activities consequently he now intends to write about.**

## Book V

If I turn my writings to the urban elite,
    What can I say? They've distinction [*honor*] and burden [*onus*].\*
The burgess's *honor* is he has great riches;
    His *onus*, he strives for ill-gotten gains.
His honor is to hold the office of mayor;\*
    His *onus*, to keep the laws of office.     660
*Honor* fades but *onus* stays; if he acts badly,
    I know *honor* won't lessen his *onus*.
The city's commons consists of two different sorts;
    They are the merchants and the artisans.
The one must have the assistance of the other
    So that there is common love between them.
For bonds constrain the two forcibly into one
    When they are thus allied by trust and love.
While steadfast love between the greater and lesser
    Lasts, the town joys and the polity thrives.     670
Concord makes prosperous the people's least affairs
    And discord turns the greatest to nothing.
While the people's union lasts, the city's mutual
    Justice will, too, and everyone applauds.
Otherwise, mutual losses vex the cities
    And profits then are harder to come by.

Just as I've heard, so I'm able to bear witness:
    Just governance scarcely sits the bench now.
The man obsessed to have the splendors of the world,
    That he enhance his name, does not know God.     680
I intend and fault specifically none but those
    Who've neglected God because of the world.
But who wishes to render the heart's just judgment
    I think will grant his own guilt before God.
For we all thus attend to profits at all hours
    That scarce one festal day remains for God.
Oh! how the Jews preserve the Lord's sacred Sabbath,
    Not buying nor selling nor seeking gain.
Divine law commands man keep the Sabbath holy,\*
    Sanctify the day by worshipping God.     690
When God rained manna once upon the wilderness,\*
    What people did then is a sign for now.
The sixth day they took double, then looked on their toil,\*
    Because the seventh day is not for work.
But all things are permitted us by modern law;
    What are sacred feasts compared with profit?

People today don't care how others make money
   As long as they can have their own profits.
Tell me who your companion is, or beloved friend,
   Whose friendship does not bring you a profit.     700
Say what burgess in the town is now free of fraud;
   If such there be, my town scarcely knows him.

## Chapter 12

**Here he talks about the two daughters of Avarice, namely Usury and Fraud, who arise in the city and provide a hidden service for the dealings of burgesses. But first he will speak about the status of Usury, who administers her own law specifically for the city's power elite.**

Oh! how subtle the sisters Fraud and Usury*
   Are, to whom townsfolk seem to cede their rights.
They, whom Mother Avarice alone has brought forth,
   By various city fathers were begot.
Usury's father is a great man rich in cash,
   But Fraud was bred by the rabble in shame.
Thus sister Usury is the more nobly born,
   Whom the rich man proclaims is his daughter.     710
She strives to hide 'neath lock and key large sums of cash
   With which she finances her crooked schemes.
This sister prospers only from another's loss,
   For the other's losses bring her profits.
This powerful sister has built mansions in town
   And yet she destroys the rural estates.
This sister enriches the burgess, but then she
   Takes the knight's gold and lays claim to his lands.*

The Lord forbade Usury by eternal law,*
   As our readings in Scripture clearly show.     720
Wouldn't he be clever who could depose a gloss
   Against this text, given by God Himself?
The merchant who proves his interest allowable
   Is able to do this in our own times.
Since nakedness bares all, Usury dresses up
   Deceitfully, concealed by her false guile.
Thus Usury's face is hidden, painted with Fraud's
   Blush so that on the outside she seem fair.
If the trickster thus change her appearance by fraud,

Book V

> Her nature stands just as it was before. 730
> So does the huckster fool God with his trickery*
>   When he hides such wickedness by his skill?
> Or is God blind, who sees everything everywhere?
>   He sees through Usury's garb and hates her.

## Chapter 13

**After he has spoken about Usury's might, now he intends to speak about Fraud's deceitfulness, which, as if by common counsel, slyly procures and arranges all the things that must be done by each and every person in buying and selling.**

> That sister does grave things, but the other, graver,
>   For she is pervasive in every place.
> Where Usury pays suit, however, Fraud does too;
>   One paves the way, the other does the job.
> Usury associates with those urbanites
>   Whose treasuries are considered peerless, 740
> But Fraud persists among all the common's tradesmen*
>   And lends them her counsel with all her might.
> She works clandestinely, for one whom she deceives
>   Suffers the harm done before he sees it.
>
> Standing outside the doors, Fraud's apprentice proclaims
>   Various wares, all that you wish to have.
> He names as many things as stars are in the sky;
>   He pulls you in with shouts of this and that.
> Those whom his words don't entice, he draws in by force;
>   "Here is," he says, "just what you seek, come on." 750
> So the apprentice pulls people in with a cry
>   And there the Master is with tricks and guile.
> For when old Fraud composes her deceptive words,
>   No one is able to escape untricked.
> If someone smart comes in, Fraud is smarter than he,
>   And if he's dumb, he's dumber when he leaves.
>
> Fraud charges double price for everything, claiming
>   That Paris or Flanders charges that much.
> Lying oaths provide what is lacking in the goods
>   Because she will wound God for a penny. 760
> For Fraud will allow no limbs to remain on Christ

When she goes after profits with her oaths.
By her skill, however, we often see mansions
   Fill up and a house hold naught of its own.
Then the burgess seeks an office deceitfully*
   So plebs will greet him upon bended knee.
So it is that a mayor rises furtively
   In his city who is minor than all.
But when the time comes that everything is laid bare,
   Dishonor subverts what had been honor.                     770
For when each gets his own, the crow clothed in the plumes*
   Of another flies naked as before.

And Fraud goes town to town to see to the wool farms;*
   From this she plans her moves in the Staple.
And doesn't Fraud seek the wines Gascony presses?*
   People say rightly that this causes harm.
Fraud dwells in the cask, draws the wine and sells it too,
   And often issues a new from an old.
Fraud also sells garments, which she'll make you look at
   In poor light, so beware, therefore, the more.                780
Let your touch do the seeing when light deceives sight
   So the draper's artful trick won't fool you.
And God forbid someone would sell spice without Fraud,
   All the while mixing old in with the new.
Fraud takes a tithing for herself upon the scales,
   Frequently, by guileful weight, a sixth part.

## Chapter 14

**Here he tells further how Fraud everywhere governs all the city's crafts and victuals by her sly management.**

Craftsmen don't want to put aside the laws of Fraud,
   By whose authority they sell their goods.
She forges cups, assays the silver and the gold,
   Takes for herself the purer from your pure.                  790
From glass she fashions jewels precious to the eye
   And gives them names that further the deceit.
If you have cloth from which you want your clothes to come,
   Fraud cuts it and keeps a piece for herself.
Though it's a simple task and she measures falsely,

## Book V

She charges more than the whole thing is worth.
But what shall I say about fur, black, white, and gray?
   Isn't it likely Fraud's helped herself first?
At first glance, Fraud measures it well enough in length,
   But tomorrow it will be a foot short.                             800
Fraud also makes feeble armor, selling it dear,
   That makes the horses of the squires lame.
She encourages the drips from tallow candles
   And, as a result, they drip constantly.
Fraud also makes saddles, leather leggings, and shoes;
   Now Fraud has caused each craft to be her own.

Then, too, Fraud sells the people meat and also fish,
   But their taste buds grieve when first they try it.
Fraud also makes bakers stand in the pillory
   Though the gallows would suit them more as thieves.           810
As the jug testifies, Fraud is mistress of beer;*
   Thetis scarcely knows how to be Ceres.
Fraud the cook prepares dishes, makes ready the roasts,
   And summons all the market to their food.
As boundless clamor echoes constantly in hell,
   So Fraud shouts her roasts in the market's ear.
Hostess Fraud rejoices for pilgrims in her inns,
   But the pilgrim groans to have it so bad.
Fraud syncopates the peck, abbreviates her cuts,
   Docking the hay, extending her profits.                           820

Since she tends the least things, Fraud sells chickens and eggs;
   Her guile rules everything in the market.
Fraud is the proctor of the commons in cities;
   When she enjoins suits, somebody will pay.
The infinite deceptions in the mouth of Fraud
   Are as many as the shores of the sea.
Fraud makes and sells facts, judges documents also,
   And stands guilty of all duplicity.
When rector, Fraud doesn't promote the common good
   As she should, but looks to her own profit.                    830
Thus it's finally clear, now barren Troth's outlawed
   From the city, that Fraud breeds all the more.
I do not say that Fraud is in charge everywhere,
   For honest tradesmen will not deal with her.

*Vox Clamantis* by John Gower: 'The Voice of One Crying'

## CHAPTER 15

**Here he talks about that malevolent and impetuous citizen who, taking upon himself the office of mayor, kindles his malice against his fellow citizens, so that he confounds and destroys the city's sound governance by his unfitness.\***

That bird is disgusting that's quick to foul with waste\*
   Its own nest, whose custodian it'll be.
Shame on the burgess who will steal his comrade's place
   And post peasants above our citizens.
A madman among the people has to be feared,
   At least while he holds a sword in his hand.              840
But a man's power must be feared the more in town
   When he rages in his judge's office.
Just as a single spark can burn down a whole house,\*
   So one bad man harms his native city.
Nature begins to groan when matters sudden change
   And grieves the unaccustomed novelty
When sudden fate lifts a poor man in the city,
   Who, though unworthy, attains high office.
The city's elite may well fear the damages
   When the novel esteem of fools lauds him.          850
Fools approve of fools and wicked men, wicked men;\*
   Intelligent men delight in the wise.
Nothing's more troubling than a baseborn man risen,
   At least when he was first born a servant.
His mind abides in the old manner of a serf
   Although fate grants him the highest status.
You can put a racing horse saddle on an ass,
   But he won't then be swifter in a race.
Crude and untaught men are not changed by offices;
   They'll be more troublesome for villeinage.         860
And as the beasts condemn the crow for perfidy,\*
   So should a city its bad citizen.
Though fickle fate advance a man without morals\*
   In a city, Fame will tell who he is.

An evil man, whom God at times lets stir things up,
   Is often the scourge of many others.
But in the end the evil redounds on his head
   That he first let loose upon the people.
An ounce of poison spoils a thousand jars of oil

Book V

    And an evil man, a thousand good ones.                                       870
One ignited coal starts many others aflame;
    A bad man does much evil where he dwells.
For when such a man has clambered to the summit*
    And wants to bend everything to his rule,
Lo! the wheel turns and who was higher in the town
    Before falls lower than everyone else.
Fraud is able to flower, but it can't bear fruit,
    Nor does its scion put roots in the soil.
In the end, when one makes himself grand by his greed,
    He'll price himself high but won't profit much.                 880
Anyone can see this by today's example,
    Yet scarce a wise man, seeing it, takes heed.

## Chapter 16

**Here he also talks about that citizen who is a gossipy whisperer and disseminator of discords among his fellow citizens. He also speaks of the various dangers that occur because of an evil tongue.**

    When a whispering man of tongues lives in a town,
        He stirs up scandals unto the folk's shame.
The man of tongues harms others just like another
    Plague, often striking just like a whirlwind.
But since his evil tongue serves sin throughout the world,
    I mean to tell what its harsh powers are.
His tongue moves suits; the suit, conflicts; conflicts, the plebs;
    The plebs, swords; swords, schisms; and schisms, death.       890
A tongue strips, a tongue puts, and a tongue devastates
    Leaders from realms, fiefs to the flames, mansions.
A tongue dissolves the bonds of marriages and makes*
    Two of the one that God had established.
Brides drive off husbands with lawsuits and husbands, brides,
    And falsely claim some wicked thing was done.
This meager body part has learned to spare no one
    And false and loose to speak both right and wrong.
This bit of ferment corrupts the entire heap;
    Stirring the mind, it moves every member.                        900
It's not for nothing double guards keep watch on it
    Lest it flow without restraint in its words.
Prudent Nature has blocked the palate up with teeth
    So, when it's shut, what's shut can be silenced.

With such sharpened points its guardian controls it
   Lest, suddenly, it act imprudently.
Outside, it gets another guard, this one of lips,
   So double door shuts double-dealer's way.
The first, a boney gate, edits its excesses,
   The second, soft and fleshy, makes words mild.                910
Yet sometimes unobserved it escapes these portals
   And gushes forth in words it can't call back.
The force of these contains a thousand disasters,
   Which swallow successes like greedy fire.

He who can say how many lights shine in the skies*
   And how many grains the dry dust contains,
Such a man is scarce wise enough that he can tell
   All the noxious seeds an evil tongue sows.
No one can tell the evils that a schemer births
   In town and the schemes his false lips provoke.             920
A busy tongue is a bad, a worse, the worst thing,
   And although it has no bones, it grinds them.*
No place is peaceful where a busy tongue governs
   And he who has no peace does not have God.
He who quarrels outside God's peace cannot be saved
   And nothing avails without salvation.
All that peace acquires for itself, discord bears off;
   What the one builds up, the other tears down.
Where love reigns, there's God; where there's no loving person,
   God won't be present to guide our affairs.                  930
A busy tongue is therefore heavier than lead,
   Beneath whose weight a city's honor sinks.
Don't let that burgess in the town who bears it ill
   Nor open up its gates to a false man.
Though this double-dealer's lips sing the town's honors,
   Still in his secret heart he bears fraud's seeds.
Happy as fish in water, wicked men rejoice
   When they see the losses others endure.
When a single person poisons the common spring,
   The plebs die and a great plague sudden comes.              940
The citizen who vexes and oppresses all
   Should suffer the pain of death or exile.
When just one tooth decays, it infects the whole head;
   When it's pulled out, the pain ceases at once.
Let a city extract any wicked burgess

## Book V

Before its civic honor has been lost,
For it is better that the one should die, lest all
   The people, struck by his cruelty, perish.

Bring, ruler of our city, the concord that gives
   Peace, for peace begets all prosperity.           950
Let your voice not thunder down upon the people;
   Nourish the city's love with pleasant words.
A light touch tames both tigers and prideful lions;*
   In time the bull endures the rustic plow.
What force cannot do, common sense can accomplish,
   Getting the job done by lightening the load.
One anchor's not enough to hold ships in a storm*
   Nor one hook enough in torrential streams.
One man cannot by himself, without some aid from
   The plebs, manage all the city's issues.          960
Nip things in the bud if you can, or wiser yet
   Do bit by bit what you can't all at once.
You'll see that the reckless days of old injuries
   Often hold more sickness than medicine.
We see that some wounds, which it was better not to*
   Have touched, become graver by their treatment.
You see mighty rivers risen from small fountains,*
   Rivers multiplied by gathered waters.
Often a wound that could be healed when inflicted,*
   Ignored for a long time cannot be helped.       970
Wickedness that is endlessly recalled renews*
   Old wounds and the least cause harms a sick man.
A badly healed scar turns back into an old wound*
   Because there was a fault in the first cure.

Just as should you but push a quenched coal near sulfur*
   It lives and a small flame will become great,
So he who rashly reawakens old anger
   Won't bear with ease what he himself provokes.
Any injury kindles an extinguished fire,*
   So anger, forgotten, returns stronger.          980
Anger creeps in, loathsome evil, and lust for gain;*
   When there's no love, it all goes wrong in town.
Charges are made, the heavens resound with complaints,*
   And everyone invokes an angry God.
It's proper that burgesses forego savage acts;*

Sweet peace suits men; fierce rage, wild animals.
Good faith is absent without love and, love withdrawn,
  Everyone in town neglects his own place.
A people separated from a town's wise men
  Takes its counsel from the very cunning.*  990
Flame and water are two lords that show no mercy;*
  An ungoverned mob is considered worse.

Not long ago, justice, peace, and concord would guide
  Citizens in politics and affairs.
"Where are they now?" you ask. Not here. "Why have they gone?"
  The reason has been spite and silver plate.
What Fraud acquires is not enduring profit:
  Love won't endure in Envy's company.
Wash away the perjuries of times past, I pray,
  Wash away yesterday's treacherous words  1000
So fortune will revive more than you could suppose
  And what today is cheap will rise in price.
Sometimes the Deity is able to be pleased;*
  When mist is driven off, the day clears up.
Peace is granted to lands in which there's honest will;
  An evil man drives all the peace from town.
Rome was the head of the world for all time, at least
  As long as common love ruled the forum.
But divided, it ebbed at once, its honor gone,*
  And its dominion lost all its glory.  1010
Athens' honor did not recede while the townsmen,
  United, likewise harbored no hatreds.
Later, when serious division rent the town,
  It had henceforth none of its old honor.
May our city, which has long shone in great honor,
  Escape that fate by God's mediation.

# NOTES TO BOOK V

On Book V generally, cf. *Mirour de l'Omme*, ll. 23592–4180.

ll. 1–10: knights ("Bellatores") are the second of the so-called "Three Estates," the first being the clergy ("Oratores"), and the third being all others ("Laboratores"). Gerard of Florenne, bishop of Cambrai, ca. 1023, earliest describes the Estates, and hence social inequality, as God's will, a view Gower shares.

l. 17: cf. *Confessio Amantis*, I. 2651–3.

ll. 19–20: cf. *Confessio Amantis*, VII. 1783–984.

ll. 53–78: cf. Gower's short poem "Est amor in glosa."

l. 79: Amans: "the loving one," or "one loving"; here generic, subsequently Gower's name for the protagonist of the *Confessio Amantis*.

ll. 83, 89: adapted from Ovid, *Metamorphoses*, 3. 422; see also *Confessio Amantis*, VI. 667–79.

ll. 113–14: *verbatim* Peter Riga, *Aurora*, II Kings 47–8.

ll. 115–16: *verbatim* Peter Riga, *Aurora*, II Kings 45–6.

ll. 117–18: *verbatim* Peter Riga, *Aurora*, Evangelium 131–2.

ll. 119–20: *verbatim* Peter Riga, *Aurora*, II Kings 43–4.

l. 121: virtually *verbatim* Ovid, *Heroides*, 4. 71.

ll. 123–4: virtually *verbatim* Ovid, *Fasti*, 2. 763–4.

l. 145: adapted from Ovid, *Ars Amatoria*, 1. 391.

l. 147: proverbial; cf. Chaucer, *CT* GenPro I. (A) 162.

l. 165: *verbatim* Ovid, *Metamorphoses*, 7. 826; see also *Carmen super multiplici viciorum pestilencia*, l. 199.

l. 168: *verbatim* Ovid, *Heroides*, 4. 52.

ll. 169–70: virtually *verbatim* Ovid, *Remedia Amoris*, 691–2.

l. 171: virtually *verbatim* Ovid, *Heroides*, 4. 161.

l. 175: cf. Matthew 15: 14; Luke 6: 39; see also *Confessio Amantis*, III. 157–8, VIII. 2129–30; *Ecce patet tensus*, 4–5.

ll. 179–80: virtually *verbatim* Ovid, *Tristia*, 5. 4. 9–10.

l. 183: Acheron = Styx, the more common name in classical Latin poetry: River separating Hades from the world of the living; the boatman Charon ferries the dead across.

ll. 185–6: *verbatim* Ovid, *Ars Amatoria*, 2. 237–8.

l. 187: *verbatim* Ovid, *Ars Amatoria*, 2. 235.

l. 193: adapted from Ovid, *Heroides*, 5. 149.

ll. 199–206: cf. *Ecce patet tensus*, 23–30.

l. 209: virtually *verbatim* Ovid, *Metamorphoses*, 10. 189.

l. 211: adapted from Ovid, *Heroides*, 16. 231.

l. 213: *verbatim* Ovid, *Heroides*, 7. 179.

ll. 215–16: cf. *Carmen super multiplici viciorum pestilencia*, ll. 207–8.

l. 221: virtually *verbatim* Ovid, *Heroides*, 2. 63.

l. 224: adapted from Ovid, *Ars Amatoria*, 3. 42.

l. 229: Galen, Roman physician (d. ca. 216 BCE), renowned in medieval Europe for his medical skills.

ll. 251–60: cf. *Mirour de l'Omme*, ll. 23917–28; *Confessio Amantis*, IV. 1620–44.

l. 257: Croesus, king of Lydia (d. ca. 547 BCE), famed for his immense wealth.

ll. 261–70: cf. *Mirour de l'Omme*, ll. 23929–40.

ll. 335–6: virtually *verbatim* Alexander Neckam, *De Vita Monachorum*, ed. Wright, II. 186, ll. 11–12.

ll. 341–2: virtually *verbatim* Alexander Neckam, *De Vita Monachorum*, ed. Wright, II. 186, ll. 13–14.

l. 349: *verbatim* Ovid, *Metamorphoses*, 2. 411.

l. 353: virtually *verbatim* Ovid, *Ars Amatoria*, 3. 481.

l. 355: adapted from Ovid, *Ars Amatoria*, 3. 295.

l. 359: virtually *verbatim* Ovid, *Ars Amatoria*, 3. 289.

l. 360: virtually *verbatim* Ovid, *Ars Amatoria*, 3. 294.

l. 361: virtually *verbatim* Ovid, *Ars Amatoria*, 3. 291.

## Notes to Book V

ll. 367–8: *verbatim* Ovid, *Ars Amatoria*, 3. 311–12.

l. 375: *verbatim* Alexander Neckam, *De Vita Monachorum*, ed. Wright, II. 186, l. 15.

l. 376. adapted from Ovid, *Ars Amatoria*, 1. 598.

ll. 377–8: virtually *verbatim* Alexander Neckam, *De Vita Monachorum*, ed. Wright, II. 187, ll. 5–6.

l. 390: virtually *verbatim* Ovid, *Ars Amatoria*, 2. 116.

ll. 399–402: adapted from Ovid, *Ars Amatoria*, 3. 163–6.

l. 403: virtually *verbatim* Ovid, *Metamorphoses*, 2. 635.

l. 405: virtually *verbatim* Ovid, *Ars Amatoria*, 2. 179.

l. 407: virtually *verbatim* Ovid, *Ars Amatoria*, 2. 185.

ll. 413–16: virtually *verbatim* Alexander Neckam, *De Vita Monachorum*, ed. Wright, II. 186, ll. 20–3.

ll. 417–19: *verbatim* Alexander Neckam, *De Vita Monachorum*, ed. Wright, II. 187, ll. 7–8.

ll. 421–8: virtually *verbatim* Alexander Neckam, *De Vita Monachorum*, ed. Wright, II. 189, ll. 17–22.

ll. 427–8: adapted from Alexander Neckam, *De Vita Monachorum*, ed. Wright, II. 189, ll. 3–4.

ll. 429–30: *verbatim* Nigel of Longchamp, *Speculum Stultorum*, ed. Mann, ll. 1367–8.

l. 438: Marcus Porcius Cato the Elder (d. 149 BC); socially conservative, he was also known as "the Censor" and "the Wise."

ll. 439–40: virtually *verbatim* Ovid, *Ex Ponto*, 1. 6. 51–2.

ll. 443–6: virtually *verbatim* Ovid, *Tristia*, 5. 2. 23–6.

l. 459: Samson, a Nazirite and so sworn never to cut his hair, was given enormous strength by God to defeat the Philistines, who bribed his lover Dalilah to betray him into their hands by cutting his hair in his sleep, thus depriving him of strength; cf. Judges 13–16. David, who cut off the head of the giant Goliath, desiring Bathsheba, arranged for the death of her husband, thus angering God; cf. II Kings 11: 1–27 (Vulgate).

l. 460: Solomon, despite his wisdom, had seven hundred wives and three hundred concubines, many from idolatrous nations; eventually he was persuaded to worship other gods, among them Astarthe and Moloch. Cf. III Kings 11 (Vulgate).

ll. 487–8: adapted from Peter Riga, *Aurora*, Deuteronomy 199–200.

l. 523: virtually *verbatim* Peter Riga, *Aurora*, Deuteronomy 201; cf. Genesis 29: 1–30.

ll. 529–30: *verbatim* Peter Riga, *Aurora*, Deuteronomy 203–4; cf. Genesis 29: 17.

ll. 533–4: cf. Genesis 29: 20.

ll. 537–40: virtually *verbatim* Peter Riga, *Aurora*, Leviticus 655–8.

ll. 561–8: cf. Genesis 3: 19.

ll. 573–82: cf. *Mirour de l'Omme*, ll. 26425–72.

ll. 575–654: Gower's complaints address conditions brought about by an extreme labor shortage following the Great Plague of 1348, when 30–40% of the population died. Prompted by complaints like Gower's, Edward III issued the Ordinance of Laborers in 1349, which established wages and price controls, required all men sixty and younger to work, and prohibited landholders from hiring others' workers for better pay.

l. 593: *verbatim* Ovid, *Metamorphoses*, 6. 318.

l. 605: i.e., the Ordinance of Laborers: see ll. 575–654 above, and note.

l. 611: *verbatim* Ovid, *Metamorphoses*, 2. 163.

l. 613: Anonymous, *Pamphilus de Amore*, l. 271; the work, a Latin verse comedy, was standard schoolboy reading; cf. *Mirour de l'Omme*, ll. 14449–60; Chaucer, *CT* VII. 1555–65 ($B^2$ *2745–53).

l. 622: i.e., the Ordinance of Laborers: see ll. 575–654 above, and note.

l. 656: *onus* = "burden," hence implicitly responsibility, but also expense, difficulty; cf. *VC* III. 1003–4, above, and note.

l. 659: the Lord Mayor of London was elected by his peers, i.e., the elite of the merchant class; the term was one year. It was expensive: the mayor was expected to entertain lavishly, thus providing more profit for the food and clothing guilds, from which many mayors originated. Cf. ll. 765–8, below.

ll. 689–90: cf. Exodus 20: 8–11.

ll. 691–4: cf. Exodus 16: 4–5.

ll. 693–4: virtually *verbatim* Peter Riga, *Aurora*, Exodus 275–6.

ll. 703–6: cf. *Confessio Amantis*, V. 4383–414.

l. 718: the rising money economy in the latter fourteenth century saw the beginning of merchants buying previously hereditary country estates.

ll. 719–20: cf. Exodus 22: 25; Leviticus 25: 36–7.

ll. 731–5: cf. Ezekiel 18: 13.

ll. 741–72: cf. *Mirour de l'Omme*, ll. 25237–72.

ll. 765–8: cf. ll. 659 above and note.

ll. 771–2: cf. Aesop, known most commonly in the fourteenth century in the Latin verse translation of Phaedrus; other versions in Odo of Cheriton ("De cornice") and Froissart's *Chronicles*.

ll. 773–4: the Staple: locations where goods of a particular kind, import or export, could be bought or sold legally, with taxes going to the crown. Wool was England's most profitable product; hence generally references to "the Staple" indicate the wool trade.

ll. 775–8: Gascony, i.e., the Aquitaine, was an English possession in Gower's time, and a major source of wine. Wine merchants notoriously adulterated wine to stretch profits.

ll. 811–12: beer is produced from water (Thetis, a water deity) and grain (Ceres, goddess of grain crops).

Ch. 15 heading: Nicholas Brembre and John of Northampton, London mayors 1377–84, are often suggested as the "cive...maliulo," but perhaps only a general type is meant here.

ll. 835–8: the cuckoo song signals the spring: ll. 835–6 are proverbial; cf. *Mirour de l'Omme*, ll. 23413–14, but not necessarily with good intent: it lays its eggs in another bird's nest, supplanting the legitimate offspring, and consequently was considered a figure of avarice: cf. Alexander Neckam, *De Laudibus Divinae Sapientiae*, ll. 865–72, *De Naturis Rarum*, LXIX (p. 118), both ed. Wright.

l. 843: proverbial – Walz, 246; cf. *Mirour de l'Omme*, ll. 10959–60.

ll. 851–2: proverbial – Smith and Heseltine, "Fool praises another."

ll. 861–2: probably Aesop; cf. ll. 771–2 above and note.

ll. 863–4: "sors fallax" = Fortune, whose wheel turns heedless of merit; here "fama" = rumor, the popular voice.

ll. 873–6: i.e., Fortune's wheel: cf. Boethius, *Consolation of Philosophy*, II. met. 1; *Mirour de l'Omme*, ll. 10943–4.

ll. 893–4: cf. Matthew 19: 6, Mark 10: 9; *VC* II. 55.

ll. 915–16: virtually *verbatim* Ovid, *Tristia*, 1. 5. 47–8.

l. 922: cf. Proverbs 25: 15, Ecclesiasticus 28: 21; *Confessio Amantis*, Prologue, Latin invocation, III. 462–5.

ll. 953–4: virtually *verbatim* Ovid, *Ars Amatoria*, 2. 183–4.

ll. 957–8: virtually *verbatim* Ovid, *Remedia Amoris*, 447–8.

ll. 965–6: *verbatim* Ovid, *Ex Ponto*, 3. 7. 25–6.

ll. 967–8: virtually *verbatim* Ovid, *Remedia Amoris*, 97–8.

ll. 969–70: adapted from Ovid, *Remedia Amoris*, 101–2.

ll. 971–2: adapted from Ovid, *Remedia Amoris*, 729–30.

l. 973: virtually *verbatim* Ovid, *Remedia Amoris*, 623.

ll. 975–6: virtually *verbatim* Ovid, *Remedia Amoris*, 731–2.

l. 979: *verbatim* Ovid, *Ars Amatoria*, 3. 597.

l. 981: *verbatim* Ovid, *Ars Amatoria*, 3. 373.

ll. 983–4: virtually *verbatim* Ovid, *Ars Amatoria*, 3. 375–6.

ll. 985–6: virtually *verbatim* Ovid, *Ars Amatoria*, 3. 501–2.

l. 990: *verbatim* Ovid, *Fasti*, 3. 380.

ll. 991–2: cf. *Confessio Amantis*, Latin verse iv. at l. 499.

ll. 1003–4: virtually *verbatim* Ovid, *Tristia*, 2. 141–2.

ll. 1009–10: refers primarily to the end of the Roman empire, but readable as the Papal Schism of 1378.

# BOOK VI

Book VI is most usefully perceived as a discussion of government considered in its three functions: judicial, legislative, and executive. It is further testimony to Gower's growing sense of the inadequacy of the three estates as a device for a socio-political analysis of England in the late fourteenth century. The book begins with a scathing account of legal practitioners, starting with the pleaders, the experts of the common law consulted by individuals involved in suits brought before the royal courts. Supposedly guarantors of the king's justice which his judges are obligated to deliver, corrupt lawyers are driven by avarice and concerned primarily with the acquisition of property, twisting the law through sophistry and trickery. The judges, sheriffs, bailiffs, and witnesses, who likewise share responsibility for the failure of justice in the realm, are attacked in their turn for their own avaricious misconduct. Although Gower's major judicial concern is the common law, he also evidences knowledge of the other legal codes – customary, civil and canon – present in fourteenth-century England.

    The legislative branch is assailed in its expression as king's councils, in which his counsellors presumably advise the monarch of the best courses of action. Although parliament was becoming increasingly important, Gower does not include it in his discussion. Legislatures were not seen in his day as the inevitable outcome of a government's perceived need for guidance from constituent assemblies. The history of the papacy, which mirrors imperial and regal courts, offers a fruitful comparison. There the synod, the *concilium generale* of the Church favored by the early reform popes, gave way from the twelfth to the fourteenth centuries to a curial development, the *consistorium* (basically a baronial council comprised of the cardinals), that became the chief advisory institution for the exercise of the legislative function. A general council of the Church could always be summoned if necessary, but perceived occasions were infrequent. This line of legislative development Gower seems to favor.

    The various counsellors of the king are discussed in two groups: the youthful companions with whom Richard surrounded himself, who comprise one aspect of his court, and the older men who formally instruct him. The latter constituted a *parvum concilium* that, at royal summons of the officials and barons, quickly could become a *magnum concilium*. This section of the poem exists in an earlier version (the A-Text) that absolves the king and his young courtiers and puts the blame wholly on his elder advisors, comprised initially of men associated with Richard's father. The later version (the B-Text) still absolves the king, but parcels out the blame for the problems of his reign equally between the two groups of counsellors.

Perhaps the best-known component of Book VI, the discussion of the executive function, is the open letter to Richard II that urges upon him the figure of his father, Edward of Woodstock (the Black Prince, as he will be known in time), as a model for his own rule. Edward, the eldest son of Edward III, who died before his father and accordingly left young Richard heir to the throne, was renowned for his warfaring prowess and great victories won in France and Spain. Although he administered the English territories in Gascony for many years, he had no particular reputation for statesmanship, and has seemed to many an inapt choice for a role model to a young monarch from a poet who sees peace as the essential precondition for good governance.

The final chapters of the Book are a wide-ranging survey of rulers good and bad, whose fates should be observed by any ruler, which provides a transition to Book VII. Structurally, these latter chapters offer a contrast between virtuous figures from the past and contemporary, vice-ridden ones. Thus, they mirror the earlier chapters' critique of the currently corrupt state of the various legal officers, all of whom have similarly betrayed their ideal callings. The positioning of this collection of rulers, whose experiences prove the poet's point about the reading of history, suggests that the end of Book VI may have been a "working conclusion" at an early stage of the poem's composition.

*Book VI*

# HERE BEGINS THE SIXTH BOOK

## Chapter 1

**Since he has discussed the error existing in all the degrees of the temporal world, now, because it is necessary that everyone be governed under the justice of the law, he intends to talk further about those who are called the ministers of justice, however much they nevertheless confound all justice with their deceits and repeatedly weaken it for worldly profit.***

Many men nowadays take their name from the law,
   On their own behalf, without title to it.
By the law of man, not of God, fictitiously,
   They falsely claim to have their name from law.
To them all love is a stranger, all sin a friend,
   And every case created for their gain.
This task and that toil must first be joined with tribute,
   Without which mutes the pleading from their tongues.
But who's open to true laws and is without guile,*
   Urges justice for his neighbor's complaint,           10
The psalmist has sung, is a very blessed man;
   But there are few such men in these our times.
The struggle for gold wastes the laws with a new sore,
   So that Justice, stricken, has lost her health.

I cry out what the people's voice cries out; none do*
   I charge but those the accusation fits.
To those in particular that greed leads astray,
   None else, I am thus writing what follows.
Beneath law's cloak lurks craft, by which law without right
   Turns out what's wished on any given day.           20
When they can twist such a law around, the pleaders
   Can change our God-given rights by their words.
All is adorned in the tinted likeness of right,
   So that an arcane assize brings more gains.
They do not care how just or unjust is a case,
   But that it be to them abundant gain.
Now when a pleader knows that right is against him,
   Then will he summon all his sly tricks up.
What he can't do by law, he cancels out with tricks;
   When he can't win a case, he worries it.           30
If he should win, custom these days demands and grants
   That he be called a learned legal man.

Unless he can by trickery disguise the laws,
  The others say his pleading has defects.
The pleading of a liar prevails thus to obscure
  The honest man's law, so it brings more gain.
When thus a pleader becomes more learned, the law
  With ruses multiplied he overwhelms.
Law is thus clear as to its form, but skilled deceit
  Becomes its essence and defeats justice.                40

This is the talky litigious tribe that prefers
  To clamor loudly in its trumped-up suits.
The pleader wants to provide service like a whore,
  Who cannot love a man without a gift.
As you can see, he is always for sale to all;
  Give him gold and you can have his body.
He never cares what a man's birth or order is,
  Whenever he can have a bit of cash.
Just as the way to Rome stands open for pilgrims
  Who come to render prayers at holy sites,           50
So does the common way to the pleaders' houses,
  On which the people go and bring them gifts.
For just as ancient tyrants chained up righteous men
  Who wouldn't offer incense to their gods,
So now the greedy pleader ties his neighbors up,
  Who are reluctant to fetch him tribute.
Thus now I see the people forced to sacrifice
  To pleaders, or things won't go well for them.
According as their means suffice, diverse peoples
  Often offer them diverse new tributes.              60
Indeed, if you lack gold it is enough for you
  Respectfully to give them silver gifts.
If you have no silver, play the good host to them,
  Whom nothing in the world can satiate.
Everything that the good earth bears, the air above,
  The sea below, they want as gifts from you.
They gather in on every side, and front and rear,
  Take everything, give nothing back to you.*

The fowler traps birds with not one snare but many;
  A single hook will catch only one fish.             70
Law has been transformed into no law, and now takes
  Its gains in not one but a thousand nets.
On all sides there's a case at law whose dangling hook

Takes gold gifts from the waters of your purse.
There's no such path that won't be probed for gain of gold,
   By wile or guile, by fancy or by force.
The deceitful spider weaves her delicate webs
   So that she can entrap her prey in them.
And if a fly comes buzzing 'round, it falls, held fast;
   The sparrow hawk, unhurt, goes from the midst.         80
Whatever flies on forceful wings escapes from it,
   Whatever weak remains wrapped in the web.
A greedy pleader wraps his neighbors, terrified,
   In law, and traps them in like circumstance.*
He persecutes defenseless and fainthearted folk;
   The law's net packs them in close together.
The simple folk fall in his webs, but, to the rich,
   The pleader's nets give way, tattered and torn.

The bat swoops in the evening to the ground, to use*
   Its wings as feet, its custom when it walks.         90
Who makes his mind rich with earthly knowledge thus makes
   Himself the equal of this winged creature,
In that he reels along the ground, seizing only
   Earthly things, ignorant of the true light.
By night the owl's said to be exact in vision,*
   By day to take less pleasure from bright light.
The sages of the law mimic this bird, since they
   Do ill by night and get no good from light.
Yet oft that prey it seizes is its death, the end
   Inevitable lies hidden in it.         100
The kite comes sudden when it hungers after chicks,*
   And guile falls often by its own deceit.
The captor thus is seized, who eats is himself eaten;
   Wretched, he loves the claw by which he's seized.

## Chapter 2

**Here he discusses those pleaders and advocates who, plundering those around them and growing rich from the goods of others, accrue huge possessions for themselves, from which, however, *as it is said, a third heir rarely takes joy.**

More than ravening Scylla gulps down the sea's waves,*
   The pleader gulps down his community.
More than the hound who seeks his prey in deepest woods,

The pleader seeks to acquire his profit.
The hound can't grip its prey more firmly by its teeth,
   In order that it may devour the flesh,                 110
Than the pleader can seize his client with the law,
   In order that he have a silver gift.
Just as the hawk is wont to oppress trembling doves,*
   The pleader presses and afflicts the folk.
Just as the frighted lamb, injured by the grey wolf,*
   Has just fled, yet isn't completely safe,
Just as the dove, its plumage smeared with its own blood,
   Fears yet the claws in which it had been clutched,
So takes the poor man fright, caught in the pleaders' snares,
   And thence cries out into the ear of God.            120

A doctor wants the people to be hurt, so that
   Another's pain should bring him joyous gain.
The pleader wants folk unruly, that he may seek
   Prosperity from litigious people.
From what you lose he gains, and if you should profit,
   He seeks from this to have his share with you.
When he has his right hand full, he reaches out his
   Left, and is never satisfied enough.
Wherever Eurus thus wild rages, on its blasts*
   It bears his tranquil sail to every strait.           130
Thus pregnant swells his cash box from another's gold,
   And, wickedly conceived, it births yet worse.
It is the way of law, when one gets swiftly rich
   In cash, to hunger after new estates.

As the she-wolf, distressed by her whelps' hungry ways,
   Seeks throughout the wide fields to find them food,
So, when his offspring are increased, the pleader schemes
   On all sides plots with which to swell his wealth.
O without rest conspiring, night and day, to snatch
   A profit everywhere, he works the court.          140
Then house to house he joins, and field to field, because*
   He wants to be alone in his own world.
Thus seizing others' eggs, he warms them, partridge-like,*
   But in the end it's clear what he deserves.
What the father has obtained by zealous effort,*
   The son disperses quickly in his vice.
The pile which the worldly sage bundled by his fraud,
   This drifty fool allows to come apart.

*Book VI*

Thus third heirs won't enjoy what wrongfully was gained;
   The world takes back those things that first it gave.    150
Isaiah says that woe will befall the pleader,*
   For wickedly he wastes the widow's home.

## Chapter 3

**Here he discusses those pleaders and advocates who, the more of them there are, the more they gulp down their community, thirst after more profit, and, weaving under color of law their subtleties, snare with their tricks the fearful innocent people.**

When thistles in large numbers spring untimely forth,
   Depleted soil produces lesser grain.
When the sow pours out her dugs to more and more young,
   Her scrawny sides become yet leaner still.
And when the law increases the pleaders' numbers,
   Then the plebs, plundered in the shires, groan more.
Just as the water's torrent floods the sunken crops,
   Plucks out what's in the ground and roots it up,    160
This greedy bunch gets, by law, all the many gains
   Of men the surface of the earth contains.
No one can be well when doctors harm the sick, add
   Injuries to injury in their frenzy.
Thus when pleaders spin their cases without justice,
   The peace will not be certain very long.
Thus things have gone in these our present days, so that
   A man will scarce escape this sickness sound.
When golden scales weigh laws, the balance won't be fair,
   And modern justice teaches this usage.    170

Chrysostom, it is written, had a golden mouth,*
   That metaphor inherent in his speech.
Powerful pleaders do, in fact, have golden mouths,
   Who now devour all things made of gold.
Spices are sold with tricky weights, so the buyer,
   Deceived by them, won't know the true value.
But now there are, behold! trickier weights by which
   The law's words are sold in its profession.
Whatsoever the laws may urge, an inner man's
   Law bears the judge's burden deep within.    180
The Lord gives everything free; misers of the law

Give out not a word unless they sell it.
If compacts make fair promises, the law should make
   Them guarantee each word, fulfill each deal.
They often ask for payment in advance, unearned,
   Whatsoever may happen in the end.
The tilted scale thus doesn't know justice's weights,
   And what should be balanced falls crookedly.
Injustice often comes in the name of Justice;
   What should be trustworthy becomes trustless.                    190
Pleaders will all maintain that the law is blessed,
   But they prove it is evil by their deeds.

If a man should pick up a straight wooden object,
   And dip it in clear water to observe,
That which was straight in line appears crooked to him.
   Lo! the law acts like my proposition.
For if I tell my pleader the law is quite plain,
   That justice cannot be denied to me,
Scheming his fee, he will subvert all that I said,
   Putting forward many impediments.                                200
From the sweetness of honey he makes bitter gall,*
   And shapes the rose to look like a thistle.
As the basilisk poisons the air with its snort,*
   From which plague all life nearby perishes,
So the man of law, his mouth full of tricky words,
   Infects that which is sound law in your ears.
As the fox frightens the sheep and the thief plunders
   The pilgrim, guile compels good faith to flee.
More kind to put a finger 'neath his sinking chin,*
   Than shove the swimmer's face 'neath waters swift.               210
I marvel that he who, by law, ought to defend
   The cases of the poor vexes their need.

How often dreams alarm men without cause, with a
   Figure of something glimpsed in sleep, not real.
How often thus the pleader, inventing hazards,
   Will fork a road where it is really straight.
He speaks to you in a doubtful manner, for none
   Of crafty mind can speak with steady voice.
He proceeds with a question designed to deceive,
   By which he makes you doubt what he doesn't.                     220
Thus by a legal fiction he makes you afraid,
   That he might turn a man to senseless brute.

*Book VI*

You take your eyes from one thing to grasp a second,
   While the law itself will dictate your case.
Pleaders are clouds that darken the heavens, whereby
   No one is able to see the sun's light.
For they obfuscate the clearest rights of the law,
   And their foul night lays claim to be the day.
Splendor loses its luster in such men, the truth
   Tells lies, and guile denies good faith exists.        230
Law raves, piety sleeps, wisdom fails, peace becomes
   A burden, and all lawsuits yield profits.
And thus law [*lex, legis*], itself from to injure [*laedo, laedis*],
   And justice, right [*ius*], from to quarrel [*iurgo*], rule the law today.
But if the people stood bonded in constant love,
   The pleader's station would be profitless.

The law in itself is good, I confess, but see
   That now its masters wrongly bend justice.
As they point out, it is illegal to hatch plots,
   But they don't do what their own justice says.        240
If law requires me to act against a pleader,
   And I seek to have my legal counsel,
The others say that they won't oppose their cronies;
   So they offend, but none can offend them.
Thus the pleader seeks everywhere the world's honors,
   Subverting justice with his lively tongue.
The law reproves others whom it will, but not those
   Neither God nor the world can keep honest.

## Chapter 4

**Here he discusses how those pleaders and advocates of the law, gradually increasing in their abilities and aspiring to the office of judge, finally attain the zenith of a judicial throne, where, as if sitting in the seat of pestilence, struck with the blindness of greater avarice, they prove to be of a worse nature than before.**

A man is an apprentice and then a Serjeant,*
   And last a judge's office marks him out.        250
If he is greedy in the first, more in the next,
   The third stage is the guiltiest of all.
And thus the law is steered by heavy reins of gold
   That now it cannot travel righteous ways.

## Vox Clamantis by John Gower: 'The Voice of One Crying'

Law is no longer free, nay blind cupidity
   Keeps it bound up in a prison of coin.
Unless a golden key unlocks its barred-up gates,
   No one will have a path to its entrance.
Not your hand knocking, nor your voice shouting, will help
   You who lack a key to speak with the law.            260
If money doesn't guide your way, nor hires for you
   The keepers of the law, you leave empty.
Neither pleader your case nor judge your just judgment
   Acknowledges, unless coin is your guide.

Three reasons chiefly cause confusion of the law,
   Whence everywhere it ruins justice's seat.
Tribute, friendship, fear, these three, denying justice,
   Conspire so nothing on earth withstands them.
Solomon says that gold blinds the judge's eyesight,\*
   And lucre contaminates his reason.                   270
And we all know that he who is the judge's friend
   Will not lose anything by his judgment.
We also know, when cases touch the powerful,
   Justice flees from decisions that raise fears.
A judge is unable to withstand dreadful threats,
   And is oft swayed by requests without threats.
When a magnate's letter drums in a judge's ears,
   His pen's might cancels rights that should pertain.
But woe above all to the wretched pauper now,
   Who goes to law and hasn't means to pay.          280
These things are known to us, that by the modern law
   Justice declines to help the poor man's case.
I dwell not on my own affairs, but hesitant,
   Ears pricked, am on the watch for wickedness.

Take our own day, when now the law, once friend to right,
   Conducts its transactions contrarily.
A mask conceals a face, a gloss confounds a text,
   Tinted law turns into classroom logic.
The world has scholars of the law without number;
   They've many leaves but rather meager fruit.\*        290
Wicked deeds are oft done beneath an honest name,
   And guile does many things in guise of right.
Such reproaches should be feared by the prudent men
   Who arbitrate the world in such cases.
Great rivers are dispersed into many small streams,

A riverbed thus drained dry of waters.
A treasury suffers eclipse from much expense;
   A rich man who won't look ahead grows poor.
Thus this richest land will shortly be impoverished,
   Unless it check the excess of the laws.                         300
Medicine cannot take away the knotty gout,*
   And law still lacks a cure for avarice.
If my purse is strong, defeated law falls silent;
   With gold to the fore, I rout all justice.
If my case is heard privately, before a lord,
   I don't need law: I witness for myself.
This wound, which has long persisted, thus ulcerates;
   It leaves no further place for a fresh sore.

## Chapter 5

**Here he speaks as if in a letter directed to those judges who, trusting in their perishable heap of riches, in no way deign to make God their helper.**

   You who manipulate your judgments of life, death,
      And property for the money they bring,                 310
   By what justice do you think you will save yourselves
      When your law has been sold for others' frauds?
O you mighty men and lovers of the false world,*
   And you who think the earth's riches are gods,
O you who thusly desire worldly distinctions,
   Whose comrade is unremitting worry,
Know that often heights await their precipitate
   Collapse, and plummet down at breakneck speed.
The lofty tree falls often from the blasts of winds;
   The seedling in its peaceful place endures.                 320
We know that lofty mountains will grow white with snows,
   Which cold and frost whirl suddenly about.
There the madness of the winds is fiercest, the while
   A vale nearby displays a pleasant mien.
Thus adversities never leave you, mighty ones;
   Neither peace nor quiet is assured you.

Tell me if ever the rich lacked an enemy;*
   Grave catastrophe more often shakes them.
Neither ivory nor purple assures sound sleep;*

Poverty lies snug on its humble straw. 330
Fear torments all misers, for they have things to lose;
   An empty shadow gives them anxious dread.
An owner is ever fearful for his gold, and*
   Thinks at every noise that thieves are at hand.
The rich man, unable to trust anyone, fears
   Weapons, robbery, poisons, and abductions.
As he seeks wealth, his wretched greed then torments him;*
   Then, when he starts to get what he sought, fear.
Thus he is wretched poor, when seeking to have wealth,
   And also when he's rich and fears its loss. 340
He lies in bed, his wakeful mind sensing problems,
   And it seethes, turning over tricky schemes.
He says, "I want to have the land of the poor man*
   Next door, for that field is next to my own."
Thus he chases orphans from their paternal homes,*
   Pursues and presses widows in the courts.
He takes delight in the poor man's valuables,
   Thinks nothing of the other man's losses.
If he could gain the world, he would not care to know
   God in the world or who that God might be. 350

O Judge, the glitter of your gold is not enough
   To dispel your mind's dark shadows, is it?
You have made the fertile gold your own, but never
   Consider your own sterile existence.
Even an honest judge, laden with the world's goods,*
   Will not climb the heights of justice with ease.
You seek to extend the long boundaries of your fields,*
   But don't think about your life's short seasons.
Why seek silver for yourself? Why place hope in gold?
   The riches of the earth belong to all.* 360
Often you see God's things given his enemies;
   There is no merit in them before God.
A pagan has them, a Jew, a savage bandit;*
   Be sure, an angry God often gives them.*
I think unimportant the things bad people have,
   The wealth of the wicked, not a great good.
How often the just man ails, the wicked prospers,
   Here but not Beyond, since Justice reigns there!
The Lord's beloved dies, the adulterer lives;*
   They aren't, however, equal in Christ's love. 370
The just grow ill, the wicked flourish in good health,*

## Book VI

But, in the end, each bears his own baggage.
Yet if a judge can get well-being in the world,
    He does not care what the end will bring him.

O you who want all, why do you forsake yourself?
    You own all things on earth except yourself.
You known to all, you who know others, not yourself,
    Don't know such knowledge profits not at all.
Therefore you should first know yourself, and then know me,
    And thus wisely reach a correct judgment.  380
You love all the world's things, abandon those of Christ,
    And trust to have enough *ex nihilo*.\*
You lose the heavens, you gain the world, you sustain
    Your worthless flesh, whence spirit perishes.
To you, perfect is empty and fickle is full,
    For such a judge perceives his task poorly.
You build towers, newly decorated chambers,
    Worship the worldly more than the divine.
You build wide, but a narrow grave will contain you,\*
    Where a closed lid will press down on your face.  390
What can I say about the judge's clothes, mansions,
    And beds, whose luxury knows no equal?
Who now would see his residences, how they've grown,
    Would say they belonged to a second Jove.
But will the pomp and glory you fashion at home
    Endure, given that you steal your profits?
For Babylon has fallen, likewise lofty Troy,\*
    And mighty Rome just barely still exists.\*

Every earthly power comes to a sudden end,
    And then forsakes its own in hasty flight.  400
Fear therefore, judge, you who climb to such high honors,
    Be mindful you stand in a crumbling place.
All that is dear to you on earth will pass from you,
    And God himself mete out your just rewards.
His equitable law will judge what you now judge
    Inequitably, and give you fair weight.
When the fearsome agent sent from the impartial
    Judge plunges you into the sulphurous lake,
Wretched you will bewail, although, alas, too late,
    That you had put your hope in such false goods.  410
Neither your gems nor gold and silver go down there,
    Nor earth's frail glory, so soon departed.

Vox Clamantis *by John Gower: 'The Voice of One Crying'*

But what I have written to the peoples' judges
   About this was in vain; I wasted words.
For justice, or the judge's impartial nature,
   Has not been seen in this our present time.
Here's the Justice; he deceives with such a title,*
   And bears without justice an empty name.

## CHAPTER 6

**Here he discusses the error of sheriffs, bailiffs, and also jurors in assizes, who each, hired by gold, back rich men's unjust cases and, without justice, falsely accuse and oppress the poor.**

Now, moreover, what can I say about sheriffs?
   Do they trespass 'gainst men in assizes?             420
The case grows gaunt from which no ointment comes dripping,
   So that their hand accordingly is greased.
If your gifts are curtailed in the assize of law,
   Right perishes and then your suit's torn up.
If your gifts, however, are assessed beforehand,
   Then you can profit from your assizes.

Like an ox that is led to the plow for a price,
   You can bring in oath-takers with a bribe.
They will also sell you perjuries for your coins;
   That's how gold defeats justice in my town.            430
Thus I see the rich man unjustly acquitted,
   And the righteous impoverished man condemned.
With vice [*vitium*], not stand-in [*vice*], "viscounts" start their name;*
   They are the deputies of the law's greed.
Thus I speak against sheriffs, conquered by bribery:
   They now do trespass against common folk.
Oath-takers don't taste anything not well seasoned
   With profit's salt you give them in advance.
The shysters seize the wool and these types take the hide,*
   So nothing's left for the poor helpless sheep.           440
Concluding finally with our high officials,
   I say that the new law thrives by the purse.
Just like a pig taking pearls in its swill, so now*
   Officials take all the rights for themselves.

What is it to sell justice if not to sell Christ,*
   Whom Judas sold with greedy treachery?

But can there be one yet like Judas in the world?
  Indeed, I think there are many like him.
We know that Judas once committed such a crime,
  And I read that he repented for it.                                450
But now everybody openly sells for bribes,
  Rejoicing that he has turned a profit.
Judas returned the evil reward he received,
  Yet it is not shown he was forgiven.
What about those who sell justice with the left hand,
  For whom each hour is like a marketplace?
Just like Gehenna's pit, which gulps and clutches fast,*
  And from out whose maw no man returns free,
There are those now who sell the laws and clutch their bribes,
  Which nobody can snatch out of their hands.                       460
And thus because they are as tenacious as hell,
  I believe hell in the end will hold them.

Or what shall I say about bailiffs, who are like
  Acheron's swift furies? Beware them more!*
Where they come in the gates, stand by for surefire loss,
  For woe is their companion in all ways.
Just as the toad cursed the harrow, thus curse I too*
  The many lawless masters of the laws.

## Chapter 7

**Here he says that, just as it is right and necessary that men exist on the earth, thus it is fit that laws be instituted for their governance, provided, however, that the keepers of the law, discerning the true from the false, should distribute in due weight to each man what is his. However, concerning the mistakes and wrongdoings lately occurring, he alleges in excuse the innocence of our king, so far as concerns the present, because of his minor age.**

The laws have been established for the trespasser,
  That every man should have his just deserts.
Yet now this good man's punished, and that wicked one,              470
  Who thrives by gold, is justified by it.
All things have their time, and each time has its seasons,*
  And therefore each cause ought to have its cause.
What does the sea bring when it swells with lofty waves,
  If not a ship borne on the flowing surge?
How fares a ship without a guiding mariner?

## Vox Clamantis by John Gower: 'The Voice of One Crying'

Without an oar, what good's a mariner?*
What is the sea, the ship, the sailor, or the oar,
  Without a port and wind apt for the seas?          480

What is a nation without law, or law without
  A judge, or what's a judge without justice?
If anyone surveys the doings in our town,
  He'll often see these three that give me fear.
All trespasses are serious, but none more grave
  Than when a just man cannot have justice.
From injustice waxes discord, and thence ceases
  Accustomed love, and so the house mutters.
If there's muttering, there'll also be division,
  And that land divided will not stand firm.*          490
And woe to whatever cannot stand by itself,
  For sudden and complete it will crash down.

For God is my witness that kingdoms divided*
  Against themselves perish, which I believe.
Therefore let all those who govern realms see to this;
  The greatest part of our fate looks to them.
Whenever kings rave, Achaeans suffer for it,*
  For an unsound head makes the limbs suffer.*
If the leader loses course, his folk, too, wander,
  The way by which they will return unsure.          500
Nations have passed away because of their king's sin,
  And records rarely teach the contrary.
But royal goodness brings the folk the joys of peace,
  For God favors a pious king's doings.
But if a king's corrupt, because the law cannot,
  God, who rules everything, will punish him.
It profits the people that each king live rightly,
  For either of two fates lies in his hands:
The good king is called the people's sole salvation;
  The evil king functions to his folk's ruin.          510
For much more harmful are the wicked deeds of him
  Whose enacted law nations must obey.

When a man is greater, his sins are all the more;*
  Then, when he falls from the heights, he's harmed more.
I see many men guilty, but those more than all
  Who carry out the law and lawless live.
When lawlessly the realm's corrupt power rages,

## Book VI

Nothing can be sadder in the whole world.
I think a beast more pious, fit in soul, than he*
   Who provides, but doesn't maintain, justice.    520
Not only wars of triumph adorn a king's rule;
   He should preserve the good laws everywhere.
A house can't be constructed without beams, can it?
   But if they've not been shaped, what good are beams?
What good's the shaping if the toiling craftsman's hand
   Isn't steady in the joining process?
If the beams have been joined, they'll support each other,
   And if they're not, no part aids another.

What use an empty land, unless folk live in it?*
   What use a folk, unless a king rule them?    530
What use a king, unless he will have sound counsel?
   What use counsels, unless a king trust them?
In our land, however, there is divisiveness,
   Since each now elects to go his own way.
The city's strife torments our fellow citizens,
   So each extinguishes the other's rights.
Masters no longer observe the law of the field,
   For who has more power shall be master.
Clergy blame the laity, and laymen, the clergy,
   And yet each one persists in its own fault.    540
Jealous of each other, each blames the other now,
   And neither side reforms its own conduct.
If you look at either estate, you'd surely say
   We have each other injured in great ways.

### A-Text

Now comes a voice, behold! that cries out to our ears*    545
   Words proclaiming we're troubled in these times,
That, as it cries, the king's court is guilty of crimes,
   That those who should take charge live lawlessly.
There's no voice raised in these days for the common good;
   Everybody just looks out for himself.*    550
Amidst the hall proceeds a throng of flatterers;
   Whatever they desire, the court concedes.
Those who presume to speak the truth, the court expels,
   Will not permit to be at the king's side.
The boy is absolved of blame, but those who should guide

His puerile reign are not without blemish.
The council, and not the king, thus grieves the land, which
   Laments, as it were, with public grumblings.
If our king were in his lifetime's mature season,
   He'd balance out the scales that lack justice.*    560
For a king's mode will moderate others, and head
   Of all justice his duty's said to be.
If a king wishes to be good, the virtuous
   Are instructed by his good character.
If bad, the king selects, rewards, esteems flunkies
   Of like lot so that they cater to him.
But this pertains to one who's reached discretion's age,
   Not to a boy, because his fault is less,
It is not nature's law, nor reason's, that childish
   Bad behavior is what injures the world.*    570
This is not guile but jest, not fraud but splendid play
   To boys; this is not the source of evil.
For Daniel says elders give rise to the evil*
   That goes forth from the madness of the world.
Old men plant all the misfortune that's in the world,
   And they sow as much poison as the plague.
For their wickedness is said to stain the image
   Of the whole world, at which God's wrath rages.
Now guile has multiplied and righteousness has failed,
   And what was honor once is reckoned shame.*    580

## B-Text

Everywhere the people's voice now shouts openly
   The fearful things I bear in timid breast.
The royal court, which is tasked with defending law,
   Instead prefers to walk on unjust paths.
The head infirm, the members all lack sound good health,*
   Yet no doctor cares for their needs today.    550
Thus a rampant disease of sins has arisen,
   Because no hand tries to pare back excess.
Thus plague's sprung up, which casts down overwhelmed virtue;
   It thrives on sin, which governs every court.

The king, an untaught boy, neglects the moral deeds
   By which a man can grow up from a boy.
Indeed there is a youthful council guides the boy,

*Book VI*

  But he heeds nothing, unless it's his will.
 The things he wants, his youthful comrades also want;
   He goes upon a path, they follow him.      560
 Vainglory makes these young comrades idle, so that
   They idly dwell beneath the royal roofs,
 Abet the boy king in his childish ways, so that
   He fails to take up the virtues' burdens.

 There are, too, greedy oldsters, who, chasing profits,
   Allow much wickedness to please the boy.
 Compliantly they yield, those who are sinful come,
   And the king's court has every vice there is.
 Sin arises on all sides of the boy, and he,
   Who's quick to learn, absorbs every evil.      570
 This is not guile but jest, not fraud but splendid sport
   To boys, yet fate springs untimely from guile.
 There are, moreover, hidden causes that no one
   On earth can know, but God himself knows well.
 A mother won't know what the fates ordain her child,
   But in the end each secret is made clear.*
 The people's voice today shouts such things on all sides,
   Put in doubt before the weight of evil.
 I'm worried by the loathsome things that I'm hearing,
   And so I bring the boy king what I write.      580

## Chapter 8*

**Since all the world's people of all ranks are governed under the justice of royal sovereignty, he consequently intends at the present time to write a kind of letter to our now-reigning king, prepared for the sake of instruction, by which he, our king, who is now in his youthful years, may be more clearly prepared for his royal responsibilities when hereafter, by mediating divine grace, he has reached his more mature years. And first he says that, although the royal power is elevated, so to speak, atop the law, nevertheless, royal clemency befits the king, because he, by adhering to good morals, should govern himself and his people in the sight of the High King as if he were a freeman subject to the laws of justice.**

 Since every liege is subject to his king's own law,
   And does him service with all his body,
 It is thus fit each liege with faithful heart should love
   Him with every fiber of his being.

The king should guide the people given to his care,
  And also govern them with proper law.
That's why in honor of my king I mean to write
  A rule of conduct drawn from many texts.

O pious king, hear what your rule of realm should be,
  Suiting to law and joined to God's justice.       590
Laws' reins in hand, I hitch you firmly to the Ark;
  Although you dread no man, be yet in dread.
For fear, a humble virtue, flees ostentation,*
  Is, so to speak, the key to the virtues.
Far better, king, that you should rule yourself by law
  Than subject to yourself all worldly realms.
Because of the world, others are subject to you;
  Because of heaven, be the Lord's subject.
So that the people, docile, serve you by the law,
  Persevere for your servants in Christ's service.    600
You who conquer others, strive to conquer yourself,
  And learn to subdue all passion's excess.
In judging others, seek to judge yourself as well;
  Give yourself the law given the commons.

You who excel others, seek to excel yourself;
  Self-ruled be king, if king you wish to be.
By what reason can one proclaim, "I am the king,"
  Who cannot rule the urgings of his mind?
He cannot bestow sound governance on others
  When he cannot be ruler of himself.                610
Though all to you permitted, seek not all to do;*
  Permitted things bring often grievous harm.
You're atop the law, but live, justly, beneath it;
  Because of you there's hope of weal for us.
Your wrath is death, you are allowed illicit acts,
  But must be guided by law's vows fulfilled.
Though something lawful may preserve your peace of mind
  Unharmed, yet, too, it may not be upright.
What is allowed is safe, but, aided by honor,
  Examine precisely what you should do.              620
Let your acts be mild if nothing else is needed,
  For harshness leads to hate and savage wars.
Let not the people's common weal escape your eye;
  By being wise avoid calamities.

*Book VI*

Old Pharaoh's life and Nero's wicked deeds teach us
   Those things from which a just king should flee far.

O good young king, devote the goodness of your youth
   So that it be given to moral ways.
What avails beauty or ancestral noble name,*
   If you've become a slave to your vices?*              630
Alexander's teacher truly taught him depraved*
   Morals, at first when he was just a lad.
The boy king learned and later, when he tried to give
   Them up, his early practice hindered him.
Babylon and Darius fell to Alexander,
   But not the evil imprint on his heart.
Thus have wise men formerly written in precepts:
   The pot is wont to hold what filled it first.*
Therefore, O king, drive vicious men away quickly,
   For habitual shames won't just depart.*            640
Applaud good men, flee wicked company, for pulled
   From pitch an injured hand will have a stain.*

## Chapter 9

**Here he tells how the king should carefully shun bad advisers, expunge completely the realm's traitors, investigate diligently the character of his ministers, and correct by due penalty, and punish severely, those whom he finds straying from justice.**

You should beware false friends enwrapped in sordid deeds,
   Who seek what's yours but don't want to love you.
Don't be elated by the bland words of the sly,
   Who will drag your esteemed name through the mud.
To hear and credit thoughtlessly the words they say
   Encourages vague fears to get their start.
A man who provokes war, promotes pillage, conspires
   To acquire the taxes of your people,              650
O king, I pray that you should close your ears to such,
   Lest your nobleness grow weak before them.
Let no avaricious man infect your royal
   Counsel, but treat him as a kind of death.
There is no evil in the world that does not lurk
   In the heart of a man who thirsts for gain.

He walks in shadows, meditating shady deals,
   Hates and assails the works of harmony.
With honey in his mouth, but venom in his heart,*
   Intending wickedness with peaceful words,            660
He is shifty, a friend to the king's enemies,
   Always venal, since he has time for gain.
A viperous and worthless sort, full of venom,
   He readies force with trickeries, snares, and crafts,
Sits in ambush and seeks to harm unwary men,
   Fashions for himself his traps in secret.
Probing the minds of men, he betrays their secrets,
   And Judas-like he counterfeits his deeds.

Consider who solicits you, O king, attempts
   To corrupt you, who urges you discard             670
God's law; see who he is and of what character,
   Or if he wants to speak the truth to you.
Probe first in mind his character, and learn if he
   Acts dubiously or with loyalty,
Or if he proposes doubtful false ideas:
   Deceitful words ever fear detection.
Be wary, pious king, when trickery is at hand;
   Beware the deeds of one who acts badly.
Many do not believe 'til something harmful wounds;
   The wise ruler sees such deeds in advance.          680
By charming songs, O king, are birds often entrapped;*
   Fly from a smooth tongue's mellifluous words.
Give good and worthy presents, O king, to good men;
   Give to the wicked what their guilt has earned.
Since Christ felt compassion, the good thief gained pardon;*
   The bad thief paid the price upon the cross.
Wrongful service draws a heavy gift at your hands;
   A man should define deeds by how they end.

If strict reason demands a crime should be punished,
   Do what a just man should in such a case.          690
Don't let false pity smooth your justice's sharp edge,
   But let your judgment accord with the crime.
A judge who's soft on crime oft brings on fierce dangers;
   Who tolerates bad men destroys the good.
To different faults let different penalties attach,
   A thousand crimes, a thousand remedies.*

## Book VI

The sword is seen to show the sign of judgment due;
   A king keeps his arms close to kill traitors.
He orders such strung up upon a high scaffold,
   Lest the status of king and law perish.           700
Act, O king, so discordant, raging plebs can't say
   Law that rules ancient rights lacks a ruler,
And lest that, in the law's absence, the mob should say
   That the shadow of the prince lends no aid.
Let Fraud die the death, consumed by its own deceit,
   So royal justice give to you renown.
Thus may the people say, "Long live our glorious king,
   Through whom peace thrives and the guilty atone."

It's advised that the sword should be always brandished,
   So crimes may come to judgment more promptly.      710
A sword that is at rest cannot restrain the world;
   Who would reign should nourish Justice with blood.
Weapons beget harmony, arms curb the greedy,*
   Just kings bear arms so that the guilty fear.
Lest officials do harm in your name's sake, be sure
   To view your people with a tender heart.
For if you are unwilling to correct your men,
   The palace is indicted for their fault.
In seizing food, the falcon falls upon its prey*
   In service to the profit of its lord.           720
Thus there are overbearing servants of the king
   Who injure the poor to his benefit.
The wretched poor who cry out to the Lord in prayer*
   Have force, for he is mindful of the poor.
Likewise a prelate, who is a keeper of souls,
   Is supposed to be forceful in office.
Thence his reckoning and final reward will rise,
   His glory or eternal punishment.
Likewise, O king, you who guide our world with your laws,
   God will reward you with your just deserts.       730
Your power is great, O king, but his is greater,
   Whose right hand balances your every deed.

## Chapter 10*

**Here he says that the king should adhere to good counsel, support and encourage the law of the Church, be fair and merciful in his judgments, and prefer his own reputation to all the wealth of the world.**

    Spurn wicked men, tend the prudent, suppress rebels,
        Aid the poor, scorn sinners, spare the guilty.
    What so you do, sink not your righteousness in sin;
        Let fame and works be more than gain and goods.
    Shape nothing for the world, O king, for which your lords
        Would think you just but God hold you guilty.
    Be eager to sustain the Church most loyally,
        For your crown should be worn with its prayers.    740
    When you attend the widow's and the pauper's plaints,
        Render gentle judgment to the wretched.
    From time to time relax the sanctions of the laws,
        Lest, in your fierceness, mercy disappear.
    Thus let your goodness deign to indulge your subjects,
        For God would often spare a tainted man.
    Assign equal taxes to lords and gentry both,
        And betray nothing secret beforehand.
    If a case should be difficult for you, recall
        In great affairs good faith is late to show.*    750
    Do not be too certain about doubtful matters;
        Hope is deceived by its own prophecy.*
    Loss is quite likely to aggrieve the human race,*
        For onset doesn't know what end will be.
    When it's necessary to treat the realm's business,*
        Let age with its experience guide your plan.
    What we say in the east will travel to the west;*
        Therefore, don't let loose tongues know your business.
    Improper counsel disturbs the royal honor,
        And stirs good peaceful times to wickedness.    760

    Age is distinguished for just laws, whence the elder
        Should seek office and give the people law.
    He is old enough in age whose wisdom affirms
        His sense, even if he is a youngster.
    I don't assert that old minds are sound or a lad*
        Foolish; age has not given its laws thus.
    Sometimes an old man will hang onto youthful ways,
        When he will affect a young man's manners.
    Therefore, good king, look into their state thoroughly,

And when you choose your men, first probe their deeds.　　　770
Who offers loyal service, not, useless, longs for
　　Gold, that one you should have for your servant.
And you can place your trust in such a one for whom
　　The king's renown is sweeter than his pay.
It is the peaceful man who is the law's best friend,
　　Free of avarice, liberal to each good.
From such a man seek your counsel, good king, so that
　　The tales of your praise overflow the earth.
Reputation soaring freely, fettered by none,*
　　Will proclaim this or that by your merits.　　　780
Know that a good name will surpass riches, preserve
　　Honor, remove scandal, thrive in glory.
Disturb a lovely bloom, it gives off a fresh scent;
　　A good man's virtue everywhere smells sweet.
Consult the doctors of the law, depart the halls
　　Of wicked men, join ever with the good.
Like grain from the harvest, like drink from a pure fount,
　　Gather your wisdom from a learned mind.

## Chapter 11

**Here he tells how the royal privilege should never fall into servitude to vice, but just as it exceeds others in power in the eyes of the people, thus by the plenitude of its virtues it should shine more fully than others in the eyes of God.**

Let no vainglory lift you up, I pray, O king,
　　For haughtiness is loathsome to the folk.　　　790
Since small flies bite, be provident in small affairs;
　　Royal scepters don't make their masters safe.
Little David defeated mighty Goliath,*
　　For humble virtue vanquishes proud hearts.
Christ, loving, raised up the humble and from his heart
　　Cast out the proud; O king, thus, pious, rule.
Let your discourse be trustworthy, your words discreet,
　　Where, when, and with whom it's appropriate.
Let your discourse, like Scripture, put trust in men's ears;
　　They won't be convinced by feigned fearsome words.　　　800
Let wrath's sudden emotion not rush upon you,
　　But judge the suits of justice soberly.
Roiling the heart, wrath takes reason's power away,
　　Negates the prudent doings of the mind.

You carry in your hands, by the law, life and death,
   Which requires you be judicious in suits.
Let greed not have the strength to corrode your good name;
   Let, rather, all earth rejoice in your gifts.
A king, who is noble, should not be the slave of
   Greed; everywhere his mark shall be largesse.       810

Let lavish alms, to your merit, care for the poor,
   By which you can appease our God the King.
Do what good you can in this brief life while you live,
   Scatter a few seeds now and you'll reap much.
Give liberally, but be cautious to whom you give;
   Believe it is a thoughtful task to give.*
Goodness that weighs out worthy gifts goes not to waste,
   For a donor's grant has godly merit.
He benefits, nor is the sea any less full,
   Who takes a little water from a stream.       820
Your alms obtained will thus duly aid the wretched,
   Nor will your sum of silver be the less.
If someone serves the poor for love of God, his gifts
   Abide a time, his fame eternal lasts.
Let your garments be divided, your gems and gold,*
   Proffer the poor what God before gave you.
The plain handmaid of God is alms, the antidote
   To death, the gate of grace, salvation's way.
It refutes the giver's sins, pleads to the Maker,
   Atones for disgraces, and prays for help.       830
Sin is the death of the soul, and death, punishment*
   For sin, but here a generous mind kills death.

Be free of gluttony, O king; your honor should
   Enjoy esteem for total purity.
For that sin damned with its stain our ancient parent,*
   By which he fell, a frail and guilty man.
This is the sin with which our ancient foe lured Christ,*
   And he, who is true king, rejected it.
Lo! Saul, wishing to fight, imposed a fast on all*
   Until he might subdue enemy spears.       840
Drive off, O king, your sloth, oppose your carnal bent,
   And stoutly take the road to righteousness.
And if your regal status stands above the plebs,
   It should in conduct thus be more noble.
O young in years, in whom is found no deception,

Book VI

> O simply noble, beware treason's darts!*
> Your youth denies that you are capable of guile,
>    Nor does it wish that you belie your birth.
> Beauty you have, birth, rank, honor, power and charm;
>    Your birth conferred these generous gifts on you.     850
> May likewise virtue tend you, fame, and manners' grace;
>    Thus live in God a full man, pious king.

## Chapter 12*

**Here he discusses how a king especially ought to abstain from the alluring enticement of the body, and how on account of divine displeasure he should delight only in his wife's lawful companionship, within the structure of sacred law.**

> O pious king, avoid blind lust above all, lest
>    It stir you with enticements of the flesh.
> Enjoy your wife according to the laws; do not
>    Deprive the sacred bed of praise and worth.
> No ancient books of kings from all the ages teach
>    That Venus pleased and realm can co-exist.
> That man might hark to Venus and his brain alike,
>    Has never been believed a likely feat.     860
> The Bible teaches you, with many instances,
>    Desire should be shunned. Take David now:
> Sin in the course of time enwrapped the king until*
>    A woman's love by force seized his whole mind.
> What sorrow from that came, or punishment ensued,
>    Still terrifies the mind of one who reads.
> Be David's sin a glass to you, in which you see
>    Another's fall may lift you up on high.
> Blessed he whom others' perils makes cautious, whence*
>    He beware in prospect the roads he sees.     870
>
> When no deceit could overcome the Hebrew folk,
>    Behold, how a woman's love trick sufficed.
> By Balaam's example you should be taught, how he
>    Showed King Balak just how the matter stood.
> He gave Balak a plan to confuse the Hebrews,*
>    The wiles of which would break their battle strength.
> "Accept counsel, O king, which you can use," he said;
>    "That people does not conquer by its might.

313

It always manages to conquer in two ways:
  Adoring God and keeping itself chaste.                      880
That you might conquer them by wit and not by war,
  Choose girls whom robes and lovely face adorn.
They'll clap their hands, cavort on foot, strum lutes, inspire
  Heat at night, pale the stars with comeliness.
Let fight the sport of love and not unyielding arms,
  Commerce with women, not the iron spear.
Let beauty conquer battle lines and girlish forms
  Tread underfoot the conquered arms of men.
Thus will the wrath of heaven's God rise against them;
  Thus will you win this nation's happy spoils."              890

The king, believing, accepted this plan, prepares
  His finest girls and their sidereal eyes,
Stages the strange fight, fends off Hebrews not with bow,
  Slays not with sword nor puts to flight with blows.
He fights not with knights' mail or with the reins of steeds,
  But rather with his lyres and women's shows.
One sings, one plays, one aids her beauty by her craft,
  So grace beguiles the eye with sidelong looks.
Her face gives off a glow, sparks shower from her eyes,
  And from her lips she offers honeycomb.                     900
These splendors rob the Hebrew people's souls; they sin;
  The wrath of God upon the sinners falls.

Take note, O king, how experience teaches you,*
  And let an old example show the way.
And see, O king, in instances of Saul the king,*
  What witchcraft woman does when she prevails.
By demon's skill the potent witch waked the prophet,*
  Forced him to stand at the king's beck and call.
Who could subject dead bodies to herself, she could
  By easy wiles subdue the living too.                        910
Who is forewarned is not deceived, O king, and thus
  Take care you rule your body without stain.
You are the king; one queen is sufficient for you;*
  Take her alone, as our cherished faith says.
Thus flee the weight of sin and hold your morals fast,
  And you will have whatever you desire.

Book VI

CHAPTER 13

**Here he now discusses and proposes to our magnificent young king the example of the Most Serene Prince, his father, saying that the king should boldly exercise the righteous valor of his arms against his enemies, where and when necessity demands it, and that he should not lose in any adversity the firmness of his countenance in the sight of others.**

> You are as well, O king, the people's champion
>   In arms; that you guard justice with valor,
> Keep in your mind as a model your father's deeds,
>   Whose living fame resounds yet everywhere. 920
> His name will never be extinguished from the earth;
>   His martial fame has outshone Hector's deeds.
> And to his praise, and to yours, I turn my writings,
>   That you recall his honor and valor.
> Just and honest, he gathered just and honest men,
>   Let no nettles contaminate the rose.
> He poured his gifts unstintingly, if merited;
>   His lavish hand came from his lavish heart.
> He plundered distant places, but kept safe his own,
>   And saw to the well-being of his folk. 930
> Indeed, if all of us should sing all his glories,
>   Our words would all be lesser than his worth.
> No reputation could encompass his merit,
>   Each voice too weak to bear the praise it ought.
> If I might briefly speak, he was as great a prince
>   As ever could be glorified by praise.
>
> France knew of him, Spain, remembering his powers,\*
>   Feared him, since he conquered her by valor.
> Storming their midst, he fell upon the enemy\*
>   Throng, and just like a lion burst his way. 940
> A wolf made gaunt with hunger, he scattered the sheep;
>   He drove, destroyed, cut down, and slaughtered them.\*
> Sober in demeanor was he, but with the blood
>   Of enemies his sword was often drunk.
> Charging, he attacked and fiercely assailed his foe;\*
>   His blade would not return dry to its sheath.
> Its hostile point was surfeited with hostile blood,\*
>   And waves of blood slaked the thirst of his arms.
> His sword would decline to loll within its scabbard;

| The blade was vomited from out its mouth. | 950 |

As a boar, driven from woods by their yapping plaint,
  Rips the coursing dogs with his deadly jaws,
So he struck the more audacious foes close by him,
  And cut them down in his sword's flashing jaws.
Just like a lion, he won every fierce battle,*
  Wasted peoples, pulled mighty castles down.
To seize his prey, he fell boldly upon his foe,
  Whose necks were subjugated by his hand.
Throughout the world his right hand suppressed haughty necks,

| The leopard therefore said to be a lion.* | 960 |

The land was peaceful under such a mighty prince;*
  No sword frightened whom that hand protected.
Beneath his vine, his fig, its leaf and shade, each man
  Was sheltered by the noble leader's sword.
The more his mighty strength increased, the more he thrived*
  Against his foe, the nobler he became.
Hold fast in mind, O king, your father's deeds, so that
  The fame he earned will be bequeathed to you.
Fortune aids and furthers those who are bold in deed,*

| Bestows the heart's desires, and even more. | 970 |

Peace surmounts every good, but when legitimate*
  Rights require, it is proper to wage war.
There is a time for war and there are times for peace;*
  In all your actions you should show restraint.
Hector and Alexander, very noble men,
  Could not stand on the wheel's unequal round.*
Surpass your father's deeds; you will be called greater,
  And every voice will shout your glory's praise.
Don't give the reins to fear in adverse times, and if

| You grieve within, be sure you grieve alone. | 980 |

If sorrow runs into your mind, pretend a face
  That simulates; let your face hide your fear.
A happy face will fright your foes and cheer your friends,*
  For it will be the herald of the mind.

## Chapter 14

**Here he says that a king should not go to war without a demonstrably just cause. Beyond that, he says that it befits a king's status to treat his subjects more with love than with the harshness of severity, nevertheless having made prudent provision for governance.**

## Book VI

The eagle, seeking heights, flies over all winged life,*
   And represents the king who's pure in heart.
Just as Sacred Scriptures witness by the minstrel
   Prophet, on heaven such have set their heart.
The Griffin, a winged four-foot animal, will seize
   Unwitting men and terrify their steeds.                          990
In this is signified all tyrants' savage deeds,
   Who gulp men's corpses down ferociously.
Better therefore is it to take the eagle's form,
   And rule a quiet realm with pious love,
Than terrorize the folk with Griffin's fearsome mien,
   For always love transcends all fearsome deeds.

Not all who fear, feel love, but every lover fears;*
   A loving folk entwine the two as one.
Love conquers everything; love is the king's defense;*
   The folk's love is glorious, God's praise on earth.             1000
The people are the king's own field; he, the tiller.
   Tilling badly, he gets thorns; if well, grain.
A king is he who performs the ruling task well;
   A tyrant, he who rules unjust by crime.
If a king lives by spoils, the people will mutter
   Curses; God's wrath will move against the king.
A just king gains both the people and God; the crown
   Of his kingdom, accordingly, sits firm.
Look in your heart, O pious king, and thus attain
   What will better prepare a king to rule.                        1010
If nobleness and noble name influence you,
   Take your own familial example.
Noble ancestrally and with a famous name,
   Match your deeds to your family's nature.
This in God's honor we plead with a common voice:
   Join heritage with nobleness of mind.

Let those men be a part of your presence whom God
   By birth, wealth, and character made the same.
And know there is one common origin of all,*
   One beginning, one ending, and one flesh.*                1020
The one who shines with virtue has nobility
   Of mind; he's base who loves an evil life.
For heaven's court venerates good morals; the just,
   But not the noble, will have God's heaven.
Remember that brotherly love, brotherly love

Alone provides and gives all things to you.
Brotherly love transcends the earth, with strength renewed
   Ascends on high and seeks the skies and stars.
Seeking to know God, it does not fear astral flight,
   In order to see the God of Zion,                                 1030
To see the mighty king and the vision of peace,
   The place of heaven, and God's great glory.
These suit a king to study long, that he by them
   More apt should be to render God just due.
Be desirous to know yourself and to love God,
   For these two things he orders you to learn.
Such are the terms by which your Creator assigned
   Your being and your mode of life to you.

## Chapter 15

**Here he says, according to the experience of Solomon, that wisdom prevails over the other virtues for the rule of a kingdom and renders the king more worthy of acceptance to God and men.**

O good young king, regard what to young Solomon
   Occurred, whence you be mindful for yourself.             1040
A lad of twelve, he got to see God in the night,*
   Since he had offered sacred gifts to Him.
God said to him, "Just ask what gift you'd have." He said,*
   "I ask good sense by which to rule my realm."
These regal words were pleasing to divine good will,
   And God delivered this response to him:
"Not length of years nor wealth, nor triumphs over foes
   You've asked, and thus is granted what you ask.
Not only wise but also rich you'll be, above
   All men the earth has held or ever will."                    1050

If you should look well, O king, into this mirror,
   You'll learn what is of greatest use to you.
From these examples it is clear: the wisdom of
   A king is needed first to rule the folk.
The years will pass away, but wisdom always stays;
   No house will fall that stands upon this rock.*
A pleasing sight, an old man cheerful as a lad;
   More pleasing yet, a youth old in his ways.
Who follows morality's steps where God wishes,

He goes before and ever guards the path. 1060
Pray God each morn a welcome day will favor you,
  Each eve, to safely pass the time of night.
A king who submits himself to the King on High,
  Obtains throughout his reign all that he seeks.

Royal scepters are held in the hands of monarchs,
  To signify their staff puts harm to flight.
Fulfill, therefore, your obligations to your law:
  Act for the honor of body and soul.
Receive good men, reject the bad, be law's lover,
  Be just, and guide your people by the law. 1070
But so that the law be useful, let Grace draw near
  Through Christ, without whom there is no good law.
Revere the law, fear ruin and nurture decency,
  Love family and be plain in spirit.
O wise king, if you savor everything wisely,
  Then you will relish your kingdom in Christ.

## Chapter 16

**Here he says how the God of Heaven, who is the King of Kings and Lord of Lords, should be worshipped with an especially pure mind by the kings of the world, and feared above all things.**

God has given all that you have, O king; nothing
  You have or ever will is from yourself.
Know that you are a creature of God; don't forsake
  His ways if you should wish to stand secure. 1080
You have a noble body, handsome every limb;*
  Let thus your spirit's worth be greater yet.
As splendid as your outer form, let your soul shine
  Within, so that your beauty be twofold.
Good looks, a fleeting gift hostile to modesty,*
  Often impede the virtues' useful path.
Beauty, the gift of God, makes many people proud,
  Although it doesn't tarnish holy men.
A pure spirit, and not good looks, earns God for you;
  The just alone receive the blessed life. 1090
It suits not a king that his mind belie his looks,
  The outside should be governed from within.

Pray, king, to God, who bestowed the realm upon you;
   Honor God, for whom others honor you.
No foe will face the king who is loyal to Christ;
   Nay, Fortune's lot, subdued, will favor him.
To make your foes fear your scepter, fear the scepter
   Of God on high, and you'll have to be feared.
Dread him on the high throne in heaven's citadel,
   Upon whose command every knee shall bend.     1100
He overthrows, exalts, saps and builds the world up,
   Carries in his hand every royal heart.
He is the King in whom throughout the world kings rule,
   He is the King without whom realms fall, crushed.
He is the King through whom death, in the end, takes all
   Kings; according to their deeds, he rewards them.

Great Caesar was more powerful than all the world;*
   An urn now holds him whom the earth did not.
Alexander also, bravest of Macedon,
   Is dust and bones held in a narrow plot.     1110
He was greater than the whole world, and now vile sand
   Covers that conquered exile's noble corpse.
Behold! for mortals nothing stays for long, behold!*
   No fame, no honor, keeps them from their deaths.
To those in tombs, vain praises bring no benefit,*
   Hell often torments famous guilty souls.
Be mindful of the future from the past, O king,
   Reflect that there is nothing fixed on earth.
And while the term of this life is granted to you,
   Always be prepared to do every good deed.     1120
To conquer earth, should you desire, be God's subject;
   Who's slave to Christ will rule his kingdom best.

## Chapter 17

**Here he tells how the king, living in the love of God and of his neighbor, ought to provision himself with all due diligence against impending death, which spares no king.**

Nature has decreed that all humans should dread death,
   Beneath whose law the whole race finds its end.
Ignorant and learned die, poor and powerful;*
   With equal end death makes us all equal.
Neither anointing nor a royal badge helps here;

They have no healing power and can't cure.
No glory in the world's affairs can be retained,
   Nor has the world then means to save itself.                       1130
Know that honors come with burdens attached, but in
   The end, the burden is more than the honor.
The more you're elevated, the more you should fear,
   For heady glory walks on a steep path.*
The life of man is thought of as a long campaign,*
   For on earth he always wages three wars.
The king who goes through the midst of battle unscathed,
   Will foolishly, incautious, often fall.
Therefore, O king, beware when you set forth, because
   You won't know if you'll find the heights or depths.          1140

Remember, all gladsome things will bid you farewell;
   The king and pauper both end up the same.
For no man can stand by himself; no man can close
   His final day with any certain end.
Betake yourself from out the world, good wayfarer*
   Begin to be, Christ's Sacred Scriptures warn.
To flee the winter of the sins, bedeck yourself
   With moral blooms and shine in virtue's light.
As if driven from Egypt land, let pitch your tents,*
   And study how to reach life's native land.                          1150
Remember, too, you're made in the Maker's likeness.
   Why? So, like him, you follow him aright.
It is, therefore, best for you that, with all your might,
   You love the God who made and redeems you.
And pray, O king, the help of such a King, that he
   Fulfill your life, himself defend your death.
Do what you wish, or good or bad, and that you'll get;
   Let God, I pray, guide you to the better.

## Chapter 18 (A-Text)

**Here he speaks in conclusion of this letter, where he prays devoutly for the king's well-being, that God happily preserve and guide his life, already flourishing in all prosperity, to the glory of God and to the benefit of the people entrusted to him forever.**

   Heaven's King, our Lord and our God, who alone time
      Founded, and alone rules the creation,*                         1160
   Who from himself brought forth the origins of things,

And was himself the beginning of all,
Who decreed that earth abide in steady movements,
   Fixed for eternity in its motion,
Who, powerful of word, brought forth the creation,
   Created and bound it by his mind's law,
Humbly I beseech that he spare my youthful king;
   May his happy realms see his hale old age.
May God forever rule and guide his youthfulness,
   Always direct his deeds to better ends.*                            1170
May no evil counsel be able to reach you,
   King, may there be no traitors in your land.
May every evil cease, lest it do harm, and may
   God give to you every good in the world.

May you be granted always in our time to hold
   The honored scepter firmly in your hand.
May that day be nigh when you, handsomest of kings,
   Will ride with four white horses, aureate.*
Such proclamations should be renewed to you as
   Once in Rome rang out in Augustus' praise.*                     1180
May the crown, enlarged, increase our leader's empire,
   May it extend his years, and guard our gates.
May you stand tall, O pious king, on conquered earth:
   May all lesser things be on your shoulders.
May the High One from above give to your right hand
   Shining gold scepters of eternal praise.
May he who gave your first realms confirm those to come,
   That you, a great man, in all honor use.
May your fortune thus forever be augmented,*
   That all the ages renew your praises.*                               1190

To your rule's glory, O king, I wrote these verses,
   Eager servant of the realm, to your praise.
Accept, O pious king, these written gifts from God
   I have made, humble in heart, in your praise.
This instruction is not so much mine, but his who
   Teaches, and whose word alone makes men taught.
O youthful virtue, royal honor, flower of youths,
   As you are valorous, I say "Vale."

Book VI

## Chapter 18 (B-Text)

**Here he briefly concludes the king's letter, saying that, just as a king shall aspire to be elevated by the privilege of his prerogatives and then rule magnificent in the presence of the people, he shall present himself just and humble in the presence of God, in order to sustain the burden of his regime with all justice. The realm will otherwise not stand because the king will totter.**

    Royal majesty is more honored above all
        When an upright king governs in his realm.            1160
    For first he pleases God and then the people's hearts
        He wins; doing so, he has a good world.
    He seeks for peace on earth and finds it, whereby in
        God's presence he will have heaven's kingdom.
    Great alive on earth, greater in Olympus dead,
        In both these places he will reign in Christ.
    A good king gets such good things from heaven's goodness,
        But otherwise he will not stay his course.

    If, avaricious, vain, and proud, a king torments
        His realm, his subject land will suffer grief.            1170
    All that pleases a king won't profit him; justice
        Without harshness grants him what's permitted.
    In the short run, a king's might will permit wonders;
        The end, however, shows his deeds were vain.
    If the king's burden is weighed against his honor,
        The honor is lesser than the burden.
    The king is obligated to dispense the laws
        Entrusted him, deny no man justice.
    But now among the plebs the voice says that, in Law's
        Absence, Guile has laid a claim on Justice.            1180
    Thus Fraud, adorned, has wormed within Justice, and thus
        Today Law secretly infects Good Faith.
    Where Law has strayed, Sin reins in kingdoms for itself,
        So the king should lend Justice assistance.

    Therefore, O king, cleanse crime from your kingdom and guide
        With wisdom what the circumstances urge.
    Restore lost communal justice, recall the law
        Into the realm, and banish every crime.
    If you wish to change the kingdom subject to you,
        First make yourself return in Christ to God.            1190

Then make the pacified people constant to you,
  Not on account of terror but by love.
Thus you'll have the hearts of your long-suffering people,
  And you shall stand noble throughout your realm.
And, while you govern your laws tempered with mercy,
  All your deeds will redound unto your praise.
If you, however, otherwise behave harshly,
  The people, who were once yours, will rebel.
I write these things, O king, for now and times to come;
  One's lot on earth is ever tinged with doubt.        1200

## Chapter 19

**Because, just as you have heard from the common voice, the characters of us moderns are changing everywhere throughout the entire world, let us consequently look at the difference, figured by examples, in the characters of those who went before us, especially in the Church, which is now divided.**

The fruits fall from the boughs, the acorns from the trees,*
  The flowers fade, the ripened grain fields die,
The lads who bear the wheat no longer bring the grain,
  And shrines now offer God incense in vain.
What was in color ripe has now turned into rot,*
  And fades the bud once wont to grow anew.
Above all cities now is Babylon renowned;
  The hand of Faith no longer bids it halt.
The virtue of the Church lies sunk anew in sleep;
  The Synagogue becomes the Bride of Christ.        1210
It's clear righteous men of old have no successors;
  The good men all have given way to death.
The evil men of yore, behold! have come again,
  So wicked is the manner of the world.

Noah the just has fallen in death, and Nimrod*
  Rises with Babel's Tower and scorns God.
Japhet has died, who concealed his sire's nakedness,*
  But scoffing Ham has revealed it today.
Abraham has died, seeking his faith's foundations,*
  But Bel is here, who fabricates new gods.        1220
Isaac has died, from whom the blessed race arose;*
  Now Ishmael, unworthy, holds it back.

## Book VI

Joseph has died, who was chaste, and Uzzah pursues*
   The flesh now in love of debauchery.
Moses has died, shining brightly in the Old Law;*
   Abiram, offending, still lives on earth.
Death has plowed Aaron's corpse under, he whom God chose,*
   And Korah's incense is envy's tinder.
Elijah has died, whose chariot climbed heaven,*
   And Dathan lives, who earned his place in hell.    1230
Micaiah has died, nor lives his like in the world,*
   Who, truthful, dares now oppose wicked men.
Zedekiah claims he is above all prophets,
   And everyone now rushes to serve him.
Elisha is no more, Naaman no longer well,*
   Lo! Gehazi wishes to have their gifts.
The dove flies from the ark, never more to return,*
   Whose role the raven now takes to himself.
And thus no one takes examples from the Old Law,*
   So that, behold! the New Law dies away.    1240

Say where those are who lately in the ranks of Christ
   Taught holy doctrine in both words and deeds.
Peter has died; now there's Liberius, whose gates*
   Simon the Magician guards with his arts.*
I think Paul upon a time converted from Saul,*
   But now I know that Saul returns from Paul.
Our words insist that Gregory's words be observed;*
   Our deeds, however, say we renounce them.
We read of Martin's gift, but since we have the deaf*
   Ears of the rich, we give none of our goods.    1250
Say where a second Tobit tends the dead on earth,*
   Or say where pity moves the modern heart.
Patient in adversity, meek in trying times*
   Was Job, and stayed the same with steady mind.
Now everyone exults in his prosperity,
   And mutters when the adverse times occur.

Benedict has died, instructor of his order,*
   But Julian, opposing him, yet lives.*
If earth's salt fails, there's naught it can be salted with;*
   The soul grows rank and reeks with fleshly sin.    1260
The wheat seed does not die, but fails to break the sod;*
   Thistles invade the land and lay it waste.*
The bud falls from the vine, which therefore bears no fruit,

But, unproductive, lies dried up and parched.
 The light from Phoebus dies, by starlight put to flight;*
   The moon, suborned, now suffers its eclipse,
 As if a new Arius, a new Jovinian,*
   Was planting heresy and sowing doubt.
 They say the day is night, the darkness also light,
   The right unjust; thus perishes all good. 1270

## Chapter 20

**Here he says that, just as the sinful lately succeeded those living virtuously in the Church, so also others have now succeeded the leaders of all the world's knighthood, lately famous for their valor, who have proven worthy neither of divine nor human praise.**

 If the keepers of divine law have gone away,
   So, too, the upright princes of the world.
 Trajan the just has died; the tyrant Nero now*
   Behold! silences all his just statutes.
 The laws' founder, Justinian, has also gone,*
   Dionysius rules that his should prevail.*
 Valentinian has died, the pure and upright,*
   And Tarquin governs with his scepter now.*
 Liberal Alexander has died, once splendid,*
   And greedy Croesus follows in his place.* 1280
 Constantine the virtuous has died, and, behold!*
   Antonius now sits upon his chair.*
 Theodosius, who husbanded the Church, has gone,*
   Leo succeeds and wants to scatter it.*
 Constantius profanes and mocks the acts of faith;*
   Tiberius' cherished faith is destroyed.*
 Julius Caesar died, who conquered realms by arms,
   Established that Rome was the head of all.
 Hannibal has died, because of whom Carthage thrived;
   Now neither Rome nor Carthage flourishes. 1290
 Hector, who was once fearsome because of his sword,
   Shies more from war than fearful Helenus.*
 Achilles has come to grief; instead rose wretched*
   Thersites, and his sword is powerless.*

 Solomon the wise died and Rehoboam lives,*
   And so youths reject their elders' prudence.
 The love of Jonathan and David sunders now,*

And envious Saul rages with hatred.*
He takes his counsel now from the Witch of Endor,*
   Because he is void of the grace of God.            1300
Now old Pharaoh's heart persists in obduracy;*
   It knows God's bitterness, but fears him not.
The scab returns upon the wound, which has not healed,*
   And what had first an evil fate has worse.
Ahithophel's perverse advice is heeded now;*
   Hushai gives counsel and none believes him.*
Envious Joab kills innocent Abner now,*
   Lets no one be his equal with the king.
Cato, who was a just judge, has left the city,*
   And, behold! Pilate judges in his place.*           1310
Righteous Abel has died, killed by his brother's sword;*
   The law confirms that this is legal now.
I see now Mordecai hanged, but Haman snatched from*
   The noose; the law permits such things these days.
The faultless Christ is crucified yet once again;*
   The thief Barabbas goes forth, a free man.
The law falls, strewn, and can't tell how to know what's right;
   Men's deeds are not ruled by spiritual strength.

## Chapter 21

**Here he speaks yet further about the same, how in place of those who were lately chaste and steadfast, others have arisen who, desiring the empty things of this world, have entirely abandoned the steadying effect of shame.**

Socrates has died, who checked vices with virtue;*
   Epicurus is here to hand them out.*            1320
Diogenes has died, forsaking vanities;*
   False Aristippus possesses this world.
Phirinus, chaste, has died, chastising his body;*
   Agladius, young lecher, lives in town.*
Troilus has died, steadfastly faithful in his love,*
   But Jason's love now cannot keep its faith.*
Faithful Medea lies content within the ground;*
   False Cressida is pleased to love two men.*
Semiramis burns impure in her loins, and now*
   Cassandra's barely able to stay chaste.*           1330
Penelope has died, so has Rome's Lucretia;*

Circe and Calypso now rule for them.\*
Justine has passed away, who scorned wicked pleasures;\*
   Thais lies ever more upon her back.\*

Now Paris' love, peaceful, is everywhere on earth,\*
   So all enjoy its pleasures without war.
Hymen no longer honors wedding vows these days,\*
   But Venus sets agendas in his beds.
Gold is betrothed, a beautiful face is prepared
   For Venus' room, ready for many men.  1340
Conjugal love and mutual care once bound a pair;
   One woman now draws five men to herself.
The law once said that two should be one common flesh;\*
   New style maintains there should be three at least.
Now Venus gives the orders, Cupid pitches camp,\*
   But chaste Love at the present has gone off.
A bird has one it loves, a female fish finds one\*
   With whom to share its joys in water's midst.
A doe follows its mate, a snake entwines a snake:
   A man and wife are even more one flesh.  1350

Where, alas, are plighted troths? Where connubial law?
   I lack answers, let someone else give them.
Iron foreheads without shame's mark are grounds for praise,
   And shame for sin has ceased to be a shame.
A blush was wont to mark the cheeks of women once;
   Shameless, they are more wanton now than men.
As silent as a jay, as chaste as a pigeon,
   They are as gentle as a thorny rose.
I trust counsel to women like water to sieves,
   And by this you can tell that I'm in love.  1360
While Jezebel rules, soothing with enticing words,\*
   Joshua will be transformed into Ahab.
Whenever heads incline to vice, the body's parts
   Succumb by force or love to evil ways.
There stands Delight, dressed in the flowers of evil,
   While Virtue's bloom lies trodden by men's feet.

# NOTES TO BOOK VI

Introduction: cf. the severe criticism of "ministers of justice" ("iuris ministri") here, with *Mirour de l'Omme*, ll. 24181–624 (lawyers), ll. 24625–816 (judges), ll. 24817–5176 (sheriffs, bailiffs, and jurors).

ll. 9–11: Psalm 14: 1–3.

l. 15: "quod plebis vox clamat": cf. *Mirour de l'Omme*, ll. 2481–3.

ll. 69–70: adapted from Ovid, *Heroides*, 19. 13.

ll. 89–94: *verbatim* Peter Riga, *Aurora*, Leviticus 735–40; cf. also Isidore of Seville, *Etymologiae*, XII. vii. 36.

ll. 95–8: virtually *verbatim* Peter Riga, *Aurora*, Leviticus 673–6.

ll. 101–2: virtually *verbatim* Peter Riga, *Aurora*, Leviticus 647–8.

Ch. 2 heading: "vix gaudet tercius heres": probably Gower has in mind Proverbs 13: 22, contextualized by Ecclesiastes 2: 26; and also ll. 145–8 below, and note.

l. 105: "Cilla": Gower interchanges Sylla and Charybdis as figures of Gluttony, following in this Alain of Lille, *De planctu Naturae*; cf. *Mirour de l'Omme*, ll. 7753–64.

l. 113; *verbatim* Ovid, *Metamorphoses*, 5. 606.

ll. 115–18: adapted from Ovid, *Metamorphoses*, 6. 527–30 (*VC* VI. 117, *Met.* 529 *verbatim*).

l. 129: "Eurus": the east wind, associated with autumn.

ll. 141–2: that is, he acquires adjoining properties to create a single, large estate for himself; cf. ll. 343–6, below, and VII. 809, and notes.

ll. 143–4: partridges were known to steal other birds' eggs to hatch; cf. Jeremiah 17: 11; in the *Bestiary*, the partridge ("Perdix") is identified with the Devil.

ll. 145–8: cf. Ch. 2 note, above.

ll. 151–2: probably Isaiah 1: 17 and 5: 22–3; cf. Luke 11: 52.

l. 171: "Chrisostomos": from the Gr. "khrusòs" (gold) + "stòma" (mouth); cf. St. John Chrysostom, one of four Greek Fathers of the Church, noted for his eloquent preaching.

l. 201: cf. Proverbs 5: 3–4.

ll. 203–4: "Basiliscus": the basilisk, a mythical serpent with a deadly glance and poisonous breath; cf. Alexander Neckam, *De naturis rerum*, Cap. CXX; *Bestiary*.

ll. 209–10: *verbatim* Ovid, *Ex Ponto*, 2. 3. 39–40.

l. 249: serjeants-at-law had the exclusive right to argue cases before the Court of Common Pleas; judges at Common Pleas and the Court of the King's Bench were drawn from their ranks. Cf. Chaucer's Man of Law, *CT* GenPro I. (A) 309–30.

l. 269: "Solomon": probably Gower has in mind Proverbs 17: 23; cf. also Exodus 23: 8, Isaiah 1: 23.

l. 290: cf. Matthew 21: 19, Mark 11: 12–14; also Luke 13: 6–9.

l. 301: *verbatim* Ovid, *Ex Ponto*, 1. 3. 23.

ll. 313–26: adapted from Alexander Neckam, *De Vita Monachorum*, ed. Wright, II. 180, ll. 17–18.

ll. 327–8: adapted from Alexander Neckam, *De Vita Monachorum*, ed. Wright, II. 182, ll. 13–14.

ll. 329–30: *verbatim* Alexander Neckam, *De Vita Monachorum*, ed. Wright, II. 181, ll. 15–16.

ll. 333–5: virtually *verbatim* Alexander Neckam, *De Vita Monachorum*, ed. Wright, II. 181, ll. 17–19.

ll. 337–41: virtually *verbatim* Alexander Neckam, *De Vita Monachorum*, ed. Wright, II. 181, ll. 21–5.

l. 343: virtually *verbatim* Alexander Neckam, *De Vita Monachorum*, ed. Wright, II. 181, l. 27.

ll. 345–6: virtually *verbatim* Alexander Neckam, *De Vita Monachorum*, ed. Wright, II. 181, ll. 29–30.

ll. 355–6: virtually *verbatim* Alexander Neckam, *De Vita Monachorum*, ed. Wright, II. 182, ll. 23–4.

l. 357: *verbatim* Alexander Neckam, *De Vita Monachorum*, ed. Wright, II. 190, l. 29.

l. 360: adapted from Alexander Neckam, *De Vita Monachorum*, ed. Wright, II. 191, l. 23.

l. 363: adapted from Alexander Neckam, *De Vita Monachorum*, ed. Wright, II. 191, l. 15.

ll. 364–5: adapted from Alexander Neckam, *De Vita Monachorum*, ed. Wright, II. 191, ll. 16–17.

l. 369: virtually *verbatim* Alexander Neckam, *De Vita Monachorum*, ed. Wright, II. 191, l. 31.

l. 371: virtually *verbatim* Alexander Neckam, *De Vita Monachorum*, ed. Wright, II. 191, l. 29.

l. 382: "ex nihilo" = "out of nothing."

l. 389: adapted from Alexander Neckam, *De Vita Monachorum*, ed. Wright, II. 192, l. 29.

l. 397: *verbatim* Alexander Neckam, *De Vita Monachorum*, ed. Wright, II. 193, l. 15.

l. 398: adapted from Alexander Neckam, *De Vita Monachorum*, ed. Wright, II. 191, l. 16.

l. 417: "Iusticarius" = "justiciar," chief minister to the king, empowered to judge in his stead; Gower satirizes the original meaning, "man of justice," contrasting it with his contemporary circumstances.

l. 433: the line contains an extended pun on "vice" and "viscounts" = "sheriffs."

ll. 439–40: cf. *Mirour de l'Omme*, ll. 25165–76.

l. 443: cf. Matthew 7: 6.

ll. 445–50: cf. *Carmen super multiplici viciorum pestilencia*, "Avaricie," ll. 246–57.

l. 457: cf. II Paralipomenon 28: 1–3, 33: 6 (Vulgate); also Jeremiah 7: 32; a general name for hell: cf. Matthew 5: 29, where the Vulgate has "gehennam."

l. 464: Acheron = Styx, the more common term in classical Latin poetry for the river separating the upper from the lower world, across which Charon ferried dead souls.

ll. 467–8: proverbial – cf. Walz, 49b; *Mirour de l'Omme*, ll. 24961–70.

l. 473: cf. Ecclesiastes 3: 1; *Confessio Amantis*, VII. 3594–5; also Chaucer, *Troilus and Criseyde*, II. 989, III. 855.

ll. 478, 479: "remus" literally "oar," but Gower may have in mind a "gubernium," i.e., a steering-oar, in European use into the sixteenth century.

ll. 490–4: cf. Matthew 12: 25; Mark 3: 24; Luke 11: 17; also *VC* III. 1721–2; 4. 1177, above.

l. 497: cf. Horace, *Epistles*, 1. 2. 14 (probably from a secondary source); *Confessio Amantis*, VII. 3925–30.

ll. 498–500: proverbial; cf. *Mirour de l'Omme*, ll. 22835–6; also l. 549, below; Walz, 241c.

ll. 513–14: proverbial; cf. Chaucer, *Troilus and Criseyde*, II. 1380–3.

l. 519: adapted from Ovid, *Metamorphoses*, 1. 76.

ll. 529–32: cf. *Confessio Amantis*, VII. 2695–9.

l. 550* (A-text): proverbial; cf. *Mirour de l'Omme*, l. 6357; Walz, 128b.

ll. 573*–4* (A-text): cf. Daniel 13: 5.

l. 549 (B-text): proverbial – Walz, 241d; also ll. 498–500, above.

l. 576: cf. Matthew 10: 26; Mark 4: 22; Luke 12: 2.

Ch. 8 heading: cf. *Confessio Amantis*, VII. 1825–48, 2709–64, 3067–94; VIII. 2109–25.

ll. 593–4: cf. Proverbs 1: 7.

ll. 611–12: cf. I Corinthians 10: 23; 6: 12.

l. 629: adapted from Alexander Neckam, *De Vita Monachorum*, ed. Wright, II. 185, l. 7.

l. 630: *verbatim* Alexander Neckam, *De Vita Monachorum*, ed. Wright, II. 185, l. 8.

ll. 631–2: i.e., Aristotle, who had a secondary reputation as a (failed) lover: cf. *Confessio Amantis*, VIII. 2705–13.

l. 638: i.e., the pot retains the taint of what first filled it; proverbial.

l. 640: proverbial.

l. 642: cf. Ecclesiasticus 13: 1; *Mirour de l'Omme*, ll. 13684–7.

ll. 659–60: virtually *verbatim* Peter Riga, *Aurora*, Machabeorum 31–2.

l. 681: proverbial – Walz, 111.

ll. 685–6: *verbatim* Peter Riga, *Aurora*, Genesis 1339–40.

l. 696: *verbatim* Ovid, *Remedia Amoris*, 526.

l. 713: adapted from Nigel of Longchamp, *Speculum Stultorum*, ed. Mann, l. 553.

ll. 719–22: virtually *verbatim* Peter Riga, *Aurora*, Leviticus 683–6.

## Notes to Book VI

ll. 723–4: virtually *verbatim* Peter Riga, *Aurora*, Leviticus 299–300.

Ch. 10: cf. *Confessio Amantis*, VII. 3873–90.

l. 750: *verbatim* Ovid, *Heroides*, 17. 130.

l. 752: *verbatim* Ovid, *Heroides*, 17. 234.

l. 753: virtually *verbatim* Ovid, *Metamorphoses*, 1. 246.

ll. 755–6: cf. *Confessio Amantis*, VII. 4135–9.

l. 757: virtually *verbatim* Ovid, *Tristia*, 4. 9. 21.

l. 765: virtually *verbatim* Ovid, *Ars Amatoria*, 3. 557.

l. 779: adapted from Ovid, *Metamorphoses*, 3. 700.

ll. 793–4: virtually *verbatim* Peter Riga, *Aurora*, I Kings 309–10.

l. 816: virtually *verbatim* Ovid, *Amores*, 1. 8. 62.

l. 825: *verbatim* Ovid, *Amores*, 1. 10. 61.

ll. 831–2: cf. Romans 6: 23.

ll. 835–6: a tradition in the Middle Ages traceable to Cassian identified gluttony as humanity's first – Adam's – sin. Gower attributes Satan's earlier fall to pride, calling it the first, and the root, of all sin: cf. *VC* III. 729–32, above; VII. 619–26; *Carmen super multiplici viciorum pestilencia*, l. 96.

ll. 837–8: cf. Matthew 4: 1–4; Luke 4: 1–4.

ll. 839–40: virtually *verbatim* Peter Riga, *Aurora*, I Kings 265–6.

l. 846: *verbatim* Ovid, *Fasti*, 2. 226.

Ch. 12: cf. *Confessio Amantis*, VII. 4215–56.

ll. 863–4: virtually *verbatim* Peter Riga, *Aurora*, III Kings 253–4.

l. 869: proverbial; a version also appears in Nigel of Longchamp, *Speculum Stultorum*, ed. Mann, l. 3893, but is rejected there by the editor as a commonplace, rather than a borrowing.

ll. 875–902: *verbatim* Peter Riga, *Aurora*, Numeri 503–34, omitting 517–18, 531–2. Peter, and Gower, follow a tradition in which Balaam (of Bosor, hence a Levite) as a false prophet encouraged Balak to use women to lure the Israelites into sin and so defeat them. Cf. Apocalypse 2: 14 (Vulgate); II Peter 2: 15; Jude 11.

l. 903: "te docet experimentum" reverses usual proverbial order of "experimentia docet," probably in an (imperfect) attempt at Leonine rhyme ("notam"/"experimentum"), although Gower also writes "docet experiencia" in Latin verses *Confessio Amantis*, I. ii; but cf. also *VC* V. 463–4.

ll. 905–10: i.e., the witch of Endor: cf. I Kings 28 (Vulgate); I Paralipomenon 10: 13 (Vulgate); *Confessio Amantis*, VI. 2384–90; and also ll. 1299–300, below.

l. 907: *verbatim* Peter Riga, *Aurora*, I Kings 535.

l. 913: cf. *Traitié pour les amantz marietz*, XVII. Refrain.

l. 937: Edward of Woodstock, called the Black Prince, captured John II, king of France, at the battle of Poitiers in 1356; in 1367 he defeated the Spanish Count Enrique II Trastámara at the battle of Nájera.

ll. 939–40: virtually *verbatim* Peter Riga, *Aurora*, Machabeorum 79–80.

ll. 942–4.: *verbatim* Peter Riga, *Aurora*, Machabeorum 92–4.

ll. 945–6: virtually *verbatim* Peter Riga, *Aurora*, Machabeorum 175, 130.

ll. 947–50: *verbatim* Peter Riga, *Aurora*, I Kings 545–6, 543–4.

ll. 955–60: virtually *verbatim* Peter Riga, *Aurora*, Genesis 1413, 1416, 1415, 1408, 1431, 1436.

l. 960: "leopardus": heraldic term for a "lion passant gardant," three of which constitute the royal arms of England. Cf. *VC* I. 263–4.

ll. 961–4: virtually *verbatim* Peter Riga, *Aurora*, Machabeorum 273–6.

ll. 965–6: virtually *verbatim* Peter Riga, *Aurora*, II Kings 33–4.

l. 969: proverbial; cf. *Confessio Amantis*, VII. 4902–3, and Latin marginal note.

l. 971: "pax super omne bonum": cf. *In Praise of Peace*, l. 78: "Pes is the chief of al the worldes welthe."

l. 973: cf. Ecclesiastes 3: 8.

l. 976: virtually *verbatim* Ovid, *Ex Ponto*, 3. 4. 86.

ll. 983–5: proverbial – cf. Walz, 119.

ll. 985–92: virtually *verbatim* Peter Riga, *Aurora*, Leviticus 635–42.

l. 997: proverbial – Walz, 178.

l. 999: "Omnia vincit amor": proverbial; cf. Chaucer, *CT* GenPro I. (A) 162; ultimately Virgil, *Bucolics*, Eclogue 10, 69.

ll. 1019–22: virtually *verbatim* Alexander Neckam, *De Vita Monachorum*, ed. Wright, p. 185, ll. 5–6, 9–10.

l. 1020: cf. Ephesians 4: 4–6.

l. 1041: *verbatim* Peter Riga, *Aurora*, III Kings 21.

ll. 1043–50: virtually *verbatim* Peter Riga, *Aurora*, III Kings 23–30.

l. 1056: cf. Matthew 7: 24–5; Luke 6: 48.

l. 1081: *verbatim* Nigel of Longchamp, *Speculum Stultorum*, ed. Mann, l. 195.

ll. 1085–6: *verbatim* Alexander Neckam, *De Vita Monachorum*, ed. Wright, II. 184, ll. 25–6.

ll. 1107–12: *verbatim* Alexander Neckam, *De Vita Monachorum*, ed. Wright, II. 193, ll. 9–14.

ll. 1113–14: *verbatim* Alexander Neckam, *De Vita Monachorum*, ed. Wright, II. 193, ll. 17–18.

ll. 1115–16: *verbatim* Alexander Neckam, *De Vita Monachorum*, ed. Wright, II. 183, ll. 13, 19.

l. 1125: proverbial; cf. *Confessio Amantis*, II. 3243–9; Walz, 152.

l. 1134: virtually *verbatim* Ovid, *Tristia*, 4. 3. 74.

ll. 1135–6: "Bella...tria": i.e., against the world, the flesh, and the devil; cf. Job 7: 1 (Vulgate).

ll. 1145–8: *verbatim* Peter Riga, *Aurora*, Numeri 180, 23–6.

ll. 1149–50: *verbatim* Peter Riga, *Aurora*, Numeri 29–30.

l. 1178* (A-text): *verbatim* Ovid, *Ars Amatoria*, 1. 214.

l. 1189* (A-text): *verbatim* Ovid, *Tristia*, 4. 5. 25.

l. 1201: virtually *verbatim* Ovid, *Metamorphoses*, 7. 586.

l. 1205: *verbatim* Ovid, *Metamorphoses*, 2. 541.

ll. 1215–40: Gower's claim here is that while all those he names from the Old Testament ("lege...vetusta") offering good examples ("exempla") have died, the wicked ones now "live," figured in contemporary behaviors, resulting in the "dying away" of the New Law ("testamentum...nouum"). Although all are biblical figures, for most of his details Gower seems to rely on the *Aurora*.

ll. 1215–16: Noah (who "found grace before the Lord," cf. Genesis 6–9, at 6: 8); Nimrod (Genesis 10: 8–9, "a mighty hunter before the Lord," subsequently blamed by Jerome and others for building the Tower of Babel [Genesis 11: 1–9], and thereby affronting God).

ll. 1217–18: Japhet and Ham are sons of Noah (Genesis 6: 10), the former covering Noah, drunk and exposed, while the latter mocked him, for which Noah cursed Ham (Genesis 9: 21–4).

ll. 1219–20: Abraham, to whom and his progeny God promised Canaan (Genesis 17: 1–8); Bel is a Babylonian – and hence false – god, revealed by Daniel, who destroys both idol and temple (Daniel 14: 1–22, Isaiah 46: 1, Jeremiah 50: 2, 51: 44).

ll. 1221–2: Isaac, whom God blesses, and Ishmael are sons of Abraham (Genesis 17: 18–21), subsequently interpreted by Paul (Galatians 4: 28–9) as spirit and flesh, respectively.

ll. 1223–4: Joseph, the favored son of Jacob and Rachel (Genesis 30: 24–5), who – among many other accomplishments – founded the Israelite tribe of Joseph, and fostered settlement by his people in Goshen (Genesis 45: 9–10). Uzzah (Oza) offended God by clutching the Arc of the Covenant, for which presumption he was killed: II Kings 6: 1–7 (Vulgate), I Paralipomenon 13: 9–10 (Vulgate). Gower seems to rely on *Aurora*, Secundus Regem 115–20 for his depiction of Uzzah's debauchery.

ll. 1225–6: for Moses, see Exodus; Abiram and his brother Dathan, along with Korah, plotted against Moses and Aaron, only to be swallowed by the earth as punishment (Numbers 16: 1–40, also cf. *Mirour de l'Omme*, ll. 2341–52).

ll. 1227–8: God appointed Aaron, elder brother of Moses, the first priest of the Israelites and his family, the Levites, continued in that role, maintaining temple rituals (Exodus 28: 1–3; Leviticus 1–2); Korah attempted to supplant Aaron and, while bearing incense to the temple, was swallowed by the earth (see ll. 1225–6 and note, above).

ll. 1229–30: Elijah, sent by God to end the worship of Baal in Israel, instituted by Ahab (III Kings 16–18 [Vulgate]), was rewarded by being brought alive to heaven in a fiery chariot amid a whirlwind (IV Kings 2: 1–11 [Vulgate]); for Dathan, see ll. 1225–6 above, and note.

ll. 1231–4: Micaiah, a minor prophet and disciple of Elijah who correctly advised Ahab not to enter battle, contradicting 400 others led by Zedekiah whose false prediction of victory brought about Ahab's death (III Kings 22: 7–38 [Vulgate], II Paralipomenon 18: 6–34, also *Confessio Amantis*, VII. 2527–694).

ll. 1235–6: Elisha, successor to Elijah who inherited twice the latter's powers, cured Naaman, a Syrian commander, of his leprosy by directing him to bathe in the River Jordan, thus convincing Naaman of the power of God (IV Kings 5: 1–19 [Vulgate]); Gehazi, servant to Elisha, pretending to represent Elisha, undeservedly sought rewards from Naaman, bringing Naaman's leprosy upon himself and his children (IV Kings 20–7 [Vulgate]).

ll. 1237–8: Noah releases a raven, then a dove, to test the safety of leaving the ark, and while the raven – a carrion eater – doesn't return, the dove does, the second time bearing an olive twig with green leaves, the third time remaining out, so that Noah knew it was safe to leave the ark (Genesis 8: 1–13).

l. 1243: Peter (Simon) the Apostle is considered the first pope, based on Matthew 16: 18; Liberius, pope CE 352–66, was believed to have deviated into Arianism, pressured by Constantine.

l. 1244: cf. Acts 8: 9–24.

ll. 1245–6: Paul the Apostle, a Pharisee originally called Saul, and a persecutor of Christians, experienced a conversion – a "rebirth in Christ" – on the road to Damascus, thereafter taking the name Paul; cf. Acts 9.

ll. 1247–8: Pope Gregory I, "the Great" (CE 590–604); probably Gower has in mind Gregory's *Liber regulae pastoralis*, in which he emphasized episcopalian responsibility for pastoral care – an idea reflected in Gregory's best-known description of a pope as "servus servorum Dei" (servant of the servants of God). Cf. *VC* III. 161 ff.

ll. 1249–50: St. Martin, bishop of Tours (CE 371–97); a Roman cavalry officer serving in Gaul at age eighteen, Martin cut his military cloak in half to clothe a freezing beggar, later dreaming that Jesus appeared to him, wearing the half-cloak and commending him for his charitable act – a vision which confirmed him in the faith.

ll. 1251–2: cf. Tobias 1: 19–21 (Vulgate).

ll. 1253–6: the "patience of Job" in the face of adversity is proverbial.

l. 1257: St. Benedict of Nursia (ca. CE 480–543) founded the first monastic order, the Benedictines, composing a Rule ("regula") directing a simple life devoid of private possessions, devoted to study, labor, and prayer, that became a model for all subsequent cloistered – or regular – orders.

l. 1258: Julian (Flavius Claudius Julianus), emperor of Rome CE 361–3; known as "the Apostate" for having renounced Christianity in favor of neoplatonic Hellenism and actively seeking to eradicate the faith from the empire.

ll. 1259–60: cf. Matthew 5: 13, Luke 14: 33–5; cf. *VC* III. 1997–8.

l. 1261: cf. John 12: 24–6.

l. 1262: "cardo": i.e., heretical sects, here possibly lollardy – cf. "lollia," *Carmen super multiplici viciorum pestilencia*, l. 29; "zizania," Matthew 13: 25; and see ll. 2267–8, below, and note.

ll. 1265–70: cf. *De lucis scrutinio, passim*.

ll. 1267–8: Arius (ca. CE. 256–336) argued for the supremacy of God the Father, contrary to the doctrine of the Trinity; countering Arianism occupied the first Council of Nicaea (CE 325). Jovinian (d. ca. CE 405), known mainly from Jerome's *Adversus Jovinanum* (where he is called "the Christian Epicurus"), rejected Christian asceticism, favoring select bodily pleasures, including clerical marriage; Gower (and others) seem to connect him with Wyclif (cf. *Carmen super multiplici viciorum pestilencia*, ll. 30–3), and later periods praised him, along with Wyclif, as a precursor of Protestantism.

l. 1273: "Troianus": Marcus Ulpius Nerva Traianus (Trajan), Roman emperor (CE 98–117), brought an era of peace and rule of law while expanding the empire to maximum size and instituting public works and social programs; for these latter, medieval legend had it that Gregory the Great convinced God to elevate Trajan from hell where, as a pagan, he had been condemned. In the Middle Ages Nero (Nero Claudius Caesar Augustus Germanicus, emperor CE 54–68) was emblematic of debauchery, tyranny, and cruelty, following descriptions by Tacitus and Suetonius.

l. 1275: "Justinianus": Justinian the Great (CE 527–65), who oversaw the codification of civil law, the *Corpus iuris civilis*.

l. 1276: "Dionisius": may be Dionysius, bishop of Alexandria (ca. CE 247–64), who briefly fell into Arianism, but later recanted, promoting the Trinity.

l. 1277: "Valentinianus": probably Valentinian III (ca. CE 419–55) Roman emperor, an ardent Christian devoted to St. Lawrence, established Rome as the western center of Christianity based on the primacy of Peter, thus ensuring papal authority.

l. 1278: "Tarquinius": Lucius Tarquinius Superbus (d. 495 BCE), the last king of Rome before popular revolt against his tyrannical rule, spurred on by his son Sixtus' (not Aruns) rape of a noblewoman, Lucretia, established the Republic. Cf. *Confessio Amantis*, VII. 4593–5130.

l. 1279: "Largus Alexander": Alexander the Great was famed for his liberality; cf. *Confessio Amantis*, VII. 3168*–79*, 5384–97.

l. 1280: "Cresus avarus": Croesus, king of Lydia (585–46 BCE), defeated by the Persian Cyrus I; his wealth was recorded by many, including Herodotus. NB: Gower's depiction of Croesus' wealth (*Confessio Amantis*, IV. 1325, V. 4730–4) may be the earliest English source for the expression "rich as Croesus."

l. 1281: "pius...Constantinus": Constantine the Great, first Roman emperor (CE 306–37) to convert to, and establish, Christianity as the state religion, convoked the First Council of Nicaea (CE 325), whereat the text of the Creed was set and proclaimed. Cf. *Confessio Amantis*, II. 3187–496.

l. 1282: "Antonius": appointed bishop of Fussola by Augustine, extorted

## Notes to Book VI

money, property, and sexual favors from his diocese; eventually removed from office by episcopal tribunal, to Augustine's discredit.

l. 1283: "Theodosius": likely Theodosius II, Byzantine emperor (CE 402–50); directed compilation of the *Codex Theodosianus*, an essential scaffolding for the subsequent *Corpus iuris civilis* of Justinian I that anchored medieval legal practices, both civil and canon.

l. 1284: "Leo": Probably Leo III "the Isaurian," Eastern Roman emperor (CE 717–41), after deposing Theodosius III; his absolute ban on image veneration brought him into bitter dispute with western Popes Gregory II and Gregory III, who maintained the validity of the practice. In the context of Wyclif's criticism of image worship, Gower's condemnation of Leo is apposite.

l. 1285: "Constancius": Constantine II, son of Constantine the Great, succeeded his father, ruling the Eastern Empire, CE 337–40. Aggressively Arian Christian, he disputed Christ's nature with the Roman popes, who followed the Nicene Creed, established by Constantine I in 325; cf. l. 1282 above, and note.

l. 1286: probably Tiberius Constantinus (Tiberius II Constantine), Eastern emperor, CE 574–82; an ardent Christian, reputedly liberal, just, and compassionate, he died of a food-related issue, possibly poison, and was succeeded by his son-in-law, Maurice; cf. *Confessio Amantis*, II. 587–1598, and Chaucer, "Man of Law's Tale," *CT* II. (B$_1$).

l. 1292: "Heleno": Helenus, son of Priam and Hecuba and brother to Cassandra, with whom he shared prophetic powers, and like whom, Dares Phrygius asserts, he pressed Priam to make peace; Apollodorus claims Helenus betrayed the secret of the Palladium to Odysseus (*Epitome*, 5. 10).

l. 1293: "Eacides": patronymic of Achilles, from Aeacus, king of Aegina and father of Peleus – hence Achilles' grandfather.

l. 1294: "Tersites": Thersites, a common soldier who mocked Agamemnon and the justification for the Trojan War: cf. *Iliad*, II.

l. 1295: "Salomon" (Solomon): cf. III Kings 4: 29 (Vulgate); "Roboas": i.e., Rehoboam, cf. III Kings 12–13, II Paralipomenon 10: 1–15 (Vulgate); cf. also *Confessio Amantis*, VII. 4027–146; *VC* II. 325–36.

l. 1297: "Ionathe...Dauid": Jonathan and David: cf. I Kings 18: 1–4 (Vulgate).

ll. 1298–300: cf. *Confessio Amantis*, IV. 1935–62; ll. 905–10 above, and note.

ll. 1301–2: "Pharaonis": cf. Exodus 10: 20.

ll. 1303–4: cf. Deuteronomy 28: 15, 27.

ll. 1305–6: "Achitofellis...Cusay" (Achitophel, Hushai): cf. II Kings 16: 16–23 (Vulgate).

ll. 1307–8: "Ioab...Abner" (Joab, Abner): cf. II Kings 3: 27 (Vulgate); but cf. also Flavius Josephus, *Antiquities of the Jews*, VII. 1.

l. 1309: "Cato": Probably Marcus Porcius Cato Uticensis, i.e., Cato the Younger (95–46 BCE), famous for his honesty.

l. 1310: cf. Matthew 27: 1–66.

ll. 1311–12: cf. Genesis 4: 1–8.

ll. 1313–14: "Mardocheum...Aman": Haman, an evil counsellor of Persian King Ahasuerus (Xerxes I, 485–65 BCE), plots to have all Jews killed, including Mordechai, but all are saved by Queen Esther, and Haman is executed for his treachery: cf. Esther 1–16.

ll. 1315–16: cf. Matthew 27: 15–23; Mark 15: 6–15; Luke 23: 17–21; John 18: 39–40.

l. 1319: Plato records Socrates exploring the claim that virtue is knowledge and vice ignorance in the *Apology*; but see also variants in the *Gorgias*, *Meno*, and *Laws*.

l. 1320: Epicurus (341–270 BCE) taught that the best life was self-sufficient, peaceful, and painless, ended by death without afterlife, all of which earned him intense condemnation by early Christians, who interpreted his ideas as amoral and licentious.

ll. 1321–2: Diogenes the Cynic (ca. 404–323 BCE) espoused poverty as an antidote to an ephemeral worldliness, begged his food and slept in a large jar or tun in the Athens marketplace; intellectually he opposed Socratic/Platonic abstraction, arguing that action, not theory, revealed virtue. Aristippus (ca. 435–356 BCE), the founder of hedonism – i.e., life's purpose is pleasure – is Diogenes' antithesis. Cf. *Confessio Amantis*, III. 1202–311, VII. 2217–323.

l. 1323: by "Phirinus" Gower intends Spurina, a Roman so virtuous that he lacerated his face, to destroy what many found a beauty too tempting; cf. *Mirour de l'Omme*, ll. 18301–12, *Confessio Amantis*, V. 6372–94. *Mirour de l'Omme*, l. 18303, Gower cites "Valiere" (i.e., Valerius Maximus, *Factorum et dictorum memorabilium*, iv. 5) as his source.

l. 1324: "Mechus...Agladius": an unknown character; possibly an allusion to the legal barring, until the reign of Severus (Marcus Aurelius Severus Alexander, CE 145–211), of Roman soldiers from marriage during the sixteen years of their service, with predictable negative consequences.

ll. 1325–8: "Troilus," a son of Priam of Troy, loved and was faithful to Cressida

## Notes to Book VI

(Crisaida) who, however, was unfaithful with Diomedes; cf. *Confessio Amantis*, V. 7597–602; Chaucer, *Troilus and Criseyde*. Jason, after winning the Golden Fleece with the help of Medea, whom he later married, only to desert her for Creusa; cf. *Confessio Amantis*, V. 3265–4222, *Traitié pour les amantz marietz*, VIII. 1–21, *Cinkante Balades*, XLIII. 1. 1.

l. 1329: "Semiramis": a (probably) legendary queen of Assyria, whose reputation as incestuous and promiscuous is traceable to Orosius, was a medieval commonplace; cf. *Confessio Amantis*, V. 1430–3.

l. 1330: "Cassandra": Daughter of Priam, promised her favors to Apollo in exchange for the gift of foresight which, once obtained, she refused the god in order to remain chaste; for this she was punished by never having her prophecies believed.

l. 1331: "Penolope" (Penelope): wife who remained faithful to Odysseus, eluding suitors for ten years while he was away at Troy; cf. *Confessio Amantis*, VI. 1471–90; "Lucrecia" (Lucretia), faithful wife of Collatinus, who, when raped by Sextus Tarquinius, killed herself to show she had continued faithful; cf. *Confessio Amantis*, VII. 4754–5123, *Traitié pour les amantz marietz*, X. 8–14, *VC* VI. 1278, above, and note.

l. 1332: "Circes" (Circe): divine sorceress who transforms Odysseus' men – but not Odysseus himself – into animals; according to Hesiod she bore him three sons, one of whom, Telegonus, later inadvertently kills him. "Calipsa" (Caliypso): nymph who keeps Odysseus prisoner on her island of Ogygia for seven years, sleeping with him every night; cf. *Mirour de l'Omme*, ll. 16669–80, *Confessio Amantis*, VI. 1391–788.

l. 1333: "Iustina" (Justine): either St. Justina of Padua, who remained firm in her chastity when tempted by the prefect Maximian, for which in frustrated rage he put her to the sword; or St. Justina of Antioch, who converted the sorcerer Cyprian after demons he sent failed to obvert her chastity; both later tortured and beheaded by Roman Emperor Diocletian.

l. 1334: "Thaisis" (Thais): reputedly mistress of Alexander the Great and later wife of his general Ptolemy I of Egypt.

l. 1335: Paris' abduction of Helen, wife of Menelaus, brought about the Trojan War.

l. 1337: "Hymeneus": god presiding over marriages.

l. 1343: cf. Genesis 2: 24.

l. 1345: adapted from Ovid, *Amores*, 1. 9. 1.

ll. 1347–9: *verbatim* Ovid, *Ars Amatoria*, 2. 481–3.

l. 1361: "Iesabel": Jezebel, Sidonian (i.e., Phoenician) wife of Ahab, who persuaded him to turn away from Yahweh to worship Baal, her deity; cf. III Kings 16: 30–1 (Vulgate).

l. 1362: "Iosue": successor to Moses who led the Israelites across the Jordan into the land of promise; cf. Joshua 1: 1–2.

# BOOK VII

Book VII pulls together the argument of the poem, which now specifies that it has discussed not the three estates but (as the first headnote puts it) "the spiritual as well as the secular degrees of society" responsible for the present state of affairs. The Book's opening lines draw a direct parallel between what can be learned from the past and England's own present difficulties:

> What is wont of late to lurk in ancient figures,
> We can verify from our own troubles.

An account of Nebuchadnezzar's dream of the shattered statue whose sole remnant is its feet, one of clay and the other of iron, is offered in evidence of the poet's reading of history. Avarice and lust, the two sins that have been the primary focus of Gower's attention throughout the poem, are shown to be deeply seated in human affairs. The iron of the shattered statue's one foot represents avarice, which characterizes the iron heart of the miser who lacks compassion. The other foot's clay stands for the lust that renders human life and institutions brittle, able to be shattered in a moment. The world, intended by God as a place of preparation for the day of judgment, has been turned upside down by humanity's misdirected desires, all the more deplorable because everything worldly is transitory, and unworthy when compared to eternal permanence. Commitment to the world and its pleasures, characterized by the seven deadly sins, leads to damnation. Commitment to Christian values leads to life everlasting. Unfortunately, Gower contends, present circumstances make clear that mankind has not learned this fundamental truth, despite the fact that God frequently sends instructive signs and portents. All parts of English society are equally guilty, and their collective failure has damaged England greatly, to the extent it is plain that the "end days" may well have come. Appropriately for a concluding commentary on such a subject, Book VII is largely eschatological in its content. The wages of sin are described in a conventional but nonetheless chilling account of the Last Judgment and the torments of hell. All sinners are urged to look to their sinful ways, repent while there is still time, and earn the joys of salvation.

The final chapter of Book VII re-establishes the poem's essential nature as an indictment, specifying again that it is a *libellus*, written in the hope that it will lead to a reinvigoration of national virtue based upon the emended conduct of every Englishman. Reiterating that his poem charges no specific individual with any fault, Gower's final message in the *Vox Clamantis* counsels: Let each look to himself.

*Vox Clamantis* by *John Gower: 'The Voice of One Crying'*

# HERE BEGINS THE SEVENTH BOOK

## Chapter 1

**After a discussion to this point of each of the spiritual as well as the secular degrees of society, throughout which sin has everywhere spread, now he intends to discuss certain ideas some hold about the feet of \*the statue that Nebuchadnezzar saw in dreams, one of which was iron, one clay, in a figure of the deterioration of this world to which at the present time we have plainly arrived, which is almost at the end of time. And first he will show the significance of the iron.**

What is wont of late to lurk in ancient figures,
   We can verify from our own troubles.
What frightened the ancients in slumber's dark shadow,
   Lo! today's unsleeping crisis now shows.
Nebuchadnezzar's golden head has been cut off,\*
   But his two feet of iron and clay still stand.
A golden people has departed from the world,\*
   A lesser one of iron sprung from it.
No great man's glorious fame flies over the earth,
   Whose honor befits both God and the world.    10
No benefactor spreads his wealth now to the poor,
   And no rich man maintains them at his board.
Scarce anyone for pity clothes the naked poor,
   Nor takes in travelers that need lodging.
No one wants to show concern for those in prison,
   And no healthy hand assists the infirm.
There's no one at the present who comes to repair
   Love's ancient bond between the contentious.

But I think that now there are mainly two reasons
   For which this world abandons righteousness.    20
Of these, lust is seen to be the first in order,
   From which arises dull torpor and sloth.
Thus nowadays it makes the knight come late to arms,
   Whom his wife strokes with love in her chamber.
And it commonly seals the lips of the clergy,
   So that they cannot chant their prayers to God.
Balaam's counsel has conquered us through our women,\*
   So God, provoked, smites the folk, who perish.
But the second cause is the age's avarice,
   Which fosters envy in the world anew.    30

It plunders, fights, murders, and nullifies the law,
   So peace, because of war, cannot return.
Outwardly, greedy lords grasp peace's benefits,*
   But inwardly their first concern is war.
When war can return him more profits than can peace,
   A miser won't love peace's benefits.
Your envy won't permit you to grant me my peace,
   For my sobs will be laughter in your ears.
It's naught to you if downtrodden people rue loss,
   When common misfortune brings you profit.            40

Thus Avarice says that she subdues our bigwigs'
   Hearts, and they say they will subdue our rights.
Thus, overwhelmed by gold, freeborn honor departs,
   Loathe to return to the seat of justice.
Thus the miser's dropsical taste for coins is clear;
   When he drinks, his thirst desires ever more.
Thus Dives does not hold rents, but is held by them,*
   And thus the lord himself serves his own serfs.
The rich man is wealthy without but poor within;
   He has nothing, which he thinks is his all.          50
The stony hardness of his mind can't melt away,
   Nor does pity's help free him from coldness.
He laughs to scorn the poor man's tears, from whose travail
   He wants to take his own peace and quiet.
Thus the miser's soul is buried beneath his coins;
   Those gods he grasps, forgetting to grasp God.

## Chapter 2

**Here he speaks mainly against misers in these times, harder than any iron, whose riches can be of no value, as he says, unless they are shared.**

Alas! Why does he pile up wealth, who wants what's his,
   When no one can even possess himself?
He can't own any property, since who is owned
   Can't own. Who doesn't own himself, owns naught.     60
Owners serve what's owned; they are owned, not owners; rents
   Own the miser; wealth lords it over lords.
Since you can't be your own, nothing is yours; no one
   Can be his own, thus what you have is naught.

## Vox Clamantis by John Gower: 'The Voice of One Crying'

If someone claims his owner's things for himself, and
  The lord's holding should then be called the serf's,
The ownings go with the re-subjugated serf,
  And he and his wealth become his owner's.
The serf accrues for his master, and not himself;
  What he owns, it's plain that his master owns.              70
Greed's slave is not his own master, and, misusing*
  His free will, has no right to anything.
When you know nothing is your own, you become rich;
  What you keep harms you, and what you share helps.

For indeed there's nobody shall be truly blessed
  Who's unable to share with his fellow.
All agree that they who can't give are destitute;
  When they fail the needy, rich men are poor.
They're rich because they have things, but they're poor because
  There's no one with whom they will share their wealth.       80
If you have large holdings, and nobody with whom
  You will share, then your plenty is nothing.
You may have looks, charm, a nice shape and a good mind,
  But they're pointless if there's nobody there.
Spend what you have, as sound usage dictates; for use
  Give your wealth, not to nourish avarice.
Grant the naked and poor the use of your excess;
  The love of kindness decorates friendship.
You manage your goods to consume or employ them;
  Be willing to employ that which you have.              90
But there's so much avarice these days, my writings
  Convey not a thing to the rich man's ears.

It's not only the magnates that become misers,
  For we know that the commons are guilty.
As a hen fills her capacious gizzard with grain,
  And gets much of her food from the least things,
The tight miser hoards up and increases his coins,
  Nothing so modest it won't yield profit.
Such a man inflicts hunger on his own belly,
  So that his purse might acquire more money.          100
Hard and stingy, with a stingy heart he preserves
  His possessions so no one shall share them.
And, lest God go there, he's lost the key to his heart,
  Where he wants to lock mercy's duties up.
Thus he can't take pleasure of his acquisitions,

And, while he has it all, he has nothing.
It's as though all of mankind have hearts of iron,*
   Since the head has been lopped from the statue.
The golden times that had prevailed are now iron,*
   And an iron nature inheres in man.                         110
And honesty's golden mean, which our forefathers*
   Cultivated, lo! greed these days destroys.

He's wretched who wants more, not he who gets less; nay,
   Who's content with what he has, has enough.
I don't condemn the rich man's riches, but approve
   Them if they are given when need requires.
Rich men aren't at fault for their money, but for not
   Benefitting their brothers nor themselves.
If their hand were generous, if they would share some
   With the poor, Mammon would be praiseworthy.*        120
But scarce a rich man lives in the world of today
   Who saves wealth to help himself and others.
The text from the Apocalypse, "Hold what you have,"*
   Is now a law that's totally enforced.
Modern hearts are now encircled by veins of flint,*
   And unyielding breasts hold lumps of iron.
Rich men don't hear the sounds of the paupers' clamor;
   Nay, they are turned to stone in their hearing.
There'll come a time when you, who now shut out the poor,
   Go to your last place, a pauper in need.                130
You have changed now, you ages, to iron from gold,*
   And whatsoever was noble is base.
Lowly greed overcomes the higher qualities;
   Honor no longer knows the throne it sat.

## Chapter 3

**Here he talks about the second part of the statue's feet, and about the significance of this part, which was brittle clay.**

Nowadays it's the last age of clay throughout earth,*
   Of which the statue's feet give me portents.
The potter's brittle clay pot is not more swiftly
   Shattered into shards, when a stone strikes it,
Than mankind's brittle circumstance now lies shattered,
   Broken by the vehemence of its sin.                    140

The laity are clay, but the clergy, more so,
  Whose wicked example occasions sin.
They prescribe flesh, their Holy Writ, for all the world,
  Where no epistle of Christ is now seen.
He who bids us subdue the flesh, we see subdued,
  And his teaching spurned by the "learned man."
The clergy itself claims a spiritual name,
  But their spirit itself has become flesh.
For they so commonly commit sins of the flesh,
  That continual use scarcely shames them.                    150
It's as if woman is lord and master of man,
  And man a handmaid slave, prone and pliant.
Weak folly falls upon the strong man and conquers,
  And he who should be wise falls, made of clay.
Since clergy march beneath Venus' rampant banners,
  She now seeks tribute from all the nations.

The French sins to which they have fallen nowadays*
  Already claim title to our houses.
All are now allowed to frequent another's wife;
  It's the plight of the nobles; it's called love.            160
It won't be sin for laymen, but great distinction,
  When men are aggrandized by adultery,
When adulterous wives court debauchery for gifts:*
  Husbands who suffer the deed are absolved.
So people now sell themselves just as though they're whores,
  When Venus' propitious hand is generous.
Thus, under the guise of false love, they are enlarged,
  And seek shameful gain through such wickedness.
But he who, prompted by a cleric, takes a wife,
  Shall, since her lover's there, give Venus more.            170
For the poor brother gets here what he'll give there, so,
  Giving or taking, he profits the more.
The age of clay causes that in brittle cases,
  Where every man now shatters easily.

But false Hypocrisy tries to hide his secret
  Frauds, and secretly does many vile deeds.
Thus he thrives in appearance by false pallor's grace,*
  So his hollow cheeks hide his sordid deeds.
But justice does not adorn the cheeks of his mind;
  Nay, pleasing the world he reproaches God.                  180
Thus nettles steal the rose's appearance, and lead

## Book VII

In gold's guise allows guile to lie hidden.
Unjust men hide behind just, cursed behind holy,
   And wicked behind those who practice faith.
They don the mantle of the virtues so it hides
   Their fault, lest anybody should shun them.
They appear shining white outside, but inside them
   Lurks the blackness of every corruption.
Thus their hate flatters the ear like the voice of peace;
   Their mouths speak friendship, but their minds, fierce threats.[1]   190
So the crow stands garbed in the feathers of the dove,
   And the falcon feigns the turtle's manner.
So Satan's spirit takes on Gabriel's aspect,*
   With a maiden's head, but a serpent's tail.
Its outward appearance shows you honeyed candies,
   Which if you taste will be, like myrrh, bitter.
Know Hypocrisy is the devil's chest, in which
   He keeps all of sin's wickedness shut up.
You can hide a needle inside a bag, but it
   Will still give a hot prick on the outside.   200
Hypocrisy can't hide so it won't show itself,
   And so that its flawed virtue isn't clear.
This vice wants to expound the gloss of its own vice;
   While it raves madly, its wrath reveals it.
It hides all the day in false piety's shadow
   As soon as you bring a charge against it.
So a wolf hidden under a lamb's fleece bares its*
   Teeth, and reveals hidden blood-stained misdeeds.
Thus virtue, conquered, labors 'neath vice's burden,
   And no freeman gets what's due him from serfs.   210
The reins of shame are slackened to please the vices,
   Who ruin the gracious path to good custom.
Thus I conclude, in short, that virtue everywhere
   Is in service, and vice has the front pews.
Every rule, turned upside down, deceives nowadays,
   And all the world is full of modern tricks.

---

[1] There is an alternate text in EHT:
   Thus a tomb made of gold gleams outside, and within
     It smells of decay, its corpse food for worms.
  DL contain both distichs.

## Chapter 4

**Here he talks yet further about the distresses, emerging in modern times, that were already figured in the varied nature of the statue's feet; indeed, he says that the aspects of the human condition that formerly had been virtuous have nowadays been changed into their opposites.**

    A bitter thing now turns sweet, a sweet thing bitter,
        Foul becomes fair, because the system fails.
    Learning becomes heresy; sins become virtues;
        Guile, genius; and stolen loot, honest gain.           220
    Holy orders become vagrant; saints, feigning mimes;
        The talkative are wise; the tongue-tied, fools.
    The easy confessor is a repeat sinner;
        His words are holy, but his deeds, wicked.
    The fox now guards the chickens; and the wolf, the lambs;
        The hawk, partridges; and the hearth, dry wood.
    Learned men and prophets are sinful counterfeits;
        Fabulous fictions please, not Holy Writ.
    Useful teaching displeases, but the sheer pleasure
        Of Venus' chatter is joy to our ears.           230
    Now love is lust and marriage is adultery,
        And sex lays down the law of chastity.
    These days the clergy have become a rabble that,*
        In the guise of clergy, explain God's ways.

    The serfs are now the lords and the lords are the serfs;
        He who's learned nothing thinks he knows it all.
    The villein feigns in his manners to be just like
        The freeborn, and shows the marks in his dress.
    A gentleman takes on the mien of such a wretch,
        And wants to partake of his boorish vice.           240
    Pomp is due measure; arrogance, righteousness; humor,
        Ribaldry; and sport, Godless diversion.
    The promotor of sins is held in regard, and
        Who opposes one's vices is his foe.
    Now a flatterer oiling your ear is beloved,
        And a forked tongue becomes an orator.
    Now an unripe boy is wiser than Cicero*
        In the king's eyes, more pleasing than Cato.
    And the blandishments of the tongue that glorify
        The world's princes you now see earn rewards.           250

## Book VII

There is no honor but the tongue's, which like Echo
  Sounds pleasing words in the ears of the king.
It faults what you fault, praises what you praise, says just
  What you say, and esteems what you esteem.
You laugh, it laughs; you weep, it will weep, and always*
  It legislates just how your face should look.
The good judgment of Philemon earns no reward,*
  Even if what his mouth says is the truth.
An infant whom first a wooly pelt protected,*
  Is covered now in flattery's linen.                     260
No court now preserves its ancient honor intact;
  No city, justice; no land, its good faith.
Arms, in which the tailor's boy now goes helmeted,
  Are more mercantile than they are noble.
The golden spur is common now, and the honor*
  Of arms is not that which it used to be.
Indeed, the proud wastrel, who lacks means to manage
  Proudly, is living everywhere from loot.

The infirmity of the realm grows, its strength ebbs,
  So that you see much chaff and little grain.            270
The rabbit-hearted hide, the lions flap their jaws;
  A leaden deed now comes with golden words.
Men are now accustomed to waste long spells of time*
  Speaking, while the day wanes away with talk.
Quarrelsome men leave unfinished, for later times,
  The needful matters that concern the realm.
We turn today into tomorrow while we talk;
  Actions called "finished" remain yet undone.
Now Pride, which scarcely stands secure on its own soil,*
  Wants other realms to be subject to it.                 280
Bold of tongue, it thunders war loud in its chambers,
  But, weak of hand, does not move to the field.
Under war's pretext, taxes grind us everywhere;
  So one might gain, I know a thousand lose.
Customary privilege has now become greedy,
  And it oppresses with hateful demands.
It pledges servants every reward beforehand,
  But won't remember when a man does well.
The old rule no longer provides a model; nay,
  Henceforth let Will, in place of Law, guide us.         290

Now gall is honey, and hatred is just like love;
   What outsides show is not what insides hold.
Jacob's soft voice and Esau's rough hand at one time*
   Deceived, but they were signs of things to come.
For what words of goodness now convey to our ears,
   Bears wickedness when action proves the deed.
Justice is gone, and her comrade, Good Faith, as well;
   Fraud and Deceit have now usurped their place.
Now friends applaud a friend's grief like an organ piece;
   If one succeeds, the other envies him.                                    300
A brother seeks to profit from a brother's loss,
   And a sister rarely lauds a sister.
A son now feels his mother is his stepmother,
   And she feels his many treacherous acts.
A daughter disparages her mother's deeds, and
   The mother scorns and detests her daughter.
A son can't wait for his father to become old,
   And he can't see clearly for his blind greed.
A father himself, he's no less wicked towards
   His sons, for whom he has no tender heart.                                310
No love spares anyone who is vulnerable;
   What two people have wished, a third denies.
The plebs remain lawless, no one defends the law,
   And no one maintains, "The laws should be kept."
A guest barely survives intact a host's plunder,*
   Or one kin another where there's profit.

Many now greet each other with abiding hate,
   And Anger chews over its own vomit.
Actions provoke hatred: while the face pleads for love,*
   The mouth offers kisses, but the hand strikes.                            320
Hearts have as many habits as the world has shapes,
   But they don't hold any long-lasting good.
Just as Proteus dissolved in the nimble waves,*
   Was now a lion, tree, goat and a boar,
Thus is the way of men inconstant nowadays,
   So I don't know how to proceed safely.
It's not easy to discern a cow from a bull,*
   The front part visible, the rear parts hid.
Thus words can't be taken at their first impressions,
   For it's the end, which hides nothing, that counts.                       330
When you're a prosperous man, you'll have lots of friends;*
   If the times become hard, you'll be alone.
As a hare saves itself by flight across the fields,

Love darts about and stays in no one place.*
Love prospered in days of old, but then grew feeble,
  So that in these days it can scarce step forth.
It has ceded the once-revered name of friendship,
  And sits like a whore in search of profit.
A prior world's honorable models are gone,
  And now there's nothing worthy of belief.*  340

Love is now single, consciously without a mate;
  With hatred for you, it loves what is yours.
Thus a hare and a greyhound don't make an item;*
  I don't know what to make of what I see.
Hatred is common now, but, phoenix-like, love lurks
  In the wasteland, all alone in the world.
Iron is harmful, but gold is yet more harmful;*
  Every man is now conquered in its wars.
What shall I say these days, when the right hand deceives
  The left? How can mankind trust in itself?  350
In every case where there is profit or pleasure,
  It's the fashion to put no trust in trust.
And thus the two-fold figure of the statue's feet*
  Shows how diverse are the deceits of men.
Losses abound, so that these days I, a freeman,
  Do not know where to find the peaceful ways.
Poverty alone will remain free from envy,*
  And nobody on earth seeks to end it.
Oh you lucky wretched paupers, who everywhere
  Are free, with peace of mind and without fear!  360
"Oh world, oh world," men say, "Oh woe unto you, world,
  You who beget ever worse disasters!"
Thus I would know what the world is in all respects,
  As it is and as it was created.

## Chapter 5

**Because everyone at present deplores the world's falsehoods, here he intends, accordingly, to discuss the state and condition of the world, as well as the wretchedness of the human condition.**

The world [*mundus*] gives itself the name, but can't be held pure
    [*mundus*]*
  By reason of all its impurities.
For it is filled with filth, full of the seeds of vice,

Full of sin, and everywhere full of guile.
The times are changed, the circumstances, the estates,*
   Are changed, and order does not long endure.                       370
Know how close and how near our ruination is,*
   Such, indeed, for which there is no relief.
Know that whatever fleeting pleasure grasps and claims*
   Falsely to be its own is as nothing.

What is our present life? Temptation, grievous war,*
   Always the battle line, the foe at hand.
The thief begrudges our wealth; war, our peace; sickness,
   Our health, and old age oppresses our flesh.
And so the charm of a lovely shape slowly dies,*
   And of the many things that charmed, none lasts.                     380
For treats have less savor, smells scarcely register,
   And the ear barely perceives loud noises.
The eyes grow dim; of the whole, only skin and bones,
   Fastened by their sinews, survive intact.
He hates summers, finds fault with winter and its cold;*
   Nothing can please a querulous old man.
He is pained now by too much cold, now too much heat,*
   And never remains in a stable state.
His tooth hurts or his neck, perhaps his tongue is stiff,*
   His spleen swells, his lung ails, his liver is vexed.                   390
His heart grows faint, his kidneys ache, his bowels are loose,
   His arms scarce move, and his sluggish legs throb.
Sickness does not suffer his body, by bitter
   Cares wracked, to keep its strength for very long.
Each part is subject to multiple diseases,*
   And the whole wretch suffers in misery.
Consumed by diseases and years, the curmudgeon
   Bewails the lengthy seasons of his life.

For every strength in which the foolish body joys
   Ceases and dies, suppressed by sundry griefs.                       400
Are you wise? Wisdom wanes with death. Are you awash
   In wealth? It vanishes in a swift rush.
Are you upright? Probity fades. Noble? Good names
   Decline. Strong? Strength is overcome by death.
And when you see yourself succumb, conquered by sins,*
   I marvel that you say and think you're strong.
Desire wages war; you succumb to its first blows,
   And put your conquered neck 'neath its vile yoke.

## Book VII

And so you serve avarice, the tumults of wrath,
   And obey ardent greed's shameful dictates.     410
So wherever you may turn your face and your mind,
   Know each thing of the flesh and world is vain.
If you ponder the flesh, you'll see in every part
   Its fragile nature, which cannot abide.
If you ponder the world, you'll see it everywhere
   Roiled by mischance in uncertain affairs.
One man bemoans his vineyard bombarded by hail,*
   Another his ships lost on the high seas.
Extravagance wrecks this one and pride another,*
   And sorrow's savage storm shakes yet a third.     420
And so the world varies variously, and one
   Whom first it elevates it hurtles down.
The place is very unstable, very much like
   The water of rivers that ebb and flow.
If it is calm, it deceives and can't be trusted;
   Its pleasures can always turn to sorrows.

Something is always absent in man's affairs, and
   This life contains nothing fully fruitful.
Before it has arrived at its end in this world,
   No life can delight in assured rewards.     430
If the blood of noble forbears has advanced you,
   Then you must grieve because you can decline.
If fate has granted you good luck, it's lost through fate;
   If bad luck ensues, fear yet even worse.
If reputation persuades you your wife is chaste,
   You must grieve that she is wont to deceive.
One bewails his faithless wife's lewdness, another*
   Fears it, deceived by baseless suspicion.
You'll fear to lose her for whom many pray and sigh,
   Or that you will not have her to yourself.     440
So you dread lest some adulterer seduce her,*
   And she will bear those whose sire you won't be.
But if the whole crowd of them should grow up decent,
   You'll grieve anew when death takes them from you.
If riches are your servant for a fleeting hour,
   You'll grieve more when someday they're snatched away.
If the spring of youth promises a lengthy life,
   You're fooled, and you'll grieve Atropos' cut.*
If wisdom empowers you with keenness of mind,
   You'll grieve when you consider Solomon.     450

If your snow-white face gleams, splashed with ruddy color,
   You'll grieve, because your bent old age draws nigh.*

Your mind won't know peace here, for within and without
   You'll wage unending war with many things.*
While you can, make up for lost time, because alas!
   Christ condemns what's done too little, too late.*
Who's done the last things of his life worse than the first,
   Who's paid too dear, let him beware of ruin.
A young man should know that life slips by on swift foot,*
   What follows not as good as what went first.       460
The wave that's passed shall not be summoned back again,*
   Nor can an hour that's passed return once more.
Because they move slowly, you think the years stand still,*
   And that time makes its journey with slow steps.
Fearing the hawk, with feathers atremble a bird*
   Dares to come weary into a man's hands.
Oh sinful old man, whom Satan awaits in hell,
   Why do you flee, why don't you come to God?
Old age's dreadful winter comes with palsied step,*
   And the lovely bloom of our youth departs.       470
Fleeting age deceives us, steals secretly away,*
   And the swift course of time flees like a ghost.

What we call the elements likewise don't endure;*
   Nay, they change and undergo diverse shifts.
Our bodies change, and we won't be tomorrow what*
   We've been or are, for time won't stay the same.
Nothing is able to endure in the same form;
   It's clear, in fact, that things change suddenly.
Behold, what was the deep is now the solid earth,*
   And what was earth, the sea's wave covers o'er.       480
Now a spring flows, and now, its flow suppressed, dries up,
   And behold! it's no longer the same place.
Iron is ground away; whetstones grow thin from use;*
   Is not frail mankind worn out even more?
Palaces for dukes that now gleam beneath the sun,*
   Were once pastures for the tilling oxen.
Castles stand now where fields once were, and where there now
   Are cultivated fields, were first castles.
Huts bedecked with boughs are castles bedecked with gems,*
   And the shire knight himself once fed his sheep.       490

And if I'd tell the realms of men, we know that no
   Prince's empire persists long in the world.

Those things that past time once did, the future will do*
   Again, and there's nothing new in the world.
Who's able to say, "I'm without care in the world,"
   And will not have cause for a thousand griefs?*
Wherever a man turns, sorrow or dread strikes him;
   None of the ranks of the world is exempt.
Oh how many tumults the hearts of kings suffer;*
   How they rage with tempestuous passions!          500
Amidst regal feasts and their many adornments,
   Consumed by fleeting dread, they waste away.*
Amidst a thousand of their weaponed attendants,
   They can't drive the dread from their fearful hearts.
Thus the impure world defiles everything with its*
   Faults, and never does anything that's pure.
It claims by antiphrasis a name for itself,*
   That it by no means has a right to share.

## Chapter 6

**Here he talks about the beginning of human creation. He also clarifies how the world was created for man to use, and man to worship God; therefore, if man does not worship his God as he ought, the world is not obliged any longer to render the services that are due to man.***

If I shall speak the truth, man alone is guilty
   Of all the wickedness the world contains.          510
Genesis teaches that when the Founder first made
   Earth, he created Adam, saying this:
"Let us make man," he said, "who is able to be
   Like us; and that he serve and worship us,
Let us breathe into him a sense of reason, love,
   Discernment, what he is and whence he comes.
Let us breathe into him knowledge of his Maker,
   That he may know and love his Creator,
Who his Author is, who gave him being and whence:
   The world attends and renders him service.          520
Man alone should explore the Supreme Mind's secrets,
   And he alone probe into everything.

But let him see that each thing he claims for himself,
   He thinks useful or deems necessary."

O the sublime glory, supreme honor, great gift,
   That man is in God's likeness, clothed in flesh!
That he's crafted on the model of his Maker,
   And comparable to his Creator!
For God created the rest by his word alone;
   This work he laid his hand on and formed it.                530
A little earth was taken up, a wee lump formed;
   What was soil before became solid flesh.
With sinews he joined the bones within together,
   To make a firm step and from it a gait.
But over these he conducted veins filled with blood,
   And he draped the flesh with both hide and hair.
He diffused life's breath throughout all of the organs,
   Apart from whose functions all limbs are still.
Man's mouth speaks, his hand grips, his foot runs, and his ears
   Listen; his eyes alone look to heaven.                     540
Man comes to life, a two-legged creature rises,
   Flesh stands, and its companion, spirit, stands, one man.
The flesh senses what pertains to flesh, the spirit*
   Longs for the high stars and seeks its place there.

When formed, man stands astonished by himself and his
   Motions, not knowing what he is and why.
His body amazes him, the way his limbs move,
   His hand's adroitness, the parts of his feet.
He stretches his limbs, shakes his arms, and with his hands
   He touches all the parts of his body.                     550
What he beholds amazes him, but he can't see
   That it is His own likeness that he bears.
He marvels at earth's face and its different shapes,
   And, since he knows no names, does not know them.
He lifts his face, raises his countenance on high,
   Ranges the heights from whence his spirit came.
He marvels at the heaven's shape and vaulted form,
   The astral motions and starry mansions.
The new sojourner stands amazed, and asks himself
   What the great bodies he sees may portend.                560
Nature, however, provides him with the knowledge,
   And he sees he is man, these things were made,
That the earth has been founded for the use of man,

That earth is his property, and he, God's.
His understanding burns with love of his Author,
And now he knows what it is to love God.

## Chapter 7

**Here he says that, since God, the Creator of all things, subjoined all the pleasures of this world to man for his use, it is proper that, just as man enjoys pleasures in accordance with the flesh, so in accordance with the spirit he should return, with grateful thanks, his wholehearted allegiance to God his Creator.**

Say, Adam, say, Mother Eve, say one and the other,
   Say whether you lack God's abundant grace.
He placed everything at your feet: sheep and cattle,
   The birds of the sky, the fish of the sea.  570
The elements, the sun, air, stars, earth, the rich sea's
   Waves and all else are well-disposed to you.
The Author of things has resolved matters so that
   All the world's creatures should attend on man.
As the creation serves him, so man, in his turn,
   Should attend on his Creator alone.
Lift your head on high and look all around your world,
   And gather all that his hands grant to you.
All are subject to you, all minister to you,
   All answer you and render obedience.  580
Who did all this for you, accomplished it for you,
   Who brought the world into being for you,
Who brought the seeds of everything out of nothing,
   And made random chaos stay orderly,
Allotting its components in four equal parts,*
   He tamed its angry motions with his skill.
Painting the starry heaven and seven planets,*
   Calling them to their places, though they fought,
The Designer, by the sun's route through the twelve signs,
   Made time pass through just as many stages.  590

After he had established the entire world,
   He adorned it with a host of blessings,
Beasts in the forests and lions upon the hills,
   Cattle on the plains, and goats on the cliffs.
He covered birds with plumage and dressed sheep in wool,

And yet that which they have is for your use.
Behold the world's delights, the gifts which the rivers
   And the wealth the sea's waves bestow on you,
The gardens with their trees, herbs and vegetables,
   Flowers, foliage, and fruitful produce.                           600
Above all, let your mind ponder him who made you,
   And how he spun goodness out of nothing.
For your spirit is his spirit, your sense is his
   Sense, and your reason is from his reason.

And when things were arranged, he put you in their charge,
   And allowed you to give them all their names.
He gave you hope of progeny in woman's love,
   An equal companion and wedlock's troth.
He made you almost his equal, made you almost,
   If I perchance might say, a second God.                         610
He took himself to heaven, handed earth to you,
   And shared with you the riches of the world.
The sky gives you the sun; the sun, light; the air, winds;
   The waves, your food; and earth, its thousand goods.
Who provides what you are from and what you have? God's
   Sweet and ample mercy does both freely.
Giving you yourself, he promised himself, and God
   Himself had nothing better he could give.

Does it thus suit any man to exalt himself
   Against commandments that God himself gave?               620
Heaven, in fact, cast down, and earth hates, the Proud One,*
   And only hell's place will be fit for him.
For by his sin the whole tribe our progenitor
   Brought forth became tainted and corrupted.
Each and every shoot was infected at the root,
   Which is why there's nothing pure in the world.
He who would cleanse the world was not yet in the world,
   Nor would the world have mercy upon him.
But he who, in his compassion, made everything,
   Restored his creation and renewed it.                           630
He took on servant's shape and redeemed his servants,*
   And what had been the devil's, he made God's.
Therefore, you should follow him with a devout mind,
   And likewise acknowledge him as your Lord.
If you follow, with all your heart, his light precept
   To avoid forbidden sin, you'll be blessed.

*Book VII*

## Chapter 8

**Here he discusses how man is called a microcosm; it follows, according to this, that the world is good or evil depending on whether man behaves well or badly.***

    O the compassion of the Lord, what power, what
      Grace, that made mankind of such consequence!
    Like the angelic host, man understands and knows*
      That God is the world's Supreme Creator.     640
    Man senses and hears, he tastes, he sees, walks, so that
      He has a kind of animal nature.
    Together with trees, man has growth, and has being,
      By his nature, in the manner of stones.
    Thus man, who alone has each, is a microcosm,
      Alone makes sacred vows to God alone.
    The man who is pure subjects the world to himself*
      As his right, and guides it for the better.
    But if he is impure, he harms all that the world
      Contains, and makes everything all the worse.     650
    He rules his world as he wants, at his own command;
      If he's good, it's good; if he's bad, it's bad.
    A microcosm does the world most grievous harm
      If he falls guilty of impurity.
    If a microcosm won't prune impurity,
      He'll worsen all the world's wounds by his sin.
    A microcosm who worships the Almighty
      Makes everything pure in human affairs.
    A microcosm who meditates on God's laws,
      Will have for himself heaven's grand kingdom.     660

    Thus it is fitting that man, born of the Maker,
      Return him worthy gifts with humble heart.
    It follows he should seek the love of his Maker,
      Should know what he is and from whence he comes.
    It follows he know, by the nature of the name,
      That, above all, he's called microcosm.
    Since he's a microcosm, he should heed himself
      When he looks into the plan of the world.
    Since he's a microcosm, he's treating mankind
      When he considers the world's origins.     670
    If he does not know himself, he won't know him by
      Or through whom he was made, and not love him.

Moreover, a two-fold substance was made for him,*
  Both spirit and flesh, from which God formed him,
In order that his spirit might serve its maker,
  The world serve the flesh, and flesh the spirit.
The flesh is a fragile handmaiden, whose mistress
  From on high is, by God's reason, the soul.
But now flesh, conquered by the world, denies reason,
  And ceases to submit to the soul's law.                                680
Thus the mistress serves, order fails, and that is lost
  Without God what should be within a man.
Dumber than a dolt, swapping heaven for the world,
  Thrusting aside gold, you would have the clay!

Why, lord of things, God's image, do you want to seek*
  Small things? Great man, you should seek what's greatest.
Earth's orb is yours, and whatsoever is enclosed*
  In it is all subject to your judgment.
Indeed, the All Father, come down from high heaven,
  Descending to earth, became man for you.                               690
Do not wish to subject yourself to sin's realm, nor*
  Pursue such possessions as swiftly flee,
But strive in your mind to transcend the lowly earth,
  Bravely seize the way to heaven above.
If you seek great things, God is great above them all,
  If good things, no one can express God's good.
Neither your birth nor your sex, nor vain adornment,
  Are of any use to you at death's door.
What availed it Plato to pierce nature's secrets*
  In his studies and to compose his books?                               700
He knew the sun's path, the sky's regions, and the moon's*
  Courses, the high vault's fixed and moving stars,
And many profound matters beyond that; but now
  The philosopher is ash, his name dead.
Whilst Hippocrates studied things and their causes,
  Saved people's lives by medicinal means,*
None of his wisdom was able to preserve him;
  Even for the doctor, death's law prevails.*
Man's nature, it's thus clear, is stronger than his skill,
  And hies to death those whom its suit pursues.                         710
Nothing is more prudent than to anticipate
  The dying that will be the end of you.
You are always on a journey; you near life's end;

Book VII

You don't know where or when it will occur.
Your road to heaven long, few days remain to you;
   Who takes up the world's burdens slows his way.

## Chapter 9

**Here he tells how man, called a microcosm, will pass from the world in death as far as his body is concerned, and just as he causes the outbreak of this world's corruption by the sin of his body while he lives, so he will be forced to undergo afterwards the decay of purification in his dead body. And first he talks about decay of the dead body from the perspective of Pride.***

What will you say when the breeze doesn't blow your hair,*
   Your gullet dries up and you've no airway,
Your face is bloodless, your eyes are listless in sad
   Cheeks, and your mouth cannot moisten itself,           720
Your tongue within it has become stuck to the hard
   Palate, blood vessels won't transmit a pulse,
Your neck won't turn, your arms aren't able to embrace
   Anything, and your foot can't take its way?

So what does the prideful man, now dead, have to say?
   Let him say now what vainglory gets him.
For all the glory of the lifeless corpse of one
   Who lately scorned others has perished now.
And since that corpse once carried itself so proudly,
   Its flesh has been interred as food for worms.           730
Not now is his eyebrow raised as if in disdain,
   Nor does his hand brush anybody off.
The strength of death has overcome what strength he had;
   Lo! a fly's backbone is stronger than his.
If beauty or comeliness did bloom in him once,
   Every beast now flees from his ugliness.
He who had been wise is anything but wise now,
   Having reached the point where he knows nothing.
The subtleties he ever sought in long study,
   Death rapidly destroyed in short order.           740
Although he had been expert in various arts,
   Skilled in their ways, he fell now on his own.
The reason of his genius died without reason;
   Death flings what was reason's into the void.
Whom books taught so much is duller than a donkey;

Not one jot or tittle stays in his mind.
His mind doesn't presume to judge anybody;
   He cannot vaunt himself because he's dead.
Who used to take office by hypocritical
   False Virtue now shows plainly what he'd been.        750
That he once knew whole families of languages
   Is no help to a corpse with muted mouth.
No organ or harp notes are delightful to him;
   No music pleases where hearing has died.
It won't help who adorned his body modishly,
   That he's lost all nature's decoration.
Neither ornate clothes nor riding atop horses
   Can glorify a corpse already stiff.
No lovely home for him, nor his servants' fawning;
   No one salutes him now before a crowd.        760
Now a serpent is his servant; the grave, his hall;
   He gets, in place of chambers, a vile pit.
Therefore, because vainglory did once deceive him,
   Nothing is left to him to make him proud.

## CHAPTER 10

**Here he talks about the corruption of the dead body viewed from the perspective of Envy.**

Who gnawed in his envy with the jaws of a dog,*
   Is now bound to be gnawed by dogs and worms.
Scorning the fame of another, which he once ruined,
   His treacherous tongue, rotted, falls silent now.
Who laughed at another's loss, and wept for his gain,
   Can't laugh now with a mouth that has no lips.        770
A heart once full of grumblings is now putrefied,
   And a burst path gapes deep into his heart.
The ambitious, who lie unpraised, can't disparage
   A comrade's glory nor promote their own.
Gall, once stirred in honey, is now stirred with itself,*
   And the flesh can't deceive without a mind.
A fiery mind filled with envious venom can't
   Prod anyone, anymore, with spite's goad.

*Book VII*

## Chapter 11

**Here he talks about the corruption of the dead body viewed from the perspective of Wrath.**

    Whom fervid wrath once inflamed when he was alive,
        No longer shakes his head impatiently.     780
    Who not long before shook his neighbors with lawsuits,
        Mute in his grave does not make any noise.
    Once very talkative, he can't even whisper;
        Death calls, he's quiet and does not answer.
    Who used to terrify the poor with fearful threats,
        Is not able to prevail against worms.
    Henceforth his fury for war will not summon him,
        Who does not have a peace treaty with worms.
    For lo! his sword will no longer be so fearsome,
        Who suffers a maggot to pierce his heart.     790
    He shan't corrupt reason by his hateful conduct,
        Who henceforth lacks the power of reason.

## Chapter 12

**Here he talks about the corruption of the dead body viewed from the perspective of Avarice.**

    O what good is avarice to the miser now?
        A narrow wooden box is all that's left.
    He sought out land for himself with such great effort,
        And now seven feet, no more, contains him.
    Who once was a robber preying upon strangers,
        Now death has taken prey like a bandit.
    He who once cast out his nets for insane profits,
        Is now caught in a net he can't escape.     800
    He gathered in many riches and hoarded them
        Tightly, but now another wastes his wealth.
    His vast estates, almost without limit, are gone,
        And of a sudden he has nothing left.
    His wife is happy with a new second husband,
        And her heart scarce recalls who went before.
    The son and heir prospers, his father forgotten,
        And not one friend of the deceased remains.
    He who joined estate to estate and field to field*

Henceforth has nothing from all his ventures. 810
One day has taken away what the years brought in,
   And a lifetime's work proves to be pointless.
Who shut his purse to the poor is now destitute,
   And abundant silver does him no good.
Neither guile nor theft, not trickery nor perjured
   False covetousness can now help his corpse.

## Chapter 13

**Here he talks about the corruption of the dead body viewed from the perspective of Sloth.**

Sloth declines to indulge any longer the man
   Who was slothful to please his body's limbs.
Who gave himself to sleep gets to sleep amply now,
   Because he can't awake from his long nap. 820
Who recently sought a soft cushion for his bed,
   Lies on top of cold earth that swarms with worms.
Who once chased after leisure, while shunning labor,
   Can't do anything now to get some help.
If once he could have learned what's good, there's no school now
   To give him wisdom, that he better grasp
The harm of possessions. Now he is left to rue
   The lengthy wasted sessions of his days.
He rarely came to church to pray, but now can't leave,
   Although he's not praying for anything. 830
Who has scattered his seed sparsely shall reap sparsely;*
   What once he could, he would now when he can't.

## Chapter 14

**Here he talks about the corruption of the dead body viewed from the perspective of Gluttony.**

The gluttony that once had been his every day,
   No longer pleasures his belly or mouth.
The guts that had been burdened by the weight of food,
   Now, emptied out, cannot hold anything.
He used to relish spices and tipple sweet wines,
   In place of which there's ordure mixed with slime.
Around his middle, where he used to store his fat,

Now lurks a snake, which gulps down all his flab.     840
The jug of his belly, which birthed his drunkenness,
  Is burst, and a toad sits in his gullet.
The dish once so savory does nothing for him now,
  And foul putrefaction fills his nostrils.
His excess, that once observed no days of fasting,
  Tastes nothing now, since his stomach has burst.

## Chapter 15

**Here he talks about the corruption of the dead body viewed from the perspective of Lust.**

O he who considered the sin of lust so sweet,
  Now has his shameful parts sucked by serpents.
He hangs no more, shamelessly, around the brothel,
  Nor can his nasty hand please by its touch.     850
He cannot flirt, with a wanton look in his eyes,
  To entice some fool to show him favor.
No beguiling songs, filled with Venus' pronouncements,
  Can delight him now with their promises.
Not for him singing or dancing in the revels;
  His throat's gone and his foot can't support him.
Dead, he can't fornicate, nor can he violate
  Virginity's glory in the body.
Whatever was desirable once now decays,
  And coitus' heat has frozen in the cold.     860
What once was a body is now a cadaver,
  And what was ashes has returned to ash.

## Chapter 16

**After he has discussed how death's decay consumes the human body in this world through the various delights of sin, he asks further about the sinful man, why he hungers and longs so ardently, to his own detriment, after the transient pleasures of the world.**

O answer me, proud man, what does pomp do for you
  When rot corrodes your limbs within the earth?
Say, you who are garbed in your silk, gold, and jewelry,
  What good will vainglory be when death comes?
Why, victor, rejoice? Victory shall abandon you,

Unless you seek to win the war on sin.
What will envy, Etna's burning son, do for you*
   When death has melted your heart and your lips?        870
What are wrath or fury supposed to avail you,
   When death comes at you with its evil rage?
What do your slothful days, months, and years do for you,
   When baneful death is lasting without end?
What can gluttonous delicacies do for you,
   When you'll be death's feast for eternity?
What do you think Venus gives you for your efforts,
   When the warmth is departed from your limbs?
What does gold profit you, rich man, the pomp of coin?
   In the end they're both swallowed by the earth.        880
All that a long, worrisome year bestowed on you,
   One brief hour snatches all at once away.
Why, O tyrant, do you conquer kings, subdue realms?
   Invincible God readies war with you.
What are fleeting fame to you, honor, useless show?
   All the world's vainglory passes away.

The undue pleasures of fools are replaced by grief,
   And tears full of sorrow dampen laughter.
Why do you boast your body's beauty or lineage?
   You go, worm food, from ashes to ashes.*        890
What if you can overcome lions with your strength?*
   Is not a flea able to disquiet you?
What except folly does the world's wisdom bring you?
   Wise men know there's no wisdom without God.
Your worthless body was made for you from the slime,
   Prone by nature to evils of the flesh.
It begins in sorrow and ends in pain. So why
   Do you attempt to exalt such a work?
Since naught of this world's body is raised to glory,
   It's not for you to glorify your flesh.        900
Nothing of your body or wealth is left to you,*
   But your merits only, if good or bad.
When that day comes that brings nothing but this body's
   Deserts, then a man shall confront his deeds.
No one by right can have here an abiding place;
   Nay, he shall go upon death's unsure ways.

Book VII

## Chapter 17

**Here he tells how all things in the world wear out like a piece of clothing, and how, in the blink of an eye, they are ended. He also speaks in particular about keeping death in mind, and the signification of its name.\***

Everything ends quickly in the blink of an eye,
   And every man passes as if through sleep.
Our worldly joys lead to everlasting sorrows,\*
   And our brief life begets the eternal.     910
I think all that can be lost seems to be nothing,\*
   And whatsoever ends, not very long.
That includes honor, wealth, reputation and youth,
   Beauty, family, strength, wife, clothing and land,
Jewels and silver, a scepter, a kingdom, and gold,
   The purple, wide estates and spacious homes,
Mighty powers, great knowledge, and empty pleasures,
   Life, and the very health of our bodies.

That the mortal body grows old just like clothing,\*
   And bent old age arrives in a swift rush,     920
That the seasons of our life always diminish,
   And that a man's day flees, smoke and shadow,\*
That life is short, death unpredictable, grievous
   Matters press us at all times in our lives –
People are able to give examples for each:
   Experience indeed teaches such things.
Who guides his acts well is king of himself, blessed;
   Who guides them poorly is a clumsy slave.
You are called "king." Why rejoice in a foolish name,\*
   You who lie beaten, a slave to your sins?     930
Why does he who rules realms serve the vices, and not\*
   Be ashamed to be the body's vile slave?
When you are soiled with sin, no garish clothes will help,
   No purple garment hide your blemishes.
It is therefore expedient that each traveler
   Go forth disburdened, light as he can be.
All things are taken from us by our passing years,
   And death, supervening, robs all our hopes.
Ash returns to ash, the body's dissolution\*
   Shows the clay matter of its beginning.     940
God knows what becomes of the soul in the future,
   If unharmed or harmed, how much and what sort.

Humans are aware that the body in this world
   Does not have the lasting use of the flesh.
The living flesh is corrupt, and, dead, is a corpse
   That's more vile than any other creature's.

O mirror of death! However many gaze in it,
   They'll see no splendor if they look closely.
The manner of our foe, of death, is so backward
   He puts a head on a par with a tail.                                950
"Death" [*mors*] is said to be from "forbidden bite" [*morsus vetitus*];
   "biting" [*mordens*]*
   Explains all of the name's signifiers.
Nothing can be more unsure in unsure matters*
   Than death's hour, nothing more certain than death.
Death tricks a man when least he expects it, and hides*
   Furtively in the man who is healthy.
No astrologer or physician is able
   To have his day prolonged by medicine.
Thus man and animal alike perish, and both
   Return to earth in the same condition.                              960
There's no exception: what is created on earth,
   Just as it lives, so it will have to die.

Come secret to chambers, death flies on furtive wings,
   Reversing, sudden, what had been before.
It plunders riches, destroys strength, and disjoins friends,
   Nor can it ever be bought off with gold.
It ruins men's affairs and summons them for their deeds,
   That reckoning come at the Judge's feet,
That same Judge who judges each one equitably,
   Whom no earthly bribes are able to sway.                            970
By his judgment, man will get for his labors due
   Rewards, without favor, for his deserts.

## Chapter 18

**Here he says that, although there is by nature one death for the just and unjust, nevertheless, the death of the just man restores his soul to eternal glory, freeing him from all his miseries.**

The just and unjust man each passes on in death,
   And earth devours each body the same way.
But their passing accords with their different merits:

## Book VII

The good man's death, sweet; the bad man's, bitter.
It's thus the happy man who, living, has done well,
   Whereby, dying, he can receive God's gifts,
The gifts, indeed, of heaven, where all joys shine bright,
   Where life will be eternal, free from grief.        980
There'll be no death, disease, toil, foe, crooked old age;
   That glad mansion above does not have these.
The King's grace will be alike to spirits on high,
   For whom he willing bore the bitter cross.

Here is the place of peace, the Almighty's reward,
   Where the day is without night and shadows,
Where God wipes away all tears and sorrow, and where
   Complaint and lament never more shall be.
Neither death nor disease, thirst, hunger, poverty,
   Nor hardship have this place as their abode.      990
There light is constant; peace, eternal; glory, lasting;
   Life, blessed; health, assured; love, forever.
Hope is there and faith, goodness, praise, grace, and virtue,
   Feeling, love, mercy, glory, looks, honor.
Youthful flesh is unblemished, old age is without
   Infirmities, wealth lacks trickery's taint.
There peace is without dread, all honor without pride,
   Rest comes without toil, health without distress.
There joys are lasting and suffering is absent,
   For a man may have all that he chooses. 1      000
Eternal life blooms there, and God's blessed presence,
   Which governs everything, is everywhere.

Should I briefly describe to you what that place is?
   There is much more than any man could say,
More than the mind's reason would be able to teach,
   Or more than the chambers of the heart hold.
How happy a place, how lauded with proper praise,
   In which all the joys are met together!
Thus, since glory there is unending, I cannot
   Compose a proper end to its praises.      1010
Here shall be the angelic host, numbers made good,*
   In the fullness of glory it once lost.
Here shall be mankind's highest honor, the body
   Arisen when the flesh is glorified.
Here all men shall rejoice forever in the Lord,
   When God himself is all things to all men.
So death takes away the hurts from the righteous man's

Flesh, and readies the soul for heaven's realm.
When a righteous man dies, he first begins to live;
   Here death gives life, restores the man who died.       1020
Here death ushers in not shame but rather honor,
   Where the dead man at rest possesses God.

## Chapter 19

**Here he talks about the double death of the sinner, the first of which destroys the body and the other which torments the soul with everlasting pains by God's fit judgment.**

Alas! How unhappy he who lived wickedly,
   So grievous torment consumes him at death.
Indeed, a twofold death is owed the wicked man;
   The first is grievous, the second more foul.
Killing the body, the first takes it from the world,
   That Death may do to it no further harm.
The second, more grievous, takes the soul to the pit,
   And renders to Satan what had been God's.*       1030
It places in doubt what worldly pleasure might be,
   And makes certain that torment is at hand,
The torment of the abyss, where every grief thrives,
   Where one is always dying, but can't die.

No voice is able to speak the wretched tortures,
   The slow torments of which are without end.
Here fear and trembling, there woe and sorrow ensue,
   The horror of endless death's endless pain.
To die in constant death or live in constant death,
   You'd say to live or die makes no difference.       1040
Alas! I repeat "death" so often since that place
   Shows the wretched nothing but death's image,
That place, which fearful hunger, which freezing and heat,
   Which dark, which night, and which night's shadow veil.
There worms gnaw the mind, and fire consumes the body
   With its heat, and there is much fearful pain.
There the torturer, who tortures always nor flags
   Ever, consumes a wretch with blazing pains.

Everything that pleased the flesh is turned upside down,
   And bitter plague twists what was sweet around.       1050
What had been lovely is fouled by repulsive shapes;

## Book VII

Torment dissolves a work that had been sound.
What had been strong is then plundered of its powers;
  There the wise are stupid, the rich are poor.
What had been the good life there becomes worms and fire;
  What was gluttony, insatiable hunger.
There sight is darkness; touch, a stinging scorpion;
  And travelers make their way in death's shackles.
As punishments, the ears are tormented with noise,
  The nose with stench, and taste with bitterness.         1060
Here's where weeping eyes, gnashing teeth, and all the limbs
  Dissolve in sorrow, where they endless grieve.
What had been life is death, and what was a body,
  Ablaze like a torch, cooks ever in fire.
And alas! God's image, that suffering soul that was
  Created pure, looks like a demon now.
There Thetis does not extinguish the lightning bolts,*
  Nor a doctor's potion soothe viper bites.
A pain like woman giving birth is constant there;
  The place seems to have no time of pardon.              1070
No one comprehends the endless torment of pain
  In hell, for grief there is beyond compare.
My soul and flesh shudder so in mind and heart that
  My palsied hand can write no more of this.

With what countenance or face, with what retinue
  Shall then appear the court's Supreme Justice?
His countenance dreadful, his face like one enraged,
  His aspect stern and boding stormy times.
The Judge's fury is brief, but his wrath, without
  Pardon or mercy, spares no punishment.                  1080
His mother, the angelic host, the apostles,
  Comprising a bench of judges, follow.
Here man and angel alike shall incur torments,
  Each punished according to his deserts.
And punishments shall make peers of those whom the love
  Of wicked sinfulness once made equals.
The bad man is distinguished from the good, the one*
  Keeping left for judgment, the other, right.

How grim the sentence given the wretched shall be,
  To die in eternal death's perdition.                    1090
This will be the Lord's Day, in whose light shall be shown*
  Clearly the secrets which now lie hidden.
This shall be the Day of Wrath, that terrible light

In which an angel will be full of fear.
If the just man will barely be saved at that point,*
   Sinner, where will you flee? By what way? None.
It thus behooves the prudent mind, in its goodness
   And its discernment, to fear wickedness.
Most happy he who shall be able to evade
   Such scourges, and live in his well-earned fame!      1100
O most happy, happy man through eternity,
   O the man saved, and O the blessed man,
Who'll be able to escape death's mighty torments,
   And experience heaven's joys with God!
Let the wise man thus sit now and reckon his deeds,
   Before that day of judgment does arrive.

## Chapter 20

**After he has discussed the joys and torments due to the good and the bad, he counsels each and every one to convert to good morals, and, contrite, without despair, confidently beg forgiveness from God for what was carelessly neglected.**

Since a slight breeze raises a feeble puff of air,
   Then an hour later threatens a downpour,
Be mindful, beloved, who, why, whence, for what you are,
   Or of what nature that you have been made,      1110
That the flesh is frail, and easily led astray,
   Prone to the worse and prompt to chase the worst.
Let the spirit scorn this world and hope for the next,
   Fixed ever on the love of its Author.
So that flesh be subject to and follow the soul,
   Let the spirit itself serve its Maker.
So that the flesh's tumult be tempered, keep death
   And its torments for the wicked in mind.
A man cannot better subdue the living flesh
   Than bear in mind what it shall be when dead.      1120
It helps to be repentant with constant weeping,*
   While the gift of weeping is granted you.
God on high does not punish one who grieves his sins,
   Which, having confessed, one repeats no more.

Therefore, let the guilty one endure the torment*
   Of this world, until all evil is cleansed.
Thus purged, he may escape, when the Judge has appeared,

*Book VII*

    That torment which endures without an end.
For who serves not God's commandments, nor bears in mind
    Life's end, is condemned to be drawn to hell.    1130
Unless Scripture deceives, surely you should know that
    Our animal nature seldom finds grace.*
For won by sin, one becomes its slave, unaided
    Has no strength to remove the yoke assumed.
Thus one who wills to sin incessantly is owed,
    Necessarily, eternal torment.

Of course, it's God's way to spare and be merciful,
    Whence, though late, take care to redeem yourself.
He has found out our falseness, but he also heals
    At last the contrite who seek out his help.    1140
Do not despair, God is merciful; nay, one who*
    Denies he's merciful, denies he's God.
A living spring, he's there for all, and as a spring*
    Can't lack water, he cannot lack mercy.
But since presumption will often ruin hopes too high,
    Keep yours at a reasonable level.
That you hope wisely, let your hope be moderate;
    Hope's reins must be guided by pious fear.*
Let fear not be excessive, since despair destroys
    Spirit; nay, fear God with the spirit's love.    1150
Let Hope not be bold, but, tinged with Fear, let her love;
    Thus Fear is Hope, and they save each other.
Yet let your pondering mind, tormented by its end
    And fearing for the worst, hope for the best.
That you live cleanly, keep last things always in mind,*
    For shafts detected early do less harm.
Look to the day, for Death's time hastens to arrive,
    And all at once he'll cast your fortunes down.

## Chapter 21

**Here he says that there are few these days who, either for love of heaven or fear of hell, renounce the pleasures of this life; instead, apart from all reason, they ardently attempt to fulfill whatever the flesh desires.**

    Who heedfully ponders all things justly, I think,
        Senses that joys in the end are in vain.    1160
But now all are so infatuated with sin,

That scarce a man is mindful of his end.
Each one tends to the body, revels in the love
　Of flesh, and forsakes the cause of the soul.
Not the glory of heaven, nor the pains of hell,
　Can now save minds from the world's corruption.
So the world, flesh, and devil everywhere mislead*
　Moderns, that scarce one knows the way of Christ.
The fragile flesh, the cunning devil, the wicked
　World now cultivate the kingdoms of men.　　　　　　　　1170
So the virtue of human reason perishes,
　Like a beast, while sin rules the body's deeds.

I say man is animal, but not rational,*
　When he lives in a brute beast's condition.
Beasts are governed, without Scripture, by a nature
　That lacks power of judgment or reason.
A man therefore is worse than a beast, when his will
　Alone unnaturally governs him.
Alas! physical strength, outside, following its
　Nature in every limb, serves the vices.　　　　　　　　　1180
And the soul's reason, conquered by the flesh's force,
　Perceives, inside, nothing about virtue.

The plebs are quick, these days, to scorn the virtuous,
　And schools explain away the work of sin.*
Those reins of virtue that once made us so blessed,
　Are controlled now by a new willfulness.
"I desire, I demand" are just like laws today
　Among those given power in the world.
The just succumb, crying, "Woe that the impious
　Weary every kingdom upon the earth."　　　　　　　　1190
Force hinders law, sin overturns morality,
　Virtue perishes, shook by sin's whirlwind.
The world is spun, the way of things is confounded,
　And great chaos envelops everything.

Thus wretched are parents in the land, and children,
　Since earthly nature scarce abides its place.
Malice and ambition, greed, fraud, fearsome passion,
　Wrath, pomposity, schism, love of praise,
Selfish honor, and very wicked love of gain,
　The evil exercise, lo! of pleasure,　　　　　　　　　　1200
Theft, armed robbery, deceit, dread and perjury
　Witness the world will henceforth be faithless.

*Book VII*

## Chapter 22

**Here he talks about various punishments, already taking place in this world almost daily because of sin, which cannot be abated without the prayers and good works of the righteous.**

    Behold! the days have come which Christ foretold would be,*
        And God's fearsome words have long since been plain.
    There have been famines, plagues, and quakings of the earth,
        Portents from the sky, and now there's a war.
    One kingdom strives to arise against another,
        Folk on folk, exposing every evil.
    Therefore man's blood has flowed nowadays like cattle's,
        Mercy lies beaten, and God allows this.         1210
    Here, too, the Avenger's smiting hand is outstretched
        To deliver the blows that no one fears.

    Our Lord's forbearing judgment bides its time, patient,
        The good, but not the evil ones, exempt.
    He whom God strikes can be safe nowhere upon earth,
        If sin does not leave him fully contrite.
    God does not wish the sinner's death, but, merciful,*
        Wants him to change, whereby he's given life.
    God is merciful, as we have it from Scripture,
        For he said of Sodom to Abraham:*         1220
    "Among so many thousands of wicked people,
        Find ten righteous, and I'll show them mercy.
    For it is mine alone to pity the wretched,
        To freely spare the many for the few."
    O God, what then shall I say to you; why are our
        Constant laments so meaningless to you?

    Aren't there now ten righteous, that He Who Bears the Stars*
        May by their merit cleanse earth's evil days?
    Unmindful of his mercy, God has forgotten,
        Sleeps (or else feigns), or his acts are obscure.         1230
    Truly I say, our God is angry, his fire strikes*
        At Jacob, and his wrath rages widely.
    Thus the Creator abhors his creature, torments
        Him for the evil deeds that He beholds.

    O, who sees in his mind's eye that our wickedness
        Continues its days at every level,

Will then be able to say that no one has seen
    Such sins long unpunished through the ages.
I don't know what estate these days is without sin,
    And what class I might consider righteous.             1240
Unless we atone willingly, I think that soon
    Our prosperity's downfall is at hand.
But since evils proceed from the highest levels,
    May God himself on high set them aright.


## Chapter 23

**Here, concluding with a summarizing recapitulation, he talks about each of the world's estates, which, deviating from the proper order, diminish and quench the virtues one by one and exercise and enhance the vices.**

Our prelates once carried on only divine works;
    Now, worldly, they don't know they have a God.
The curate once served in his cure, but traveling
    Abroad he now wanders every nation.
Priests who were once chaste have now become lecherous;
    The leisure that they seek causes much harm.          1250
Scholars once learned morality through their studies;*
    Now the university is defiled.
Insoluble love, like zeal, bound monks together;
    Now Envy seeks to make cloisters its own.
Once austerity subdued friars in their flesh,
    But now their easy *regula* spares them.
The knightly class was once quick with its courtesy,
    But now it's sluggish, since it lives badly.
The merchant once sought a fair profit for himself,
    But now he seeks to have his gains by fraud.          1260
A simple spirit had been the farmer's hallmark;
    Now his heart is uncontrollably fierce.
Law, once impartial in its justice, spared no one,
    But silver's force subdues it everywhere.
The peerage is weakened by less-than-peerless acts,
    And every traveler pursues his own road.

Thus humble Mercy is eroded and Pride reigns;
    Spite comes nimbly, but Love is paralyzed.
Ferocious Wrath abides, and docile Patience leaves,

>     Inaction lives, and Duty perishes. 1270
> Ebriety rules tables, not Sobriety,
>     And food-stuffed Drunkenness revels in sin.
> Modest Chastity formerly was wont to hide
>     Her loins, and now Lust wants to expose them.
> A liberal hand once scattered gifts to the needy;
>     Now, miserly, it clutches a shut purse.
>
> Say into how many sins Pride alone has plunged
>     The world to benefit diverse evils.
> Say how many armies, following their standards,
>     Gnawing Envy subdues with fearful force. 1280
> Say how many people strive with covetous hands,
>     Or rapacious minds, denying God's law,
> How Gluttony lolls in delights, how Torpor fouls
>     Fools in the world with carnal adultery.
> Because the world has overwhelmed the sin-stained flesh,
>     The flesh consumes every bit of the soul.
> The world's false charm has subjugated everything,
>     But it can't purify impure humans.

## Chapter 24

**Now, at the end of his book, he addresses more particularly that country in which he was born, where, as if in mourning, he laments how at the present time ancient honors and virtues have been sapped in many ways, as he says, by a host of successive errors.**

>     All the world's realms the Lord established for himself,
>         Which bear their standards in the name of Christ, 1290
>     I love, but most of all I love my own country,
>         In which my birth fashioned my beginnings.
>     Whatever other lands may do, I'm not disturbed,
>         Because I live afar, distant from them.
>     But if my native land, which took me in, its child,
>         Within whose realm I ever fixed remain,
>     Should suffer anything, my heart and soul suffer,
>         And she'll not bear her losses without me.
>     I'm nigh overwhelmed by the weight of her troubles;
>         I stand if she stands; if she falls, I fall. 1300
>     At all events, therefore, I lament the discords
>         That, as others say, currently harm her.

## Vox Clamantis by John Gower: 'The Voice of One Crying'

There's one thing, in my opinion, that most of all
   Can now be called evil's fountain and source.
Alas! Since Justice has departed, fugitive,*
   Her comrade Peace has gone elsewhere with her.
Peace, which at one time used to give Justice kisses,
   Now flees the land, since the law perishes.
Many harmful masters take power for themselves,
   Force and Will rule, and no one observes rights.         1310
Now laws follow, without right, where the magnate goes,
   But the people shall then bear the burden.
I'm not so much physically tormented, but
   I have property I may scarcely use.

Adultery these days scarcely offends a bit,
   For all the flesh demands is permitted.
And even if Venus prevails in other lands,
   They make up for it with other merits.
They have positive law that gives to all equal
   Judgment, and concludes cases without guile.         1320
Status or sex, bribery, pleas, fear or whatever
   Cannot deprive the least man of his rights.
And so Justice redeems in some measure the sin
   Of Flesh, which falls by its frail condition.
But we in this country are conquered not only
   By Flesh's goad, with which man is prodded,
But the Law, ignoring right, exceeds its limits,
   And thus our country goes so far astray
Along crooked paths that, they say, there'll be no more
   Order in our localities. So God         1330
Visits these parts with his vengeance, such as has been
   Seen at no time since the world's beginning.
Albeit no one land is happy in all things,
   In ours right now his rod is very fierce.
Look – clamor everywhere: I don't complain alone.
   It's wrong to leave such glaring crimes unsaid.
Our law deceives; deceived myself, I weep as well,
   For my country is filled with serious wrong.

Fate scatters us everywhere, accused and oppressed,
   Whom she was never wont to use cruelly.         1340
Our land, which once had riches from every metal,
   Is no longer worth its own weight in lead.
She, worthier than silver and the tawny gold,
   Who birthed nobles, is scarce worth a farthing.*

## Book VII

Whoever came here not so long ago would say,
   "We have come to your ports, abundant land."
But now you are thought barren, and you are, because
   You are lacking both morals and riches.
Where shall I turn, seeking relief for sad affairs?
   Not any anchor holds our vessel now.*                        1350
Thus my country, which was steadfast, is weakened by
   Unjust judgments, denying rights to men.
Thus our Britannia, as if widowed, renders
   Error tribute and stands apart from God.
Thus she who had been virtuous is now vicious;
   Once a lawgiver, she's a lawless beast.
Thus she who'd been lavish now endures poverty;
   Who'd been holy becomes Venus herself.
She is bestrewn with salt, who had been filled with fruits,
   And she who was the rose is like the thorn.                  1360
She who'd been beautiful is now thought a monster;
   She's head to tail, so all tread upon her.
A wicked stepmother spawns foul scandals anew,
   Who was a mother and host praised by all.
Who was once an angel now works all the angles,
   And hangs about in shadows, veiled in filth.
Our country, whose sister, as they say, had been Fame,
   Is more infamous than all other lands.
Who had been worthier above all upon earth
   Is now laid low, as if God is elsewhere.                     1370
She yields whatever fame she had by her backward
   Course, and she lies rejected, unsteady.
Squabbling error moves the fixed, fells the high, wears down
   What's strong, and strews countless widespread evils.
Nobles grow indolent and clergy, lax; cities
   Quarrel; the laws are lawlessly severe.
The unruly mob murmurs; accustomed to sin,
   Its abuse grows; thus the whole land's in pain.
I think the earthen foot attacks the golden head,*
   And the wolf fears the lambs, that have no horns.          1380
God views the earth only through the merits of men,
   And man accordingly authors his times.

O land barren of morals, devoid of counsels
   Sound, injured and lacking medication,
Say, where hides these days the fortune that once you thought
   To be without equal throughout the world.
If Lachesis meted out a deceitful fate,*

## Vox Clamantis by John Gower: 'The Voice of One Crying'

She comes now to make good her treacherous deal.
And now Aurora grows wan with your black venom,*
   Whose light shone bright on others in the world.           1390
Now the flower of your youth, which grew profusely,
   Withers, and you die, aged by all your sins.
Now that loathsome bird, herald of coming trials,
   The prophet owl, prophesizes your fate.*
God knows that this matter should be worthy of note,
   So far from his esteem this place now stands.
I know our land has grown proverbial to all,
   And everyone remarks it's like a mirror.

Such things happen in all lands by the laws of Fate,
   They say, but I don't think it is like that.               1400
It's not Fortune that makes such things bound to happen,
   Nor Fate, but our deserts for evil deeds.
But who now thinks it is Fate and wants to expunge
   Her, let purge his sins and she'll be expunged.
God's ready grace will come to those who now seek it,
   For God turns to those who return to him.
When the land's pious behavior proclaimed the peace,
   And Justice supported her own actions,
When Faith remained firm and Love endured without stain,
   Then, since Peace bloomed, Fate brought everything good.    1410
Now, therefore, let our life be renewed in our God,
   Lest perchance our fate should be more evil.
Let us offer the Lord of Lords the age-old prayers,
   That the Lord render mercy to his own,
Through whom peace, honor, and wholesome times will return,
   Which are now fugitive because of sin.

Who'd like to see the good old days come back again,*
   Should give up his old ways and start anew.
God is mild with the meek and stern with the wicked,
   So anyone can have God by merit.                   1420
Therefore, Lord, let thy grace aid us in thy mercy,
   Which once brought indulgence to the guilty.
Let thy mercy receive us, lest the nations say,
   "Where's your Lord, who's wont to be merciful?"
Grant our tears a hearing, I pray, Merciful One,
   For without you, you know we have no help.
Exert now your grace on behalf of our failings;
   Do not dwell upon our previous sins.

Your grace has never been slow to come to our aid;
    Where is that now, which was our salvation?        1430
We are the sinners, and you are the Redeemer,
    And your goodness knows that we are your work.
If man should sin much, you're able to forgive more;
    Our ways give you matter for your pardon.
Should you hurl thunderbolts as often as men sin,
    The world shall survive for but a short time.
Thus when you survey the earth dependent on you,
    O Creator, let your world be peaceful.
We, dear God, your servants, though dilatory now,
    Believe that you, not Fortune, are our God.        1440
We know you alone should be worshipped above all;
    Thus you alone have mercy on us, God!

## Chapter 25

**Here he tells how he conceived, not so much by himself but from the common voice of the folk, as if in a dream, what he wrote about the world's errors in this indictment. However, he advises, finally, that whoever feels himself culpable should repent and, before worse times befall us, correct himself with a humble heart.**

I've composed these verses that the spirit uttered
    During my sleep. That was a heavy night.
Yet I've not written these lines as the book's author,*
    But rather give you to read what I've heard.
I've written them not out of presumptuousness,
    But as the folk's voice gave them to my ear.
May he whom his mind troubles be vexed by that voice,
    That he the better tend his prior faults.        1450
But he who perceives himself unscathed should go quit
    Thence, and may each stand on his own merits.
It's not my purpose to fault whom sins don't burden;
    Hence, none is harmed unless perchance guilty.
Therefore don't be troubled, for a galled horse declines
    To bear the saddle's weight, not one that's sound.
I don't accuse anyone specific of sin's
    Burden, but let man probe within himself.
I've not distrained anyone with bitter charges,
    Nor do my verses indict anyone.        1460
Waking, I've finished the writings I got in sleep,

### Vox Clamantis *by John Gower: 'The Voice of One Crying'*

Good things for the good, and bad for the bad.
For all groan that the world is tormented by God's
   Vengeance for the gravity of our sin.
Let the wicked man, therefore, amend his fault from
   A contrite heart, before we are consumed.

The man who keeps his heart pure sets the world aright;
   Let him read these words, that he rule his heart.
What I've written is the people's voice, but you'll see
   That God is there where the people clamor.          1470
The good man hears what is good, the bad ignores it;
   Let the good, given to good, hear these words.
Let the bad know them, who henceforward may be good;
   And let the good seek them to be better.
The world can't harm a righteous one who's of good faith,
   But at a slip, the world resorts to force.
Just as each one behaves in life, so goes the world;
   Thus everyone should stand against evil.
Sin is indeed widespread, as virtue is corrupt,
   Since it's not purged, but perpetuated.               1480
The dooms are deserved that are given in the end.[2]

---

[2] Lines 1479–81 are replaced in DLTH$_2$ by the following distich:
I myself am worse than all men, but may the world's
   Founder forgive me through the Holy Spirit. Amen.

# NOTES TO BOOK VII

Ch. 1 heading: "statue, quam Nebugodonosor viderat in sompnis": cf. Daniel 2: 31–44.

ll. 5–8: cf. *Confessio Amantis*, Pro. 585–662; see below ll. 106–12, 136–40, 353–4, 1379.

ll. 7–8: see note to ll. 109–10, below.

ll. 27–8: cf. Numbers 31: 16.

ll. 33–42: the magnates' wish to prolong the Hundred Years' War, to profit from plunder and ransom, was not shared by the commons, heavily taxed to subsidize the fighting, who gained nothing; see also ll. 279–84, below.

ll. 47–54: "Dives": cf. *Confessio Amantis*, VI. 975–1109.

ll. 71–4: cf. Luke 16: 11–13.

ll. 109–10: both are proverbial, based ultimately on Daniel, and on Ovid, *Metamorphoses*, 1. 89–150, who describes the Four Ages of Man as Golden, Silver, Bronze, and Iron. Ovid's source was likely Hesiod, *Works and Days*, ll. 109–201. See also ll. 7–8, above.

l. 111: "Aureus...modus probatis": Aristotle's Golden Mean; cf. *Nichomachian Ethics*, II.

l. 120: "Mammon": cf. Matthew 6: 24, Luke 6: 13.

l. 123: cf. Apocalypse 2: 25.

ll. 125–6: virtually *verbatim* Ovid, *Tristia*, 1. 8. 41–2.

l. 131: virtually *verbatim* Ovid, *Metamorphoses*, 15. 260–1; see also note to ll. 109–10 above.

ll. 135–40: see note to ll. 5–8, above.

ll. 157–60: "Gallica peccata": Possibly a reference to "courtly love," from the country of origin, which in one iteration declared marriage an obstacle to true love: cf. Andreas Capellanus's (likely satirical) *De arte honesti amandi*.

ll. 163–78: cf. *Mirour de l'Omme*, ll. 8917–40; *Traitié pour les amantz marietz*, XVII, XVIII.

ll. 163–4: possibly an allusion to Alice Perrers and Edward III.

ll. 177–8: "in facie ficti palloris": pallor was considered evidence of a lover's sincerity, and also of true clerical holiness.

ll. 193–4: "aspectum Gabrielis...caput ancille": Although referred to as a man in Daniel 8: 15–16, as an angel Gabriel had no gender, and was frequently depicted in contemporary visual arts with feminine features.

ll. 207–8: cf. Matthew 7: 15.

ll. 233–4: possibly an allusion to John Ball (cf. *VC* I. 793), or more likely a general allusion to lollard preachers.

ll. 247–8: adapted from Nigel of Longchamp, *Speculum Stultorum*, ed. Mann, ll. 37–8.

ll. 255–6: adapted from Ovid, *Ars Amatoria*, 2. 201–2.

ll. 257–8: "Philemonis": cf. Ovid, *Metamorphoses*, 8. 616–724.

l. 259: adapted from Ovid, *Metamorphoses*, 2. 680–1.

l. 265: "Fulvus...talus": Alludes to the presentation of spurs, part of the ceremony of creating a new knight. Gold spurs became part of the English coronation ceremony for Richard I (Lionheart) in 1189; may also refer to a papal order of knighthood first conferred by Charles IV, Holy Roman Emperor, in 1357.

ll. 273–4: virtually *verbatim* Ovid, *Tristia*, 5. 13. 27–8.

ll. 279–84: see note to ll. 33–42, above.

ll. 293–4: cf. Genesis 27.

ll. 315–16: adapted from Ovid, *Metamorphoses*, 1. 144–5.

l. 319: virtually *verbatim* Ovid, *Amores*, 3. 11. 43.

ll. 323–4: virtually *verbatim* Ovid, *Ars Amatoria*, 1. 761–2.

ll. 327–8: *verbatim* Ovid, *Fasti*, 4. 717–18.

ll. 331–2: adapted from Ovid, *Tristia*, 1. 9. 5–6.

l. 334: *verbatim* Ovid, *Ars Amatoria*, 3. 436.

l. 340: virtually *verbatim* Ovid, *Tristia*, 1. 8. 8.

l. 343: greyhounds were bred for hare coursing, a sport popular in medieval England.

l. 347: virtually *verbatim* Ovid, *Metamorphoses*, 1. 141.

l. 353: see note to ll. 5–8, above.

## Notes to Book VII

ll. 357–8: proverbial; cf. *Mirour de l'Omme*, ll. 3337–41; Walz, 106b.

l. 365: the line translates a pun on "mundus" = "world" and "mundus" = "clean, pure"; cf. notes to ll. 505–8, 647–60, below, *VC* III, Pro. 100, *Mirour de l'Omme*, ll. 26590–8.

ll. 369–70: proverbial.

l. 371: *verbatim* Nigel of Longchamp, *Speculum Stultorum*, ed. Mann, l. 579.

ll. 373–4: virtually *verbatim* Nigel of Longchamp, *Speculum Stultorum*, ed. Mann, ll. 583–4.

ll. 375–6: *verbatim* Alexander Neckam, *De Vita Monachorum*, ed. Wright, p. 177, ll. 15–16.

ll. 379–83: virtually *verbatim* Alexander Neckam, *De Vita Monachorum*, ed. Wright, II. 183, ll. 29–30, 184, ll. 1–3.

l. 385: *verbatim* Alexander Neckam, *De Vita Monachorum*, ed. Wright, II. 184, l. 17.

l. 387: *verbatim* Alexander Neckam, *De Vita Monachorum*, ed. Wright, II. 195, l. 25.

ll. 389–92: virtually *verbatim* Alexander Neckam, *De Vita Monachorum*, ed. Wright, II. 197, ll. 5–8.

ll. 395–6: *verbatim* Alexander Neckam, *De Vita Monachorum*, ed. Wright, II. 197, ll. 9–10.

ll. 405–10: *verbatim* Alexander Neckam, *De Vita Monachorum*, ed. Wright, II. 186, ll. 5–10.

ll. 417–18: *verbatim* Alexander Neckam, *De Vita Monachorum*, ed. Wright, II. 196, ll. 3–4.

ll. 419–20: virtually *verbatim* Alexander Neckam, *De Vita Monachorum*, ed. Wright, II. 196, ll. 20–1.

ll. 437–8: *verbatim* Alexander Neckam, *De Vita Monachorum*, ed. Wright, II. 196, ll. 1–2.

ll. 441–2: virtually *verbatim* Alexander Neckam, *De Vita Monachorum*, ed. Wright, II. 189, ll. 9–10.

l. 448: "Attropos": oldest of the three Fates in Greek and Roman belief (the others being Clotho, who spins the thread of human life, and Lachesis, who measures it), Atropos decided how and when each would die, cutting the thread to effect it; see also l. 1387, below.

l. 452: adapted from Ovid, *Ars Amatoria*, 2. 670; cf. *Carmen super multiplici viciorum pestilencia*, l. 186.

l. 454: adapted from Ovid, *Tristia*, 2. 236.

l. 456: cf. Luke 16: 19–31.

ll. 459–60: adapted from Ovid, *Ars Amatoria*, 3. 65–6.

ll. 461–2: *verbatim* Ovid, *Ars Amatoria*, 3. 63–4.

ll. 463–4: *verbatim* Ovid, *Tristia*, 5. 10. 5–6.

ll. 465–6: virtually *verbatim* Ovid, *Ex Ponto*, 2. 2. 35–6.

l. 469: *verbatim* Ovid, *Metamorphoses*, 15. 212.

l. 471: *verbatim* Ovid, *Metamorphoses*, 10. 519.

l. 473: *verbatim* Ovid, *Metamorphoses*, 15. 237.

ll. 475–6: adapted from Ovid, *Metamorphoses*, 15. 215–16.

ll. 479–80: adapted from Ovid, *Metamorphoses*, 15. 263–4.

l. 483: *verbatim* Ovid, *Ars Amatoria*, 3. 91.

ll. 485–6: virtually *verbatim* Ovid, *Ars Amatoria*, 3. 119–20.

ll. 489–90: adapted from Ovid, *Fasti*, 1. 203–4; "senator," l. 490, borrowed from Ovid, here translated as "shire knight," as a contemporaneously equivalent.

ll. 493–4: cf. Ecclesiastes 1: 9.

l. 496: *verbatim* Ovid, *Remedia Amoris*, 572.

ll. 499–500: *verbatim* Alexander Neckam, *De Vita Monachorum*, ed. Wright, II. 181, ll. 3–6.

ll. 502–4: *verbatim* Alexander Neckam, *De Vita Monachorum*, ed. Wright, II. 181, ll. 9–10.

ll. 505–8: "Mundus" can have two meanings, "world" and "pure." The play on both creates antiphrasis ("antifrasim," l. 507), i.e., obviously intending the opposite of what is said. Cf. also ll. 361–4, above, ll. 647–60, *VC* III, Pro. 100, *Mirour de l'Omme*, ll. 26590–8, containing the same pun.

Ch. 6 and 7 headings: cf. Genesis 1: 296–2: 25; also *Confessio Amantis*, VIII. 1–58, *Mirour de l'Omme*, ll. 85–180.

ll. 505–10: cf. *Mirour de l'Omme*, ll. 26785–844.

ll. 507–8: contains an implicit pun on "mundus": see notes to ll. 366, 505–8, above.

ll. 543–4: cf. Romans 8: 5.

l. 585: "partes quatuor equas": i.e., the four elements, fire, air, earth, and water.

ll. 587–90: i.e., the firmament of stars, the planets constrained within their orbits, the Zodiac, and the twelve months of the year; cf. *Confessio Amantis*, VII. 699–709, 953–78, Psalm 8: 4–10.

ll. 621–2: cf. Isaiah 14: 11–15.

ll. 631–2: cf. Mark 10: 45; Luke 22: 26–7.

Ch. 8 heading: The notion of the human being as a microcosmic universe can be traced to Plato and Plotinus, and to Arab philosophy; the early Scholastics, especially the Victorines, promoted it; subsequently Aquinas, whose concept Gower mirrors, refined it: cf. *Summa Theologica*, I. 91. 1, I–II. 17. 8. Obj. 2.

ll. 639–60: cf. Gregory I ("the Great"), *Moralia in Job*, 6: 16; *Confessio Amantis*, Pro. 943–58, *Mirour de l'Omme*, ll. 26869–940.

ll. 647–60: see note to ll. 505–8, above.

ll. 673–6: cf. *Traitié pour les amantz marietz*, I. 1–21.

ll. 685–6: *verbatim* Alexander Neckam, *De Vita Monachorum*, ed. Wright, II. 197, ll. 17–18.

ll. 687–90: *verbatim* Alexander Neckam, *De Vita Monachorum*, ed. Wright, II. 197, ll. 25–8.

ll. 691–4: virtually *verbatim* Alexander Neckam, *De Vita Monachorum*, ed. Wright, II. 197, ll. 33–4, II. 198, ll. 1–2.

l. 699: *verbatim* Alexander Neckam, *De Vita Monachorum*, ed. Wright, II. 193, l. 23.

ll. 701–5: *verbatim* Alexander Neckam, *De Vita Monachorum*, ed. Wright, II. 193, ll. 25–9.

l. 706: *verbatim* Alexander Neckam, *De Vita Monachorum*, ed. Wright, II. 193, l. 32.

l. 708: adapted from Alexander Neckam, *De Vita Monachorum*, ed. Wright, II. 194, l. 4.

Ch. 9 heading: With Gower's depiction of death in Ch. 9, cf. Ecclesiastes 9: 1–6.

ll. 717–24: adapted from Ovid, *Metamorphoses*, 6. 303–9.

l. 765: snakes and dogs commonly symbolize Envy in medieval visual arts; cf. "Invidia" in the painting of the Sins by Hieronymus Bosch, in the Prado Museum.

l. 775: proverbial – Walz, 36b.

## Vox Clamantis by John Gower: 'The Voice of One Crying'

ll. 809–10: cf. Isaiah 5: 8; see also *VC* VI. 343–6, above, and note.

l. 831: cf. II Corinthians 9: 6, Galatians 6: 8.

l. 869: "Ethne": Etna is Gower's favorite figure for Envy; cf. *Confessio Amantis*, II. 149–66.

l. 890: cf. Genesis 18: 27, Job 30: 19, Ecclesiastes 3: 20.

ll. 891–2: cf. *Mirour de l'Omme*, ll. 1784–8; the quotation originates with Augustine, *Tractates on the Gospel of John*, I. xv.

ll. 901–2: cf. the morality play *Everyman*.

Ch. 17 heading: "mundi...vestimentum veterascunt": cf. Isaiah 51: 6; also Isaiah 50: 9, Psalm 101: 27 (Vulgate); and l. 919, below.

ll. 909–10: *verbatim* Alexander Neckam, *De Vita Monachorum*, ed. Wright, II. 178, ll. 23–4.

ll. 911–18: virtually *verbatim* Alexander Neckam, *De Vita Monachorum*, ed. Wright, II. 179, ll. 1–8.

l. 919: see note to Ch. 17 heading, above.

ll. 919–24: *verbatim* Alexander Neckam, *De Vita Monachorum*, ed. Wright, II. 180, ll. 5–10.

l. 922: cf. Job 8: 9.

ll. 929–30: *verbatim* Alexander Neckam, *De Vita Monachorum*, ed. Wright, II. 180, ll. 11–12.

ll. 931–2: *verbatim* Alexander Neckam, *De Vita Monachorum*, ed. Wright, II. 180, ll. 15–16.

ll. 939–40: on the combination of ashes and clay, cf. Genesis 18: 27, Job 30: 19.

l. 951: a triple pun on "mors" (death), "morsu vetito" (forbidden bite) and "mordens" (biting): i.e., the bite in Eden of the forbidden fruit brought death into the world.

ll. 953–4: cf. Bernard of Clairvaux, Epistle 105 ("To Romanus, Sub-Deacon of the Roman Curia").

ll. 955–6: cf. *Mirour de l'Omme*, ll. 11404–9; probably derived from Hélinant de Froidmont, *Vers de la Mort*, XV. 10–11.

ll. 1011–12: the notion that at Judgment Day the fallen angels will be replaced in some fashion by holy men was not unique to Gower, but rather is traceable to Augustine (e.g., *Enchiridion*, IX. esp. 28–30), whom Gower usually follows; the idea remained a subject of scholastic debate, however: e.g., cf. Anselm, *Cur Deus Homo*, I. XVIII.

## Notes to Book VII

l. 1030: cf. Matthew 22: 21, Mark 12: 17, Luke 20: 25.

l. 1067: "Thetis": sea nymph, one of the fifty Nereids, hence a water goddess; mother (with the Phthian Peleus) of Achilles; here used metonymically for water; cf. *VC* V. 812.

ll. 1087–8: cf. Matthew 25: 32–3; also *VC* IV. 693.

ll. 1091–2: cf. Matthew 10: 26–7, Luke 12: 2.

l. 1095: cf. Genesis 18: 22–33; see also ll. 1220–4, below and note.

ll. 1121–2: "Fletibus assiduis": By the fourteenth century, weeping had become evidence of penitential piety, with biblical roots (cf. Psalms 41: 4, 79: 6, 101: 10 [Vulgate]) and promoted in the mystical tradition (e.g., *Dialogue* of Catherine of Siena, *Scale of Perfection* of Walter Hilton, *Book of Margery Kempe*).

ll. 1125–8: *verbatim* Peter Riga, *Aurora*, Deuteronomy 243–6.

l. 1132: virtually *verbatim* Peter Riga, *Aurora*, Exodus 200.

ll. 1141–2: Despair was considered a form of Sloth, here of insufficient belief; cf. *Confessio Amantis*, IV. 3389–514.

ll. 1143–4: cf. John 7: 37–9.

ll. 1148–54: "timore": "timor domini," or "holy fear," the last of the seven gifts of the Holy Spirit given to Christ, but the first (i.e., given in reverse order) to humanity; cf. Isaiah 11: 2–3.

l. 1155: "novissima": cf. the Four Last Things, i.e., Death, Judgment, Heaven, and Hell.

ll. 1167–8: "mundi.../ caro...demon": i.e., the World, the Flesh, and the Devil, the three sources of temptation; cf. Ephesians 2: 2–3, Thomas Aquinas, *Summa Theologica*, Q.47 A.13. Obj. 3; these three structure the first third of the *Mirour de l'Omme*, ll. 37–18420.

l. 1173: cf. Aristotle, *Nichomachean Ethics*, 1. 13, *De Anima*, 3. 11.

l. 1184: "scola": that is, the training given to clergy: cf. ll. 1251–2, below.

ll. 1203–10: cf. Matthew 24: 7; also Apocalypse 6 and 8.

ll. 1217–18: that God will forgive the penitent sinner is a Christian cornerstone: cf. Mark 2: 17, I Timothy 1: 15–16, Luke 15: 7, 10.

ll. 1220–4: cf. Genesis 18: 22–33; see also l. 1095, above.

l. 1227: cf. Job 9: 8–9.

ll. 1231–2: cf. Psalm 77: 21 (Vulgate).

ll. 1251–2: cf. l. 1184, above, and note.

ll. 1305–8: cf. Psalm 84: 11.

l. 1344: "Nobile que genuit": refers to the gold noble, a coin first minted 1344–6, under Edward III; initially valued at 6s. 8d. the noble was steadily reduced in size and weight, first in 1346–51, again in 1351–77, to maintain the same exchange value, bringing charges of debasement.

ll. 1350–9: the verse here changes to leonine couplets before reverting to hexameters.

ll. 1387–8: see l. 448, above, and note.

l. 1389: adapted from Ovid, *Metamorphoses*, 7. 209.

l. 1394: "bubo propheta": to hear an owl in the night was a proverbial harbinger of death. The *Bestiary* equates owls with the Jews, who refused to believe, and thus were condemned to darkness and death.

l. 1417: *verbatim* Ovid, *Fasti*, 4. 596.

l. 1445: "ut auctor": i.e., "as an authority"; Gower claims only to be reporting what he's heard.

# THE *CRONICA TRIPERTITA*

In four of its eleven known manuscripts, the *Vox Clamantis* is attached following Book VII via a perfunctory prose colophon to what Gower called "A chronicle in three parts." Known now as the *Cronica Tripertita*, these verses are a fierce and partisan condemnation of Richard II, reflecting strong Lancastrian leanings. The *Cronica*'s matter is largely derived from the records of the parliament convened in 1399 especially to depose Richard in favor of Henry IV – the so-called "Record and Process."[3] It is clear that, like the *Visio Anglie* added at its beginning, the *Cronica* was conceived as a separate poem and subsequently conjoined to the *Vox Clamantis*. Unlike the *Visio*, however, the *Cronica* differs both metrically and in tone from the *VC* proper, and no attempt was made to incorporate it as an eighth Book. It is doubtful Gower intended the *Cronica* to serve as a conclusion to his longer poem. The four manuscripts that contain it (Oxford, All Souls College MS 98, Macaulay's base text; London, British Library, MS Cotton Tiberius A. iv; London, British Library, MS Harley 6291; Glasgow, University Library, Hunterian MS T.2.17) seem to be compendia prepared by scribes for patrons, and thus unlikely to have been overseen, or known, by Gower himself – the same is true of Oxford, Bodleian Library, MS Hatton 92, a fifteenth-century copy in which the *Cronica* appears alone. Consequently, here we translate the colophon, but not the *Cronica* itself.

**\*Here ends the *libellus* called *The Voice of One Crying*, based most notably upon the article of the first misfortune that famously befell, as if from God's rod, the unfortunate Richard the Second in the beginning of his reign in England, as you have heard. And now, furthermore, because he was not remorseful but hardened to the tyrant's manner, he did not leave off scourging his realm ceaselessly with constant oppressions until the scourge of divine punishment, not undeservedly, put an end to him with his deposition. \*Three nobles of the realm were particularly implicated in this, namely Thomas Duke of Gloucester, commonly called the Swan, Richard Earl of Arundel, called the Horse, and Thomas Earl of Warwick,**

---

[3] For the Latin text, see *The Deposition of Richard II, "The Record and Process of the Renunciation and Deposition of Richard II" (1399) and Related Writings*, ed. David R. Carlson, Toronto Medieval Latin Texts 29 (Toronto: Pontifical Institute of Medieval Studies, 2007).

**whose name was the Bear. Together with certain other prominent men who followed them, they arose manfully that they might destroy the supporters of the royal malice, strong in hand and righteous in spirit, to the glory of God and the wellbeing of the realm, just as the writer intends to disclose more plainly in the following chronicle, which is in three parts.**[4]

Prose colophon to *Cronica Tripertita*, which follows *Vox Clamantis* in four of the five known manuscripts containing it, including Oxford, All Souls College, MS 98, Macaulay's base text, which he wrongly believed was compiled under Gower's supervision. The prose link itself is probably not Gower's work.

Swan: badge originally of the Bohun family, adopted as Lancastrian following marriages of Thomas of Gloucester to Eleanor de Bohun, and Henry Bolingbroke (Henry IV) to Mary de Bohun, surviving heirs of the last Bohun earl; Gower's effigy wears an "SSS" collar with a pendant swan. Bear: badge of Thomas de Beauchamp, 12th Warwick earl – a bear with ragged staff. Horse: badge of Richard Fitzalan, 4th earl of Arundel (and perhaps why arms of later earls bore two horses as supporters). Both Bear and Horse identified in a "prophecy," in verse, recorded by Thomas Walsingham, *Chronica Maiora* for 1397 (ed. Taylor, Childs, Watkiss, II, 72–3); cf. also Walsingham, *Annales Ricardi Secundi et Henrici Quarti, regum Anglie*.

---

[4] MSS EDTH$_2$ omit the link to the *Cronica Tripertita*, ending only "Explicit libellus qui intitulatur *Vox Clamantis*." L has only "Explicit liber intitulatus *Vox clamantis*."

# APPENDIX 1: THE EPISTLE TO ARUNDEL

The Epistle is known from a single manuscript, Oxford, All Souls College MS 98, which served G.C. Macaulay as the base text for his edition of most of the poems in Latin. It contains, along with the Epistle and the *Vox Clamantis*, the *Cronica Tripertita*, *Rex celi Deus*, *H. aquile pullus*, *O recolende*, the *Carmen super multiplici viciorum pestilencia*, *Tractatus de lucis scrutinio*, *Est amor*, the *Traitié pour essampler les amantz marietz*, *Quia unusquisque*, *Eneados bucolis*, *O Deus immense*, *Quicquid homo scribat*, and *Dicunt scripture*. Although Macaulay thought the manuscript "was certainly written and corrected under the direction of the author, and remained for some time in his hands, receiving addition from time to time," more recent scholarship (most notably that of Malcolm Parkes) has shown most of Macaulay's guesses to be unfounded.[1] This is especially true of the Epistle, which Macaulay and most subsequent scholars, following him, believed "seems to relate to this volume in particular," thereby providing evidence that All Souls MS 98 "was eventually presented to Abp. Arundel."

In fact, All Souls MS 98 is an assemblage of poems independently copied in two different scripts by five different scribes, the major texts, such as the *Vox Clamantis*, originally as stand-alone works. In Parkes's view, the composite volume never belonged to Gower, but rather was brought together for a patron-owner after Gower's death. It was thus not the "librum" mentioned in ll. 1 and 8, nor the "scriptum" of ll. 3 and 14, given to Arundel. As for the Epistle itself: the single copy, along with remains of its original quire, was bound into what is now All Souls MS 98 sometime after 1490, since the Vellum Inventory prepared at the College in that year fails to record its presence.[2] Based on the evidence of its disparate decorative elements, including the illuminated "S" with its image of a bishop (perhaps a "portrait" of Arundel, by the illuminator Herman Scheerre), the Epistle was probably copied in its original form in the later 1390s – but if the

---

[1] M.B. Parkes, "Patterns of scribal activity and revisions of the text in early copies of works by John Gower," in *New Science Out of Old Books: Studies in Manuscripts and Early Printed Books in Honour of A.I. Doyle*, ed. Richard Beadle and A.J. Piper (Aldershot: Scholar, 1995), 81–121.

[2] On the date, see R.F. Yeager, "Gower's 'Epistle to Archbishop Arundel': The Evidence of Oxford, All Souls College, MS 98," in *Manuscript and Print in Late Medieval and Early Modern Britain: Essays in Honour of Professor Julia Boffey*, ed. Tamara Atkin and Jaclyn Rajsic (Cambridge: D.S. Brewer, 2019), 12–34.

*Appendix 1: The Epistle to Arundel*

illuminator of the "S" was indeed Scheerre, production could have occurred up to 1419, when Scheerre closed his London workshop.

As we have it, the text of the Epistle in All Souls MS 98 has been heavily revised. Fourteen full lines are written over erasure, as are several individual words and phrases – another indication of an earlier original with a different text that may have gone to the archbishop. Were that the case, then the likeliest candidate for the unnamed "librum/scriptum" would be the shorter, 1397 version of *Carmen super multiplici viciorum pestilencia*, not the *Vox Clamantis* or any other of the poems in All Souls MS 98.

**With a devout heart, John Gower, old and blind, has sent the following epistle to his esteemed Lord and Most Reverend Father in Christ, Lord Thomas of Arundel, Archbishop of Canterbury, Primate of All England and \*Legate of the Apostolic See. Whose office for the governance of His Church may our Lord Jesus Christ guide and blissfully preserve, the son of the glorious Virgin who with God the Father and the Holy Ghost lives and reigns, God forever and ever. Amen.**

    Thomas, Thomas's heir, I give you my humble self,\*
    And write what follows to present this book to you.\*
    Be heedful of this work that I present to you,
    And, as you contemplate it, let it stir your mind.
    The divided curia seen these days in Rome\*
    Turns joy into sorrow because it is corrupt.
    And because Christ's law mourns in this sorrowful time,
    I send you this book, that should be read as a plaint.\*
    But grant, you who bear the light of divine healing,
    A cure for those sorrowing, that it bring them joy.        10
    Since the light has ceased, and the Faith darkens elsewhere,\*
    Shine your light, you our Phoebus, upon our affairs,\*
    And so that you shine bright and glow with your power,
    I offer for your light this work that I've written.
    I think it won't be in vain, if you look clearly,\*
    With a judicious spirit, in such a mirror.
    I'm almost blind, but though I can't see what goes on,\*
    I see you in my mind and hold you in my heart.
    Although crooked old age has twisted my worn out
    Body, it allows that my mind remains zealous,\*        20
    And thus zealous in Christ I persist in this work,
    In which I'll write for you the world's manifest deeds.

*Appendix 1: The Epistle to Arundel*

Hence, father, I pray, while I work on my writings,
You put at ease the spirit of a zealous mind.
I have ever loved you as a father, whereby
I've hoped your special grace would be mine in the end.
Because my sight has now been reft from my body,*
Let your light shine and guide the footsteps of my soul,
Let my wretched body, old and miserable,*
Helped by you, its protector, not be confounded.       30
And so, my guardian in life and death alike,*
Take me, by your suffrage, blinded, along with you.
Your honorable light, that shines from noble stock,*
Must needs not lie hidden beneath the world's ashes.*
  Let Arundel shine with a new light, like the sun,*
Which brought you forth and which first nursed you at its breast.
You're named at birth Thomas, since you are To[tus] Mas [completely masculine];*
Whence finished by God [with *tus* = frankincense], you are kept from every stain,
And thus a prelate now, sanctified by Christ's law,*
You keep the law by which you keep yourself from stain.       40
Your light in our day is bright, unspotted by sin,
And shines clearly since no dishonor obscures it.
Let England rejoice that it merits such a lamp,
Where those who would live well follow your example.
Through you all love will prosper, and anger withdraw,*
And under your care all our days are prosperous.
And since your light thus increases and fills the earth,
May God grant such a light be yours eternally.
This is what Gower asks, who is and will be yours.

# NOTES TO THE "EPISTLE"

Prologue: "apostolice sedis legato": Arundel seems to have been appointed "legate to the Holy See" ca. 1391, by Boniface IX; cf. *Calendar of Close Rolls*, 1392 to 1396, pp. 399, 401–2; and 1396–9, p. 61. Less likely is his appointment to the cardinalate in 1390, as reported in the *Continuatio Eulogii* (and its possible, now-lost source) which probably confused the two offices.

l. 1: "Thome, Thomas": The comparison is with Arundel's predecessor, Thomas Becket, Archbishop of Canterbury from 1162–70, when at the behest of Henry II he was assassinated in the Cathedral during mass. Their dispute was over royal prerogative and Church autonomy. Gower's comparisons with Becket were not infrequent, often to emphasize the degeneration of the current Church (e.g., *VC* III. 79) and also to signal martyrdom in defense of the Church. Cf. Sudbury, *VC* I. 1055–78; also l. 37 and note, below.

l. 2: "librum" here and in l. 8 should be understood in conjunction with "scriptum" in ll. 3 and 14, which together suggest a range of possibilities for the form taken by the Epistle at its original presentation.

l. 5: "curia divisa": i.e., the Western Schism, 1378–1417, that produced rival popes in Avignon (Clement VII) and Rome (Urban VI), supported by France and England, respectively. Cf. *VC* III. 3–6.

ll. 8–11: written over erasure.

l. 11: "lux cessit": i.e., the "darkness" brought about by the divided Church. Cf. *Tractatus de lucis scrutinio*, ll. 1–8.

l. 12: "Phebus": Phoebus Apollo, the god of the sun, and hence of light; cf. l. 35, below, where Arundel is compared to the sun – likely here also Richard, whose badges included the sun, as did his self-designed tomb, and ship sails on his return from Ireland in 1395.

ll. 15–16: "In speculo": a mirror reflects both outward images (cf. l. 22, below) and inward – in it, one sees the self – hence implicitly a device suggesting introspection.

l. 17: "mere" ("wholly"), the only word written over erasure here, probably replaced "fere" ("nearly"), thus pointing to an earlier version of the Epistle, ca. 1397, co-terminal with Arundel's elevation from Archbishop of York to Canterbury; cf. l. 27, below, and note.

Notes to the "Epistle"

l. 20: written over erasure.

ll. 26–34: written over erasure.

ll. 27–8: Play here on "divisus" ("separated, reft") and "visus" ("sight') likely influenced the tenor of the image; see note to l. 17, above.

ll. 33–4: For the underlying image that Christ's light should not be hidden under a covering ("a bushel"); cf. Matthew 5: 14–15; Mark 4: 21; Luke 11: 33, 8: 16. Gower's use of "sub cinere" ("beneath ashes") is unique and undoubtedly pointed.

ll. 35–6: Arundel was a long-term favorite of Richard II's, who appointed him chancellor twice (1386–9, 1391–6), Archbishop of York (1388–97), and Archbishop of Canterbury (1396–7), before turning on him, sending him into exile.

ll. 37–8: The three puns here, on "Mas": "manly" and "tus" = frankincense, used to sanctify the temple and as an offering to God (cf. Exodus 30: 34, Leviticus 2: 1, 16, respectively). As the second gift of the Magi, frankincense represented worship.

l. 39: "prelatus": Arundel was three times a prelate during Richard's reign, as bishop of Ely (1373–88), Archbishop of York (1388–96), Archbishop of Canterbury (1396–7), and a fourth time, when Henry IV restored him to Canterbury in 1399.

l. 45: "ira recedet": possibly alludes to the conflict between the Appellants and Richard, in whose mind animosity was still strong in 1397.

# APPENDIX 2: KNOWN MANUSCRIPTS OF THE *VOX CLAMANTIS*

(Bracketed letters indicate sigils assigned to each MS by G.C. Macaulay.)
Twelve manuscripts of the *Vox Clamantis* are currently known. These are:

1. Dublin, Trinity College, MS D.4.6 (214). First quarter of the fifteenth century. [T]
    Contains *Quia unusquisque*. One of two witnesses of (apparently) the earliest form of the poem, Hatfield House being the other (see below). A poor copy with significant scribal errors.

2. Glasgow, University Library, Hunterian MS 59 (T.2.17). Ca. 1400. [G]
    Contains *Cronica Tripertita, Quia unusquisque, Carmen super multiplici viciorum pestilencia, De lucis scrutinio, Est amor, O deus immense, Ecce patet tensus, Rex celi deus* (preceded by "Nota Epistolam quam Johannes Gower dum adhuc vixit in laudem Serenissimi principis sui Henrici quarti statim post coronacionem suam ad modum orationis forma subsequente deuote composuit. R [similar small initial] Ex celi deus et dominus qui tempora solus"), *O recolende, H. aquile pullus, Quicquid homo scribat* [*In fine*], *Unanimes esse, Henrici Regis annus fuit, Presul ouile regis, Cultor in ecclesia, Dicunt scripture, Traitié pour ensampler les amantz marietz; Eneidos bucolis* (probably by Gower), full-page archer image with verses *Ad mundum mitto* (fol. 6v), full page image of a draped bier, two angels above holding shield bearing Gower arms, verses *Ora[ntibus] pro anima* [*Armigeri scutum*] (fol. 129v), blot (possibly erased) of a third, full-page image now missing and too blurred to identify (fol. 131v).

3. Hertfordshire, Hatfield House MS, privately owned (Marquess of Salisbury). Second quarter of the fifteenth century. [H$_2$]
    Contains *Vox Clamantis* only. With Trinity College apparently the poem in its earliest form, possibly preceding Trinity, which sometimes agrees with revised MSS. A more professional copy than Trinity, with ornamental margins in the first few folia. Notable in having belonged to William Cecil, 1st Lord Burghley, containing his notes.

4. Lincoln, Cathedral Library, MS A.72 (235). First quarter of the sixteenth century. [L$_2$]
    Contains *Vox Clamantis* without *Visio* (ll. 165–2150), *Carmen super multiplici viciorum pestilencia, De lucis scrutinio, Lex docit auctorum* (latter

*Appendix 2: Known Manuscripts of the* Vox Clamantis

part of *Est amor*), *Quis sit vel qualis* (nine leonine lines added to *Traitié* in London, British Library MS Additional 59495 [*olim* Trentham], and in Oxford, Bodleian Library, MS Digby 294), *H. aquile pullus*; also *Inter saxosum montem* (unlikely by Gower, of undetermined meaning). Copied from Oxford, Bodleian Library MS Laud (Misc.) 719 (see below), including space left (fol. 21) for image, corresponding to archer drawing in Laud (fol. 21r).

5. London, British Library, MS Cotton Tiberius A.iv. Late fourteenth century. [$C_2$]
   Contains *Cronica Tripertita, Quia unusquisque, Carmen super multiplici viciorum pestilencia, Rex celi deus, H. aquile pullus, O recolende, De lucis scrutinio, Orate pro anima, O deus immense, Henrici regis, Unanimes esse, Presul ouile regis, Cultor in ecclesia, Dicunt scripture, Eneidos bucolis* (probably by Gower); also full-page archer image with verses *Ad mundum mitto* (fol. 9v). *Vox Clamantis* in a single hand, multiple hands in the MS identified by Macaulay, *Works*, IV, lxiii–iv, who deems MS "unquestionably independent." Notes by Robert Cotton.

6. London, British Library, MS Cotton Titus A.xiii. Third quarter of the sixteenth century. [C]
   Contains *Vox Clamantis* Prologue–III, l. 116 only; copied by William Lambard(e) from Oxford, Bodleian Library, MS Digby 138 (see below).

7. London, British Library, MS Harley 6291. Late fourteenth century. [H]
   Contains *Cronica Tripertita, Quia unusquisque, Carmen super multiplici viciorum pestilencia, Rex celi deus, H. aquile pullus, O recolende, De lucis scrutinio, Orate pro anima, O deus immense, Henrici regis, Unanimes esse, Presul ouile regis, Cultor in ecclesia, Dicunt scripture, Eneidos bucolis* (probably by Gower) – that is, contents replicate those in BL MS Cotton Tiberius A.iv, except no archer image nor *Ad mundum mitto*. Multiple missing pages from *VC* text, e.g., begins at I. l. 502. Some lines missing from *VC* text written in margins, side and bottom. Macaulay, *Works*, IV, liv–lv, identifies nine hands.

8. Oxford, All Souls College, MS 98. Late fourteenth century. [S]
   Contains *Cronica Tripertita, Quia unusquisque, Carmen super multiplici viciorum pestilencia, Rex celi deus, H. aquile pullus, O recolende, Tractatus de lucis scrutinio, O deus immense, Est amor, Quicquid homo scribat, Traité pour ensampler les Amantz Marietz* (lacks opening lines to Balade III. 3), *Quia unusquisque, Unanimes esse, Presul ouile regis, Cultor in ecclesia, Dicunt scripture, Eneidos bucolis* (probably by Gower), and the sole copy of the "Epistle" to Archbishop Thomas Arundel. At least five hands involved. Base text for Macaulay's edition.

9. Oxford, Bodleian Library, MS Digby 138. Second quarter of the fifteenth century. [D]

*Appendix 2: Known Manuscripts of the* Vox Clamantis

Contains *Vox Clamantis* only. Lacking multiple lines ("deficit versus in copia" in margins), these probably missing from exemplar. Lambard(e)'s copytext for BL MS Cotton Titus A.xiii (see above). Macaulay, *Works*, IV. lxvii, posits a common source for this MS and MS Laud (Misc.) 719 (below), as well as a further source for MS Digby 138, as it – unlike MS Laud (Misc.) 719 – contains the *Visio*.

10. Oxford, Bodleian Library, MS Laud (Misc.) 719. Second quarter of the fifteenth century. [L]
    Contains *Vox Clamantis* without *Visio* (ll. 165–2150), *Carmen super multiplici viciorum pestilencia, De lucis scrutinio, Est Amor* (long version), *H. aquile pullus, Quis sit vel qualis* (nine leonine lines added to *Traitié* in London, British Library MS Additional 59495 [*olim* Trentham], and Oxford, Bodleian Library, MS Digby 294), *Ad mundum mitto*; also *Inter saxosum montem* (unlikely by Gower, of undetermined meaning). Line drawing of archer aiming at globe (fol. 21r), crudely resembling archer images in Glasgow, University Library, Hunterian MS 59 (T.2.17) and London, British Library, MS Cotton Tiberius A.iv. Exemplar for Lincoln, Cathedral Library, MS A.72 (235) (see above). One scribe throughout. Macaulay, *Works*, IV. lxvii posits a common source for MS Laud (Misc.) 719 and Oxford, Bodleian Library, MS Digby 138 (above).

11. Oxford, Bodleian Library, Hatton 92. First half of the fifteenth century. [H$_3$] Contains *Vox Clamantis, Cronica Tripertita, H. aquile pullus, O recolende, Rex celi deus*.
    Contains also prose incipit/explicit variously cobbled from MSS London, British Library MS Additional 59495 (*olim* Trentham) and CHG. Two hands throughout, one for the text, the other for the margins.

12. San Marino (California), Huntington Library, MS HM 150 (*olim* Ecton). Late fourteenth or very early fifteenth. [E]
    Contains *Carmen super multiplici viciorum pestilencia, De lucis scrutinio, O deus immense, Cultor in ecclesia, Unanimes esse, Dicunt scripture, Ad mundum mitto*; omits *Presul ouile regis*, which suggested to Macaulay (IV. lxvi) that "the MS was written before 1402." Unique image of an archer aiming at a trisected globe (moon and stars, forest, water) surmounted by a cross and attached white banner with red cross (fol. 13v), differing, though clearly derived, from images in Glasgow, University Library, Hunterian MS 59 (T.2.17) and London, British Library, MS Cotton Tiberius A.iv. One hand throughout.

# BIBLIOGRAPHY

*Works have been chosen for general accessibility and readability, giving preference to editions translated into English, wherever possible.*

### PRIMARY SOURCES

Andreas Capellanus. *De arte honesti amandi* (*The Art o Courtly Love*) Ed. and trans. Frederick Locke (New York: Ungar, 1978).
Anonymous. *Anonimalle Chronicle 1333–1381.* Ed. and trans. V.H. Galbraith. (Manchester: Manchester University Press, 1927).
Anonymous, *Anonimalle Chronicle 1307-1334 from Brotherton Collection MS 29.* Ed and trans. Wendy Childs and John Taylor. (Leeds: Yorkshire Archaeological Society, 1991).
Anonymous. *Pamphilius de Amore, comédie de latine du XIe siècle.* Ed. M. Ad. Baudouin (Paris: Firmin Didot, 1874).
Anselmus, St. *Prologium; Monologium; an Appendix on Behalf of the Fool by Gaunilon; Cur Deus Homo.* Ed. and trans. Sidney Norton Deane. (Philadelphia: Open Court, 1961).
Aristotle. *Nichomachian Ethics.* Ed. Martin Ostwald. (New York: Bobbs-Merrill, 1962).
Aquinas, Thomas. *Basic Writings.* 2 vols. Ed. Anton C. Pegis (New York: Random House, 1944).
Augustine, Aurelius Hipponensis, St. *City of God.* Ed. and trans. Henry Bettenson. (Harmondsworth: Penguin, 1972).
—Confessions. Ed. and trans. William Watts. 2 vols. Loeb Classical Library (Cambridge, MA: Harvard University Press, 2014).
—"Tractates on the Gospel of John." *Commentaries, Homilies, and Sermons on St. John's Gospel and First Epistle.* Trans. Fr. Seraphim. (New York: 2008)
Avianus. *The Fables of Avianus.* Ed. and trans. David R. Slavitt. (Baltimore: Johns Hopkins University Press, 1993).
*The Bestiary: A Book of Beasts.* Ed. White, T. H. (New York: Capricorn, 1954).
Boethius, Anicius Manlius Severinus. *The Consolation of Philosophy.* Ed. and trans. Richard H. Green (Indianapolis: Bobbs Merrill, 1975).
Chaucer, Geoffrey. *The Riverside Chaucer.* 3$^{rd}$ ed. Ed. Larry D. Benson, et al. (Boston: Houghton Mifflin, 1987).
Colonne, Guido delle. *Historia Destructionis Troiae.* Ed. and trans. Mary E. Meek (Bloomington and London: Indiana University Press, 1974).
Cretensis, Dictys. *Ephemeridos belli Trojani.* Ed. Ferdinand Otto. (Leipzig: Teubner, 1872).

Crow, Martin and Clair C. Olson, eds. *Chaucer Life-Records*. (Oxford: Clarendon Press, 1966).
*Deposition of Richard II*, "The Record and Process of the Reunciation and Deposition of Richard II (1399) and Related Writings. Ed. David R. Carlson. (Toronto: Pontifical Institute of Medieval Studies, 2007.)
Eccleston, Thomas of. *De adventu fratrum minorum in Angliam*. Ed. A. G. Little (Manchester: Manchester University Press, 1911).
Froidmont, Hélinand de. *Les Vers de la Mort*. Ed. Fr. Wulff and Em. Walberg (Paris: Firmin Didot, 1905).
Froissart, Jean. *Chroniques*. Available online at https://www.dhi.ac.uk> onlinefroissart
Godfrey, of Viterbo. *Pantheon Gotfridi Viterbiensis...* (Basel, ex Officina Iacobi Parci 1559). [accessed 2023 at books.google.com]
*Gospel of Nicodemus*, ed. H. C. Kim (Toronto: Pontifical Institute of Medieval Studies, 1973).
Gough, Richard. *Sepulchral Monuments in Great Britain: Applied to Illustrate the History of Families, Manners, Habits, and Arts, at the Different Periods from the Norman Conquest to he Seventeenth Century*. 2 vols. (London: J. Nichols 1796).
Gower, John. *See* also Macaulay, G. C.
—*The Minor Latin Works*. Ed. and trans. R. F. Yeager. (Kalamazoo, MI: Medieval Institute Press, 2005).
—*The French Balades*. Ed. and trans. R. F. Yeager. (Kalamazoo MI: Medieval Institute Press, 2011.
Gregory I (The Great). *The Book of Pastoral Rule*. Ed, and trans. G. Denacopoulus (New York: St. Vladimir's Seminary, 2007).
—*Liber regulae pastoralis*. Ed. Ernst Bredt. (Leipzig: Priber, 1873).
—"Moralia in Job." *Forty Gospel Homilies*. Ed. and trans. David Hurst. (Kalamazoo, MI: Cistercian Publications, 1990).
Hesiod. *The Works and Days. Theogony. The Shield of Heracles*. Ed. and trans. Richmond Lattimore. (Ann Arbor: University of Michigan Press, 1991).
Insulis, Alanus de (Alain of Lille). *De planctu Naturae* [The Plaint of Nature]. Ed. James J. Sheridan. (Toronto: Pontifical Institute of Medieval Studies, 1980).
Isidore of Seville. *Etymologiae. The Etymologies of Isidore of Seville*. Trans. Stephen A. Barney, W. J. Lewis, J.A. Beach, Oliver Berghof. (Cambridge: Cambridge University Press, 2010).
—*Isidori Hispalensis Episcopi. Etymologiarum sive originum*. Ed. W. M. Lindsay. 2 Vols. (Oxford: Clarendon Press, 191; rpt. 1971)
Jean, le Senschal. *Les Cent Ballades: Poème du XIV$^e$ Siécle*. Ed . Gaston Raynaud (Paris: Firmin Didot, 1905).
Jerome, *Adversus Jovinianum*. Available online at https://www.newadvent.org>fathers
Josephus, Flavius. *Jewish Antiquities*. 9 vols. Ed. and trans. Henry St. John Thackeray and Ralph Marcus. Loeb Classical Library. (Cambridge, MA: Harvard University Press, 1926/1963).
Knighton, Henry. *Chronicle 1337–1396*. Ed. and trans. G. H. Martin. (Oxford: Clarendon Press, 1995).

Lorris, Guillaume de and Jean de Meun, *Le Roman de la Rose*. 3 vols. Ed. Félix Lecoy. (Paris: Champion, 1974).

Macaulay, G. C., ed., *The Complete Works of John Gower*, 4 vols., (Oxford: Clarendon Press, 1899–1902): I, *The French Works*, II and III, *The English Works*, IV, *The Latin Works*.

*Mirour de l'Omme*. (See also Macaulay).Trans. William Burton Wilson (East Lansing, MI: Colleagues Press, 1992).

Monmouth, Geoffery of. *The History of the Kings of Britain* [*Historia regem Britanniae*]. Ed. and trans. Lewis Thorpe (Harmondsworth: Penguin, 1966).

Neckam, Alexander. *De vita monachorum*. In *The Anglo-Latin Satirical Poets and Epigrammatists of the Twelfth Century*. 2 vols. Ed. Thomas Wright. (Cambridge: Cambridge University Press, 2013). II, 175–200.

—*De laudibus divinae sapientiae, De naturis rarum*. Ed. Thomas Wright. (London: Rolls Series, 1863).

Nigel of Longchamp. *Speculum Stultorum*. Ed. and trans. Jill Mann (Oxford: Oxford University Press, 2023).

Ovid (Publius Ovidius Naso). *Metamorphoses*. Ed. and trans. Frank. J. Miller. 2 vols. Loeb Classical Library. (Cambridge, MA: Harvard University Press, 1977).

—*Fasti*. Ed. and trans. James G. Fraser; rev. G. P. Goold. Loeb Classical Library (Cambridge, MA: Harvard University Press, 1967).

—*Tristia and Ex Ponto*. Ed and trans. A. I Wheeler; rev. G. P. Goold. Loeb Classical Library. (Cambridge, MA: Harvard University Press, 1965).

—*Heroides and Amores*. Ed and trans. Grant Showerman; rev. G. P. Goold. Loeb Classical Library. (Cambridge, MA: Harvard University Press, 1977).

—*The Art of Love* [*Ars Amatoria*] *and Other Poems*. Ed. and trans. J. H. Mozley. Loeb Classical Library. (Cambridge, MA: Harvard University Press, 1969).

Pennington, Kenneth. "Introduction to the Courts." In *The History of Courts and Procedures in Medieval Canon Law*. Ed. Wilfried Hartmann and Kenneth Pennington (Washington, D.C.: Catholic University Press of America, 2016).

Petrarch, Francis. (Francesco Petrarca). *De remediis utriusque fortunae*. Ed., with commentary, Rudolf Schottländer. (Munich: Fink, 1975).

Riga, Peter. *Petri Rigae, Aurora*. 2 vols. Ed, Paul Beichner. (South Bend, IN: University of Notre Dame Press, 1965).

Saint-Amour, William de. *De periculis novissimorum temporum*. Ed. and trans. G. Geltner (Paris/Louvaine: Peeters, 2008).

Stockton, Eric W., ed. and trans. *The Major Latin Works of John Gower: The Voice of One Crying and the Cronica Tripertita*. (Seattle, WA: University of Washington Press, 1962).

Valerius Maximus. *Factorum et dictorum memorabilium*. Available online at onlinebooks@pobox.upenn.edu

Virgil (Publius Virgilius Maro). *Aeneid I-VI, Eclogues. Georgics*. Ed. and trans. H. R. Fairclough. Loeb Classical Library. (Cambridge, MA: Harvard University Press, 1969).

—*Aeneid VII–XII. Appendix Vergiliana*. Ed. and trans. H. R. Fairclough. Rev, G. P. Goold. Loeb Classical Library. (Cambridge, MA: Harvard University Press, 2000).

Voragine, Jacobus de (*Legenda Aurea*) *The Golden Legend of Jacobus de Voragine: The Great Collection of the Legends of Saints Translated from the Medieval*

*Latin.* Ed and trans. Ryan Granger and Helmut Ripperger (New York: Arno Press, 1969).

Walsingham, Thomas. *Chronica Maiora.* 2 vols. Ed. and trans. John Taylor, Wendy R. Childs, and Leslie Watkiss. (Oxford: Clarendon Press, 2011).

—*Historia Anglicana.* [*Chronica Monasterii S. Albani Thomae Walsingham, quondam monachi S. Albani, Historia Anglicana 1381–1422*] Ed. H. T. Riley (London: Rolls Series, 1864).

Wyclif, John. *Tractatus de civili dominio. Liber Primus.* Ed. R. L. Poole (London: Trübner, 1885).

SECONDARY SOURCES

Bennett, Michael. "John Gower, Squire of Kent, the Peasants' Revolt, and the *Visio Anglie.*" *Chaucer Review* 53 (2018): 258–82.

Boas, George. *Vox Populi: Essays in the History of an Idea.* (Baltimore: Johns Hopkins University Press, 1969).

Carlin, Martha. "Chronology of Gower's Life Records," in *Historians on John Gower*, ed. Stephen H. Rigby with Siân Echard. (Cambridge: D.S. Brewer, 2019).

Carlson, David R., ed. and A.G. Rigg, trans. *Poems on Contemporary Events: The Visio Anglie (1381) and Cronica Triperta (1400).* (Toronto: Pontifical Institute of Medieval Studies, 2011).

Curtius, Ernst Robert. *European Literature and the Latin Middle Ages.* Trans. Willard R. Trask. Bollingen Series 36 (New York: Harper & Row [1953] 1963).

Oman, Charles. *The Great Revolt of 1381.* New ed. with new introduction and notes by E. B. Fryde. (Oxford: Clarendon Press, 1969).

*Oxford Dictionary of English Proverbs.* Compiled W. S. Smith, intro. Janet E. Heseltiine. (Oxford: Clarendon Press, 1948).

Parkes, Malcolm B. "Patterns of scribal sctivity and revisions of the text in early copies of works by John Gower, in *New Science Out of Old Books: Studies in Manuscripts and Early Printed Books in Honour of A. I. Doyle.* Ed. Richard Beadle and A. I. Piper (Aldershott: Scholar Press, 1995), 81–121.

Rigg., A. G. *A History of Anglo-Latin Literature 1066–1422* (Cambridge: Cambridge University Press, 1992).

Smith, William G. and Jant E. Heseltine. *The Oxford Dictionary of English Proverbs*, rev. Sir Paul Harvey. 2nd ed. (Oxford: Clarendon Press, 1948)

Walz, Gotthard. *Das Sprichtwort bei Gower mit Besonderem Hinweis auf Quellen und Parallelen.* (Nördlingen: Beck, 1907)

Whiting, B. J. *Chaucer's Use of Proverbs.* (Cambridge, MA: Harvard University Press, 1954).

Wickert, Maria. *Studien zu John Gower* (Cologne: Kölner Universitäts-verlag, 1953). Trans. Robert J. Meindl, Studies in John Gower, 2nd ed. (Tempe, AZ: ACMRS, 2016).

Yeager, R. F. "Gower's 'Epistle to Archbishop Arundel'; The Evidence of Oxford, All Souls College MS 98," in *Manuscript and Print in Late Medieval and Early Modern Britain: Essays in Honour of Professor Julia Boffey.* Ed. Tamara Atkin and Jaclyn Rajsic (Cambridge: D. S. Brewer, 2019), 12–34.

## FURTHER READING

Bertolet, Craig E., *Chaucer, Gower, Hoccleve and the Commercial Practices of Late Fourteenth-Century London* (Burlington, VT: Ashgate, 2013).
Cady, Diane, *The Gender of Money: Value and Economy in Late Medieval England* (Cham: Springer, 2019).
Carlson, David R., "A Fourteenth-Century Anglo-Latin Ovidian: The *Liber exulis* in John Gower's *Visio Anglie* (*Vox clamantis* 1.1359–1592)," *Classica et Mediaevalia* 61 (2010), 293–335.
Carlson, David R., *John Gower: Poetry and Propaganda in Fourteenth-Century England* (Cambridge: D.S. Brewer, 2012).
Carlson, David R., *Gower and Anglo-Latin Verse* (Toronto: Pontifical Institute of Medieval Studies, 2021).
Donavin, Georgiana, *John Gower's Rhetoric: Classical Authority, Biblical Ethos, and Renaissance Receptions* (Turnhout: Brepols, 2022).
Echard, Siân, ed., *A Companion to Gower* (Cambridge: D.S. Brewer, 2004).
Fisher, John H., *John Gower, Moral Philosopher and Friend of Chaucer* (New York: New York University Press, 1963).
Fonzo, Kimberly, *Retrospective Prophecy and Medieval English Authorship* (Toronto: University of Toronto Press, 2022).
Fredell, Joel, *Fictions of Witness in the Confessio Amantis* (Cham: Springer, 2023).
Giancarlo, Matthew, *Parliament and Literature in Late Medieval England* (Cambridge: Cambridge University Press, 2007).
Itô, Masayoshi, *John Gower the Medieval Poet* (Tokyo: Shinozaki Shorin, 1976).
Irvin, Matthew W., *The Poetic Voices of John Gower: Politics and Personae in the Confessio Amantis* (Cambridge: D.S. Brewer, 2014).
McCabe, T. Matthew N. *Gower's Vulgar Tongue: Ovid, Lay Religion, and English Poetry in the Confessio Amantis.* (Cambridge: D. S. Brewer, 2011).
Meindl, Robert J., "Gower's 'Speculum Iudicis': Judicial Corruption in Book VI of the *Vox Clamantis*," in *John Gower: Others and the Self*, ed. Russell A. Peck and R.F. Yeager (Cambridge: D.S. Brewer, 2017), 260–82.
Meindl, Robert J., "Nuisance and Trespass in the *Vox Clamantis*: Sheriffs, Jurors and Bailiffs," *Interdisciplinary Journal for Germanic Linguistics and Semiotic Analysis* 20 (2015), 181–213.
Mitchell, J. Allan, *Ethics and Exemplary Narrative in Chaucer and Gower* (Cambridge: D.S. Brewer, 2004).
Nicholson, Peter, *Love and Ethics in Gower's Confessio Amantis* (Ann Arbor: University of Michigan Press, 2005).
Peck, Russell A., *Kingship and Common Profit in Gower's Confessio Amantis* (Carbondale and Edwardsville: Southern Illinois University Press, 1978).
Pearsall, Derek and Linne Mooney, eds., *A Descriptive Catalogue of the English Manuscripts of John Gower's Confessio Amantis* (Cambridge: D.S. Brewer, 2021).

Rigby, Stephen H. and Siân Echard, eds., *Historians on John Gower* (Cambridge: D.S. Brewer, 2019).

Sáez-Hidalgo, Ana, Brian W. Gastle and R.F. Yeager, eds., *The Routledge Research Companion to John Gower* (Abingdon: Routledge, 2017).

Simpson, James, *Sciences and the Self in Medieval Poetry: Alan of Lille's Anticlaudianus and John Gower's Confessio Amantis* (Cambridge: Cambridge University Press, 1995).

Van Dijk, Conrad, *John Gower and the Limits of the Law* (Cambridge: D.S. Brewer, 2013).

Watt, Diane, *Amoral Gower: Language, Sex, and Politics* (Minneapolis: University of Minnesota Press, 2003).

Yeager, R.F., ed. and trans., *John Gower: The Minor Latin Works with In Praise of Peace*, ed. Michael Livingston (Kalamazoo, MI: Medieval Institute, 2005).

Yeager, R.F. and Brian W. Gastle, eds., *Approaches to Teaching the Poetry of John Gower* (New York: Modern Language Association, 2011).

Yeager, R.F., *John Gower's Poetic: The Search for a New Arion* (Cambridge: D.S. Brewer, 1990).

# INDEX

Aaron 175, 325, 336
Abraham 324, 336, 377
Absalom 100, 114
Acheron 129, 258, 282, 301, 331
Acteon 27; see also Ovid, *Metamorphoses*
Adam 77, 103, 160, 172, 185, 230, 268, 333, 357, 359
Adultery 132, 348, 350, 379, 380
*Aeneid* 3, 74, 110, 405
Aesop 285
Ahab 100, 328, 336, 342
Alain of Lille, *De planctu Naturae 83*, 184, 329, 404
Alexander 1, 113, 114, 239, 282, 283, 285, 307, 316, 320, 326, 338, 341; see also Macedonians; Gog and Magog
Alexander Neckam, *De Vita Monachorum*, 239, 243, 244, 248, 330, 331, 332, 334, 335, 387, 388, 389; *De naturis rerum* 330
Amans 80, 250, 255, 256, 257, 258, 281
Anne of Bohemia 252
Apocrypha 117; Acts of Peter 187; Pseudo-Clementine 187; Nicodemus (Gospel of) 117, 404
Archbishop 10, 11, 12, 42, 78, 79, 118, 119, 186, 195, 395, 396, 398, 399, 401, 406
Aristotle 1, 332, 391, 403
Arius 237, 249, 326, 337; see also Jovinian; Wyclif, lollards
Ark 28, 75, 100, 115, 136, 176, 188, 306, 325, 336, 337
Arundel, Thomas, Archbishop viii, 186, 393, 394, 395, 396, 397, 398, 399, 401
Asmodeus 100; see also Titivollus
Augustine 113, 159, 193, 242, 338, 339, 390, 403
Avianus 76, 403,
Avignon 119, 185, 189, 193, 398; see also Babylonian Captivity, Great Schism
Azariah 100, 115

Babel 61, 335
Babylon 99, 299, 307, 324
Babylonian Captivity 119; see also Avignon, Great Schism
Balaam 110, 140, 333
Barabbas 327

Bathsheba 246, 283; see also David, Uriah
Bear 394; see also Beauchamp, Thomas, Earl of Warwick
Beauchamp, Thomas, Earl of Warwick 393, 394; see also Bear
Bellatores 281; see also Laboratories, Oratories
benefit of clergy 201; see also clergy
Benoît de Sainte-Maure, *Roman de Troie* 78, 80
Bernard, St. 203, 213, 237, 242, 249, 390
Bible:
  Old Testament:
    Genesis 71, 76, 77, 79, 83, 84, 85, 87, 114, 115, 116, 117, 185, 188, 189, 194, 195, 196, 200, 201, 244, 245, 248, 284, 332, 334, 335, 336, 337, 340, 341, 357, 386, 388, 390, 391
    Exodus 75, 79, 111, 113, 114, 115, 116, 117, 186, 187, 194, 195, 198, 199, 200, 201, 284, 285, 330, 336, 339, 391, 399
    Leviticus 185, 187, 194, 196, 197, 198, 199, 200, 201, 242, 248, 284, 285, 329, 332, 334, 336, 399
    Numbers (Numeri) 23, 26, 110, 113, 114, 116, 186, 189, 198, 199, 200, 201, 230, 248, 333, 335, 336, 385
    Deuteronomy 73, 110, 112, 187, 189, 192, 197, 199, 248, 284, 339, 391
    Joshua 98, 112, 130, 328, 342
    Judges 114, 132, 283
    I Kings (I Samuel) 78, 117, 192, 194, 198, 240, 333, 334, 339
    II Kings (II Samuel) 199, 246, 281, 283, 334, 336, 340
    III Kings 114, 115, 116, 200, 248, 283, 333, 334, 335, 336, 339
    IV Kings, 113, 115, 200, 336, 339
    I Paralipomenon 334, 336
    II Paralipomenon 115, 331, 336, 339
    Tobias (Tobit) 98, 112, 114, 325, 337
    Esther 100, 115, 340
    Job 93, 111, 112, 168, 195, 247, 273, 279, 325, 335, 337, 389, 390, 391, 404

## Index

Psalm(s) 71, 76, 85, 112, 114, 117, 188, 189, 194, 195, 197, 201, 247, 329, 389, 390, 391, 392
Proverbs 82, 194, 195, 199, 286, 329, 330, 332, 406
Ecclesiastes 111, 117, 194, 196, 329, 331, 334, 388, 389, 390, 391
Sapientiae 285, 405
Ecclesiasticus 242, 286, 332
Isaiah 35, 112, 115, 137, 187, 191, 194, 293, 329, 330, 336, 389, 390, 391
Jeremiah 191, 201, 329, 331, 336
Ezekiel 189, 192, 285
Daniel 14, 71, 72, 99, 113, 114, 115, 137, 242, 304, 332, 336, 385, 386
Hosea (Osee) 195, 225
Joel 137, 192, 407
Jonah 62, 99, 114
Zephaniah (Sophonias) 246
Machabeorum 77, 79, 114, 332, 334
New Testament:
Matthew 75, 79, 80, 83, 85, 110, 111, 113, 114, 116, 117, 158, 186, 188, 189, 190, 191, 192, 193, 194, 195, 196, 197, 198, 200, 201, 239, 242, 244, 245, 246, 247, 248, 282, 285, 330, 331, 332, 333, 335, 337, 340, 385, 386, 391, 399, 407
Mark, 75, 80, 110, 111, 116, 152, 158, 170, 190, 192, 193, 195, 196, 197, 198, 200, 244, 245, 285, 312, 328, 330, 332, 340, 389, 391, 399
Luke 75, 87, 110, 111, 116, 158, 186, 187, 190, 191, 192, 193, 194, 195, 196, 197, 198, 200, 201, 239, 241, 244, 249, 282, 329, 330, 332, 333, 335, 337, 340, 385, 388, 389, 391, 399
John 110, 116, 117, 151, 158, 184, 187, 188, 189, 191, 193, 194, 195, 196, 197, 200, 201, 240, 244, 337, 340, 390, 391
John (of Patmos) 71, 72
Acts 85, 187, 188, 191, 192, 193, 195, 200, 241, 337
Romans, 82, 188, 192, 197, 247, 333, 388
I Corinthians 116, 184, 188, 189, 192, 194, 197, 198, 200, 239, 247, 332
II Corinthians 111, 191, 192, 195, 197, 390
Galatians 195, 198, 239, 245, 336, 390
Ephesians 191, 194, 334, 391
I Peter 197
II Peter 333
Apocalypse 35, 72, 77, 86, 193, 245, 333, 347, 385, 391
Bishops 113, 118, 120, 185, 188, 192, 197, 202, 220, 244
Blackheath 10, 12, 77
Black Prince 78, 288, 334; see also Enrique II Trastámara, Nájera, Edward III
Boccaccio 184, *Filocolo, Filostrato*; see also Chaucer, *Troilus and Criseyde*
Boethius 88, 111, 112, 114, 117, 285, 403; *Consolation of Philosophy* 111, 112, 114, 117, 285, 403
Bohun 394 ; see also Henry IV; Thomas, of Woodstock
Bordeaux 1: see also Richard II
boys (in the cloister) 169, 219, 231, 244
Brembre, Nicholas 252, 285
Brunellus, Burnel, Burnellus 21, 73, 201, 203, 236, 237, 249; see also Nigel of Longchamp
Brutus 66, 85, 86,
*Bucolics* 334
bull of Minos 22
bulls of Colchis 22
Burley, Simon 1; see also Richard II

Caesar 120, 142, 150, 190, 192, 320, 326, 338
Cain 35, 44, 76
Canon law 87, 119, 120, 121, 197, 201, 203, 243, 244, 405
Canons 136, 202, 213, 214, 242, 243; Augustian 242, 243; Black 243; White 243
*Canterbury Tales (CT)* x, 72, 76, 186, 187, 191, 196, 200, 242, 244, 281, 284, 330, 334, 339; see also General Prologue, "Wife of Bath's Tale," "Summoner's Tale," "Tale of Melibee"
Cardinals 118, 119, 185, 287
Cassandra 45, 79, 327, 339, 341
Cassian 333
Catherine of Siena 391
Cato xiii, 6, 141, 264, 283, 327, 340, 350
Cats 27
Centaurs 22
Cephalus 27, 75
Cerberus 26, 75

*Index*

Chance 39, 41, 49, 51, 54, 67, 94, 96, 97, 109; see also Destiny, Fate
Charybdis 60, 83, 329; see also Scylla
Chaucer 3, 4, 5, 7, 72, 76, 77, 121, 122, 184, 186, 187, 191, 200, 242, 244, 249, 281, 284, 330, 331, 332, 334, 339, 341, 403, 404, 406; *Canterbury Tales*, General Prologue, "Wife of Bath's Tale", "Summoner's Tale", "Melibee", *Troilus and Criseyde*,
Circe 36, 76, 328, 341
Cistercians 242, 249, 404: see also White canons
Class-consciousness, three estates 1, 4, 7, 18, 39, 49, 57, 59, 69, 91, 92, 118, 122, 164, 250, 268, 269, 272, 281, 284, 287, 292, 343, 354, 365, 369, 378; see also Bellatores, knights, knighthood, gentry, Oratores, clergy, Laboratores, peasants, serfs, plebs, villeins, yeomanry, legal practitioners, judges, mercantile community, sheriffs.
Clergy 1, 6, 88, 118, 119, 120, 124, 125, 133, 134, 135, 136, 137, 138, 139, 140, 141, 143, 144, 147, 148, 150, 152, 153, 155, 158, 159, 161, 165, 171, 181, 183, 185, 187, 192, 193, 196, 201, 202, 203, 204, 230, 234, 236, 237, 238, 247, 253, 281, 303, 344, 348, 350, 381, 391; see also papacy, cardinals, archbishops. bishops, monks, nuns, mass priests, parish priests, friars, benefit of clergy, Rule of St. Augustine, Rule of St. Benedict, Francis of Assisi
cock 29, 30, 169
common law 121, 153, 182, 197, 201, 287
Constantine (emperor) 114, 134, 188, 190, 326, 337, 338, 339; see also Donation of
Cormorant 168, 197
Croesus 260, 282, 326, 338
Cupid 178, 328; see also Venus

Dalilah 283; see also Samson
Daniel 14, 71, 72, 99, 113, 114, 115, 137, 242, 265, 304, 313, 332, 336, 385, 386
Dante, *De Monarchia* 120
David 99, 100, 136, 137, 138, 157, 191, 230, 246, 311, 313, 326, 339; see also Bathsheba, Uriah

Death (personification) 28, 33, 47, 49, 54, 69, 107, 145, 149, 150, 177, 325, 362, 365, 368, 372, 373, 375, 390; see also Four Last Things
*De civili dominio* 198, 406; see also Wyclif, John
Decretals 120, 163, 213, 242
Deposition 2, 393
Despenser, Henry, Bishop of Norwich 11, 121, 189
Destiny 97; see also Chance, Fate
Diana 27, 66, 86
Diogenes 327, 340
Dog 25, 26, 27, 28, 32, 36, 40, 46, 75, 162, 166, 316, 364, 389
Donation of Constantine 114, 188, 190; see also Constantine; Valla, Lorenzo

Edward II 195, 246
Edward III 1, 4, 246, 247, 284, 288, 386, 392; see also Black Prince, Hundred Years' War.
Ekron 28
Eli 100, 115, 120, 156
Enrique II Trastámara 334, Nájera ; see also Black Prince
Envy (personification) 111, 145, 208, 364, 368, 378, 379, 389, 390
Etna 368, 390
*Everyman* 390

Faith, Hope, and Charity 6, 137, 184
Fate, Fates xiii, 41, 45, 49, 51, 53, 54, 55, 59, 61, 62, 64, 66, 94, 95, 96, 97, 100, 122, 141, 225, 235, 259, 260, 276, 280, 288, 302, 305, 327, 355, 380, 381, 382, 387; see also Chance, Destiny
feast of Corpus Christi 11, 12, 39, 77
Fitzalan, Richard, Earl of Arundel; see also Horse
Flanders Crusade 136, 189, 273; see also Despenser
Flemings 80
Flies 30, 31, 32, 36, 38, 60, 75, 311
Fortune (personification) 32, 47, 54, 65, 66, 88, 89, 92, 93, 94, 96, 97, 100, 101, 108, 109, 111, 112, 118, 122, 141, 260, 266, 285, 316, 320, 382, 383; see also Fate
Four Ages of Man 385
Four Last Things 391; see also Death
Four-part map 199
Fourth Lateran Council (1215) 87, 192

Foxes 27, 28
Franchisers 251
Francis of Assisi, Franciscans 11, 195, 229, 231, 233, 245, 246, 247, 249, 405; see also clergy, friars
Fraud (personification) 42, 145, 161, 200, 213, 251, 272, 273, 274, 275, 277, 278, 280, 309, 323, 348, 352
French sins 348
Friars 6, 195, 200, 202, 203, 223, 224, 225, 226, 227, 228, 229, 230, 231, 232, 233, 234, 235, 236, 237, 245, 246, 251, 272, 273, 274, 275, 277, 280, 309, 323, 352, 376, 378
Frog 30, 31, 75, 237
Froissart, Jean 76, 80, 404; see also Hundred Years' War
Furies (personification) 57, 59, 76

Galen 259, 282
Gander 29, 30, 36
Gaunt, John 10, 77, 120, 211, 252; see also Savoy Palace
Gelasian dyarchy 120
General Prologue x, 76, 186, 187, 242, 281, 330, 334
Genius (character) 202, 220, 244, 250
Gentry 1, 4, 48, 250, 251, 265, 266, 267, 268, 310
Geoffrey of Monmouth, *Historia regem Britanniae* 77, 85
*Georgics* 74, 405
Geryon 27
Golden Legend (*Legenda Aurea*) 75, 113, 114, 186, 241, 242, 405; see also Jacobus de Voragine
Gluttony (personification) 127, 206, 207, 213, 329, 333, 366, 373, 379
Godfrey of Viterbo xii, xiii, 3, 72, 76, 77, 85, 112, 114, 115, 191, 240, 404; *Pantheon*
Gog and Magog 35, 113; see also Alexander
Good Parliament 250
Gower:
  *Carmen super multiplici viciorum pestilencia* 116, 281, 282, 331, 333, 337, 338, 387, 395, 396, 400, 401, 402
  *Confessio Amantis* 5, 6, 7, 71, 72, 73, 74, 76, 77, 80, 82, 110, 111, 112, 113, 114, 115, 116, 117, 187, 188, 189, 190, 192, 193, 195, 196, 198, 199, 202, 241, 242, 246, 247, 250, 281, 282, 284, 286, 331, 332, 333, 334, 335, 336, 338, 339, 340, 341, 385, 388, 389, 390, 391
  *Cronica Tripertita* viii, 2, 5, 9, 77, 393, 394, 395, 400, 401, 402, 405, 406
  *Mirour de l'Omme* 1, 4, 5, 6, 7, 71, 83, 110, 111, 112, 113, 114, 115, 185, 187, 188, 193, 194, 195, 196, 197, 198, 199, 201, 239, 241, 242, 243, 245, 246, 247, 248, 281, 282, 284, 285, 329, 331, 332, 336, 340, 341, 385, 387, 388, 389, 390, 391, 405
Grace 42, 91, 100, 107, 174, 176, 224, 256, 258, 264, 305, 312, 313, 314, 319, 327, 335, 348, 359, 361, 371, 375, 382, 383, 397
Gratian (emperor) 120
Great Rising of 1381 2, 9, 72; see also Blackheath, boar of Kent, Jack Straw, John Ball, Henry Despenser, Smithfield, Wat Tyler, William Walworth
Great Schism 119, 185; see also Avignon, Rome

Ham 199, 324, 335
Hales, Robert 11, 77, 78, 79, 119
Hawkwood, John 188; see also Visconti, Bernabò, White Company
Hecuba 27, 41, 78, 339
Helenus 42, 45, 78, 326, 339; see also Sudbury, Simon
Hélinand de Froidmont, *Vers de la Mort* 241, 390, 404
Henry IV 2, 6, 7, 393, 394, 399; see also Bohun, Swan
Hercules 22, 24, 74
Hilton, Walter 391
Homer 159
Horeb 113
Horse 20, 39, 41, 110, 155, 157, 260, 275, 276, 322, 364, 383, 393, 394; see also Fitzalan, Richard, Earl of Arundel 394
Hundred Years' War 385; see also Froissart, Jean; Edward III
Hypocrisy (personification) 213, 348, 349

Isabella of Valois 246
Ishmael 324, 336
Isidore of Seville 35, 190, 199, 329

Jacob 110, 156, 162, 191, 267, 336, 352, 377

## Index

Jacob's ladder 180
Jacobus de Voragine 75, 113, 114, 186; see also *Golden Legend*
Japhet 199, 324, 335
Jason 22, 327, 341
Jay 33, 34, 37, 63, 327, 328
Jeremy 137
Jerusalem Collections 192
Jews 117, 234, 271, 340, 392
John the Baptist 6, 7, 72, 110
Jovinian 237, 249, 326, 337; see also Wyclif
Julian (emperor), the Apostate 325, 337
Justice 39, 43, 44, 45, 48, 66, 128, 146, 147, 159, 160, 171, 172, 180, 203, 207, 251, 253, 270, 271, 280, 287, 289, 290, 293, 294, 295, 296, 297, 298, 300, 301, 302, 303, 304, 305, 306, 307, 309, 311, 314, 315, 323, 329, 331, 345, 348, 351, 352, 373, 378, 380, 382
Justinian (emperor) 326

kiss of peace 197
kite 29, 291
knights 41, 79, 120, 124, 143, 162, 230, 247, 250, 253, 255, 259, 281, 314; knighthood 250, 253, 259, 265, 266, 326, 386
Korah 99, 325, 336

Laboratores 281; see also Bellatores, Oratores
Leah 267
Lollards 6, 186, 246; see also Wyclif
Lust 88, 92, 128, 129, 131, 170, 171, 172, 174, 176, 179, 212, 213, 216, 217, 248, 254, 264, 279, 313, 343, 344, 350, 367, 379

Macedonians, Macedon 99, 320; see also Alexander
Magog 35, 113
Mammon 131, 347, 385
Mass priests 118, 121
Maure (St. Maure) 213
Meleager 24
*mens rea/actus reus* 201
Merciless Parliament 252
Microcosm 12, 361, 363
Minotaur 22
Mohammed 150; see also *Qur'an*

Monk, Monks 6, 136, 186, 198, 202, 203, 204, 205, 206, 207, 208, 209, 210, 211, 212, 213, 214, 215, 216, 217, 218, 219, 239, 240, 241, 242, 245, 246, 378
Moses 98, 99, 106, 113, 130, 131, 132, 136, 160, 325, 336, 342

Nebugodonosor (Nebuchadnezzar) 9, 100, 343, 344, 385; see also Daniel
Neptune 11, 13, 22, 63

Nereids 391
Nero (emperor) 326, 338
Nessus 22
New Law 103, 107, 175, 179, 325, 335
New Troy (London) 10, 38, 39, 79
Nicene Creed 85, 115, 339
Nigel of Longchamp (Nigellus Wireker), *Speculum Stultorum* 3, 73, 74, 75, 76, 80, 110, 112, 186, 187, 189, 190, 191, 195, 196, 197, 201, 203, 240, 241, 244, 245, 246, 249, 283, 291, 332, 333, 335, 386, 387, 405; see also Brunellus
Nimrod 324, 335
Northampton, John of 251, 252, 285
Nun, Nuns 187, 202, 203, 219, 220, 221, 222, 244

Old Law 133, 139, 152, 156, 175, 176, 193, 325, 386, 405
Oratores 281
Ordeals of God 192; see also benefit of clergy
Ordinance of Laborers 247, 284
Ovid:
  *Amores* 73, 74, 75, 77, 80, 84, 186, 197, 244, 333
  *Ars Amatoria* xiii, 3, 74, 77, 80, 81, 85, 111, 116, 191, 194, 195, 240, 241, 242, 243, 244, 247, 281, 282, 283, 286, 333, 335, 341, 386, 387, 388, 405
  *Remedia Amoris* 81, 86, 200, 244, 281, 286, 332, 388
  *Ex ponto* 3, 71, 74, 81, 82, 85, 86, 112, 184, 190, 194, 245, 283, 286, 330, 334, 388
  *Fasti* xiii, 3, 72, 73, 75, 76, 78, 79, 80, 81, 82, 83, 84, 85, 86, 110, 186, 192, 240, 243, 245, 246, 247, 281, 286, 333, 386, 388, 392, 405

*Metamorphoses* xii, 3, 72, 73, 74, 75, 76, 77, 78, 79, 80, 81, 82, 83, 84, 85, 86, 111, 112, 184, 186, 240, 241, 247, 248, 281, 282, 283, 284, 329, 332, 333, 335, 385, 386, 388, 389, 392, 405
*Tristia* 3, 71, 72, 73, 78, 79, 81, 82, 83, 84, 85, 86, 111, 112, 184, 200, 244, 246, 282, 283, 285, 286, 333, 335, 385, 386, 388, 405
Owls 28, 30, 58, 392

Palladium 42, 339
Papacy 118, 119, 287; Gelasius 120; Sylvester I 99, 114, 188; Gregory I (the Great) 113, 249, 337, 389, 404; Leo III 339; Leo IX 118; Gregory VII 118; Paschal II 185; Innocent III 118, 120, 195, 203, 245, 246; Gregory XI 119, 188; Clement VII 119, 185, 189, 193, 398; Urban VI 119, 185, 189, 398; Boniface VIII 120
Paris, Matthew, *Chronica Majora* 114
Parish priests 118
Pater noster 197
Paul of Tarsus (St. Paul, apostle) 200
Paul of Thebes 200
Peasants 5, 10, 13, 38, 46, 47, 72, 143, 203, 210, 251, 268, 276, 406; see also plebs, serfs, villeins
Perrers, Alice 386
Peter Comestor 114
Peter Riga, *Aurora* 77, 78, 79, 81, 83, 84, 86, 111, 112, 113, 115, 116, 117, 185, 186, 187, 188, 189, 192, 194, 195, 196, 197, 198, 199, 200, 201, 240, 242, 248, 281, 284, 329, 332, 333, 334, 335, 391
Petrarch, Francis, *De remediis utruisque fortunae* 112, 405
Pharisees 160, 201, 232, 246
Philemon 351, 386
*Piers Plowman* 194, 200
Plague of 1348 (Black Plague) 247, 251, 278, 284, 304, 372
Pleader 287, 289, 290, 291, 292, 293, 294, 295, 296
Plebs 1, 34, 42, 43, 45, 49, 106, 130, 226, 274, 277, 278, 279, 293, 309, 312, 323, 352, 376; see also peasants, serfs, villeins
Poitiers 113, 334
poll tax 11, 78

positive law (*lex positiva*) 120, 132, 133, 134, 135, 141, 151, 152, 187, 193, 230, 380
Prelates 118, 120, 124, 125, 126, 127, 128, 129, 130, 131, 134, 135, 139, 142, 147, 151, 153, 156, 159, 160, 161, 187, 378
Priam 41, 45, 339, 340, 341
Prudentius 75, 184
Pseudo-Aristotle, *Secretum Secretorum* 1

Qur'an 192; see also Mohammed

Rachel 147, 267, 336
Raphael 98
Raven 29, 181, 229, 325, 336
Record and Process 2, 393
Red Sea 113
Rehoboam 100, 326, 339
Richard II 1, 2, 4, 5, 78, 84, 136, 246, 287, 288, 393, 404; see also Record and Process, Anne of Bohemia, Isabella of Valois, Thomas Rushook, Deposition, Burley, Simon
Rome 15, 41, 98, 99, 113, 114, 118, 119, 134, 158, 167, 168, 185, 188, 280, 290, 299, 322, 326, 337, 338, 396, 398; see also Great Schism, Avignon; Babylonian Captivity
Rule of St. Augustine 242; see also Clergy
Rule of St. Benedict 239, 240, 241, 242, 244, 246,; see also Clergy
Rushook, Thomas 246

Samson 114, 283; see also Dalilah
Saturn 98, 112, 150, 192
Saul 100, 312, 314, 325, 327, 337; see also Witch of Endor
Savoy Palace 10, 11, 77, 78
Scylla 56, 60, 61, 62, 64, 65, 69, 83, 255, 291; see also Charybdis
Semiramis 327, 241
Serf 10, 12, 14, 32, 39, 41, 44, 51, 69, 212, 251, 258, 269, 276, 345, 346, 349, 350; see also peasants, plebs, villeins
Serjeants-at-law 330
Serlo of Wilton 249
Ship 10, 11, 12, 13, 56, 57, 58, 59, 60, 61, 62, 63, 64, 65, 67, 143, 159, 301, 302, 398; see also Tower of London
Simon Magus 110, 187

Simony 120, 153, 187, 195
Sinon 91, 110, 111
Sirens 256, 262
Sloth (personification) 217, 312, 344, 366, 391
Smithfield 10, 11, 76, 85; see also Great Rising of 1381
Southwark 4, 7, 10, 242; see also St. Mary Overey; Gower, Augustinian canons,
Spurina 340
St. Ambrose 120
St. John Clerkenwell 10, 11
St. Mary Overey 7, 242; see also Gower, Augustinian canons, Southwark
Staplers 251
Statute of Laborers 247, 251
Sudbury, Simon, Archbishop 10, 11, 12, 78, 79, 119, 398; see also Helenus
Summoner, "Summoner's Tale" 186, 187, 191, 200; see also *Canterbury Tales*, Chaucer
Susannah 100; see also Daniel
Swan 393, 394; see also Henry IV, Thomas of Woodstock, Duke of Gloucester
Sybil 35
Synagogue 105, 133, 234

Temple (London) 10, 11, 40, 78, 79
Theodosius (emperor) 326, 339
Thomas of Woodstock, Duke of Gloucester 393, 394; see also Swan; Bohun
Titivollus 228, 247; see also Asmodeus
Tower of London 10, 11, 12, 56, 60, 78, 79, 225, 324; see also Ship
Trajan (emperor) 326, 338
Tribes of Israel 113
*Troilus and Criseyde* 5, 112, 184, 331, 332, 341; see also Chaucer
Tyler, Wat 10, 11, 12, 13, 74, 76, 84, 85

Ulysses 35, 36, 41, 76; see also Circe
University scholars 118
Uriah 227, 246; see also Bathsheba, David
Usury 248, 251, 272, 273

Valla, Lorenzo 188; see also Donation of Constantine
Valentinian (emperor) 326, 338
Venantius Fortunatus 116
Venus 18, 40, 72, 78, 127, 128, 129, 160, 165, 167, 169, 178, 202, 208, 211, 220, 227, 241, 253, 258, 263, 264, 313, 328, 348, 350, 367, 368, 380, 381; see also Cupid
Vespasian (emperor) 30, 75
Villeins 11, 31, 33, 38, 41, 269, 270; see also peasants, plebs, serf
Virgil xiii, 7, 74, 110, 112, 334, 405; see also *Aeneid*, *Bucolics*, *Georgics*
Visconti, Bernabò 188; see also Hawkwood, John, White Company
*vox populi, vox dei* 87, 184, 195, 204, 406

Walworth, William 11, 85
Wasps 30, 31, 37, 75; see also Vespasian
Westminster 11
White Company 188; see also Visconti, Bernabò, Hawkwood, John
Wife of Bath, "Wife of Bath's Tale" 196, 244; see also *Canterbury Tales*, Chaucer
Witch of Endor 327, 334; see also Saul
women/woman 48, 131, 152, 164, 166, 167, 169, 172, 183, 202, 203, 205, 216, 217, 219, 220, 221, 222, 228, 243, 248, 250, 253, 254, 255, 258, 259, 260, 261, 262, 263, 264, 313, 314, 328, 333, 344, 348, 360, 373
Wrath (personification) 160, 254, 355, 365, 373
Wyclif, John 6, 120, 186, 189, 192, 193, 194, 198, 201, 249, 338, 339, 406; see also Arius, Jovinian, lollards

# VOLUMES ALREADY PUBLISHED

I     *Concordance to John Gower's Confessio Amantis*, edited by J.A. Pickles and J.L. Dawson, 1987

II     *John Gower's Poetic: The Search for a New Arion*, R.F. Yeager, 1990

III     *Gower's Confessio Amantis: A Critical Anthology*, Peter Nicholson, 1991

IV     *John Gower and the Structures of Conversion: A Reading of the Confessio Amantis*, Kurt Olsson, 1992

V     *Fathers and Daughters in Gower's Confessio Amantis: Authority, Family, State, and Writing*, María Bullón-Fernández, 2000

VI     *Gower's Vulgar Tongue: Ovid, Lay Religion, and English Poetry in the Confessio Amantis*, T. Matthew N. McCabe, 2011

VII     *John Gower, Poetry and Propaganda in Fourteenth-Century England*, David R. Carlson, 2012

VIII     *John Gower and the Limits of the Law*, Conrad van Dijk, 2013

IX     *The Poetic Voices of John Gower: Politics and Personae in the Confessio Amantis*, Matthew W. Irvin, 2014

X     *John Gower in England and Iberia: Manuscripts, Influences, Reception*, edited by Ana Sáez-Hidalgo and R.F. Yeager, 2014

XI     *John Gower: Others and the Self*, edited by Russell A. Peck and R.F. Yeager, 2017

XII     *Historians on John Gower*, edited by Stephen H. Rigby and Siân Echard, 2019

XIII     *Studies in the Age of Gower: A Festschrift in Honour of Robert F. Yeager*, edited by Susannah Mary Chewning, 2020

XIV     *John Gower in Manuscripts and Early Printed Books*, edited by Martha Driver, Derek Pearsall and R.F. Yeager, 2020

XV     *A Descriptive Catalogue of the English Manuscripts of John Gower's Confessio Amantis*, Derek Pearsall and Linne Mooney, 2021

www.ingramcontent.com/pod-product-compliance
Lightning Source LLC
Chambersburg PA
CBHW051554230426
43668CB00013B/1845